A

2500

1500

WALL TAPPINGS

WALL

TAPPINGS

An Anthology of Writings by Women Prisoners

*

edited by

JUDITH A. SCHEFFLER

Northeastern University Press · BOSTON

Northeastern University Press

Library of Congress Cataloging in Publication Data

Main entry under title:
Wall tappings.
  Bibliography: p.
  1. Women prisoners—Biography. 2. Prisoners'
writings. 3. Literature—Women authors. 4. Political
prisoners—Biography. I. Scheffler, Judith A., 1949–
HV6245.W345 1986   365'.43'0922 [B]   85-21506
ISBN 0-930350-85-5 (alk. paper)

Designed by David Ford

Composed in Trump by Crane Typesetting Service, Inc.
Printed and bound by Kingsport Press, Kingsport,
Tennessee. The paper is Miami Book, an acid-free
sheet.

MANUFACTURED IN THE UNITED STATES OF AMERICA
91 90 89 88 87 86   5 4 3 2 1

For Carl and Margaret Scheffler and Michael Neely

Contents

*

CONTENTS

P A R T 5

"I sense the great weight of the society/pressing down on the little box of room I lie in/alone/forgotten/like my sisters in prison": Solidarity with Other Women   257

Preface

*

In *Silences* Tillie Olsen calls for a reconsideration of the literary canon. Borrowing from Virginia Woolf, she theorizes, "The greatness of literature is not only in the great writers, the good writers; it is also in that which explains much and tells much (the soil, too, of great literature)."[1] Women's prison literature invites the reader to test Olsen's theory by applying it to a little-known body of works that explain much and tell much. Few of these works have been accepted into the literary canon; "greatness" in prison texts requires definition from another point of view. These works tell about the lives of silenced, imprisoned women and reveal a whole facet of women's experience usually considered too unpleasant or too atypical for attention. These are the marginal texts in a tradition of marginal texts. In a society that devalues women's writing in general, what is the position of women's prison texts? Collectively, they proclaim the continuity between the personal and the social aspects of literature by women.

Anthologies of prison literature include celebrated works by male prisoners, but few works by women. Therefore, these anthologies paint a distorted picture of prison life by failing to address women's concerns, which often differ from those of men. Women have much to say about the prison experience—and have been saying it for hundreds of years. The purpose of this anthology is to provide a forum for women's voices to be heard individually, and to demonstrate the cumulative wealth of writing that has until now been buried.

Readers should not assume that there is a standard format, style, or content in prison texts; an understanding of the historical and cultural context of the works is essential to appreciate fully each writer's particular prison environment as well as her method of describing her imprisonment. Furthermore, it is impossible to represent the entire body of women's prison literature in one anthology, and this work does not purport to do so. My purpose rather is to call attention to this neglected body of literature and to encourage the reader's own process of discovery in a journey that, owing to the wealth of material available, may lead in many directions that cannot be explored here.

In order to present the range of existing works, the scope of the anthology is broad. I have tried to include all of the genres used by women prison writers: autobiography, memoirs, letters, diary, essay, journalism, character sketches, fiction, and poetry. Selections include works from the United States, England, and South Africa and English translations of works from France, Germany, Russia, and Chile. While recognizing the inadequacy of translations, I have included these works in order to emphasize that this body of literature is international. Furthermore, I have selected works ranging from the seventeenth century to the present to demonstrate the vitality of prison literature over time and to highlight the roots of contemporary texts.

Each selection begins with a biographical introduction and a bibliography of all the author's works. Selections were written either during the woman's incarceration or at a later date about her incarceration, and each focuses on how the writer, as a woman, personally regarded imprisonment and adapted to her surroundings by work, special interests, or sheer mental effort, and especially by communicating with others both within prison and outside. Purely political treatises and works that do not discuss the prison experience are not included.

The fact that educated women and political activists figure prominently among the authors represented in this anthology requires explanation, since the majority of incarcerated women throughout history have been poor and uneducated. In general, prisoners—whether men or women—do not write, and throughout the history of prisons, few works by the poor and uneducated have survived, if indeed they ever *were* written. However, women imprisoned for political reasons often *do* write, and their works are doubly interesting, for they often discuss the plight of their sister inmates with the same fervor and immediacy that they use in describing themselves. It would, indeed, be preferable to have more firsthand accounts by poor and working-class imprisoned women, so that we might hear them tell their experiences in their own voices. Nevertheless, we owe a debt to the many politically active women who have sensitively depicted the lives of their silenced cell mates.

In contrast to the historical norm of prison writings, contemporary women's prison literature shows an exciting awakening of poor, working-class, and minority women to the satisfactions of writing. In America, for example, prison writing workshops and inmate-managed newsletters are encouraging a wider group of women to write and have their works read by other inmates and the public. Latin American testimonies, although mostly oral interviews rather than written pieces, are being published and distributed worldwide. Women prisoners of all classes are gaining the courage, confidence, and resources to speak and write in their own voices.

When women inmates write, they often reject the term "prisoner," with its connotation of shame, and they question the justice of the society that has imprisoned them. Most selections in this anthology are by women generally considered political prisoners, but some are by women who committed nonpolitical crimes, such as forgery, and who might even consider themselves deserving of punishment. The writers unite, however, in condemning an institution that labels them worthless and attempts to destroy their humanity in the name of justice. In this sense, each of the writers is, explicitly or implicitly, a political prisoner, and writing itself becomes a part of her protest. Carol Muske, a New York poet who has conducted writing workshops in women's prisons, explains: "Publishing is part of the art of not bowing."[2]

Women's prison writing constitutes an unexplored body of literature that merits investigation by the researcher as well as the general reader. Because these works differ in many important ways from the "classics" written by male prisoners, providing unique, firsthand views of women's prison experience in various nations and eras, they are valuable, untapped primary source material for researchers in literature, sociology, criminology, legal studies, and women's studies. The general reader and the incarcerated woman or man will also find much of interest here.

NOTES

1. Tillie Olsen, *Silences* (New York: Dell, 1978), p. 45.
2. Carol Muske, "The Art of Not Bowing: Writing by Women in Prison," *Heresies* 1 (January 1977): 30–34.

Acknowledgments

*

I am grateful to the many people who have contributed to this book in important ways. The pathbreaking work of H. Bruce Franklin, Elissa D. Gelfand, and Paul Lauter in reconstructing the literary canon has been an invaluable source of inspiration and guidance. Their generous and practical support helped to make this book a reality. Above all I appreciate their belief that this project is needed.

Special thanks go to my colleagues Valarie Arms and Julia Epstein for their encouragement and always perceptive suggestions. The bibliographical research of my graduate research assistants, Ann-Adele Wight and Amy Neil, was professional and resourceful.

This book owes much to the assistance and advice of numerous librarians. In particular I want to thank Nancy Halli of the Historical Society of Pennsylvania, and Richard Binder of Drexel University. The Interlibrary Loan staff of Drexel University has been instrumental in helping me compile the Annotated Bibliography. I am indebted to Robin Barnes, Merrill Stein, and especially Deidre Harper.

For their assistance in providing biographical data and information on works by women prisoners, I thank Grant Allen Anderson of the Historical Department of the Church of Jesus Christ of Latter-day Saints, Salt Lake City; Jane Begos, editor of *Women's Diaries*; Susan L. Boone of The Sophia Smith Collection, Smith College; David Braham of Amnesty International—International Secretariat; Joseph Bruchac of Greenfield Review Press; Nick Caistor of Writers and Scholars Educational Trust, London; Pat Case of Temple University's Contemporary Culture Collection; Sandra L. Chaff of the Medical College of Pennsylvania Archives; Mara L. Crowell of the Oswego County Historical Society (N.Y.); Karlene Faith; Renny Golden; Paul Gordon of the Education Department of Arthur Kill Correctional Facility; Axel Guwe of the Academy of Arts and Humanities, Seaside, Calif.; Ramon Hodel of Amnesty International–U.S.A. James H. Hutson of the Library of Congress Manuscript Division; Jesus Alerio Ibarra; David King of the Rare Book Department of the Free Library of Philadelphia; J. Richard Kyle of the Swarthmore College Peace Collection; Rita Lawn and Philip Balla of PEN American Center; Edward Lyon of The George Arents Research Library at Syracuse University; Sally M. Miller; Aurora Levins Morales; The New York Public Library, Rare Books and Manuscripts Division and Newspaper Department; David Rothenberg of the Fortune Society; Elizabeth Shenton of the Schlesinger Library; Richard A. Schrader of the Southern Historical Collection at the University of North Carolina; Nicola Johnson of the Suffragette Papers Collection at the Museum of London; Gloria F. Waldman; Meta Winter; S. Wong of Women's International Resource Exchange (WIRE); and Laura X of Women's History Research Center, Inc.

For clerical and word processing support I thank Paulette Williams, Lettitia Dolores, and Nelson Vecchione.

My association with the Pennsylvania Prison Society over the years has taught me much about prisons and prisoners; the idea for this book germinated in my work with the Prison Society in the Philadelphia County Prisons. I am especially grateful to former Executive Director Rendall Davis, Renee Evans, Janet Leban, Rena Nassau, and Norman Pearson for showing me a humane approach to the ancient problem of imprisonment. Joan Leiby of the Philadelphia Probation Office has shared with me her sensitive perspective during many thoughtful discussions.

Nancy Waring, my editor, has helped give life and shape to this project. Her suggestions often probed to the heart of complex issues, and our discussions have always been productive.

My greatest debt is to my parents, Margaret and Carl Scheffler, and to my husband, Michael Neely, who read the manuscript and helped make this a better book. Their love and faith in me has been an unfailing source of strength and light.

WALL TAPPINGS

Introduction

*

1 April 1957, Leningrad

In the fearful years of the Yezhov terror I spent seventeen months in prison queues in Leningrad. One day somebody "identified" me. Beside me, in the queue, there was a woman with blue lips. She had, of course, never heard of me: but she suddenly came out of that trance so common to us all and whispered in my ear (everybody spoke in whispers there): "Can you describe this?" And I said: "Yes, I can." And then something like the shadow of a smile crossed what had once been her face.[1]

Russian poet Anna Akhmatova (1889–1966), long suppressed and harassed by censors and police in her native land, was never imprisoned, but her senses were finely attuned to the suffering around her. In *Requiem* she writes of her own anguished attempts to visit her son in Stalin's prisons. She voices the need of the silenced to communicate their experience, and stresses the invaluable function of the writer, whose words speak for those who cannot. The simple but powerful scene described above characterizes women's prison literature, with its clear link between the craft of writing and the society in which the writer lives and works.

All women's prison texts are political, each speaking in its own way for silenced women behind bars and beyond prison walls. Many women prison writers are political activists who speak for fellow victims of society's repression.[2] Others, imprisoned for criminal offenses, express the general plight of the incarcerated woman through accounts of their own pain. Still others, despising the criminal women they have been forced to live with, seem totally absorbed in the task of justifying their own lives before society; yet even their works reveal much about the social condition and status of women.

The marginal texts of women's prison literature increasingly demand attention.[3] Prison literature by men, for example, is often cited for its rich imagery and influence; however, works by women prisoners are

[3]

much more obscure. And since works by women as well as by prisoners lie outside the mainstream of great literature, women's prison texts are doubly marginal. Few people have access to these works or even know of them, and, consequently, a prison author and her audience in "polite" society remain widely separated.

This "double marginality" makes the investigation of women's prison literature extremely exciting from the standpoint of recent directions in feminist scholarship. The need to consider race and class as well as gender in revising the literary canon has been a growing concern among feminist literary critics, who call for nothing less than a reexamination of aesthetic and social assumptions behind our responses to works.[4] Feminist criminologists share these concerns about the dynamics of class, race, and gender in the criminal justice system.[5] Women's prison literature lies at the heart of this issue, since its authors are the female dispossessed—in society, in the canon, and—until recently—even in feminist scholarship. Considerations of class, race, and gender are central to an understanding of these texts. They demonstrate that opening the canon to writing by women is not enough; authors who have been excluded by reason of race or low socioeconomic class must also share in the reconstruction of our concept of "great literature."

H. Bruce Franklin makes a similar point about American prison literature, particularly that of black men, in *Prison Literature in America: The Victim as Criminal and Artist*: "I believe that this book leads inevitably to a fundamental redefinition of American literature, its history, and the criteria appropriate to evaluating all literary works produced within the United States."[6] Feminist criticism and criticism of prison literature converge in a reading of women's prison literature, and highlight the need to reevaluate traditional aesthetic criteria.

A major undertaking of feminist literary criticism, the rediscovery of lost texts, is central to research in women's prison literature, where works have been mostly forgotten. Here, it is instructive to look in two directions simultaneously: at points that unify these texts, and at individual distinctions. After reading several prison texts by women, one recognizes the special value of considering these writers as a *group* rather than as isolated authors of lost texts or as notable individuals. The sense of solidarity within the texts becomes increasingly strong in recent prison works, underscoring the communal nature of much of the writing.

Women's prison literature is political, communal, and radical because women's prisons are paradigmatic of women's position in society. Michel Foucault, writing primarily of men's prisons, describes the modern trend toward objectification of the institutionalized prisoner, who is treated as a faulty mechanism that must be repaired.[7] Even more striking is prison's objectification of women, who are already treated as objects in the society outside. If women are generally vulnerable in normal society, their vulnerability is acute in prison. Critic Elissa Gelfand explains how writings by French women demonstrate this effect of imprisonment. She sees women's texts from French prisons as unique because they are written "under explicitly sex-specific social conditions." They show "an unusually clear interplay between society and text, or, more precisely, between social and literary representations of the same cultural myths surrounding criminal women."[8]

If the situation of individual female inmates is seen as a paradigm of women's position in general, it might be useful to regard a women's prison as a "microsociety," where women adapt to the deprivations of imprisonment by assuming roles analogous to their roles in society.[9] In reflecting their authors' views of this microcosm, women's prison texts offer a unique perspective about women's life in society in general.

THE PRISON INSTITUTION AND THE WOMAN PRISONER

The "concrete womb" of prison, to use Kathryn Burkhart's telling metaphor, is a modern, paradoxical institution. "It is a place we send people for *change*. We expect them to grow and become responsible on literally concrete ground."[10] The concept of imprisonment has evolved over centuries, with prison as an institution being a relatively recent development. Since the liberal awakening in the 1960s to the civil rights of minorities and the oppressed, the American public has become more aware of this generally ignored institution and the grievances of prisoners, many of whom have brought class action suits to protest their overcrowded, inhumane conditions.

Prisons before the eighteenth century were largely holding places for the condemned before execution; loss of liberty was not itself a punishment. Foucault describes the shifting locus of power from the king to society in the treatment of offenders in France.[11] Placing this shift in the eighteenth century's revolutionary ferment, he notes a transition from excessive demonstrations of the king's absolute power over the body of the offender during torture and execution, to society's discipline of the body of the offender by restriction of rights in prison.[12] Under either system, control over the body is the issue. And as prisons evolved as institutions reflecting and advancing an industrial society's goals, that control became more individualized. As society becomes more and more intent upon "normalizing" its members, explains Foucault, institutions such as schools, hospitals, the military, and prisons ensure this regulation at all levels. From the start, the purpose of prisons as institutions has been to reform deviants as well as to deprive them of liberty. The offender, no longer the enemy of the sovereign but rather a traitor or a social misfit, has to be made to conform.

With the establishment of a prison system, the individual offender became an object of scientific interest. Control of inmate behavior was maintained by measuring the skull to identify criminal traits, classifying vices, probing social and psychological background, and observing every action.[13] In his classic study, *Society of Captives*, Gresham Sykes presents prison as a totalitarian society that forces contact among many individuals. A "maximum security prison represents a social system in which an attempt is made to create and maintain total or almost total social control."[14]

A counterforce balancing prison's controls is reform. According to Foucault, this movement has proceeded simultaneously with prisons themselves: "The prison has always formed part of an active field in which projects, improvements, experiments, theoretical statements, personal evidence and investigations have proliferated. The prison institution has always been a focus of concern and debate."[15]

The history of reform in American prisons for women is distinctive in several ways. Historian Estelle Freedman explains that three principles characterized the independent movement for women's prison reform in the late nineteenth century: the separation of female from male prisoners, based upon the belief in women's moral superiority and men's corrupting influence; the provision of feminine care and facilities, based upon the concept of separate sexual spheres; and the management of women's prisons by female staff and administrators.[16]

While these reforms undoubtedly improved prison conditions for women, they also generated problems that continue to plague women's correctional institutions today. Training was restricted to moral and domestic education rather than useful occupational skills, even after twentieth-century criminologists began to discern the economic basis of female crime. To foster desirable domestic, maternal virtues, women's institutions were constructed as homelike cottages and located in rural areas far from urban corruption. This remoteness meant a lack of educational and training programs and isolation for inmates whose families lived in the city.

Perhaps the most destructive aspect of women's treatment in prison is the dependency that the disciplinary system encourages. While this lack of adult responsibility also characterizes men's institutions, women prisoners in particular complain that the system treats them like children.[17] This atmosphere of absolute dependency promotes female stereotypes, stifles individual initiative and creativity, and helps to explain why so few female prisoners write. Freedman describes the problem this presents for the researcher:

> The most difficult problem in prison history is reconstructing the inmate experience. Although quantitative data tell something about who went to prison and why, they do not record feelings. Most statements about inmates come from reformers and officials, and thus must be read with care.[18]

Nevertheless, texts by women prisoners have played a part in the history of women's prison reform, with American Socialist Kate Richards O'Hare (*In Prison*) and British suffragette Lady Constance Lytton (*Prisons and Prisoners*) among the most notable writers who used their prison experience to advocate reform.[19] Recent, outspoken writings by female inmates in America are part of this inmate reform tradition that rejects stereotypes in an attempt to get to the heart of prison issues.

The relative scarcity of prison texts by women can also be partially explained by the small number of female prisoners. Women have always constituted a small segment of the total prison population. For example, United States Department of Justice figures for 1981 show that the 14,000 women in state and federal prisons accounted for only 4 percent of the total prison population.[20]

Who is the female prisoner today? According to recent studies in the United States, she is young (the majority are under thirty), black, and poor, and she is a mother and the breadwinner in the household.[21] American and British researchers agree on the types of crimes committed by women: British sociologist Carol Smart explains that adult women are characteristically imprisoned today for shoplifting and prostitution, while adolescent females are imprisoned for being promiscuous and ungovernable. Women's offenses are usually not violent, and victims of homicides by women are generally family and lovers, rather than strangers.[22]

Smart attributes the relative scarcity of research on women's crime to the fact that it has not seriously threatened society. Even recent research on the etiology of female crime is still rooted in theories of biological and psychological determinism and misogynous myths about woman's innate evil and fragility, mostly ignoring the economic basis of crimes committed by women.[23] Classical studies of the female criminal, from that of Lombroso and Ferrero (1895) to that of Otto Pollak (1950; 1961), employ stereotypes.[24] Pollak is to be credited for bringing women's criminology to the attention of contemporary researchers, but even he accepted myths about women. In his theory of the "masked character of female crime," he attributes women's low rate of reported crime to what he considers their innate ability to deceive, manifested, he contends, when they feign pleasure during sex.[25] His influence has been widespread; as recently as 1969, a rather sensational study of women's crime, *How Could She Do That?*, made a similar statement:

> Among insects, the female of certain species is more deadly than the male; among human beings, her poison is of but equal potency, but when she chooses to use it, the victim is often caught unaware, for her sting is well concealed.[26]

Louise Michel, heroine of the Paris Commune of 1871, was imprisoned many times throughout her life as a political activist. Her experiences as a prisoner helped her to empathize with imprisoned women who suffered from poverty and the prejudices of a criminal justice system that based its judgments upon sexist stereotypes. Her memoirs describe the nineteenth-century woman's predicament:

> All the women reading these memoirs must remember that we women are not judged the same way men are. When men accuse some other man of a crime, they do not accuse him of such a stupid one that an observer wonders if they are serious. But that is how they deal with a woman; she is accused of things so stupid they defy belief. If she is not duped by the

claims of popular sovereignty put forth to delude people, or if she is not fooled by the hypocritical concessions which hoodwink most women, she will be indicted. Then, if a woman is courageous, or if she grasps some bit of knowledge easily, men claim she is only a "pathological" case.[27]

Thus, women were viewed as inferior either morally or mentally, but in both cases they were seen as controlled by their biology. The consequences of those stereotypes are still being felt by imprisoned women.

The myth of women's emotional weakness and irrational nature has led to several problems and inequities in their treatment within the criminal justice system. Writers like Pollak have perpetuated the theory that women are given chivalrous treatment by males in the court and correctional systems, but recent researchers challenge this view and find that women may be treated even more harshly for certain offenses, especially those of a sexual nature.[28] Another problem women face is the analogy drawn between mental illness in women and criminal behavior in men. According to this theory, emotional problems in women lead to mental illness, but those in men lead to crime. Relatively few women therefore turn to crime, the reasoning goes, and those who do are particularly aberrant.[29]

A recent criminological theory, quite hotly disputed by researchers and the media, is the effect of the women's movement on the incidence and nature of female crime. The research of criminologist Freda Adler (1975) is particularly cited for its argument that the feminist movement has led to increased crime by women.[30] Adler posits a "liberated female criminal" who, desiring to emulate men, has entered the realm of traditionally male crimes, complete with violence. On the other hand, in her 1975 study, Rita J. Simon expects a rise in white collar crime since more women are working, but she does not foresee an increase in violent crime. Because women's violence stems from frustration and is directed primarily at family members, Simon expects that increased education and employment should actually lower the level of violent female crime. Simon explains her view of how the women's movement has affected crime:

If one assumes that the changes in women's roles, in their perceptions of self, and in their desire for expanded horizons that began in the latter part of the sixties will not be abated, either by external events such as a major economic depression or by internal processes whereby women examine their situation and decide that their happiness lies in the traditional pursuits of homemaking, wifely companionship, and motherhood, then we would expect that one of the major by-products of the women's movement will be a higher proportion of women who pursue careers in crime.[31]

The theory of a causal link between women's liberation and crime raised a storm in the mid-1970s and was soon criticized as reactionary and dangerous to the women's movement. Critics cite several points overlooked in the simplistic theory of the new female criminal: (1) statistics on crime rates require careful interpretation and are easily distorted; (2) changes in law and police policy may lead to increased arrests and convictions of women, which may be mistaken for increased crime; (3) criminologists, corrections officials, and mental health professionals are simply paying more attention to women's crime now; (4) the women's movement seeks equality with men, but female criminals do not necessarily strive to imitate male violence; (5) most female inmates come from a lower socioeconomic class and have little interest in the women's movement; and (6) most women's crimes are property offenses, demonstrating that their actions have an economic basis, motivated by poverty.[32] Rather than relying on simplistic theories of female crime, criminologists are recognizing the need for attention to "the wider moral, political, economic and sexual spheres which influence women's status and position in society."[33]

THE CONVERGENCE OF TWO MARGINAL TRADITIONS: WOMEN'S LITERATURE AND PRISON LITERATURE

Because women's prison literature takes the reader doubly out of the accepted literary canon, we must consider the works in the context of two separate marginal traditions in order to understand the silence of most imprisoned women and the obscurity of most texts they have managed to write. Discussing women's literature and prison literature in the same context offers possibilities for rich discoveries, for each helps to explain the silence of the other.

Before the eighteenth century's establishment of imprisonment as a form of punishment, broadsides and pamphlets recorded the lives and executions of criminals and the condemned. Foucault notes the ambiguity of these texts. They served those in power as a form of ideological control over the people by presenting examples of crime, punishment, and repentance. On the other hand, they transformed criminals into folk heroes who achieved glory even in their infamy. With the rise of prisons and the changing perception of crime from offense against the ruler to betrayal of society, a new literature of crime supplanted these broadsides. Accounts of crimes by the masses were relegated to the newspapers, while the new literature glorified crime as a fine art, practiced by the great and powerful classes and epitomized by the intellectual confrontation between criminal and detective. As the institution of prison began to objectify inmates in its discipline process, their biographies left the pages of heroic folk literature and entered the charts of case studies.[34]

Literature written in prison, like earlier works written in cells or dungeons that were holding places before punishment, was mostly written by educated political prisoners. Many of these works have become accepted as part of the world's great literature, and their authors, almost exclusively male, are noteworthy historic and literary figures: Mohandas Gandhi, Oscar Wilde, Silvio Pellico, Miguel de Cervantes, Saint Thomas More, François Villon, and Jean Genet. During World War II Isidore Abramowitz compiled *The Great Prisoners: The First Anthology of Literature Written in Prison*; he saw prison writing as an inspirational testimony to human endurance and hope:

> If the great names appear here, and in some of the great papers and manifestos of the spirit, it is because what began as an experimental formula for exploring a bypath of literature flowered into an odd but effective commentary on our intellectual adventure in the west.[35]

Abramowitz takes the traditional Western male perspective and gives little attention to women and Third World writers. However, his point may be adapted to explain the significance of women's prison writing, which makes "an odd but effective commentary" on women's intellectual adventure.

Analysis of women's prison literature is aided by H. Bruce Franklin's discussion of American prison literature by black males. This body of works combines two major streams of convict narrative in America:

slave narratives and personal confessionals of an individual's life in crime. Few political prisoners before early twentieth-century anarchists wrote autobiographies, but Franklin finds that by mid-nineteenth century, confessionals by common criminals had turned from their emphasis on moral example or mere entertainment to protests of social injustice. The choice of the term "prisoner" over the traditional label "criminal" and the objection to being identified by number demonstrate this awakening political consciousness. By the 1920s, works demonstrating prisoners' humanity, intelligence, and social concerns began to threaten prison authorities, who attempted to suppress prison writing during the Great Depression. Few works by women inmates were published because, theorizes Franklin, few women were imprisoned, and their crimes, stemming from dismal poverty, did not lend themselves to descriptions of adventure.[36]

Up until the twentieth century, the majority of prison narratives in America were written from the white male perspective. However, in the twentieth century, works by black American prisoners became prominent. In these works the white prison narrative tradition joined with black slave narratives that focused on the slave's awakening consciousness. The special perspective of the slaves' writings leads to a basic difference in the prison works of black and white men. While white prison writers began with an emphasis on the individual "I" and later recognized the suppression of prison's social subclass and of workers in general, black prison writers began with the knowledge that prison was an updated form of slavery meant to control a whole people, not only an individual. The latter point of view generated a "collective aesthetic" that identifies the writer as a representative of the people rather than as a solitary artist. Franklin explains that this aesthetic often conflicts with generally accepted literary standards, for its emphasis is often on the power of the text to motivate its readers to action rather than on originality and literary artifice.[37]

To what extent are women's prison texts analogous to those of black men? Both differ from the white masculine mode of writing from a position of power. Though works by women prisoners before the twentieth century often turned inward to the self, their contemporary prison texts have a strong similarity to black writing in the growing trend toward women's solidarity. However, while a comparison with the tradition of prison literature, especially that of blacks, gives insight to characteristics of women's prison literature, it should be noted that the most widely acclaimed works in the prison tradition are written by men. Therefore, attention to the *female* literary tradition, itself marginal, is needed to complement the perspective gained from reading prison texts by black men.

Elaine Showalter, discussing the works of British women writers, comments on the limitations of the canon:

> There are many reasons why discussion of women writers has been so inaccurate, fragmented, and partisan. First, women's literary history has suffered from an extreme form of what John Gross calls "residual Great Traditionalism," which has reduced and condensed the extraordinary range and diversity of English women novelists to a tiny band of the "great," and derived all theories from them. . . . Criticism of women novelists, while focusing on these happy few, has ignored those who are not "great," and left them out of anthologies, histories, textbooks, and theories. Having lost sight of the minor novelists, who were links in the chain that bound one generation to the next, we have not had a very clear understanding of the continuities in women's writing, nor any reliable information about the relationships between the writers' lives and the changes in the legal, economic, and social status of women.[38]

As a group, and to a large extent as individuals, women prison authors are among the most forgotten writers, yet they certainly provide a wealth of "information about the relationships between the writers' lives and the changes in the legal, economic, and social status of women." Women prisoners epitomize the plight of the silenced female writer, who has recently drawn so much concern from feminist scholars.

In the starkest sense the woman prisoner lacks Virginia Woolf's "Room of One's Own" and must contend with a lack of privacy, money, and education and the demoralizing effects of anonymity. The general lack of decent writing conditions for women is acute in a woman's prison, where regimentation and dreary routine sap creative energy, and where privacy loses all meaning. Most female inmates, who generally have a below-average formal education, do not express themselves in writing. For most poor and minority women prisoners, writing was not seen as an option before imprisonment, and once released, these women usually face the same problems of basic survival that they knew before incarceration, and have little time, encouragement, or motivation to write their prison stories.

In order to write, any woman, and especially the woman prisoner, must escape society's restrictions against female artistic creation or written self-expression. Sandra M. Gilbert and Susan Gubar call the tension felt by the female artist the "anxiety of authorship."[39] Moreover, women must combat the illusion of absolute literary standards, since they live on the margins of the male culture and power that create the standards.[40] Too often the result is silence.

In *Silences* Tillie Olsen calls class, economic circumstance, and race "those other traditional silencers of humanity."[41] Women prisoners, with the exception of some political activists, display a unique combination of all those elements that work against expression and against acceptance of their work by the literary establishment. Even if a woman prisoner from a background of poverty does succeed in publishing her work, she is likely to experience the "one-book phenomenon" Olsen describes. Ex-prisoners may be unproductive writers because even when the prison experience gives the individual an unprecedented opportunity and the motivation to write, the released woman meets a hostile society that barely grants her employment or the means to survive, and the writing of her memoirs has no place in this new life. She becomes the most extreme victim of Olsen's "discontinuity," the tendency of women to be easily distracted by everyday demands or others' needs.[42]

Feminist critics find that women writers who do break the silence often express their ideas through a deceptive code.[43] One of the fundamental codes, according to Annis Pratt, is that of "marriage as archetypal enclosure." Her description of the restrictions imposed on women by marriage reads like the pains of imprisonment described by Gresham Sykes in his study of a maximum-security prison: loss of erotic freedom, of intellectual freedom, and of freedom to come and go.[44] The image of marriage in literature as presented by Pratt, Gilbert, and Gubar is clearly that of a prison—either a literal one or the figurative prison of madness, domesticity, or the "cult of true womanhood."[45] French women's prison texts, according to Gelfand, clearly demonstrate this coding technique. These female writers do not angrily challenge society, as in classic male prison texts:

> . . . rather than engage in an overt dialectic with the values of their times, women, who have never created those values, covertly subvert and contest them; instead of seeking to give wholeness to an incoherent world

women search within themselves for unity; and, far from attempting to conquer hostile space by appropriating it, women generally observe and respect it. Indirection and coded contestation, a search for self, and an acknowledgement of surroundings characterize women's prison writing.[46]

Increasingly, today's women prison writers do not code their images; the prison is direct and real. As the "titanic outcast," to use Nina Auerbach's term for the fallen woman,[47] the imprisoned female writer assumes a sort of freedom and power in her ability to create without the deception of codes. The use of forthright, uncoded statements is found in the writings of many contemporary prisoners, as well as in works by earlier prisoners who wrote from a firm religious or political conviction. Consider the proclamation of Black Panther Ericka Huggins:

> How often do women awake
> in the prison of marriage,
> of solitary motherhood
> alone and forgotten[48]

Huggins's prison is a literal one, and she calls upon her sisters, black and white, to acknowledge that theirs is quite literal too. Ironically, if the woman prisoner is afforded the opportunity to write, her work often reveals her situation more directly than does that of the woman on the outside. She is, in a sense, more free to write truthfully.

The concept of a female subculture offers a new dimension to discussion of women's prison literature.[49] Faragher and Stansell define subculture as a "habit of living . . . of a minority group which is self-consciously distinct from the dominant activities, expectations, and values of a society."[50] Though women can hardly be called a minority, it is their marginal position with respect to the mainstream society that is being stressed here. In prison populations, women definitely are a minority; female prisoners are also a minority among the general population of women. Thus, their works may be best understood in the context of their marginal position. Critics are finding that this focus by women writers on their marginality can be a source of strength and creative insight if it represents a conscious decision to center attention on women rather than a failed attempt to write like men.[51] Here, the positive model of an earlier female writer's success is encouraging. For imprisoned women, the example of other women who have described their prison experiences to the world can be especially meaningful, and from this female subculture, a body of literature with its own characteristics has arisen.

CHARACTERISTICS OF WOMEN'S PRISON TEXTS

During those few days we were baptized, and the Holy Spirit bade me make no other petition after the holy water save for bodily endurance. A few days after we were lodged in prison; and I was in great fear, because I had never known such darkness. What a day of horror! Terrible heat, thanks to the crowds! Rough handling by the soldiers! To crown all I was tormented there by anxiety for my baby. Then Tertius and Pomponius, those blessed deacons who were ministering to us, paid for us to be removed for a few hours to a better part of the prison and refresh ourselves. Then all went out of the prison and were left to themselves. [My baby was brought to me], and I suckled him, for he was already faint for want of food. I spoke anxiously to my mother on his behalf, and strengthened my brother, and commended my son to their charge. I was pining because I saw them pine on my account. Such anxieties I suffered for many days; and I obtained leave for my baby to remain in the prison with me; and I at once recovered my health, and was relieved of my trouble and anxiety for my baby; and my prison suddenly became a palace to me, and I would rather have been there than anywhere else.[52]

This passage from "The Passion of Saint Perpetua," a third-century Christian martyr from Carthage, vividly illustrates qualities that separate women's prison writing from men's. Her interest is in the concrete reality of the prison environment and especially in her relationship with those who are close to her. As one critic explains, hers is "the Christian woman's point of view, with its constant references to child-bearing, nursing, food, the drinking of milk, and so on."[53] Her focus is simultaneously upon eternity and the moment, with its physical discomforts and family responsibilities.

Most readers' impressions of prison writing come from the dominant tradition of the famous male prison authors, who, as mentioned earlier, are represented in general literature as well as in prison anthologies. Richard Lovelace's poem "To Althea from Prison," with its famous line "Stone walls do not a prison make," is a staple of British literature anthologies. It also graces the title page of John Alfred Langford's more specialized 1861 anthology, *Prison Books and Their Authors*. The editor includes only male writers and declares the works of these prisoners to be edifying reading: "Truly a noble record of the power of the mind to make its own kingdom—a perennial teaching of the benign influence of sorrow, and a glorious monument of genius are the world's Prison Books."[54] Langford's comment imitates the literature it praises in its elevated, cerebral tone. In the mental transformation of her prison to a palace, Perpetua to some extent shares Lovelace's triumph; however, men's prison writings in general are much more concerned with images of transcendence and rebellion. Freedom has different meanings for Lovelace and Perpetua. Lovelace neglects the lover in his love poem in favor of a discourse on the abstract concept of freedom; freedom for Perpetua comes when she nurses her baby, as only then can she celebrate the paradox of a palatial prison.

Patricia Meyer Spacks makes a useful distinction between social *limitations* that discourage artistic creation by women, and *limits*, such as mortality, placed on men, who interpret them as challenges and "gain existential dignity by defying them."[55] Women prisoners face both limitations and limits, while imprisoned men use Promethean endurance as a metaphor for the universal limits imposed on humanity and the glory inherent in a battle against overwhelming odds.

In *The Romantic Prison*, Victor Brombert analyzes the image of the prison as used in French texts written by men from the Romantic era to the present.[56] The Romantics saw prison as a paradoxical space simultaneously providing suffering and the seclusion from worldly affairs desired by the poet. Prison fostered individualism, encouraged the rebel in his quarrel with society, and inspired dreams of transcendence. Whether the focus of the writer/artist was inward, through meditation, or outward, through imaginative flight, the basic image was that of spiritual and intellectual freedom. Many of the authors Brombert discusses, including Proust, Sartre, and Kafka, were not actually imprisoned, but favored imprisonment as an image for a state of mind they wished to project. With Camus and Genet, the figure of the prisoner as social rebel became a prominent influence on other modern writers. The "notion of a happy captivity"[57] is consistent with the religious nature of much early prison literature, and is therefore expressed by Perpetua also, but her primary focus is clearly on her actual association with others during her imprisonment, and only subsequently on spiritual and intellectual freedom.

Thus we see that a basic difference separates male and female prison writers' treatment of the freedom/captivity opposition. The incarcerated male, aware of his separation from a distracting society, may view his imprisonment as a situation in which he is mentally free to write even though he is physically bound. He may claim that prison gives him genuine freedom. For the woman prisoner, this paradox is not at all a standard image, since she never knew on the outside the physical and social freedom that men enjoy. She does not share the luxury of verbal play with the word *freedom*. Instead, she records—perhaps for the first time—her understanding that she is and always has been a prisoner. While the male prisoner has exchanged literal freedom in society for a figurative freedom in prison, she has traded virtual imprisonment in society for actual imprisonment. This explains the images of imprisonment and escape that are common in nineteenth-century literature by women who had never seen the inside of a prison,[58] and these images become quite literal in women's texts written behind bars and walls.

However, silenced by the lack of education and poverty that brought them to prison in the first place, and then by the sensory deprivation of the prison environment itself, the vast majority of women in prison do not write. "What are rights without means?" Tillie Olsen aptly quotes novelist Rebecca Harding Davis.[59] Newspaper reporter Kathryn Burkhart explains that she hesitated to write *Women in Prison*, her study of daily life in women's correctional institutions, because she felt that this was a job for inmates who could relate their experiences firsthand. But the women themselves encouraged her:

> As one older woman said, "Baby, you gotta be the voice for us. Cause according to society, we ain't got no voices. Numbers can't talk—everybody knows that. Besides that, we get so used to this whole thing we can't even *see* a lot of it. It's too close. You got some perspective."
>
> "We haven't never had the chance to tell our side of the story," another jail-weary woman said. . . . "I always thought I'd try to write a book about all this but I never got past the title: *Jail Ain't Shit.*"[60]

What, then, motivates the relatively few women prisoners who do write? Their work functions on personal, social, and political levels—sometimes simultaneously—and their intended audiences vary with their purposes. On the most personal level, women prisoners write because they believe their experience is worth communicating, and they may or may not envision any outside reader among their contemporaries or posterity. They write to confirm their own sense of worth, a sense of worth that is essential for any woman writer, but especially for the female outcast, relegated to one of society's most degrading institutions.

The variety of motivations for writing by women prisoners is treated in more detail within the section introductions of this anthology. Social and political circumstances and the woman's own background account for differences in writers' purposes. The desire to vindicate the self before a hostile society motivates authors of some texts, particularly those written before the twentieth century. On the other hand, commitment to a political, social, or religious cause is a very different reason to write, and it inspires texts where the writer's self receives little attention.

Some women, particularly political activists, enter prison with such self-confidence that they do not feel a need for self-justification. In this case, imprisonment encourages the woman to record her story, often to advocate social reform. Nineteenth-century British suffragettes such as Lady Constance Lytton, for example, underwent frequent and often brutal imprisonments, which figured dramatically in the memoirs and histories they later wrote.[61] (Throughout this book *suffragette*, rather than *suffragist*, is used to refer to the women who worked in the militant arm of the British woman suffrage movement. Suffragette is the term they used to describe themselves; suffragists were nonmilitant supporters of woman suffrage.) Patricia McConnel, imprisoned in a number of American jails and in the Federal Penitentiary for Women at Alderson, West Virginia, also advocates prison reform. She did not come to prison as a political activist and she writes that she "deserved to be in jail." Witnessing the "extreme cruelty, both physical and psychological, of penal institutions" led her to write her short fiction long after her release:

> I started writing these stories about 19 years ago to cleanse myself of horrors and to do a service for my society and women by bringing these conditions to light. . . .
>
> I have come to appreciate writing as a powerful tool for therapy and growth. I believe that in a very literal sense, it has saved me.[62]

For some women, prison ironically opens doors for repressed talents and subdued personalities. A case in point is Ethel Rosenberg. Putting questions about her alleged espionage aside, she undeniably discovered her voice in prison. Her letters, addressed to family but also intended for publication, provided an opportunity for expression denied her in the roles of daughter, housewife, and mother. When faced with a pressing need to defend her integrity and save her life, Rosenberg found a subject and a voice through her isolation from the society that limited her to conventional roles and standards. Her execution in 1953 makes it impossible for readers to know whether she would have continued to grow beyond her beginning efforts to write, but her case exemplifies how prison can promote writing from silence.

The most basic reason for all prison writing is the human need to communicate. Choosing writing as a medium allows contact with a wider audience, but it stems from the same visceral need as do attempts to communicate through other means in prison. Although imprisonment itself forcibly separates the inmate from her family, friends, and social environment, isolation can take much more extreme forms within the prison.

Human beings subjected to sensory deprivation and social isolation have always struggled to combat restricted communication. The panopticon, for example, was an eighteenth-century architectural design by Jeremy Bentham that imposed a clever system of "communication" benefiting only the administration. From a central tower, all cells could be observed, but the prisoner could neither see the observer nor contact the inmate in the next cell. "He is seen, but he does not see; he is the object of information, never a subject in communication," writes Foucault.[63] This isolation was a means of thought control as well as physical discipline, since the administration could monitor all ideas and messages conveyed to the inmate.

For prisoners with the educational background, materials, and opportunity to write, communication may take a variety of forms, ranging in sophistication from the publishable book to the outlawed prison "kite," a communication medium common in women's institutions.[64] Kites are notes that function as poetry, news, courtship, and political communication when they are passed between women.[65] The subversive nature of kites in the eyes of prison administrators became apparent in the trial of Ericka Huggins, when her messages to sister prisoners were exhibited in court as evidence against her.[66]

Wall tapping is the most ancient of all systems of prison communication. No mere cliché from romantic novels, this system has been responsible for saving the sanity, if not the lives, of prisoners throughout centuries around the globe. The British suffragettes defiantly tapped "No Surrender!" to encourage their sisters who were being forcibly fed. A striking story illustrating both the significance of wall tapping and the influence of one woman prison author on another comes from *Journey into the Whirlwind*, the memoirs of Eugenia Ginzburg, who was imprisoned in Stalin's prisons and camps for seventeen years. Ginzburg, at first ignorant of the code, could not benefit from the tapping of a fellow sufferer in the next cell. She launched her own life-sustaining communication after recalling an explanation of the code that she had read years earlier. Ginzburg's countrywoman Vera Figner had described in her memoirs the code she used to survive her twenty-year solitary confinement in the Schlüsselburg Fortress. Fifty years later, her message saved Ginzburg.

The woman who has the means to communicate through writing in prison must choose a form for her work. The overwhelming majority of women prisoners throughout the world write confessional works— letters, diaries, memoirs, and autobiographies. The confessional mode is especially congenial if the woman did not write before imprisonment. For some, personal formats allow the self-justification that is their motivation for writing; for others, they enhance a bold affirmation of the writer's personality and beliefs.

In any case, confessional works display a fascinating variety of ways that female prisoners create a "self" through writing to sustain and express themselves during imprisonment. In an environment where women are treated like children, the incarcerated woman writer can maintain some control over her world by ordering reality according to her own perceptions and organizing principles. In letters and memoirs she constructs a persona that, to varying degrees, can challenge the prevailing stereotypes of the woman prisoner. In their memoirs, Vera Figner and Eugenia Ginzburg testify that wall tapping saved them by restoring the power to communicate. With communication came consciousness, strength, and pride in their intelligence. Writing, like the more basic medium of tapping, instills a sense of autonomy and pride.

Gelfand has shown that French women's prison texts generally follow confessional formats. Society often responds to female crime by accusing the woman of "desensitization" and a lack of femininity. An imprisoned woman can defend herself against unjust labels by writing a confessional text that presents a picture of an integrated, sensitive personality. In their defense before society, concludes Gelfand, many French women prison writers, from the eighteenth century to the present, actually reinforce female stereotypes to convey an impression of their social conformity to standards of acceptable female behavior. They *use* stereotypes for their own purposes, examining their own past lives and employing their knowledge of social conventions as a guide in their defense.[67]

Readers of women's prison letters and memoirs, particularly those written before the twentieth century, should not expect to find the universalizing of personal experience that characterizes men's autobiography, any more than they would find this approach in women's autobiographical narratives written outside prison. Distinctions made by critics between confessional writings by men and women are useful to readers of women's prison texts. Whereas men tend to set their lives' events in the context of the political atmosphere of the time and attribute great significance to their activities, women are more concerned with personal relationships and justifying themselves, particularly in the role of writer.[68] Perhaps this is why many women prisoners such as O'Hare and Rosenberg choose the letter form, even when they expect that the letters will be circulated among supporters or even published: Letters allow them to write their prison stories boldly under the guise of intimate communication with family and friends.

Women's confessional forms in the twentieth century have become more straightforward, however, with fewer apologies for taking on the conscious role of writer and more assertions of the writer's intention to record her life for others to read.[69] Even earlier works by political prisoners often show this confidence, perhaps because they felt the support of others in their cause and a motivation to communicate that surpassed any personal reticence. Their works provided an appropriate means of channeling the aggression and anger that underlie much women's writing.[70] Of all society's institutions, prison demands the most extreme form of deception; prisoners must simultaneously deny and use their feelings to survive physically, emotionally, and mentally. Women have known social limitations on the outside; in prison these limitations could build into explosive tensions. Prisoners who can express their tensions in writing, and even serve as spokeswomen for their silenced sisters, find a constructive outlet for their anger.

Other forms are also used by women prison writers, particularly those who write to promote a cause or those who consider writing as their vocation or avocation. American journalist Anna Louise Strong, like Agnes Smedley an advocate for the Chinese Communists, wrote a serial account of her imprisonment in Russia for the *New York Herald Tribune*. In addition to writing letters to family and friends, American Socialist Kate Richards O'Hare published *In Prison*, her report on observations of conditions and practices in the Missouri State Penitentiary, where she served a one-year sentence in 1919 for protesting American involvement in World War I. Although her letters do give her personal response, O'Hare made clear to the prison administration upon her admission her intent to make a sociological study of her fellow inmates. She did, in fact, later publish her study and submit it to the president.[71]

Impersonal approaches are often taken by prisoners who write to advance a cause, such as the early Quaker women prisoners who wrote tracts detailing their sufferings in the seventeenth century. A more contemporary example is Barbara Deming's *Prison Notes*, where her personal response to an Albany, Georgia, jail cell is not nearly so important as her message about the civil rights activism that led her there and the story of why she dared to practice nonviolent protest.

Many prisoners of both sexes have become conscious of the political aspects of the criminal justice system; in the United States, for example, a disproportionate number of male and female inmates are black. This awareness leads some prison writers to abandon autobiographical forms and identify with the silenced inmates around them. Such writers today often use literary genres of poetry and fiction, but over the centuries these have not generally been major forms of writing for women prisoners. In writing poetry and fiction, as with expository writing, the author to some extent objectifies her personal experience of incarceration, this time projecting it onto a character or a scene or expressing it through the imaginative constructs of literature. Most women's prison poetry and fiction were written only recently, perhaps because prisoners today feel less need to justify their lives in autobiographical forms.

Poetry has become a popular genre for male as well as female prison writers, many of whom now have access to writing workshops sponsored by university or community groups. The poetry selections by Carolyn Baxter (from the New York Correctional Facility for Women) and Norma Stafford (from the California Institution for Women) originated in workshops for women prisoners. The perspective of poetry written in these workshops varies with the personal styles and concerns of their members. The simple, declarative forms and vernacular diction of contemporary black poetry suit Baxter's purpose much more effectively than the more self-directed mode of memoirs. In contrast, Stafford's poetry, closer to her personal pain, speaks for her sister inmates by revealing her own struggles and victories. The introduction to Part 5 discusses these prison writing workshops further.

Short fiction and novels are relatively rare among women's prison texts, but fiction can be especially effective in helping the author achieve distance from her experience in order to convey it to those outside. Albertine Sarrazin, imprisoned for theft and prostitution, became a noted French writer of fiction in the 1950s and 1960s. Unlike earlier French imprisoned women writers, she directly stated her defiance of social rules. Sarrazin figures prominently as the imprisoned heroine of her works, but the fictional form allows her to depart from the emphasis on self that is characteristic of memoirs to explore the injustices of the contemporary French prison system as she knows it. Gelfand finds that Sarrazin's confident image of herself as a writer rather than as a criminal exemplifies the current affirmative attitude of women writers in general.[72] Patricia McConnel, the recipient of a recent grant from the National Endowment for the Arts, has been compiling a collection of stories based upon her personal experiences as an inmate in American prisons for women. It has taken years, she notes, to achieve the distance she feels is necessary to express her message, which, like Ericka Huggins's poetry, supports reform and declares unity with all who are oppressed.[73] Though the events and characters are autobiographical, McConnel's use of fiction rather than a confessional format allows her to protest prison injustices as well as affirm her faith in the survival of simple human decency in prison, without the risk of self-pity or self-absorption.

The variety of material selected for this anthology is presented best in a thematic organization. Five major parts highlight notable concerns of women prison writers, and selections are arranged chronologically within their respective parts. These five categories are by no means the only divisions appropriate to the study of women's prison literature, nor do the selections always fit neatly into one category. However, these divisions provide a useful tool to enable the reader to grasp the differences between the texts while also being aware at times of their overlapping themes. Variety of nationality, era, point of view, form, and style complements the similarity of these fundamental, recurring themes. The works are further united by their choice of realism over abstraction, whether the subject is prison food or spiritual growth.

Although contemporary women prisoners continue to write about each of the five themes, those highlighted in the first two parts are among the most ancient. Part 1 focuses on women prisoners' concerns to oppose misogynous criticisms, set the record straight, and vindicate themselves before their families, their contemporaries, or posterity. In Part 2 the writers' causes and beliefs take precedence over accounts of personal suffering or injustice.

Parts 3 through 5 deal more directly with the writers' imprisonments themselves. Part 3 offers several views of prison conditions and interrogation procedures in various countries. This topic is so basic that it forms the background for almost all prison writing. Part 4 examines coping strategies and methods of psychological survival within women's prisons. The writers here are concerned with combating attempts to break spirit and body. The selections conclude in Part 5 with a theme that receives increasing attention in recent prison writing: solidarity among sister inmates.

One intriguing aspect of women's prison literature is its theme of relationships among women as opposed to the prominent marriage theme of women's novels. Imprisoned women do, of course, write about their relationships with children, spouses, lovers, parents, prison guards, and administrators, but perhaps nowhere else in women's literature is the opportunity so rich to explore the dynamics of women's friendships, conflicts, prejudices, and mutual support.

Another kind of solidarity, transcending time and place, links women prisoners through the works they have written or those that have been written about them. Names of earlier prisoners echo in later works, forming an informal *Who's Who* of great women prisoners through the ages. Tracing the influences is fascinating. Ethel Rosenberg, referring to her martyrdom, compares herself to Joan of Arc, while Ericka Huggins and Socialist Elizabeth Gurley Flynn both are inspired by Rosenberg herself. Angela Davis and Huggins sustain each other through their writings while incarcerated in separate prisons. Ginzburg is joined by British suffragette Evelyn Sharp and British–Hungarian physician Edith Bone in admiration of Vera Figner. While in New York's Tombs prison, Agnes Smedley met Mollie Steimer and corresponded with Margaret Sanger, two activists whose work is also noted by Emma Goldman. Moreover, during her imprisonment, Goldman formed a supportive friendship with Kate Richards O'Hare and read an account of the tzar's prisons by Catherine Breshkovskaya, "Little Grandmother" of the Russian Revolution. In addition, Goldman was influenced by Figner and Louise Michel, and she regretted the brutal death of Rosa Luxemburg.

Whether held in solitary confinement or not, these female prisoners are obviously not alone. Their connections through writing argue for the existence of not only a *body* but also a *tradition* of women's prison literature. Perhaps Vera Figner speaks for all women prison writers as she explains her motivation and the mutual benefits of writing: "Yet though my book speaks of the past and contributes nothing to the practical life of the present moment, a time will come when it will be of use. The dead do not rise, but there is resurrection in books."[74]

NOTES

1. Anna Akhmatova, *Requiem and Poem without a Hero*, trans. D. M. Thomas (London: Paul Elek, 1976), p. 23.

2. Carolyn Forche, American poet and journalist, notes the dialectic of poetry as art and as social message and states that their division is false, in "Sensibility and Responsibility," in *The Writer and Human Rights*, ed. Toronto Arts Group for Human Rights (Garden City, N.Y.: Anchor/Doubleday, 1983), pp. 22–25.

3. For a discussion of marginal texts, see Priscilla B. P. Clark, "Literature and Sociology," in *Interrelations of Literature*, ed. Jean-Pierre Barricelli and Joseph Gibaldi (New York: MLA, 1982), pp. 107–122; H. Bruce Franklin, *The Victim as Criminal and Artist: Literature from the American Prison* (New York: Oxford Univ. Press, 1978), 2d ed., in 2 vols.: vol. 1, *Prison Literature in America: The Victim as Criminal and Artist* (Westport, Conn.: Lawrence Hill, 1982), vol. 2, *American Prisoners and Ex-Prisoners: Their Writings: An Annotated Bibliography of Published Works, 1798–1981* (Westport, Conn.: Lawrence Hill, 1982); Tillie Olsen, *Silences* (New York: Dell, 1978).

4. For works discussing revision of the literary canon, see Paul Lauter, "Reconstructing American Literature: A Synopsis of an Educational Project of the Feminist Press" *MELUS* 11, no. 1 (Spring 1984): 33–43; Wayne Charles Miller,

"Toward a New Literary History of the United States," *MELUS* 11, no. 1 (Spring 1984): 5–25; Marianne Whelchel, "Transforming the Canon with Nontraditional Literature by Women," *College English* 46, no. 6 (October 1984): 587–597; Sydney Janet Kaplan, "Review Essay: Literary Criticism," *Signs* 4, no. 3 (Spring 1979): 514–527; Annette Kolodny, "Dancing through the Minefield: Some Observations on the Theory, Practice and Politics of a Feminist Literary Criticism," *Feminist Studies* 6, no. 1 (Spring 1980): 1–25; Lillian Robinson, presentation at MLA Convention, New York City, December 1983.

5. See, for example, Nicole Hahn Rafter, *Partial Justice: Women in State Prisons, 1800–1935* (Boston: Northeastern Univ. Press, 1985); Dorie Klein, "The Etiology of Female Crime," *Issues in Criminology* 8, no. 2 (Fall 1973): 3–30, reprinted in Freda Adler and Rita J. Simon, *The Criminology of Deviant Women* (Boston: Houghton Mifflin, 1979), pp. 58–81; Carol Smart, *Women, Crime and Criminology: A Feminist Critique* (London: Routledge & Kegan Paul, 1976).

6. Franklin, *Prison Literature in America*, p. xxix.

7. Michel Foucault, *Discipline and Punish: The Birth of the Prison*, trans. Alan Sheridan (New York: Vintage, 1979).

8. Elissa Gelfand, "Imprisoned Women: Toward a Socio-Literary Feminist Analysis," *Yale French Studies* 62 (1981): 185–203.

9. Esther Heffernan, in *Making It in Prison: The Square, the Cool, and the Life* (New York: Wiley-Interscience, 1972), pp. 184–185, discusses the microsociety as well as the formal organization of women's prisons.

10. Kathryn W. Burkhart, *Women in Prison* (Garden City, N.Y.: Doubleday, 1973), p. 425.

11. Foucault, *Discipline and Punish*.

12. *On Crimes and Punishments* (1764), by an aristocratic Italian, Cesare Beccaria, is acknowledged to have been a leading force in the movement toward humane punishment in the West. Beccaria concludes his treatise with this general theorem about appropriate punishment: "In order for punishment not to be, in every instance, an act of violence of one or of many against a private citizen, it must be essentially public, prompt, necessary, the least possible in the given circumstances, proportionate to the crimes, dictated by the laws." *On Crimes and Punishments*, trans. Henry Paolucci (Indianapolis, Ind.: Bobbs-Merrill, 1963), p. 99.

13. Foucault, *Discipline and Punish*.

14. Gresham M. Sykes, *The Society of Captives: A Study of a Maximum Security Prison* (Princeton, N.J.: Princeton Univ. Press, 1958; reprint, New York: Atheneum, 1968), pp. xii–xiv.

15. Foucault, *Discipline and Punish*, p. 235.

16. Estelle B. Freedman, *Their Sisters' Keepers: Women's Prison Reform in America, 1830–1930* (Ann Arbor: Univ. of Michigan Press, 1981), pp. 45–46. See also Rafter, *Partial Justice*, for a discussion of women's prison reform.

17. For further discussion of prison conditions stemming from sex role stereotypes, see Nicole Hahn Rafter and Elizabeth A. Stanko, ed., *Judge, Lawyer, Victim, Thief: Women, Gender Roles, and Criminal Justice* (Boston: Northeastern Univ. Press, 1982); Freedman, *Their Sisters' Keepers*; Burkhart, *Women in Prison*, pp. 128–129; Clarice Feinman, "Sex Role Stereotypes and Justice for Women," *Crime & Delinquency* 25, no. 1 (January 1979): 87–94; Feinman,

Women in the Criminal Justice System (New York: Praeger, 1980), pp. 27–29; Rose Giallombardo, *Society of Women: A Study of a Women's Prison* (New York: Wiley, 1966), pp. 6–8; Margery L. Velimesis, "The Female Offender," *Crime and Delinquency Literature* 7, no. 1 (March 1975): 94–112. Smart, in *Women, Crime and Criminology*, pp. 140–141, discusses her study of British prisons and their similar problems arising from female stereotypes.

18. Freedman, *Their Sisters' Keepers*, p. 100.

19. Foucault, in *Discipline and Punish*, pp. 234–235, notes that there is a history of former prisoners' taking a hand in prison reform through accounts of personal experience.

20. Statistics are from Rafter, *Partial Justice*, p. 177. Cathy Spatz Widom, in *Sex Roles and Psychopathology* (New York: Plenum, 1984), p. 184, cites 13,000 women or 3.9 percent of the American prison population in 1980.

21. Helen Greene, "Black Women in the Criminal Justice System," *Urban League Review* 6, no. 1 (Fall 1981): 55–61; Velimesis, "The Female Offender"; Rafter, *Partial Justice*, pp. 177–178; Ruth M. Glick and Virginia V. Neto, *National Study of Women's Correctional Programs* (Washington, D.C.: National Institute of Law Enforcement and Criminal Justice, 1977).

22. Smart, *Women, Crime and Criminology*, pp. 16–18.

23. The problem of the use of stereotypes in recent research is discussed in Smart, *Women, Crime and Criminology*, pp. 2–4. These stereotypes are also discussed in Rafter and Stanko, *Judge, Lawyer, Victim, Thief*, pp. 2–7.

24. Smart, *Women, Crime and Criminology*, p. 27.

25. Otto Pollak, *The Criminality of Women* (Philadelphia: Univ. of Pennsylvania Press, 1950; reprint, New York: Barnes, 1961), p. 10.

26. Edith deRham, *How Could She Do That?: A Study of the Female Criminal* (New York: Potter, 1969), p. 337.

27. Louise Michel, *The Red Virgin: Memoirs of Louise Michel*, trans. Bullitt Lowry and Elizabeth Ellington Ganter (University, Ala.: Univ. of Alabama Press, 1981), p. 139.

28. Pollak, *The Criminality of Women*, p. 151. The theory of chivalrous treatment is countered by Rafter, *Partial Justice*, pp. 178–179; Smart, *Women, Crime and Criminology*, pp. 131–140; Feinman, *Women in the Criminal Justice System*, pp. 22–25; Etta A. Anderson, "The 'Chivalrous' Treatment of the Female Offender in the Arms of the Criminal Justice System: A Review of the Literature," *Social Problems* 23, no. 3 (February 1976): 350–357.

29. Smart, *Women, Crime and Criminology*, pp. 146–158.

30. Freda Adler, *Sisters in Crime* (New York: McGraw-Hill, 1975).

31. Rita J. Simon, *Women and Crime* (Lexington, Mass.: Heath, 1975), p. 1.

32. For a discussion of the effect of women's liberation on women's crime, see Widom, *Sex Roles and Psychopathology*, pp. 192–195; Glick and Neto, *National Study of Women's Correctional Programs*, pp. xxiii, 172; Smart, *Women, Crime and Criminology*, pp. 24–26, 70–74; Coramae Richey Mann, *Female Crime and Delinquency* (University, Ala.: Univ. of Alabama Press, 1984), pp. 15–20, 107–111; Darrell J. Steffensmeier, "Crime and the Contemporary Woman: An Analysis of Changing Levels of Female Property Crime, 1960–75," *Social Forces* 57, no. 2 (December 1978): 566–584; Steffensmeier, "Sex Differences in

Patterns of Adult Crime, 1965–77: A Review and Assessment," *Social Forces* 58, no. 4 (June 1980): 1080–1108; Margaret L. Anderson, *Thinking about Women: Sociological and Feminist Perspectives* (New York: Macmillan, 1983), pp. 189–193; Joan McCord and Laura Otten, "A Consideration of Sex Roles and Motivations for Crime," *Criminal Justice and Behavior* 10, no. 1 (March 1983): 3–12; Velimesis, "The Female Offender"; Feinman, *Women in the Criminal Justice System*, pp. 17–22; Feinman, "Sex Role Stereotypes and Justice for Women," p. 91; Jane Roberts Chapman, *Economic Realities and the Female Offender* (Lexington, Mass.: Lexington Books, 1980), pp. 39–72, 183–185; Anne Campbell, *Girl Delinquents* (New York: St. Martin's, 1981), p. 231; Eileen B. Leonard, *Women, Crime, and Society: A Critique of Theoretical Criminology* (New York: Longman, 1982), pp. 10–43.

33. Smart, *Women, Crime and Criminology*, pp. 72–76, 185. Radical criminologists, such as Dorie Klein, stress the significance of economic factors in analyzing crime patterns. See Klein, "The Etiology of Female Crime," and Klein and June Kress, "Any Woman's Blues: A Critical Overview of Women, Crime and the Criminal Justice System," *Crime and Social Justice: A Journal of Radical Criminology* 5 (Spring–Summer 1976): 34–49.

34. Foucault, *Discipline and Punish*, pp. 66–69, 192–193.

35. Isidore Abramowitz, ed., *The Great Prisoners: The First Anthology of Literature Written in Prison* (New York: Dutton, 1946; reprint, Salem, N.H.: Ayer, 1977), p. xviii.

36. Franklin, *Prison Literature in America*, pp. 124–178, 236–237.

37. Ibid., pp. 100–101, 142–149, 236–237, 243–251.

38. Elaine Showalter, *A Literature of Their Own: British Women Novelists from Brontë to Lessing* (Princeton, N.J.: Princeton Univ. Press, 1977), pp. 6–7.

39. Sandra M. Gilbert and Susan Gubar, *The Madwoman in the Attic: The Woman Writer and the Nineteenth-Century Literary Imagination* (New Haven: Yale Univ. Press, 1979), pp. 46–51. Susan Gubar has had direct experience teaching in a women's prison. See her account in Gubar and Ann Hedin, "A Jury of Our Peers: Teaching and Learning in the Indiana Women's Prison," *College English* 43, no. 8 (December 1981): 779–789.

40. For a discussion of the dilemma of women writers facing absolute standards, see Joanna Russ, *How to Suppress Women's Writing* (Austin, Tex.: Univ. of Texas Press, 1983).

41. Olsen, *Silences*, p. 24.

42. An excellent dramatization of the released female prisoner's economic and social plight is *Getting Out*, a play by Marsha Norman (New York: Avon, 1979). The book jacket explains that ". . . the idea for *Getting Out* came from her experience working with children in a state mental hospital."

43. See, for example, Gilbert and Gubar, *The Madwoman in the Attic*, p. 75.

44. Annis Pratt, *Archetypal Patterns in Women's Fiction* (Bloomington, Ind.: Indiana Univ. Press, 1981), pp. 45–48. Sykes's *Society of Captives* is discussed further in the introduction to Part 3.

45. For a discussion of the cult of true womanhood, see Barbara Welter, "The Cult of True Womanhood: 1820–1860," *American Quarterly* 18 (1966): 151–174.

46. Elissa Gelfand, *Imagination in Confinement: Women's Writings from French Prisons* (Ithaca, N.Y.: Cornell Univ. Press, 1983), p. 110.

47. Nina Auerbach, *Woman and the Demon: The Life of a Victorian Myth* (Cambridge, Mass.: Harvard Univ. Press, 1982), pp. 159–161.

48. Ericka Huggins, "I wake in middle-of-the-night terror," *Off Our Backs: A Women's News Journal* 2, no. 8 (April 1972), p. 17.

49. See, for example, the discussion of female subculture in Elaine Showalter, "Review Essay: Literary Criticism," *Signs* 1, no. 2 (Winter 1975): 435–460; Showalter, "Feminist Criticism in the Wilderness," in *Writing and Sexual Difference*, ed. Elizabeth Abel (Chicago: Univ. of Chicago Press, 1982), pp. 9–35; and Showalter, *A Literature of Their Own*.

50. Johnny Faragher and Christine Stansell, "Women and their Families on the Overland Trail to California and Oregon, 1842–1867," *Feminist Studies* 2 (1975): 150–166.

51. See Showalter, "Feminist Criticism in the Wilderness," pp. 28–34.

52. "The Passion of SS. Perpetua and Felicitas," in *Some Authentic Acts of the Early Martyrs*, ed. E. C. E. Owen (Oxford: Clarendon Press, 1927), pp. 79–80. Reprinted by permission of Oxford University Press.

53. Herbert Musurillo, *The Acts of the Christian Martyrs* (Oxford: Clarendon Press, 1972), p. xxvi.

54. John Alfred Langford, *Prison Books and Their Authors* (London: William Tegg, 1861), p. 5.

55. Patricia Meyer Spacks, *The Female Imagination* (New York: Knopf, 1975), pp. 196–197.

56. Victor Brombert, *The Romantic Prison: The French Tradition* (Princeton, N.J.: Princeton Univ. Press, 1978).

57. Brombert, *The Romantic Prison*, p. 17.

58. See Gilbert and Gubar, *The Madwoman in the Attic*, on images of imprisonment and escape in men's and women's literature in the nineteenth century.

59. Rebecca Harding Davis, from "Life in the Iron Mills" (1861), quoted in Olsen, "Rebecca Harding Davis: Her Life and Times," Introduction to *Life in the Iron Mills*, by Rebecca Harding Davis (Old Westbury, N.Y.: Feminist Press, 1972), reprinted in Olsen, *Silences*, p. 49.

60. Burkhart, *Women in Prison*, p. 16.

61. For a discussion of the suffragettes' awareness of their own worth as their motivation for writing, see Kathleen Dehler, "The Need to Tell All: A Comparison of Historical and Modern Feminist 'Confessional' Writing," in *Feminist Criticism: Essays on Theory, Poetry and Prose*, ed. Cheryl L. Brown and Karen Olson (Metuchen, N.J.: Scarecrow, 1978), pp. 339–352.

62. Patricia McConnel, letter to Judith Scheffler, 2 March 1985.

63. Foucault, *Discipline and Punish*, p. 200.

64. Lee H. Bowker, "Gender Differences in Prison Subcultures," in *Women and Crime in America*, ed. Lee H. Bowker (New York: Macmillan, 1981), p. 414.

65. Giallombardo, in *Society of Women*, pp. 142–143, discusses the importance of these functions of kites.

66. Donald Freed, *Agony in New Haven* (New York: Simon & Schuster, 1973), pp. 139–140.

67. Gelfand, *Imagination in Confinement*, especially pp. 120–121.

68. For a further discussion of men's and women's autobiography, see Spacks, "Selves in Hiding"; Robert A. Fothergill, *Private Chronicles: A Study of English Diaries* (London: Oxford Univ. Press, 1974); Mary Grimley Mason and Carol Hurd Green, *Journeys: Autobiographical Writings by Women* (Boston: G. K. Hall, 1979); Estelle C. Jelinek, "Introduction: Women's Autobiography and the Male Tradition," in *Women's Autobiography: Essays in Criticism*, ed. Estelle C. Jelinek, pp. 1–20; Elizabeth Winston, "The Autobiographer and Her Readers: From Apology to Affirmation," in *Women's Autobiography: Essays in Criticism*, ed. Estelle C. Jelinek, pp. 93–111.

69. Winston, "The Autobiographer and Her Readers," pp. 93–94, notes this shift in works published after 1920.

70. For a discussion of anger in women's writing, see Spacks, "Selves in Hiding"; Spacks, *The Female Imagination*; Russ, *How to Suppress Women's Writing*.

71. Kate Richards O'Hare, *In Prison* (New York: Knopf, 1923; reprint, Seattle, Wash.: American Library, no. 30; Univ. of Washington Press, 1976); *In Prison, being a report by Kate Richards O'Hare to the President of the United States as to the conditions under which women federal prisoners are confined in the Missouri State Penitentiary, under the authority of the United States Department of Justice and the United States Superintendent of Prisons. Based on the author's experience as a federal prisoner from April 14, 1919, to May 30, 1920.* (St. Louis, Mo.: F. P. O'Hare, 1920).

72. See detailed discussion of Sarrazin's work in Gelfand, *Imagination in Confinement*, pp. 214–238; Gelfand, "Albertine Sarrazin: The Confined Imagination," *L'Esprit Créateur* 19, no. 2 (Summer 1979): 47–57; Gelfand, "Albertine Sarrazin: A Control Case for Femininity in Form," *French Review* 51, no. 2 (December 1977): 245–251; Gelfand, "Imprisoned Women: Toward a Socio-Literary Feminist Analysis."

Sarrazin's "confessional" work, *Journal de Prison 1959*, has not been translated into English.

73. McConnel, letter to Judith Scheffler, 1 April 1983.

74. Vera Figner, *Memoirs of a Revolutionist*, trans. Camilla Chapin Daniels (New York: International, 1927), p. 5.

PART 1

"Preserve the remembrance
of what I was":
Vindication of Self

*

They were as obdurate as rocks. I have always observed that the female, who seems to have been made for tenderness, and piety, and moral courage, when really depraved and fallen, is not only the wickedest, but the most hard and unmanageable of beings.

That was how the Rev. James Bradley Finley, chaplain of Ohio Penitentiary, described his visit with female prisoners in 1846.[1] He was not alone in his opinions; misogynous characterizations of imprisoned women are as old as prisons themselves.[2] In the face of such hostility and sexist criticism, some inmates who write of their imprisonment focus on self-justification. In fact, it is primarily this need to vindicate the self that motivates some women prisoners to write in the first place. Ostensibly, they write privately to family and friends or to a public audience of their contemporaries, but overwhelming prejudice often drives these women to address a presumably more enlightened and just posterity. In the following selections, which span three centuries, Madame Roland, Rose Greenhow, Ethel Rosenberg, and Gabrielle Russier defend themselves through writing.

Many female prisoners have written to combat criticisms that they are monsters or fallen women. Elissa Gelfand proposes that this motivation, based upon a conflict between individual self-image and social stereotypes, explains the solipsism of most eighteenth- and nineteenth-century prison texts by French women.[3] An example from the time of the French Revolution is by Madame Roland, wife of the French minister of the interior. A refined and educated woman, Madame Roland was offended by her imprisonment "in the midst of murderers and women of the town." In her memoirs, *An Appeal to Impartial Posterity*, she deplores her forced association with "this scum of the earth" and carefully presents her case as a respectable, feminine woman, wrongfully thrown among genuine criminals whose acts shame their sex.

Madame Roland purports to tell the truth to posterity in her memoirs, knowing that she cannot expect justice in her time. Her strategy is to offer an account of her exemplary character and past. She implies that, because she has led a virtuous life according to the prevailing social definition of femininity, and because she is so obviously superior to imprisoned prostitutes and criminals, her current predicament must be unjust.[4] As an intellectual force behind her husband and the Girondists, Roland cannot argue that she lacks intellectual aspirations, but she is careful to show how she moderates and tailors them to conform to standards of appropriate female behavior. The proof is her own past and her unimpeachable method of educating her beloved daughter, for whom she desires a refined sensibility, judiciously chosen amusements, and modest accomplishments.

Another political prisoner, Confederate spy Rose Greenhow, mixes propaganda with self-vindication in her writing. Greenhow's prison memoirs, adapted from her diary after her release, were published very successfully in England during the Civil War, and at times Confederate rhetoric seems to dominate the book. Yet works like Greenhow's differ significantly from those by male political prisoners, for whom personal and political subjects are often more clearly separated. So-called political charges against women are commonly mixed with disparaging references to their betrayal and violation of femininity. Greenhow's response to the sexual implications in the political accusations is characteristic of some women prison writers, in that she emphasizes the *self* instead of writing a purely political treatise.

In *My Imprisonment and the First Year of Abolition Rule at Washington*, Greenhow exemplifies this intricate weaving of the personal and political. As a popular Washington hostess with a spy ring operating from her home, she became a wartime role model for young Southern women. Greenhow readily contributed to the writing of her own legend in her memoirs, where she appears as a dominant figure in the city's Confederate intelligence network. Her text combines a proud personal account with unflinching propaganda.

Accustomed to directing espionage from her home, Greenhow was anything but a docile prisoner, judging from her own account as well as those of her contemporaries. Union descriptions of Greenhow must, of course, be read with skepticism, but Confederate associates as well remarked on her power and ambition. Shortly after her arrest, a Union report stated that she "possessed an almost superhuman power, all of which she has most wickedly used to destroy the Government."[5] But the Greenhow described by Provost Marshal of Washington William E. Doster, supervisor of the Old Capitol Prison, is more annoying than formidable: "Her carriage was graceful and dignified, her enunciation too distinct to be natural, and her manners bordering on the theatrical." She was a troublesome "intermeddler with politics" who had dreams of glorious martyrdom.[6] Fellow Confederate spy and prisoner Augusta Heath Morris seems to agree, complaining of "the cabal formed against me by Mrs. Greenhow . . . she is drowned by mean ambition of being known [as the only one] in the good work and jealous of everything that surpasses her in loyalty and courage." Even in prison Greenhow reveled in the role of infamous spy as she continued to send messages in cipher. "Greenhow enjoys herself amazingly," Morris wrote with mixed sarcasm and envy.[7]

These charges against Greenhow imply an unseemly masculine ambition and an indomitable, adventurous spirit. They contrast ironically with previous charges that as a successful spy she used sexual attraction to elicit secrets from unwary government and military officials. Her defense, interestingly enough, relies on her own use of a female stereotype: Southern womanhood. *My Imprisonment* projects a consistent persona of Greenhow as the female champion of the Confederacy, defending and exemplifying Southern civilized values against a barbaric and petty North. According to her, the Abolitionists have plunged the nation into a new Dark Age, and she must accept her status as an imprisoned public spectacle, subjected to the rudeness of her keepers, the indignity of curiosity seekers, and the insults of the sensational press.

Greenhow records her contempt for the Union as well as for fellow Confederate prisoner Catherine Virginia Baxley, who Greenhow claims abandoned feminine grace in prison and indulged in embarrassing displays of uncontrolled emotion before the enemy. Baxley, according to Greenhow, was an insult to Southern womanhood. Like the "scum" in Roland's prison, she was a convenient foil for the writer's flattering display of self.

The need to defend herself against misogynous stereotypes persists for the modern woman prisoner as well, as demonstrated by the prison letters of Gabrielle Russier, a teacher who committed suicide in 1969 after enduring imprisonment without trial in Marseilles, France. Russier was not a political prisoner like Greenhow or Roland, who were supposedly arrested for political crimes but were unofficially punished for overstepping their limits as women. Instead, Russier was charged with immorality, stemming from her affair with a sixteen-year-old male student. Nevertheless, in a very real sense she *was* a political prisoner—a prisoner of a judicial and penal system that could hold an adult woman in preventive detention for her affair with a male minor, but would not imprison an adult man if the situation were reversed. Even the Dominican nuns visiting her in prison advised Russier to think of herself as a political prisoner.[8]

Russier's failure to grasp the political implications of her case was her undoing. The overwhelming disgrace of her detention precipitated a depression she could not fight. Letters to her parents and friends and to her ex-husband and father of her twin children chronicle with raw pain the progressive nightmare of her imprisonment. Her frank confusion and inability to comprehend what was happening to her caused her greatest anguish:

> You were wrong when you told me that truth grows in the shadow of prisons. They are keeping me here for motives I don't understand, that have nothing to do with reality, and I can't go on not understanding. I envy the girls who know what they've done, what they are being held responsible for.[9]

Like Roland and Greenhow, Russier held herself distant from the other women, who knew why they were there and, by implication, deserved to be there. In her letters Russier is totally involved in a mystified self-examination; she presents herself as harmless, naive, sensitive, and—most of all—undeserving of the fate that has befallen her from external, implacable forces. Yet an insoluble conflict is reflected in Russier's letters, because she came to fear more than anything "the shock of getting out. Learning to live again." Driven to the edge of sanity, she pleads her lack of fitness for both prison and the street. Russier did self-imposed "hard time," unlike inmates who learn to accommodate themselves to the realities of the system by gradually losing their

attachment to life outside. She contributed to her own emotional destruction by denying her inmate role and affiliation with those around
her.[10]

After Russier's death, Raymond Jean commented that Russier was
destined to be broken by society because she stubbornly and naively
refused to enjoy her affair in private and would not admit her mistake
in court, in fact insisting that she had done no wrong. She was guilty,
he explains, "of not accepting the rules of the game. . . . She never saw
that she was being blamed less for the things she had done than for the
manner in which she did them."[11] Yet because her rebellion was more
naive than brazen, she found neither strength nor comfort in the traditional male rebel's disdain for social stigma. She helped society punish
her for unorthodox female behavior, and her letters record her failure
to present a self-defense strong enough for her ego to accept.

An attitude that links the writings of Roland, Greenhow, and Russier
is their response to sexism. Although contempt for fellow inmates is
not their primary theme, each of these writers defends herself at least
partly by denouncing the women around her and implying her own
moral superiority. They respond to sexism with classism, and—in
Greenhow's case—with racism as well. This attitude contrasts mark-
edly with the solidarity that resounds in the selections in Part 5. In
general, vindication of self gives way in contemporary women's prison
texts to proudly proclaimed solidarity.

The prison correspondence of Ethel Rosenberg is an interesting exception to the pattern outlined above. She was condemned, along with
her husband, Julius, for atomic espionage and for nothing less than
causing the Korean War and altering "the course of history to the disadvantage of our country."[12] As if this were not enough, Rosenberg was
also condemned as an unnatural mother who orphaned her children by
refusing to confess. Explaining his unorthodox denial of clemency to a
woman, President Eisenhower stated, "it goes against the grain to avoid
interfering in the case where a woman is to receive capital punishment.
Over against this, however, must be placed one or two facts that have
greater significance. The first of these is that in this instance it is the
woman who is the strong and recalcitrant character, the man is the
weak one. She has obviously been the leader in everything they did in
the spying."[13] To counter the inherent sexism of the charges and vin-

dicate herself, Ethel Rosenberg did not resort to the racism and classism used by many women prisoners who write in self-defense, as exemplifed in the writings of Roland, Greenhow, and Russier. Though she spent much of her three-year imprisonment in solitary confinement, Rosenberg did have contact at first with other women in the New York Women's House of Detention, and rather than setting herself apart, she identified with these outcast women. Socialist Elizabeth Gurley Flynn, imprisoned there in 1951, recalls, "We were told when she left the House of Detention there was not a dry eye in the place."[14]

Two themes dominate in letters written to Rosenberg's family: her maternal concern for the welfare of her young sons and her civic concern for American and even global justice. These themes work together as Rosenberg's vindication of self. The subsequent publication and international distribution of her letters raise intriguing questions about the prison writer's stance vis-à-vis multiple audiences. Critics have questioned the sincerity of these "personal" letters, which at times sound like so much political rhetoric. The juxtaposition of the personal and the political, particularly in letters to small children, makes many readers uncomfortable.[15]

Looking further at the context of the letters sheds light on Rosenberg's writings. Although she had been politically active before her marriage, Rosenberg assumed the role of housewife and mother expected by society in the 1940s and 1950s. Inner conflicts that stemmed from her strained relationship with the Greenglass family led her to seek psychiatric counseling after her children's birth. In the early days of her incarceration, a psychiatrist feared that Rosenberg's isolation might cause her to suffer a "prison psychosis,"[16] but the letters, on the contrary, show Rosenberg discovering great reserves of strength as she challenges American justice and addresses her testimony to her children and to the world. While the rhetorical flourishes seem at times amateur, the letters may be seen as the work of a fledgling writer finding her voice as she addresses the familiar audience of her family as well as the formidable audience of the world and of posterity.

This blend of the personal and the political in Rosenberg's letters creates a tension that is not as prominent in men's prison writings, where the political rhetoric, even in family letters, is more acceptable to most readers. A condemned man might be expected to write his political legacy to his sons, whereas a woman is expected to write more personally, as Roland does. Rosenberg, however, combines political testimony with concern for her children. The public persona jars with the maternal voice, unsettling the reader. The letters are discomforting because Rosenberg does not subscribe to the separation of public and private spheres expected of women.[17] Though she entered prison as a housewife, imprisonment ironically gave her the opportunity to return to a more active engagement in public affairs through the medium of her letters.[18] If she had once struggled to find her place between the two spheres, prison seems to have given her life a unity she had not known before.

Whatever the stated charges against imprisoned women, sexist stereotypes constitute some of the most damaging and least easily defeated criticisms. Writing in self-defense may not reduce prison sentences or save lives, but to some extent it mitigates the pain of imprisonment for women prison authors.

NOTES

1. James Bradley Finley, *Memorials of Prison Life* (Cincinnati: L. Swormstedt and A. Poe, 1855; reprint, New York: Arno, 1974), pp. 60–61.

2. The particular criticisms may vary over time. For example, Nicole Hahn Rafter, in *Partial Justice: Women in State Prisons, 1800–1935* (Boston: Northeastern Univ. Press, 1985), pp. 3–51, 157–175, describes how reformatories in late-nineteenth- to early-twentieth-century America proposed to make "promiscuous women" conform to ideals of "true womanhood." Before reformatories were established, women in early- and mid-nineteenth-century state prisons were regarded as monsters rather than as errant, redeemable fallen women. See also Rafter and Elizabeth A. Stanko, *Judge, Lawyer, Victim, Thief: Women, Gender Roles, and Criminal Justice* (Boston: Northeastern Univ. Press, 1982), pp. 2–7.

3. Elissa D. Gelfand, *Imagination in Confinement: Women's Writings from French Prisons* (Ithaca, N.Y.: Cornell Univ. Press, 1983), pp. 28–30.

4. Gelfand, *Imagination in Confinement*, pp. 130–152, 224. See also Gelfand, "A Response to the Void: Madame Roland's 'Memoires Particuliers' and Her Imprisonment," *Romance Notes* (Fall 1979): 75–80.

5. E. J. Allen, letter to Brig. Gen. Andrew Porter, Provost Marshal, November 1861, quoted in *The War of the Rebellion: A Compilation of the Official Records of the Union and Confederate Armies, Additions and Corrections* to 2d ser., vol. 2 (Washington, D.C.: Government Printing Office, 1902), p. 567.

6. William E. Doster, *Lincoln and Episodes of the Civil War* (New York: Putnam, 1915), pp. 79, 80–82.

7. Augusta Heath Morris (Mason), letter to Col. Thomas Jordan, 24 February 1862, and letter to Col. B. T. Johnson, *Present*, 19 February 1862, quoted in *The War of the Rebellion: A Compilation of the Official Records of the Union and Confederate Armies*, 2d ser., vol. 2 (Washington, D.C.: Government Printing Office, 1897), p. 1349.

8. Gabrielle Russier, letter to R. J., 16 May 1969, *The Affair of Gabrielle Russier* (New York: Knopf, 1971), pp. 147–149.

9. Russier, letter to Albert, 30 May 1969, *The Affair of Gabrielle Russier*, pp. 163–164.

10. See Thomas E. Arcaro, "Self Identity of Female Prisoners: The Moral Career of the Inmate," *Humanity and Society* 8, no. 1 (February 1984): 73–89, for a discussion of women's process of adjustment to the inmate role.

11. Raymond Jean, "For Gabrielle," in *The Affair of Gabrielle Russier*, pp. 112–115, 119.

12. Judge Irving R. Kaufman's sentencing remarks, as quoted in Ronald Radosh and Joyce Milton, *The Rosenberg File* (New York: Holt, Rinehart & Winston, 1983), pp. 283–284.

13. President Dwight D. Eisenhower, letter to son John, Tuesday, 16 June 1953, quoted in Miriam Schneir and Walter Schneir, *Invitation to an Inquest* (Garden City, N.Y.: Doubleday, 1965), p. 242; latest edition New York: Pantheon, 1983.

14. Elizabeth Gurley Flynn, *The Alderson Story: My Life as a Political Prisoner* (New York: International, 1963), pp. 18–19.

15. For example, Robert Warshow, "The 'Idealism' of Julius and Ethel Rosenberg," *Commentary* 16, no. 5 (November 1953): 413–418, criticizes the letters.

The Rosenbergs' letters have been considered a touchstone of their characters; commentators have used these documents to support their arguments about the guilt or innocence of the couple. Allen Weinstein, "The Symbolism of Subversion: Notes on Some Cold War Icons," *Journal of American Studies* 6, no. 2 (1972): 165–179, writes, "The popularity of their 'Death House Letters' canonized the Rosenbergs among radicals as martyred saints even before their execution" (p. 171). Radosh and Milton, *The Rosenberg File*, p. 340, note the letters' "tremendous impact" in the United States and abroad.

16. Letter from Dr. Frederic Wertham, in Robert Meeropol and Michael Meeropol, *We Are Your Sons: The Legacy of Ethel and Julius Rosenberg* (Boston: Houghton Mifflin, 1975; reprint, Champaign: Univ. of Illinois Press, 1986), p. 59.

17. For a discussion of public/private spheres, see Margaret L. Anderson, *Thinking about Women: Sociological and Feminist Perspectives* (New York: Macmillan, 1983), pp. 280–282; Barbara Ehrenreich and Deirdre English, *For Her Own Good: 150 Years of the Experts' Advice to Women* (Garden City, N.Y.: Anchor/Doubleday, 1978), pp. 1–29.

18. Ellie Meeropol and Beth Schneider, "The Ethel Rosenberg Story," *Off Our Backs: A Women's News Journal* 5, no. 8 (September–October 1975): 5.

MARIE JEANNE (MANON) PHLIPON, MADAME ROLAND DE LA PLATIÈRE (1756–1793)

Manon Phlipon received an early appreciation for the arts from her father, an engraver. She began a "proper" female education in the arts in their bourgeois French home, and at the age of eleven completed her education in a convent. When she was twenty-five she married a middle-aged scholar, Jean Marie Roland. They had one daughter. Serving as secretary for her husband, who was minister of the interior, she met and entertained the most prominent political leaders of the day, including the Girondists, at her home.

Though she affirmed her Republican sentiments and her hope for the French Revolution, on May 31, 1793, Madame Roland was arrested without a specific charge. She was taken from her Paris home and imprisoned in the Abbey and St. Pelagie prisons. While there, she wrote several works, including her memoirs, in which she took pains to clear her name for posterity by emphasizing her morality and normal femininity, despite the vicious charges that she had stepped outside her natural sphere by engaging in politics. She was taken to the Conciergerie prison on November 1, 1793, where she was tried and found guilty of conspiring with the Girondists against the Republic. Observers praised her for her dignified bearing on the way to the guillotine. Her husband committed suicide shortly after hearing of her execution.

Note: Biographical information is from *An Appeal to Impartial Posterity: By Madame Roland, Wife of the Minister of the Interior: or, a Collection of Tracts Written by Her During Her Confinement in the Prisons of the Abbey, and St. Pelagie, in Paris*, translated from the French original, first American edition (corrected), 2 vols. (New York: Robert Wilson, 1798); Elissa D. Gelfand, *Imagination in Confinement: Women's Writings from French Prisons* (Ithaca, N.Y.: Cornell Univ. Press, 1983); Winifred Stephens, *Women of the French Revolution* (London: Chapman & Hall, 1922).

WORKS BY MADAME ROLAND

An Appeal to Impartial Posterity: By Madame Roland, Wife of the Minister of the Interior: or, a Collection of Tracts Written by Her During Her Confinement in the Prisons of the Abbey, and St. Pelagie, in Paris. Translated from the French original. First American edition (corrected). 2 vols. New York: Robert Wilson, 1798; reprint, New York: AMS, forthcoming (1986).

The Private Memoirs of Madame Roland. Edited by Edward Gilpin Johnson. Chicago: McClurg, 1900; reprint, New York: AMS, 1976.

The Works (never before published) of Jeanne-Marie [sic] Phlipon Roland, wife of the ex-Minister of the Interior, containing her philosophical and literary essays written previous to her marriage, her correspondence, and her travels. To which are annexed the Justificative documents relative to her imprisonment and condemnation. The whole preceded by a preliminary discourse, interspersed with notes, illustrative and explanatory, by L. A. Champagneux. Translated from the French. London: J. Johnson, 1800.

Madame Roland's Memoirs

From *An Appeal to Impartial Posterity*, New York:
Robert Wilson, 1798.

Abbey Prison, June 1793

Rising about noon, I considered how I should arrange my new apartment. With a clean napkin I covered a little paltry table, which I placed near my window, intending that it should serve me for a bureau, and resolved to eat my meals on a corner of the chimney-piece, that I might keep the table clean, and in order, for writing. Two large hat-pins, stuck into the boards, served me as a port manteau. In my pocket I had Thomson's Seasons, a work which I was fond of on more than one account; and I made a memorandum of such other books as I should wish to procure. First, Plutarch's Lives of Illustrious Persons, which at eight years of age I used to carry to church instead of the Exercises of the holy week, and which I had not read regularly since that early period: then Hume's History of England, and Sheridan's Dictionary, in order to improve myself in the English language. I would rather have continued to read Mrs. Macaulay; but the person who had lent me some of the first volumes, was not at home; and I should not have known where to enquire for the work, as I had already tried in vain to get it from the booksellers. I could not avoid smiling at my peaceful preparations; for there was a great tumult in the town: the drums were continually beating to arms, and I knew not what might be the event. At any rate, said I to myself, they will not prevent my living to my last moment: more happy in my conscious innocence, than they can be with the rage that animates them. If they come, I will advance to meet them, and go to death as a man would go to repose.

The keeper's wife came to invite me to her apartment, where she had directed my cloth to be laid, that I might dine in better air. On repairing thither, I found my faithful maid, who threw herself into my arms, bathed in tears, and half suffocated by her sobs. I could not avoid melting into tenderness and sorrow. I almost upbraided myself with my previous tranquillity, when I reflected on the anxiety of those who were attached to me; and when I described to myself the anguish first of one friend, and then of another, my heart was rent by the keenest sensations of grief. Poor woman! how many tears have I caused her to shed! and for what does not an attachment like her's atone? In the common inter-course of life she sometimes treats me roughly, but it is when she thinks me too negligent of what may contribute to my health or happiness; and when I am in distress, the office of complaining is her's, and that of consoling mine. There was no getting rid of so inveterate a habit. I endeavoured to prove to her that, by giving way to her grief, she would be less capable of rendering me service; that she was more useful to me without, than within the walls of the prison, where she begged me to permit her to remain; and that, upon the whole, I was far from being so unfortunate as she imagined, which indeed was true. Whenever I have been ill, I have experienced a particular kind of serenity, unques-tionably proceeding from my mode of contemplating things, and from the law I have laid down for myself, of always submitting quietly to necessity, instead of revolting against it. The moment I take to my bed, every duty seems at an end, and no solicitude whatever has any hold upon me: I am only bound to be there, and to remain there with res-ignation, which I do with a very good grace. I give freedom to my imagination; I call up agreeable impressions, pleasing remembrances, and ideas of happiness; all exertions, all reasonings, and all calculations, I discard; giving myself up entirely to nature, and, peaceful like her, I suffer pain without impatience, and seek repose or cheerfulness. I find that imprisonment produces on me nearly the same effect as disease; I am only bound to be in prison, and what great hardship is there in it? I am not such very bad company for myself. . . .

St. Pelagie, August 8, 1793

More than two months have I been imprisoned, because I am allied to a worthy man, who thought proper to retain his virtue in a revolution, and to give in exact accounts though a minister. For five months he solicited in vain the passing of those accounts, and the pronouncing of judgment on his administration. They have been examined; but, as they have afforded no room for blame, it has been deemed expedient to make no report on the subject, but to substitute calumny in its place. Roland's activity, his multifarious labours, and his instructive writings, had procured him a degree of consideration which appeared formidable; or so at least envious men would have it, in order to effect the downfall of a man whose integrity they detested. His ruin was resolved upon, and an attempt was made to take him into custody at the time of the insurrection of the 31st of May; the epoch of the complete debasement of the national representation, of its violation, and of the success of the decemvirate. He made his escape, and in their fury they fastened upon me; but I should have been arrested at any rate; for though our persecutors know that my name has not the same influence as his, they are persuaded that my temper is not less firm, and are almost equally desirous of my ruin.

The first part of my captivity I employed in writing. My pen proceeded with so much rapidity, and I was in so happy a disposition of mind, that in less than a month I had manuscripts sufficient to form a duodecimo volume. They were intitled Historical Notices [henceforth referred to as *Historic Notices*], and contained a variety of particulars relative to all the facts, and all the persons, connected with public affairs, that my situation had given me an opportunity of knowing. I related them with all the freedom and energy of my nature, with all the openness and unconstraint of an ingenuous mind, setting itself above selfish considerations, with all the pleasure which results from describing what we have experienced, or what we feel, and lastly with the confidence, that, happen what would, the collection would serve as my moral and political testament.

I had completed the whole, bringing things down to the present moment, and had entrusted it to a friend, who rated it at a high price. On a sudden the storm burst over his head. The instant he found himself put under arrest, he thought of nothing but the danger, he felt nothing but the necessity of averting it, and without casting about for expedients, threw my manuscript into the fire. This loss distressed me more than the severest trials have ever done. This will easily be conceived, when it is remembered that the crisis approaches, that I may be murdered tomorrow, or dragged, I know not how, before the tribunal which our rulers employ to rid them of the persons they find troublesome; and that these writings were the anchor to which I had committed my hopes of saving my own memory from reproach, as well as that of many deserving characters.

As we ought not, however, to sink under any event, I shall employ my leisure hours in setting down, without form or order, whatever may occur to my mind. These fragments will not make amends for what I have lost, but they will serve to recall it to my memory, and assist me in filling up the void on some future day, provided the means of doing so remain in my power.

Prison of St. Pelagie, Aug. 9, 1793

The daughter of an artist, the wife of a man of letters (who afterwards became a minister, and remained an honest man), now a prisoner, destined perhaps to a violent and unexpected death, I have been acquainted with happiness and with adversity, I have seen glory at hand, and I have experienced injustice.

Born in an obscure station, but of honest parents, I spent my youth in the bosom of the fine arts, nourished by the charms of study, and ignorant of all superiority but that of merit, of all greatness but that of virtue.

Arrived at years of maturity, I lost all hopes of that fortune, which might have placed me in a condition suitable to the education I had received. A marriage with a respectable man appeared to compensate this loss; it served to lay the foundation of new misfortunes.

A gentle disposition, a strong mind, a solid understanding, an extremely affectionate heart, and an exterior which announced these qualities, rendered me dear to all those with whom I was acquainted. The situation into which I have been thrown has created me enemies; personally I have none: to those who have spoken the worst of me I am utterly unknown.

It is so true that things are seldom what they appear to be, that the periods of my life in which I have felt the most pleasure, or experienced the greatest vexation, were often the very contrary of those that others might have supposed: the solution is, that happiness depends on the affections more than on events.

It is my purpose to employ the leisure of my captivity in retracing what has happened to me from my tenderest infancy to the present moment. Thus to tread over again all the steps of our career, is to live a second time; and what, in the gloom of a prison, can we do better than to transport our existence elsewhere by pleasing fictions, or by the recollection of interesting occurrences?

If we gain less experience by acting, than by reflecting on what we see and do, mine will be greatly augmented by my present undertaking.

Public affairs, and my own private sentiments, afforded me ample matter for thinking, and subjects enough for my pen during two months imprisonment, without obliging me to have recourse to distant times. Accordingly, the first five weeks were devoted to my *Historic Notices*, which formed perhaps no uninteresting collection. They have just been destroyed; and I have felt all the bitterness of a loss, which I shall never repair. But I should despise myself, could I suffer my mind to sink in any circumstances whatever. In all the troubles I have experienced, the most lively impression of sorrow has been almost immediately accompanied by the ambition of opposing my strength to the evil, and of surmounting it, either by doing good to others, or by exerting my own fortitude to the utmost. Thus misfortune may pursue, but cannot overwhelm me; tyrants may persecute, but never, no never shall they debase me. My *Historic Notices* are gone: I mean to write my *Memoirs*; and, prudently accommodating myself to my weakness, at a moment when my feelings are acute, I shall talk of my own person, that my thoughts may be the less at home. I shall exhibit my fair and my unfavourable side with equal freedom. He who dares not speak well of himself is almost always a coward, who knows and dreads the ill that may be said of him; and he who hesitates to confess his faults, has neither spirit to vindicate, nor virtue to repair them. Thus frank with respect to myself, I shall not be scrupulous in regard to others: father, mother, friends, husband, I shall paint them all in their proper colours, or in the colours, at least in which they appeared to me.

While I remained in a quiet and retired station, my natural sensibility so absorbed my other qualities, that it displayed itself alone, or governed all the rest. My first objects were to please and to do good. I was a little like that good man, Mr. de Gourville, of whom Madame de Sévigné said, that the love of his neighbour cut off half his words; nor was I undeserving of the character given me by Sainte-Lette, who said, that though possessed of wit to point an epigram, I never suffered one to escape my lips.

Since the energy of my character has been unfolded by circumstances, by political and other storms, my frankness takes place of every thing, without considering too nicely the little scratches it may give in its way. Still, however, I deal not in epigrams; they indicate a mind pleased at irritating others by satirical observations; and, as to me, I never yet could find amusement in killing flies. But I love to do justice by the utterance of truths, and refrain not from the most severe, in presence of the parties concerned, without suffering myself to be alarmed, or moved, or angry, whatever may be the effects they produce. . . .

St. Pelagie, August 20, 1793

My courage did not sink under the new misfortunes I experienced;* but the refinement of cruelty with which they have given me a foretaste of liberty, only to load me with fresh chains, and the barbarous care with which they took advantage of a decree, by applying to me a false designation, as the mode of legalizing an arbitrary arrest, fired me with indignation. Feeling myself in that disposition of mind when every impression becomes stronger, and its effect more prejudicial to health, I went to bed; but as I could not sleep, it was impossible to avoid thinking. This violent state, however, never lasts long with me. Being accustomed to govern my mind, I felt the want of self-possession, and thought myself a fool for affording a triumph to my persecutors, by suffering their injustice to break my spirit. They were only bringing fresh odium on themselves, without making much alteration in the situation I had already found means so well to support: had I not books and leisure here as well as at the Abbey? I began indeed to be quite angry with myself for having allowed my peace of mind to be disturbed, and no longer thought of any thing, but of enjoying existence, and of employing my faculties with that independence of spirit which a strong mind preserves in the midst of fetters, and which thus disappoints its most determined enemies. As I felt that it was necessary to vary my occupations, I bought crayons, and had recourse to drawing, which I had laid aside some time. Fortitude does not consist solely in rising

---

*Madame Roland had been briefly released from prison, then rearrested.—*Ed.*

superior to circumstances by an effort of the mind, but in maintaining
that elevation by suitable conduct and care. Whenever unfortunate or
irritating events take me by surprise, I am not content with calling up
the maxims of philosophy to support my courage; but I provide agreeable
amusements for my mind, and do not neglect the art of preserving health
to keep myself in a just equilibrium. I laid out my days then with a
certain sort of regularity. In the morning I studied the English language
in Shaftsbury's Essay on Virtue, and in the poetry of Thomson. The
sound metaphysics of the one, and the enchanting descriptions of the
other, transported me by turns to the intellectual regions, and to the
most touching scenes of nature. Shaftsbury's reason gave new strength
to mine, and his thoughts invited meditation; while Thomson's sensibility, and his delightful and sublime pictures, went to my heart, and
charmed my imagination. I afterwards sat down to my drawing till
dinner time. Having been so long without handling the pencil, I could
not expect to acquit myself with much skill; but we always preserve
the power of repeating with pleasure, and of attempting with facility,
whatever in our youth we have practised with success. Accordingly, the
study of the fine arts, considered as a part of the education of young
women, ought, in my opinion, to be less directed towards the acquisition
of distinguished talents than to inspiring them with the love of employment, making them contract a habit of application, and multiplying
their means of amusement; for it is thus we escape from that *ennui*
which is the most cruel disease of man in society; and thus we avoid
the quicksands of vice, and seductions still more to be feared than vice
itself.

I will not then make my daughter a professor *(une virtuose):* I shall
ever remember that my mother was afraid of my becoming too great a
musician, or of my devoting myself entirely to painting, because she
desired, above all things, that I should be fond of the duties of my sex,
and learn to be a good housewife, in case of my becoming the mother
of a family. My Eudora then shall learn to accompany herself in a pleasing manner on the harp, or to play with ease on the *forte piano;* and
shall know enough of drawing, to enable her to contemplate the masterpieces of art with pleasure, to trace or imitate a flower which delights
her, and to shew taste and elegant simplicity in the choice of her ornaments. It is my wish that the mediocrity of her talents may excite
neither admiration in others, nor vanity in herself. It is my wish that

she may please rather by her collective merit, than astonish at the first glance, and that she may rather gain affection by her good qualities, than applause by her brilliant accomplishments. But, good heavens! I am a prisoner and a great distance divides us! I dare not even send for her to receive my embraces; for hatred pursues the very children of those whom tyranny persecutes; and no sooner does my girl in her eleventh year appear in the streets with her virgin bashfulness, and her beautiful fair hair, than wretches, hired or seduced by falsehood, point her out as the offspring of a conspirator. Cruel wretches! they well know how to break a mother's heart.

Could not I have brought her with me?——I have not yet said what is the situation of a prisoner at Sainte Pelagie.

The wing appropriated to females, is divided into long and very narrow corridors, on one side of which are little cells like that which I have described as my lodging. There, under the same roof, upon the same line, and only separated by a thin plastered partition, I dwell in the midst of murderers and women of the town. By the side of me is one of those creatures who make a trade of seduction, and set up innocence to sale; and above me is a woman who forged assignats, and with a band of monsters to which she belongs, tore an individual of her own sex to pieces upon the highway. The door of each cell is secured by an enormous bolt, and opened every morning by a man who stares in impudently to see whether you be up or in bed: their inhabitants then assemble in the corridors, upon the staircases, or in a damp or noisome room, a worthy receptacle for this scum of the earth.

It will be readily believed that I confine myself constantly to my cell; but the distance is not great enough to save the ear from the expressions which such women may be supposed to utter, but which without hearing them it is impossible for any one to conceive.

This is not all: the wing where the men are confined, having windows in front of, and very near the building inhabited by the women, the individuals of the two sexes of analagous character, enter into conversation, which is the more dissolute, as those who hold it are unsusceptible of fear: gestures supply the place of actions, and the windows serve as the occasions of the most shameful scenes of infamous debauchery.

Such is the dwelling reserved for the worthy wife of an honest man!—If this be the reward of virtue on earth, who will be astonished at my contempt of life, and at the resolution with which I shall be able to look death in the face? It never appeared to me in a formidable shape; but at present is not without its charms; and I could embrace it with pleasure, if my daughter did not invite me to stay a little longer with her, and if my voluntary *exit* would not furnish calumny with weapons against my husband, whose glory I should support, if they should dare to carry me before a tribunal. . . .

October 18, 1793

To my daughter

I do not know, my dear girl, whether I shall be allowed to see, or to write to you again. REMEMBER YOUR MOTHER. In these few words is contained the best advice I can give you. You have seen me happy in fulfilling my duties, and in giving assistance to those who were in distress.—It is the only way of being happy.

You have seen me tranquil in misfortune and in confinement, because I was free from remorse, and because I enjoyed the pleasing recollections that good actions leave behind them. These are the only means that can enable us to support the evils of life, and the vicissitudes of fortune.

Perhaps you are not fated, and I hope you are not, to undergo trials so severe as mine; but there are others against which you ought to be equally on your guard. Serious and industrious habits are the best preservative against every danger; and necessity as well as prudence command you to persevere diligently in your studies.

Be worthy of your parents: they leave you great examples to follow; and if you are careful to avail yourself of them, your existence will not be useless to mankind.

FAREWELL, my beloved child, you who drew life from my bosom, and whom I wish to impress with all my sentiments. The time will come when you will be better able to judge of the efforts I make at this moment to repress the tender emotions excited by your dear image. I press you to my heart.

Farewell, my Eudora

To my faithful servant Fleury

My dear Fleury, you whose fidelity, services, and attachment, have been so grateful to me for thirteen years, receive my embraces, and my farewell.

PRESERVE the remembrance of what I was. It will console you for what I suffer: the good pass on to glory when they descend to the grave. My sorrows are about to terminate; lay aside yours, and think of the peace which I am about to enjoy, and which nobody will in future be able to disturb. Tell my Agatha that I carry with me to the grave the satisfaction of being beloved by her from my infancy, and the regret of not being able to give her proofs of my attachment. I could have wished to be of service to you—at least let me not afflict you.

Farewell, my poor Fleury, farewell!

ROSE O'NEAL GREENHOW (1815?–1864)

Rose O'Neal Greenhow, a native of Montgomery County, Maryland, spent her adolescence in Washington, D.C. She lived with an aunt who ran the Congressional Boarding House in the Old Capitol Building, which had served temporarily as the Capitol and later was used for the Old Capitol Prison. As a young woman Rose was known for her beauty, captivating wit, and charm, and she began to establish friendships with powerful men, including South Carolina Senator John C. Calhoun, whose political ideas inspired her unshakable loyalty to the Confederacy. Her marriage in 1835 to Robert Greenhow, translator for the State Department, enabled her to entertain most of the nation's major political figures in her home. After her husband's death in 1854, she was recruited by Confederate Colonel Thomas Jordan to spy for the South at the start of the Civil War. The greatest contribution of this fashionable Washington hostess/spy is said to be information that led to General Beauregard's victory at the Battle of Bull Run in 1861.

When federal agent Allan Pinkerton arrested her on August 23, 1861, Greenhow swallowed the paper cipher she carried and destroyed as much other evidence as she could. Since several other women were engaged in espionage, Greenhow's house on Sixteenth Street was temporarily converted to "Greenhow Prison" for female political prisoners. Early in 1862 she was transferred to the Old Capitol Prison, where she was recorded as a "dangerous, skillful spy." She and her eight-year-old daughter, Rose, shared a room equipped with a sewing machine and writing materials. On June 2, 1862, Greenhow and fellow inmates Catherine Virginia Baxley and Augusta Heath Morris (Mason) pledged not to return north of the Potomac River during the war and were sent to Richmond. Jefferson Davis ordered payment of $2,500 for Greenhow's services to the South.

In August 1863, Greenhow traveled to England where she promoted the Confederate cause and published the memoirs she had fashioned from her prison diary. The purpose of her return trip on the British blockade-runner *Condor* is a matter of speculation; she was probably carrying messages to the South. When the ship ran into a storm and was threatened with capture by the Union, Greenhow demanded to go ashore. Her boat capsized, and she drowned on October 1, 1864. Greenhow's body, still bearing a reticule containing the heavy gold proceeds from her successful book, washed ashore in Wilmington, North Carolina, and was buried with honors.

Note: Biographical information is from James D. Horan, *Desperate Women* (New York: Putnam, 1952); Ishbel Ross, *Rebel Rose: Life of Rose O'Neal Greenhow, Confederate Spy* (New York: Harper & Bros., 1954); Ross, "Rose O'Neal Greenhow," in *Notable American Women* ed. Edward T. James (Cambridge, Mass.: Belknap, 1971); *The War of the Rebellion: A Compilation of the Official Records of the Union and Confederate Armies*, 2d ser., vol. 2 (Washington, D.C.: Government Printing Office, 1897), p. 1349, and *Additions and Corrections* to 2d ser., vol. 2 (1902), p. 577.

WORKS BY ROSE O'NEAL GREENHOW

Papers: Correspondence, National Archives, Washington, D.C.; 1860–1864 Papers, Manuscript Department, Perkins Library, Duke University, Durham, N.C.; 1863–1864 Papers, North Carolina Division of Archives and History, Raleigh, N.C.
My Imprisonment and the First Year of Abolition Rule at Washington. London: Richard Bentley, 1863.

My Imprisonment

From *My Imprisonment and the First Year of Abolition Rule at Washington* (London: Richard Bentley, 1863)

Whether a faithful record of my long and humiliating imprisonment at Washington, in the hands of the enemies of my country, will prove as interesting to the public as my friends assure me it is to them, I know not. It is natural for those who have suffered captivity to exaggerate the importance and interest of their own experiences; yet I should not venture upon publishing these notes and sketches merely as a narrative of indignities heaped upon myself personally. It is hoped that the story may excite more than a simple feeling of indignation or commiseration, by exhibiting somewhat of the intolerant spirit in which the present crusade against the liberties of sovereign States was undertaken, and somewhat of the true character of that race of people who insist on compelling us by force to live with them in bonds of fellowship and union. . . .

*The idea of the Yankees at first was to hold me up conspicuously before the eyes of the public as a terrible example and a warning. In this they signally failed, for I became, even amongst their own people, an object of interest. And one of their own papers, the 'New York Times,' some months later, said, 'Had Madam Greenhow been sent South immediately after her arrest, as we recommended, we should have heard no more of the heroic deeds of Secesh women, which she has made the fashion.'

On the 7th of September my child was taken very ill. In consequence I wrote to Provost-Marshal Porter, asking that my family physician might be allowed to visit her. With *characteristic humanity* he refused, and proposed to send me one of his own creatures, whom I declined to receive, preferring to trust her life to the care of the good Providence which had so often befriended me.

A few days after, a Dr. Steward† was introduced. He was a vulgar, uneducated man, bedizened with enough gold-lace for three field-marshals; and endowed with a considerable degree of 'modest assurance.' He evidently expected, by affected *bonhomie*, to overcome my repugnance to his visits; but he reckoned without his host, for, if my confessor had come to me under such auspices, I should think that the devil had been tampering with him, and refuse to receive him. . . .

‡After the lapse of some half-hour I was taken up to the room which had been selected for me by General Porter. It was situated in the back building of the prison, on the north-west side, the only view being that of the prison-yard, and was chosen purposely so as to exclude the chance

*At this point Greenhow was imprisoned in her home, "Greenhow Prison."—*Ed.*
†This is doubtless a misspelling, since Greenhow refers to him throughout the book as Stewart.—*Ed.*
‡Greenhow was moved from "Greenhow Prison" to the Old Capitol Prison.—*Ed.*

of my seeing a friendly face. It is about ten feet by twelve, and furnished in the rudest manner—a straw bed, with a pair of newly-made unwashed cotton sheets—a small feather pillow, dingy and dirty enough to have formed part of the furniture of the Mayflower—a few wooden chairs, a wooden table, and a glass, six by eight inches, completed its adornment: soldiers' rations being only allowed me by this magnanimous Pennsylvanian, who was doubtless driving a good trade by his patriotism. The second day of my sojourn in this dismal hole a carpenter came to put up bars to the windows. I asked by whose order it was done, and was informed by the superintendent that General Porter not only ordered it, but made the drawings himself, so as to exclude the greatest amount of air and sunlight from the victims of abolition wrath. Wood* remonstrated against the bars, saying that they had not been found necessary; whereupon Porter said, 'Oh, Wood, she (alluding to me) will fool you out of your eyes—can talk with her fingers,' &c. But to speak of myself—the door of this den is locked and barred, and the sentinels pacing up and down before it.

I had scarcely entered my cell, when this same Dr. Stewart came in, attended by his hospital steward. I received him very coldly, and he withdrew after showing himself.

On the 21st Dr. Stewart came in again, with his hospital steward, very unceremoniously—for I had no fastening on my door. He seemed determined to disturb my equanimity. I was in bed, not having arisen. The customs of our people made this seem a great outrage to me, so I told him that I trusted that his sense of delicacy would prevent his future visits to me, unless I desired his presence; that I supposed that I had been sufficiently explicit upon former occasions; that his Government had deprived me of my liberty, but that they could not force upon me civilities—and I supposed that his visit was intended as such—which I, from principle, declined to receive. With that he spread himself like a *Basha* with three tails, discoursed fluently upon the dignity of his position, and concluded by saying it was his pleasure to come; to which I replied, 'It is mine not to receive you.' As he went out, he said to the guard in a very loud voice, '*I am the first person who has made that woman feel that she is a prisoner, and I will yet reduce*

---

*William P. Wood, superintendent of the Old Capitol Prison.—*Ed.*

her to the condition of the other prisoners.' I thereupon sent for the superintendent, to make my protest against this renewed impertinence. In the course of the day he obtained authority to exclude 'Materia Medica' from my presence.

Extracts from notes kept in the Old Capitol:—

25th.—I have been one week in my new prison. My letters now all go through the detective police, who subject them to a chemical process to extract the treason. In one of the newspaper accounts, prepared under the direction of the secret police, I am supposed to use sympathetic ink. I purposely left a preparation very conspicuously placed, in order to divert attention from my real means of communication, and they have swallowed the bait and fancy my friends are at their mercy.

How I shrink from the notoriety which these dastards force upon me: for five months I have had a daily paragraph. One would think that curiosity would have been satiated; but not so. And I have the uneasy consciousness that every word I utter will appear with exaggeration in the newspapers. Even my child of eight years is deemed of importance enough to have her childish speeches recorded. Well! I bide my time, confident in the retributive justice of Heaven. Rose is subject to the same rigorous restrictions as myself. I was fearful at first that she would pine, and said, 'My little darling, you must show yourself superior to these Yankees, and not pine.' She replied quickly, 'O mamma, never fear; I hate them too much. I intend to dance and sing "Jeff. Davis is coming," just to scare them!'

January 28.—This day, as I raised my barred windows, and stood before one of them to get out of the smoke and dust, &c. the guard rudely called, 'Go away from that window!' and raised his musket and levelled it at me. I maintained my position without condescending to notice him, whereupon he called for the corporal of the guard. I called also for the officer of the guard, who informed me that I 'must not go to the window.' I quietly told him that, at whatever peril, I should avail myself of the largest liberty of the four walls of my prison. He told me that his guard would have orders to fire upon me. I had no idea that such monstrous regulations existed. To-day the dinner for myself and child consists of a bowl of beans swimming in grease, two slices of fat junk, and two slices of bread. Still, my consolation is, 'Every dog has his day.'

January 30.—I wonder what will happen next. My child has been ill for several days, brought on by close confinement and want of proper food. Just now I went to the door and rapped, that being the prescribed manner of making known my wants. The guard came. 'What do you want?' 'Call the corporal of the guard,' I said. 'What do you want with him?' 'That is no business of yours; call him?' 'I won't call him.' 'You shall' (rap, rap, rap). The guard—'G——d d——n you, if you do that again I will shoot you through the door.' 'Call the corporal of the guard!' Here horrid imprecations followed. I thereupon raised the window and called, 'Corporal of the guard.' The ruffian called also, finding that I was not to be terrified by his threats. But, when the corporal came and opened the door, I was seized with laughter, for there stood the Abolitionist blubbering like a child, that *he had 'not orders to shoot the d——d Secesh woman, who was not afraid of the devil himself.'*

I sent for the officer of the guard, who was Lieutenant Carlton, of Zanesville, Ohio, and reported this outrage. He said that the guard had acted by his orders in refusing to call the corporal of the guard, and that he had no idea of allowing his non-commissioned officers to act as servants, &c. I told him that my child was ill, and I demanded the use of a servant; whereupon he told me that a servant should not be allowed me, save morning and night. I replied, 'Very well, sir. I will resort to the window, then, as my only expedient.' A servant after this was sent, but had to perform her functions with a sergeant of the guard standing over her. I told Lieutenant Carlton that I would report him to the Provost-Marshal, which I accordingly did, and the following is a copy of my letter: . . .*

M'Clellan† did me the honour to say that I knew his plans better than President Lincoln or his Cabinet, and had caused him four times to change them—this was a matter of public notoriety amongst the Yankees, and fully believed. But he gave me credit sometimes for more information than I possessed. I was, of course, a close observer of the smallest indications, and often drew accurate conclusions without having any precise knowledge on the subject. I was in Washington, as the Indian savage in the trackless forest, with an enemy behind every bush.

---

*Greenhow gives the text of her indignant letter.—*Ed.*
†Union General George McClellan.—*Ed.*

My perceptive faculties were under a painful tension, and every instinct was quickened to follow the doublings and windings of the ruthless foe who was hunting my race unto death; and, of course, no word or indication was lost upon me.

I was very often at this period intruded upon by large parties of curious Yankees, who came with passes from the Provost-Marshal, or Governor of the district, to stare at me. Sometimes I was amused, and generally contrived to find out from these parties what was going on. One set of men came, introducing themselves as friends of Mrs. Timothy Child's—as if this would furnish a passport to a Southern woman's confidence. This party affected to be literary, one of whom was editor of a Rochester journal: informed me that I was detained on account of my talents 'as a writer,' and classed me with Mdme. de Sevigné. Another large party came a few days after this: the women, very smartly dressed, helped themselves very unceremoniously to cake which had been just sent to my little one. A woman of this party, who claimed Boston as her residence, made quite a furious onslaught upon me, and said to me, 'Confess that it was love of notoriety which caused you to adopt your course, and you have been certainly gratified, for there is no one whom everybody has such a curiosity to see'—became very much excited, and said a great deal more. I told her that I had not supposed her object in visiting my prison was for the purpose of making a personal attack upon me, but that she did not surprise me. And afterwards I requested the superintendent not to allow any more of these parties to have access to me; for the fishwomen of Paris in the French Revolution were before my mind, and I feared that the next party might come armed with sticks or knives. The superintendent told me that numbers daily came to the prison who would gladly give him ten dollars a-piece to be allowed to pass my open door, so as to obtain a view of the 'indomitable rebel,' as I was sometimes called in their papers. This was being 'damned to immortality.' . . .

One day, on going down in the yard, the market-cart of the superintendent had just come in. My friend Charlie, who drove it, said, 'Will you take a ride?' I immediately got in—the other female prisoners following my example—exclaiming, 'I am off for Dixie!' and Charlie drove rapidly around the yard. It is impossible to describe the panic and confusion which ensued. All the prisoners rushed to the windows to enjoy the scene. The officer of the guard, Captain Gilbert, also rushed out, crying with might and main, 'Stop that *wehickle!*' The guard were doubled all around the yard, and, I believe, were actually preparing to fire upon us. After driving around the enclosure two or three times, we drew up in front of our redoubtable captain, who verily believed that an escape had been meditated, and that his timely intervention had alone frustrated it. . . .

The guard were at this time often extremely insolent, and questioned the slightest rule of privilege, so that it was necessary to make constant appeals to the officer on duty. One day, on going down, the guard very rudely placed his musket before me, and said, 'You shall not go down that way,' and ordered me to go by a dirty back stair, which was not the usual route. I immediately sent for the officer of the guard, Lieutenant Miller, who passed me down. Some time after the woman Baxley, and the one *calling herself* Mrs. Morris, or *Mason*, attempted to go down, and were also stopped by the guard, with whom they entered into an angry contest, and resolved in defiance to force their way through them. Morris was pushed into a corner, and held there by a bayonet crossed before her, whilst the more daring of the two, Baxley, seized on the musket that obstructed her passage, and attempted to pass under it. The guard cursed her. She struck him in the face, which caused his nose to bleed, and he knocked her down and kicked her. Attracted by the commotion, I went up, under escort of Lieutenant Miller, when this statement was given to me and to the officer by the women, amidst sobs and cries—the guard, also, who witnessed it, giving substantially the same account. Thus it will be seen that I must have suffered much from this humiliating association. Captain Higgins came up to speak with me on the subject, greatly mortified at the occurrence, and said that he would punish the guard if he could have any justification in doing so. I told him that I thought it was a case which he could not take cognisance of, as he could only regard it as a fight between a prisoner and a guard, in which the prisoner was the aggressor. Captain Higgins then implored those prisoners to have no words with his guard, but to appeal to him in case of insolence or disrespect, and that they should be summarily punished.

Ethel Rosenberg

ETHEL ROSENBERG (1915–1953)

Ethel (Greenglass) Rosenberg, the only daughter of Orthodox Jewish immigrant parents, was born on the Lower East Side of New York City. She was an imaginative, intelligent young woman restricted by poverty and her position as the older sister in a family that doted on her younger brother, David. Determined to succeed, she found work as a stenographer during the Depression and became politically active as a union organizer at the National New York Shipping and Packing Company, where she helped lead a strike in 1935.

She shared this progressive consciousness with Julius Rosenberg, an engineering student whom she married in 1939. As a housewife and mother, Rosenberg was troubled with anxieties about her health, family finances, and her two young sons, Michael and Robert. In 1949 she began psychiatric treatment "to discover the sources of her anxiety," which were determined to be her long-standing conflict with the Greenglass family rather than problems with Julius or their sons.

During the McCarthy era, when concern over Russian advancements in atomic weaponry was high, a series of arrests and trials of alleged atomic spies made international headlines. In July 1950 Julius Rosenberg was arrested upon the accusation of Ethel Rosenberg's brother, David Greenglass, who admitted to stealing atomic secrets from Los Alamos and claimed that Julius had directed his espionage. Ethel was arrested after her testimony before a grand jury in August 1950. She spent over seven months in the Women's House of Detention in New York City before coming to trial with Julius in March 1951. After their conviction, they were sentenced to death by Judge Irving R. Kaufman, who accused them of causing the Korean War and altering "the course of history to the disadvantage of our country." At Sing Sing, Ethel was held in solitary confinement for two years and was the only prisoner on the women's wing of death row. She was permitted weekly visits with Julius, who was not held in solitary, and they had infrequent visits with their children.

During their imprisonment, the Rosenbergs wrote many letters to each other, their attorney, Manny Bloch, and their sons. Their letters were published in 1953 and 1954 by the National Committee to Secure Justice in the Rosenberg Case, in order to encourage a public demand for clemency and to raise funds for the Rosenberg children.

On June 19, 1953, despite world-wide protests, the Rosenbergs were electrocuted at Sing Sing. Information from recently opened FBI files on the case strongly suggests that the government had no evidence against Ethel Rosenberg, that her conviction was intended to pressure her into informing against Julius, and that her refusal to "confess" forced the government to carry out an execution originally planned only to frighten her.

Note: Biographical information is from Michael Meeropol and Robert Meeropol, *We Are Your Sons: The Legacy of Ethel and Julius Rosenberg* (Boston: Houghton Mifflin, 1975; reprint, Champaign: Univ. of Illinois Press, 1986); Ronald Radosh and Joyce Milton, *The Rosenberg File* (New York: Holt, Rinehart & Winston, 1983); Walter and Miriam Schneir, *Invitation to an Inquest* (Garden City, N.Y.: Doubleday, 1965; latest edition, New York: Pantheon, 1983).

WORKS BY ETHEL ROSENBERG

Letters. In *We Are Your Sons: The Legacy of Ethel and Julius Rosenberg*, by Michael Meeropol and Robert Meeropol. Boston: Houghton Mifflin, 1975 (reprint, Champaign: Univ. of Illinois Press, 1986). This book by the Rosenbergs' sons (they use their adoptive parents' surname) includes a large collection of unedited letters written between 1950 and 1953.

The Death House Letters of Ethel and Julius Rosenberg. New York: Jero, 1953.

The Testament of Ethel and Julius Rosenberg. New York: Cameron & Kahn, 1954. Revised and enlarged edition of *The Death House Letters.*

The Long Nightmare

From Michael Meeropol and Robert Meeropol, *We Are Your Sons*, Houghton Mifflin, 1975. Used by permission of Michael and Robert Meeropol.

July 29, 1951

Hello, darling,

I scarcely know how to begin, my mind is in such a turmoil. Fortunately, my scribbling kept me so well-occupied this weekend that it passed much more quickly than I had hoped. Lee's* visit, too, was tremendously helpful along these lines; the picture she drew of the

*Lena Rosenberg, sister of Julius.—*Ed.*

[60]

children's reactions, however, pleased me none too well and served to dramatize their very real need for proper emotional reorientation.

All the same, dearest, there is a most gratifying upsurge of parental feeling and eagerness to see them which should do a good deal to promote the kind of atmosphere in the counsel room which we so fervently desire. Sweetheart, I shall do all that is within my power to set them at ease and prepare them for your coming; do try to lay aside some of the anxiety, meanwhile. Believe me, I am trying to convince myself, at the same time!

Hah! You can't make me jealous with your boats and trains; I have an envelope full of rare specimens collected with painstaking care by that intrepid hunter of wild insects, namely, your wife! Dearest! Daddy, how sweet and thoughtful of you to have hit on such a splendid plan! It's just the thing, particularly for Robby, who methinks may be a little shy and strange with us . . .

There is a great deal more that will come to me later in the day as I walk slowly about the yard and ruminate, that I'll be simply aching to share with you. Oh, yes, if he neglects to question me as to the form of the death penalty, this lovely job will fall to you, in which case answer him briefly but unequivocally that it is painless electrocution, which we feel, of course, will never come to pass. You can explain it in terms of a highly magnified electric shock that anybody might sustain through contact. Believe me, my loved one, children are what their parents truly expect them to be. If we can face the thought of our intended execution without terror, so then will they. Certainly, neither of us will seek to dwell on these matters, unduly, but let's not be afraid, and they won't, either. I am utterly convinced that that's all there is to it! All my love, darling—

Ethel

August 16, 1951

My very dearest Sweetheart,

I believe I attempted to describe somewhat, the last time I wrote, the latest frame of mind toward which I seem to be gradually progressing. Actually, it is a very difficult mood to capture on paper, since there are quite a few apparently unrelated facets that comprise its format, that yet are all one and the same thing. For example, I have the curious feeling of living in a world beyond whose walls no other exists; in jail terminology, I've "made it," I've "arrived," because the "street" no longer contributes the magnet, the painfully plaguing goal, it once did. The carefully restricted demarcations of the area in which I am permitted, have dissolved because there is no longer any other area. I am conscious of a need to remain immersed in my own being that amounts to an actual resistance to showing my thoughts and feelings. Oh, I make plans about the children, Manny, and Dr. ———, but it's all so mechanical, it's as though I don't really believe these events will actually transpire; they are dreams I have yet to dream. I am withdrawn into myself and a lethargic lassitude envelopes me, yet there is awareness of a stronger bond with you and all these others, if anything, just because I don't feel so driven to overtake you and them. In other words, this outside world which I have to all intents and purposes, renounced, is more sharply with me than ever, by dint of the fact that the situation of which I am presently a part holds so much less strangeness and terror for me than it did.

I know it's all very paradoxical and maybe my brain is so worn with poking and pulling that it cannot function keenly enough to properly expound the particular ideas that have been streaming back and forth across it, of late. So take them for what they are worth to you, and perhaps I'll try my luck another time, along these lines . . .

Ethel

7:30 A.M. Feb. 26 [1952]

My dear one,

Last night at 10:00 o'clock, I heard the shocking news.* At the present moment, with little or no detail to hand, it is difficult for me to make any comment, beyond an expression of horror at the shameless haste with which the government appears to be pressing for our liquidation. Certainly, it proves that all our contributions in the past regarding the political nature of our case, have been amazingly correct.

My heart aches for the children, unfortunately they are old enough to have heard for themselves, and no matter what amount of control I am able to exercise, my brain reels, picturing their terror. It is for them

---

*The appeal of the Rosenbergs' case had been turned down.—*Ed.*

I am most concerned and it is of their reaction I am anxiously awaiting some word. Of course, Manny will get here just as soon as he puts in motion proper legal procedure for our continued defense, but meanwhile, my emotions are in storm, as your own must be.

Sweetheart, if only I could truly comfort you, I love you so very dearly. . . . Courage, darling, there's much to be done.

Your devoted wife,
Ethel

March 4, 1952

Dearest children,

Did Aunt Lena tell you of her visit to me and of my messages of love to you both? Darlings, I am so sorry you had to be disappointed; I am just as unhappy about it all as you are. However, if you think we're licked, you just don't know your Mommy and Daddy! So do the best you can to get used to waiting all over again, but give yourself time because it's very hard not to mind. Daddy and I understand only too well just how hard it is and we're slightly bigger and stronger than you are. Nevertheless, let's not forget the old team cheer: "The Rosenbergs are re-e-a-l hot!" And more and more wonderful people are beginning to realize this and are pitching in to help send us home to you where we belong.

The snow is whirling outside my window as I sit at my writing table and wonder what my pussies might be doing at this moment. The other day when I was outside in the yard, the snow that had fallen the night before looked so much like the icing on a birthday cake, that I couldn't resist "printing" letters in it with my right foot. By the time I was through, all our initials were outlined clearly, M.R., R.R., E.R., and J.R. Do you remember how we used to tease Daddy by calling him, "J.R. the wonder dog"?

Speaking of birthday cake reminds me of a certain date, (March 10) when my dear Michael will be nine years old. I wish I could really tell you how happy I should be to celebrate the day with you and Robby in person. But since this is not possible I can only say that I shall be thinking of you both and loving you with all my heart.

Mike dear, what a perfectly wonderful picture of you I received; you know, the one that was taken in school. Since Robby doesn't attend school yet, I told Aunt Lena to make arrangements to have a good picture done of him outside, so that I can see my boys just as they are right now whenever I get hungry for a glimpse of them.

Robby dear, how do you like the drawings Daddy made for you? I didn't see them but I bet they must be swell. I am hoping you have fun on Mike's birthday. When you are five on May 14th, he will enjoy yours, too.

Again, all my love, my very dearest children.

Mommy—

September 25, 1952

Sweetest children,

You are exactly that, you know; since Saturday, I've been walking on air, remembering how you looked and what you said. How wonderfully satisfying it was to squeeze you in my arms and exchange loving kisses. As a matter of fact, I plan to have all the Rosenbergs, short and tall, fat and skinny, spend one solid week doing nothing else but, sometime in the near future, the nearer the better, of course! When Daddy was in to see me on Wednesday, we babbled like a couple of kids ourselves, marveling first over one of you and then over the other, and we dearly wish for you to know how proud we are of the fine job both of you are doing, each in his own individual way, just the most worthwhile job anyone, be it adult or child, *can* do—that of growing and changing and developing, into healthy, happy people . . .

All my love—
Mommy—

Sept. 28, 1952

Dearest children,

What a glorious day it was to celebrate a birthday. I awoke to find a gold sun bright in a clear blue sky. A mild breeze wafted in gently from the Hudson and it was heavenly good to fill the lungs with sweet, fresh air. Overhead the sea gulls floated by on indolent, gray wings, and only the sound of the starlings, possibly scolding, broke the all-pervading stillness. I walked quickly about the peaceful yard, stopping every now and then to inspect the bits of green stuff struggling up through the cracks in the concrete, and trying to imagine what you two might be up to, this fine morning! My goodness, I thought, that's right; I am 37 years old today, old enough to have chalked up to my credit a grand family, a worthwhile life, and a host of wonderful friends; old enough also to realize why I must spend my birthday alone, but strong enough, too, to know without any doubt whatever, that those artificially induced storms about which Ben* told you, will at long last no longer be permitted to rage at the expense of decent mankind. This day I spend apart from loved ones is all the proof I need that there is no loneliness too great to withstand, no task too difficult of accomplishment, for the establishment of that kind of world that will give all peoples the opportunity to live and work and grow together, in love and in dignity and in peace! Know then, my two dearest dears, that bitterly as I missed you, (and there's no two ways about it, I'll have to go on missing you until we're all together at last), know then that I was gladdened because I understood the necessity to accept my responsibility for your dear sakes, just as it warmed me to remember all the other countless parents who are standing up for their families! Our precious children deserve no less than that! . . .

Robby, darling, would you please make a few pictures for me? I should like very much a drawing of the "wolfie" and the bear with the long nails, and the one of the doorknob and the two bell buttons. And you, Mike, honey, compose a poem—or if you'd rather draw something, too, I should be delighted. Such presents would bring you closer to me and make me ever so happy!

Your Daddy is fine and sends all his love— And so does your Mommy!—X X X X X X X X X X X X X X X X X X X X X X X X

June 17, 1953†

Dear Manny,

Please send this letter to the kids or phone it in to them or send by messenger in as short a time as possible as I don't know where they are staying now.

*Michael and Robby were living with their parents' friends Ben and Sonja Bach at this time.—*Ed.*
†This is misdated. She wrote it on the 16th.

My dearest darlings,

This is the process known as "sweating it out," and it's tough, that's for sure . . .

Maybe you thought that I didn't feel like crying too when we were hugging and kissing goodbye, huh, even though I'm slightly older than 10. And maybe you thought I was just too matter of fact to stand, when your outraged feelings demanded acknowledgement in kind. Darlings, that would have been so easy, far too easy on myself; and I had to resist a very real temptation to follow your lead and break down with you. As I say it would have been only too easy, but it would not have been any kindness, at all. So I took the hard way instead of the easy, because I love you more than myself, and because I knew you needed that love far more than I needed the relief of crying.

Instead, I reassured you, as well as I could, in the minutes we had, and promised to write. There is one thing among many others I'd like you to know. The kisses are there between Daddy and myself even though we may not exchange them presently.* And while it would be sweet to be able to do so, it is only to the degree that parents are able to give each other and their children the strength and encouragement to cope with their problems and to "sweat it out" if need be, it is only to that degree, I say, that people really love.

I know, sweethearts, an explanation of this kind cannot ever substitute for what we have been missing and for what we hope to be able to return to, nor do I intend it as any such thing. Only, as I say, we need to try to remain calm and free from panic, so that we can do all we can to help one another to see this thing through! . . .

All my love and all my kisses—

Mommy

[June 19, 1953]

Dearest Sweethearts, my most precious children,

Only this morning it looked like we might be together again after all. Now that this cannot be, I want so much for you to know all that I

---

*At one prison visit I [Michael] had said, "I never saw Mommy and you kiss" (obviously referring to them not kissing in prison).

have come to know. Unfortunately, I may write only a few simple words; the rest your own lives must teach you, even as mine taught me.

At first, of course, you will grieve bitterly for us, but you will not grieve alone. That is our consolation and it must eventually be yours.

Eventually, too you must come to believe that life is worth the living. Be comforted that even now, with the end of ours slowly approaching, that we know this with a conviction that defeats the executioner!

Your lives must teach you, too, that good cannot really flourish in the midst of evil; that freedom and all the things that go to make up a truly satisfying and worthwhile life, must sometimes be purchased very dearly. Be comforted then that we were serene and understood with the deepest kind of understanding, that civilization had not as yet progressed to the point where life did not have to be lost for the sake of life; and that we were comforted in the sure knowledge that others would carry on after us.

We wish we might have had the tremendous joy and gratification of living our lives out with you. Your Daddy who is with me in the last momentous hours, sends his heart and all the love that is in it for his dearest boys. Always remember that we were innocent and could not wrong our conscience.

We press you close and kiss you with all our strength.

Lovingly,
Daddy and Mommy
Julie   Ethel

P.S. to Manny: The Ten Commandments religious medal and chain and my wedding ring—I wish you to present to our children as a token of our undying love.

P.S.—to Manny

Please be certain to give my best wishes to——.* Tell him I love and honor him with all my heart— Tell him I want him to know that I feel he shares my triumph— For I have no fear and no regrets— Only that the release from the trap was not completely effectuated and the qualities I possess could not expand to their fullest capacities— I want him

---

*Our mother's psychiatrist.

to have the pleasure of knowing how much he meant to me, how much he did to help me grow up— All our love to all our dear ones.

Love you so much—

Ethel

[June 19, 1953]

Dear Manny,

These are some notes I want you to give to ————*. They are attached to this letterhead. There are also a few last notes for you—the one beginning with quote from Geo. Eliot. Dearest person, you and ———— must see to my children. Tell him it was my last request of him. They must have professional help if needed and he must see that they are tested to find if it is needed.

All my heart I send to all who held me dear. I am not alone—and I die "with honor and with dignity"†—knowing my husband and I must be vindicated by history. You will see to it that our names are kept bright and unsullied by lies—as you did while we lived so wholeheartedly, so unstintingly—you did everything that could be done—We are the first victims of American Fascism.

Love you,

Ethel

Geo. Eliot said "This is a world worth abiding in while one man can thus venerate and love another—"

Honor means you are too proud to do wrong—but Pride means that you will not own that you have done wrong at all—

I cry for myself as I lie dead how shall they know all that burned my brain and breast—

The fat's in the fire to say nothing of the books—(my best to Pop Bloch)‡

---

*Our mother's psychiatrist.
†At one of her last meetings with Manny our mother said she shivered from head to foot when she thought of getting into that chair and having the current run through her, but "I will die with dignity"
‡Alexander Bloch, with his son Manny, defended the Rosenbergs.—*Ed.*

GABRIELLE RUSSIER (1937–1969)

Gabrielle Russier was raised as a French Protestant by her American mother and her father, a Parisian lawyer. In 1967 she began teaching French literature at the Lycée Saint-Exupéry in Marseilles. She lived in an apartment with her twin children, Valérie and Joël, after her divorce from Michel Nogues. As a teacher she was an anomaly. Very small and slight of build, at the age of thirty she looked no older than her students. According to standards of behavior in French education, she was unusually familiar with her students, who affectionately called her *Gatito*, Spanish for "little cat." She even joined them in the student riots of 1968.

Her legal problems began in the fall of 1968 when her affair with Christian Rossi, her sixteen-year-old student, came to the attention of his parents, university professors who attempted to force a separation by sending Christian to a boarding school. Russier nevertheless attempted to maintain the liaison; when Christian ran away from school she was arrested on charges of "having caused a minor to leave home" and was held in preventive detention. The experience was shocking to the naive Russier, who did not understand that the sort of forbidden relationships common in literature would not necessarily be accepted in real life. She refused to divulge Christian's whereabouts, and was released only after he came out of hiding.

Christian responded badly to the psychiatric treatment demanded by his father. After he ran away again, Russier was arrested and held without trial in Les Baumettes prison, Marseilles, from April to June 1969. Russier's letters show her pain and confusion during her imprisonment with poor female criminals. She was tormented by financial problems and her inability to understand what she had done wrong. When her trial in July ended in a suspended sentence, which the prosecution immediately appealed, she sought relief from stress in a rest home. She committed suicide upon her return home in August.

The Russier case was a cause célèbre, widely debated in the French media. *To Die for Love*, a film based on the story, was quickly planned. One legal consequence of the case was a law restricting the use of preventive detention. *L'affaire Russier* has evoked criticism of the French educational and judicial systems and of women's status in French society.

Note: Biographical information is from introductions by Mavis Gallant and Raymond Jean in *The Affair of Gabrielle Russier*, by Gabrielle Russier, trans. Ghislaine Boulanger (New York: Knopf, 1971; originally published as *Lettres de Prison* [Paris: Éditions du Seuil, 1970]).

WORKS BY GABRIELLE RUSSIER

The Affair of Gabrielle Russier. Preface by Raymond Jean. Introduction by Mavis Gallant. Translated by Ghislaine Boulanger. New York: Knopf, 1971. Originally published as *Lettres de Prison* (Paris: Éditions du Seuil, 1970).

Letters from Prison

From *The Affair of Gabrielle Russier*. Reprinted by permission of Éditions du Seuil.

May 5, 1969

Dear Gilberte*

I made up my mind to write you despite the absence of mail because I'm afraid that if you see me again one day—if in spite of everything you see me again—you will be disappointed. I have forced myself to stay in good spirits up till the present, but now I can't go on anymore, for so many reasons I can't go into here. I am just about in the state I was in when I had dinner at your house, except there is no cure here. On the contrary, everything is done to reinforce a depression which had already made its presence felt earlier, and against which I have done nothing but fight for six months until it's made me ill. Human resistance is inexhaustible and yet sometimes I wonder if I'm not going to be completely beyond help after all this. Don't be too upset. Don't mention it. But I don't want you to expect too much of me—in all probability you will have a lot to do helping me get back to the way I used to be.

The people around me are stronger, perhaps it's because they're used to this type of thing, of clinging to values which don't exist for me and which they will find again outside.

And then, at the very bottom of my serenity in the beginning there must have been the idea that despite everything, this could not last

*A neighbor and colleague at the Lycée Nord de Marseille—*Ed.*

because I had done nothing to deserve it, which would be easy to prove.

Now I have the feeling that once here it's unimportant whether or not you had reasons for coming, it's unimportant whether you're innocent or guilty, you are in a hole, and you go lower and lower. I'm losing my memory of everything. I feel a little as though I were dead. And this letter is also a last effort to try and explain something. I've seen too much, heard too much, I should like to fall into an endless sleep, to forget, but I don't even know if I could. And what hurts me most is that the others find everything normal, what they did before, what they find here, what they'll do again afterward. So much unawareness.

Don't say this to Madame R., tell her it's all right and that I send a kiss to Joël.

Forgive me for writing you so sadly. But it helps to speak to someone. And then afterward, if I'm not too far gone, you'll help me come back to life, won't you?

With love

And a smile—a last little smile,

> Gabrielle

> May 12, 1969

Dear Gilberte

Your letter did me so much good. I haven't received anything for a very long time, and I assume that you haven't received the letters I wrote you either where I asked you to take care of my rent, my car, of Joël, and to send me some laundry. I do hope they forwarded my drawings to Joël all the same, and that he isn't too upset. And perhaps by now you have the letters from the good days, when I was managing to keep on top of things.

They gave me some medicine, I'm better. Don't worry, above all don't worry.

I feel as though I'm in a hole because the world here is so special, and also because I know the real difficulties will begin when I get out. How can I explain it to you—there is a certain sense of security here, you've lost all responsibilities. When I think of what is waiting for me outside I'm afraid, and yet I should so love to see a tree, a real one. That's why being inside is such torment, the thought that I'll have to

leave means more torment. Difficult to explain, I shall try later, but certain things are impossible to get across. But don't worry, and tell the others not to worry. Could you send me by mail with the name of the sender written on the outside, a package (small) with
—colored felt-tipped pens
—deodorant and dry shampoo
—a large crochet hook.
And another with wool (there's some at home) and my nylon overall. That way I'll get it faster because packages which are brought are only distributed on Mondays.

It took me a long time to get to know you, Gilberte, you frightened me a little, I didn't dare open up. And then through the days I learned to have confidence and I was at ease with you. You are sensible, upright, and that helped me so much. It's true, you only understand when you love, so I'm going to wait patiently for my lucidity to return. And today I'm pulling myself together as I did the evening when we talked together at length about the SNES.* Because I have your letter and it tells me I'm not mad; because you are alive and that'll make me forget what I see here, and what I see is dreadful—it's not tangible but it's in their minds. So many disturbed people—in any case devoted to failure. I'll explain to you. Your dependability, your sense of humor will help me . . . and *Teorema.* Above all that's what I can't stand, what I'm frightened of not being able to forget. Everything is soiled and you know, Jansenist that I am, I can't put up with that. Will I always be fifteen years old? I am incapable of looking at all this with detachment, except when I think that one day I shall get out, but then fresh torment because I don't think I shall be able to stand living as I did these last months, in a comfortable prison continually being spied upon and everything that that means. If I could be sure that everything will be cleared up, I think I would be able to hold out for a long time, a long time. I'm going to try to believe it but I'm afraid of being disillusioned, there's been so much of that already.

Tell your mother, of whom I was very fond, that since I can't get the first rose, I'm sending her a petal from the one that has been helping me to survive for several days.

*National Syndicate for Secondary Education.—*Ed.*

Tell everyone who deserves it that I'm thinking of them and that, in the stupid way of those whose life slips by them, I am sorry I didn't understand them better, and that the red tortoise is moving forward shakily, but it is moving forward, if it falls down it will get up again.

With love

Gabrielle

May 13, 1969

[To her parents]

In this so special world which you can only understand if you have lived in it, I try to roll myself into a ball, to see nothing, to hear nothing. I look at my syringa blossom and the sky outside, a little pale, a little sad. Spring has not really come back this year, and the approaching summer will without doubt lack the brightness of the summers that went before. I try not to think of the future, to live from day to day.

Marseilles is a rotten town. And yet I loved Provence so much. I loved Marseilles too, sparkling in the night, and the Estaque, and the boat, on which we had set our sights, sleeping in the port. It was called *The Misunderstood.*

So much has happened since that day in May when you left St. Charles Station, papa. Everything had been in the works for some months even then, but nothing had been said. Each of us thought he was dreaming. So many things, so many friends. It would fill several books. But then, at least this will serve to measure the strength and price of friendship, when it is true. And we shall try to forget the others, the wolves.

I don't regret anything except having dragged so many people into what appears today to be a disaster. Tell me you know "that you only see clearly with your heart," that we are now in the black hole of appearances and ugliness, but that truth, in its simplicity, will return with the sun. Tell me that you aren't too sad. For such a long time we have lived with the barrier of space between us. And yet, since February '58, eleven years ago already, we have always been together. I am with you—not in sadness and misery—I should like you to have the calm I feel at this moment, to tell you I'm waiting for you, and that nothing can happen to us. With a smile

And love

Gabrielle

May 13, 1969

[To her parents]

The atmosphere here is as you would imagine. The guardian angels are kind, but the company pretty awful. I'm all right in my cell and leave it as little as possible. The best moments are with the choir and at mass. The chaplain is a Dominican, like the sisters who come to visit us and who are marvels of serenity and understanding. I hope I shall be able to pay them a visit afterward at Saint Zachary where they live.

Saint Zachary, those were the good times of our walks together when we were discovering Provence. I am going to try and be strong so that those times will come again, so that we shall find Saint Victoria again just as it is turning mauve, so that we can pick everlasting flowers.

Since I live partly in the company of Baudelaire and Rimbaud and partly with the rabble, I don't really know where I am. I can no longer tell if what I'm writing is lucid, reasonable.

But I should like to be able to say to you, as before,

till tomorow

till always

I send you my love

Gabrielle

May 16, 1969

Dear old Michel*

I hope that the last week of your vacation went off well. At the time when you must have been traveling, I came to vacation here, where I have been living since April 25. I did not write you before so as not to upset you, but I am doing so now because I guess you will have been brought up to date if you went to see Joël. Moreover, I don't know when you will receive this letter, the mail seems to be held up somewhere and for my part I receive virtually nothing.

Above all don't worry about me, although I have not received the packages I requested, I'm not bad, and for the rest I have done nothing to justify my presence here. My father's attorney will confirm this to you by telephone if you want to be reassured, or my Marseillais attorney, Monsieur Raymond Guy. If you have time, send me some postcards so

*Her ex-husband.

I can decorate my cell a bit. For the last two days I have been alone and my morale is better than before, I am trying to organize myself, to work. The impatient nature you once knew is learning patience.

I'm writing you because I'm worried about the children. Joël is in the same place he was during the Easter vacation. I write to him but I don't know if he gets my letters. If you have a moment, go and say hello to him and above all reassure him because I'm certain he understood that I was coming here.

I have also written Valérie, but since she knows absolutely nothing I talk to her about the rain and good weather. I hope she doesn't notice that my letters do not correspond with hers. They are kind enough here not to put the "censored" stamp on what I write her (the sisters open the mail in Savoy). Write her. She gets back the 10th or 11th, if I haven't gotten out (you never do know when you're getting out of here) someone must go and fetch her at the station. You could find out the date of her return by telephoning the Social Security Department Camps Service at the beginning of June. I think that Madame R. will agree to take her with Joël. You could then pay Madame R. (against receipt) for the whole of June; she is not rich and I was only able to give her 100 francs when I left.

I interrupted myself because I just received my first package—some wool, some Scotch tape, a little laundry, a drawing I liked—life is beautiful.

They've been giving me a hard time for months, they are trying to wear me down, but although I'm fading little by little, I don't think they will ever stop me from experiencing the joy that one discovers in little things—a flower, a smile, an occasional silence.

We have shared good and bad times before. Don't be too angry with me for making you share bad times again. *Don't worry.* Take care of Joël, send cards to Valérie (packages are not allowed). You'll see, a day will come when we can smile with them once more, for real this time. I relish the idea of having a drink at Le Grillon with you. I'll put on a dress in your honor, you won't have to drag an androgynous hippie to the Cours Mirabeau.

Bise*

Gabrielle

*The bise is a warm little wind which blows from the Gobi Desert, it fights against the storm . . . and it will win.

Friday, May 16, 1969

Dear Gilberte

I'm writing you again, as you have permitted, although I haven't received anything from you. There is one sign that Saint Antoine exists—I just received the second package I asked for (there's absolutely no trace of the first) and I thank whoever sent or brought it.

Life had already picked up: I have been alone in a cell for two days, and feel so much better in my solitude. Yesterday I came back to life a bit, I moved the furniture, cleaned the walls, organized my refuge. And now I have my parcel, a clean dress, the picture by Luc on the wall, my own little corner. I'm OK, ready to hold out for a long time. Tell those who deserve it at the lycée not to worry. I hope too that you, Gilberte, have not had too many problems because of me, materially or spiritually. I know from experience that it's harder for those who are outside than for those inside. But your sense of humor, your determined spirit, will stop you, I'm sure, from following my tracks down the road to depression. Above all I do hope my disappearance has not affected your mother's morale too deeply. Tell her I send her a kiss, that I think of her, that I try to be like her by always keeping myself neat and clean (that's not always easy here) and leading my life with care and attention to detail, by trying to chase away depression when it sneaks up on me. And I value my good fortune at being able to write and read. But I would very much like not to be able to hear anymore because these ladies, my coprisoners, have conversations (through the windows) that I won't forget for a long while.

I shall at least have learned to do each act slowly, patiently, and God knows, if indeed there is a God, that was not my wont.

In short, a little life in slow motion, that won't do any harm. But unfortunately I imagine that now, as I begin to part with my earlier illusions, they will start making me come out of my shell.

I can visualize the little red shoes and our first conversation last year, going down toward St. Louis for a coffee. I was very, very intimidated. Now you mean a lot to me—and it's not because I am in prison. But perhaps it is because I'm in prison that I dare tell you.

And then, it has always seemed to me that I don't deserve people looking after me. At the moment I accept it—make a virtue of necessity—but afterward . . .

[76]

Afterward I think I shall take up the bag I came with and go lose myself in the crowd, or beside the water. I have learned to do without everything or nearly, I have also learned not to take on responsibilities anymore since I collapsed under their weight. And since I don't know how to steer a middle course . . . That's the danger here—the shock of getting out. Learning to live again. I shall want to walk, walk without a destination, without money, without anything. To lose myself, to disappear, I'm frightened of the day when they will uproot me from this world where, when all is said and done, we are protected. Especially now that I am alone; the convent, the "rest." Difficult not to say "I" all the time. Because "outside" is a more and more diffuse memory—sometimes painfully nostalgic—that one drives away so as not to be hurt by it. However, I should like to continue to write you because I find that writing for oneself is—I don't know—absolutely absurd. Even if I'm aware that sending these epistles is absurd too.

I shall try not to "run away" when I get out. So that this experience will at least make some sense for those who come after me. But the temptation will be great.

Thank you for being there. For helping me not to forget that the earth exists. My love to everyone. Tell them that the lycée coffee was good! Tell them too that true fidelity is that of ideas. And that is why I'm here.

With love

Gabrielle

P A R T 2

"We were stronger afterward than before":
Transcendence through Causes and Beliefs
beyond the Self

*

Most women's prison literature explores the writer's personal response
to incarceration or describes her prison environment and lifestyle. Whether
she focuses directly on herself or shifts her gaze to her sister inmates,
the basic subject is the reality of imprisonment. Some writings, however, transcend this focus on the immediate situation to discuss another
topic that consumes the writer's attention: the cause or belief that
brought her to prison in the first place. In these works, the fact of imprisonment is decidedly secondary and is mentioned only to enhance
the argument by demonstrating the prisoner's professed dedication to
a political, social, or religious cause. And, as is the case with the other
prison literature of women, this type of writing firmly grasps the concrete; the writer transcends imprisonment without ethereal flights into
theory or abstract philosophical arguments.

Both male and female prisoners who write about a cause usually
intend to support an audience of fellow believers or to persuade a neutral
or hostile audience. Imprisonment underscores the merit of a cause that
can elicit such commitment despite injustice and hardship. In texts by
both men and women, the *self* of the writer is usually subordinated to
the cause, but the subordination is particularly distinctive in this type
of women's prison literature, since it is generally more complete; it is
more likely that the male writer will place a secondary emphasis on
his own story.

Patricia Meyer Spacks's discussion of women's autobiographies sheds
some light on this issue.[1] Discussing the works of five politically active
women—Emmeline Pankhurst, Dorothy Day, Emma Goldman, Eleanor
Roosevelt, and Golda Meir[2]—Spacks notes that their autobiographies,
with the exception of Emma Goldman's, show how women lose their

sense of self, as many men tend to do. The four selections in this section similarly demonstrate the authors' overriding sense of a larger, external purpose that eclipses the self. The selections show, however, that women writers often stress the concerns of *women* working for a cause, even while they downplay their own personal histories.

Focusing on an external cause at the expense of self is a centuries-old theme in women's prison literature. The following excerpt from "The Passion of Saint Perpetua" offers an early and vivid illustration, in her account of a vision on the day before her martyrdom in the amphitheater at Carthage in 203 A.D.:

And I saw a huge crowd watching eagerly. And because I knew that I was condemned to the beasts, I marvelled that there were no beasts let loose on me. And there came out an Egyptian, foul of look, with his attendants to fight against me. And to me also there came goodly young men to be my attendants and supporters. And I was stripped and was changed into a man. And my supporters began to rub me down with oil, as they are wont to do before a combat; and I saw the Egyptian opposite rolling in the sand. And there came forth a man wondrously tall so that he rose above the top of the amphitheatre, clad in a purple robe without a girdle with two stripes, one on either side, running down the middle of the breast, and wearing shoes curiously wrought made of gold and silver; carrying a wand, like a trainer, and a green bough on which were golden apples. And he asked for silence, and said: "This Egyptian, if he prevail over her, shall kill her with a sword; and, if she prevail over him, she shall receive this bough." And he retired. And we came near to one another and began to use our fists. My adversary wished to catch hold of my feet, but I kept on striking his face with my heels. And I was lifted up into the air, and began to strike him in such fashion as would one that no longer trod on earth. But when I saw that the fight lagged, I joined my two hands, linking the fingers of the one with the fingers of the other. And I caught hold of his head, and he fell on his face; and I trod upon his head. And the people began to shout, and my supporters to sing psalms. And I came forward to the trainer, and received the bough. And he kissed me, and said to me: "Peace be with thee, my daughter." And I began to go in triumph to the Gate of Life. And I awoke and I perceived that I should not fight with beasts but with the Devil; but I knew the victory to be mine. Such were my doings up to the day before the games. Of what was done in the games themselves let him write who will.[3]

Confidence in the truth for which she dies prevails in Perpetua's victory, where an anonymous chosen daughter of God triumphs, and not Perpetua the individual. In fact, it is the truth, and not a person at all, that triumphs in Perpetua's testimony. Her narrative is remarkable for its omission of references to her personal identity; even her sex is changed, though the female pronoun continues to be used. The text does not, however, launch into an abstract discussion of Perpetua's Christian philosophy. Instead, she chooses to convince her reader through recitation of visions recounted with simplicity and dignity.

Similar techniques are used in British Quaker Katharine Evans's account of her religious trials in seventeenth-century Malta.[4] The works of Evans and Sarah Cheevers, her companion in the ministry, belong to the early Quaker movement's literature of "sufferings," which emphasized the cause rather than the writer. Written explanations of the principles for which they suffered enabled members of the Religious Society of Friends to combat religious intolerance without violating their peace testimony. Since the form of sufferings tracts was quite standardized and, after 1672, subject to approval by the London Yearly Meeting (the largest central body of Quakers), there was relatively little room for expression of the writer's personality.[5] Still, the spiritual and physical power that these Quaker women possessed shines through their writings even though they used impersonal, standard forms of expression.

High drama charges Evans's account of the classic battle between good and evil that she and Cheevers lived. The lines are clearly and absolutely drawn: the Lord Inquisitor and his accomplices "with a black Rod" represent the Devil, while Evans and Cheevers stand fast in the Light. Although we see little of Evans's *self*, she is far more than a cardboard figure. She demonstrates the toughness that made leaders of so many seventeenth-century Quaker women. Despite failing health, she refuses to be moved from her airless "inner Room" and separated from Cheevers, but her joy in her strength bears no trace of ego: "We were stronger afterward than before, the Lord God did fit us for every Condition."

Prison writing about a cause generally employs public formats, such as Quaker sufferings tracts, rather than the personal, confessional formats of diaries or memoirs. The author wishes to announce rather than to justify her imprisonment. Madame Roland's need to justify herself before an impartial posterity is absent from these confident but relatively selfless prison writings.[6] During the civil rights era Margaret Sanger, for example, wrote a magazine article for the Methodist journal *Together* (1960) to explain her imprisonment, which had taken place four decades earlier. The piece, which concerned Sanger's fight to give women access to birth-control information, was a timely reminder of past struggles. Although there is relatively more of the author's ego involved in this article than in the other three selections, Sanger exercises considerable restraint in discussing her motivation, emotional involvement, personal sacrifice, and victory in her crusade. Instead, she gives voice to the powerless women whom she sought to serve and presents a compelling case for the cause itself.

Civil rights activist Barbara Deming, also writing in the 1960s, presents the most theoretical of the four selections in her discussion of nonviolence. *In Prison* includes few personal references, yet it does not lack passion. Like Katharine Evans, Deming states her beliefs with intense feeling, and her confidence never wavers. Evans and Deming feel no shame at their imprisonment; rather, they condemn the immorality of their captors. Deming differs from Evans, though, in that she sees her jailers as human beings and tries to understand their point of view. To give her nonviolent philosophy a more personal tone and a sense of immediacy, Deming uses the form of a letter to a friend who has objected to her "wasteful" actions. This form is consistent with the message itself, which emphasizes the application of her philosophy to Deming's walk through the South. In its blend of theory and practice, her letter resembles Martin Luther King Jr.'s widely known "Letter from Birmingham Jail." Deming, however, writes not as a civil rights leader but as part of the rank and file; her point of view is not that of a black man, but that of a white woman who has felt the hatred of white Southern townspeople as well as that of white female inmates who scorn her alliance with blacks. The difficulties of her position add weight to her argument for the viability of nonviolence in solving complex social problems.

The final selections, from the Chilean resistance movement of the 1970s, are testimonies of the authors' experiences as representative of the collective experience of their people. Anonymity is more than a security measure for the writer: it is a reinforcement of the message that the writer belongs to a community of imprisoned and oppressed women who speak collectively through her. She provides the voice; the experience is shared by all.[7]

Latin American women's written testimonies, at least those translated into English, are very scarce. Most testimonies take the form of interviews or begin as interviews that are later written as narratives by collaborating authors.[8] Many testimonies do not get written at all because of fear of reprisal or because the woman, tortured and physically humiliated, finds it difficult to publicize her painful experience within a society that considers her somehow to blame for the violation of her body.[9] Ana Guadalupe Martinez of El Salvador's Revolutionary Democratic Front (FDR) explains the psychological aspect of women's physical torture:

> In the case of women, sexual abuse, the constant pawing, and the threat of rape are among the principal ways used by the repressive apparatus to demoralize. The mere fact of feeling an assassin's hands on your body causes revulsion and anguish. Even though I had known that all this would happen, it was a brutal, horrible experience.[10]

However, testimonies proclaim that the pain and humiliation of torture are by no means the whole story of political prisoners. When women who have endured this trauma are afterward imprisoned in camps such as Tres Alamos in Chile, they put their revolutionary theory to practice in the most inauspicious of environments. Communal organization of work, leisure, domestic tasks, and child care makes prison existence bearable while it creates, in a microcosm, the society that the women and their *compañeros* (male comrades) have struggled to build. The challenge these women face is to maintain morale and momentum upon release, despite exile's disruption, grief over comrades who have disappeared, and resistance by *compañeros* who are uneasy with new female roles.

Literature of commitment is among the most articulate, unambiguous, and positive of all women's prison writings. Many of the causes supported in this literature are shared by men and women alike, so that gender differences are not always prominent in this type of prison writing. Still, the unique aspects of women's experiences as activists and as prisoners underscore the perspective of each selection in this section.

NOTES

1. Patricia Meyer Spacks, "Selves in Hiding," in *Women's Autobiography: Essays in Criticism*, ed. Estelle C. Jelinek (Bloomington, Ind.: Indiana Univ. Press, 1980), pp. 112–132.

2. The first three of these women have written about their prison experiences. See entries in the Annotated Bibliography.

3. Excerpt from "The Passion of SS. Perpetua and Felicitas." From *Some Authentic Acts of the Early Martyrs*, ed. E. C. E. Owen (Oxford: Clarendon Press, 1927), pp. 84–85. Reprinted by permission of Oxford University Press.

4. See Judith Scheffler, "Prison Writings of Early Quaker Women," *Quaker History* 73, no. 2 (Fall 1984): 25–37.

5. For a discussion of Quaker sufferings literature, see Luella Wright, *The Literary Life of the Early Friends, 1650–1725* (New York: Columbia Univ. Press, 1932), pp. 74–97.

6. Some writers, like Margaret Sanger, also wrote more personal, autobiographical works.

7. A similar message is stated in the Preface to *Slave of Slaves: The Challenge of Latin American Women*, by the Latin American and Caribbean Women's Collective, trans. Michael Pallis (London: Zed Press, 1980), p. 5: "We have sought to show that it is quite possible to write as a group and that ideas are no one's private property."

8. See, for example, Domitila Barrios de Chungara with Moema Viezzer, *Let Me Speak! Testimony of Domitila, a Woman of the Bolivian Mines*, trans. Victoria Ortiz (New York: Monthly Review Press, 1978); Margaret Randall, *Sandino's Daughters: Testimonies of Nicaraguan Women in Struggle*, ed. Lynda Yanz (Vancouver, Canada: New Star, 1981); Comite Jane Vanini, *Women in Resistance* (Berkeley, Calif.: Support Committee for Women in the Chilean and Latin American Resistance, n.d.), which includes an interview with Gladys Diaz; *I, Rigoberta Menchu: An Indian Woman in Guatemala*, ed. Elisabeth Burgos-Debray, trans. Ann Wright (New York: Verso/ Schocken, 1984); Ana Guadalupe Martinez, *Las Cárceles Clandestinas de El Salvador* (Libertad por El Secuestro de un Oligarca, 1978).

9. Ximena Bunster, presentation in the "Women and Human Rights" session, Women's Studies Conference, University of Pennsylvania, Philadelphia, March 1985.

10. Ana Guadalupe Martinez, *Las Cárceles Clandestinas de El Salvador*, excerpt translated in *Women and War: El Salvador* (New York: Women's International Resource Exchange Service, 1981), pp. 24–26.

KATHARINE EVANS (?–1692)

English Quaker Katharine Evens and her husband, John, "a Man of considerable Estate," lived near Bath in Englishbatch, Somerset. She was a housewife whose fervent commitment to the beliefs of the Religious Society of Friends inspired her traveling ministry. As was the custom in the early years of this religious movement, husband and wife traveled separately, and Evans's frequent companion in the ministry was Sarah Cheevers (or Chevers), a housewife from Wiltshire. Like other early Quakers, Evans was persecuted throughout her extensive travels. Between 1655 and 1658 she was jailed in Exeter, banished from the Isle of Wight and the Isle of Man, whipped in Salisbury, and attacked in Warminster.

While on a journey to Alexandria and Jerusalem in 1659, Evans and Cheevers were arrested by the Inquisition when their ship stopped at Malta and they boldly preached there. They were initially confined in the English consul's house, but were later transferred to the Inquisition's prison and pressured to convert to Roman Catholicism. Defying their captors, Evans and Cheevers instead preached to the other prisoners. Their most severe test came when Evans, whose fragile health was suffering from the lack of air in their small room, was offered a separate, cooler room. They refused to be parted, but after nine months they were forced to separate. To earn money for expenses in prison, Evans and Cheevers were allowed to knit and darn clothes for other prisoners, and, more important, they were permitted to write letters of spiritual encouragement to family and other Friends at home.

Meanwhile, in England, attempts were being made to secure the women's release. Sea captain Daniel Baker traveled to Malta but was unable to help them. However, when George Fox, founder of the Society of Friends, appealed to powerful English nobles, the release followed promptly. While at the consul's house awaiting passage home, Evans and Cheevers continued to proclaim their message. They arrived home in 1662, after three and a half years. Cheevers died shortly afterward, in 1664, and Evans's husband died in prison the same year, but Katharine Evans lived many more years and continued in the ministry.

Note: Biographical information is from Joseph Besse, ed., *A Collection of the Sufferings of the People Called Quakers* (London: Luke Hinde, 1753); Mabel R. Brailsford, *Quaker Women 1650–1690* (London: Duckworth, 1915); William C. Braithwaite, *The*

Beginnings of Quakerism, 2d ed. (Cambridge: Cambridge Univ. Press, 1955); Cicely Veronica Wedgewood, "The Conversion of Malta," *Velvet Studies* (London: J. Cape, 1946).

WORKS BY KATHARINE EVANS

A Brief Discovery of God's Eternal Truth. London: R. Wilson, 1663.

"Isle of Malta, Anno 1661." With Sarah Chevers. In Chapter 13 of *A Collection of the Sufferings of the People Called Quakers*, edited by Joseph Besse, vol. 2. London: Luke Hinde, 1753.

This is a Short Relation of Some of the Cruel Sufferings . . . of Katharine Evans & Sarah Chevers. . . . London: R. Wilson, 1662.

A Sufferings Tract

From "Isle of Malta, Anno 1661."

The Day that we were had from the *English* Consul's to the Inquisition, there came a Man with a black Rod, and the Chancellor and Council, and had us before their Lord Inquisitor, and he asked us, *Whether we had changed our Minds yet?* We said, *Nay, we should not change from the Truth.* He asked, *What new Light we talked of?* We said, *No new Light, but the same the Prophets and Apostles bore Testimony to.* Then he said, *How came this Light to be lost ever since the Apostles Time?* We said, *It was not lost, Men had it still in them, but they did not know it, by reason the Night of Apostacy had and hath overspread the Nations.* Then he said, *If we would change our Minds, and do as they would have us do, we should say so, or else they would use us as they pleased.* We said, *The Will of the Lord be done.* And he rose up, and went his Way with the Consul, and left us there. And the Man with the black Rod, and the Keeper, took us and put us into an inner Room in the Inquisition, which had but two little Holes in it for Light or Air; but the Glory of the Lord did shine round about us. . . .

But he did thirst daily for our Blood, because we would not turn, and urged us much about our Faith and the Sacrament, to bring us under their Law, but the Lord preserved us. They said, *It was impossible we could live long in that hot Room;* for the Room was so hot and so close, that we were fain to rise often out of our Bed, and lie down at a Chink of the Door for Air to fetch Breath, and with the Fire within, and the Heat without, our Skin was like Sheep's Leather, and the Hair did fall off our Heads, and we did fail often; our Afflictions and Burdens were so great, that when it was Day we wished for Night, and when it was Night we wished for Day, we sought Death, but could not find it. We desired to die, but Death fled from us. We did eat our Bread with Weeping, and mingled our Drink with our Tears. We did write to the Inquisitor, and laid before him our Innocency and our Faithfulness in giving our Testimony for the Lord amongst them, and I told him, *If it were our Blood they did thirst after, they might take it any other Way, as well as smother us up in that hot Room.* So he sent for the Friar, and he took away our Inkhorns, (they had our Bibles before). We asked, *Why they took away our Goods?* They said, *It was all theirs, and our Lives too if they would.* We asked, *How we had forfeited our Lives to them?* They said, *For bringing Books and Papers.* We said, *If there was any Thing in them that was not true, they might write against it.* They said, *They did scorn to write to Fools and Asses, that did not know true* Latin. And told us, *The Inquisitor would have us separated because I was weak, and I should go into a cooler Room, but* Sarah *should abide there.* I took her by the Arm, and said, *The Lord hath joined us together, and Wo be to them that shall part us: I chuse rather to die here with my Friend, than to part from her.* The Friar was smitten, and went away, and came no more in five Weeks, and the Door was not opened in all that Time. Then they came again to part us, but I was sick, and broke out from Head to Foot. They sent for a Doctor, who said, *We must have Air, or else we must die.* So the Lord compelled them to go to the Inquisitor, and he gave Order for the Door to be set open six Hours in the Day. They did not part us in ten Weeks after. But O the dark Clouds, and the sharp Showers, the Lord did carry us through! Death itself had been better than to have parted in that Place. They said, *We corrupted each other, and that they thought when we were parted, we would bow to them,* but they found it otherwise. We were stronger afterward than before, the Lord our God did fit us for every Condition. They came and brought a Scourge of small Hemp, and asked us, *If we would have any of it?* They said, *They did whip themselves till the Blood came.* We said, *That could not reach the Devil, he sat upon the Heart.* They said, *All the Men and Women of* Malta *were for*

[87]

us *if we would be* Catholicks, *for there would be none like unto us.* We said, *The Lord had changed us into that which changeth not.* They said, *All their holy Women did pray for us, and we should be honoured of all the World, if we would turn.* We said, *We were of God, and the whole World did lie in Wickedness, and we denied the Honour of the World, and the Glory too.* They said, *We should be honoured of God too, but now we were hated of all.* We said, *It is an evident Token whose Servants we are, the Servant is not greater than the Lord, and that the Scripture was fulfilled, which saith,* All this will I give thee, if thou wilt fall down and worship me.

At Another Time the *English* Friar shewed us his Crucifix, and bade us *Look there.* We said, *The Lord saith,* thou shalt not make to thyself the Likeness of any Thing that is in Heaven above, or in the Earth beneath, or in the Waters under the Earth, thou shalt not bow down to them, nor worship them, but me the Lord thy God only. He (the Friar) was so mad, that he called for Irons to chain *Sarah,* because she spake so boldly to him: She bowed her Head, and said, *Not only my Feet, but my Hands and my Head also for the Testimony of Jesus.*

They fought three Quarters of a Year to part us, before they could bring it to pass, and when they did part us, they prepared a Bed for *Sarah,* and removed her to another Room. When we were parted, they went from one to another, thinking to intangle us in our Talk, but we were guided by the same Spirit, and spake one and the same Thing in Effect, so that they had not a Jot or a Tittle against us, but for Righteousness-sake. Our God did keep us by his Power and Holiness out of their Hands. . . .

There was a poor *Englishman,* who hearing that *Sarah* was in a Room with a Window next the Street, which was high, got up and spoke a few Words to her: They came violently and haled him down, and cast him into Prison upon Life and Death. And the Friars came to know of us, *Whether he had brought us any Letters?* We said, *No.* I did not see him. They said, *They did think he would be hanged for it.* He was one they had taken from the *Turks,* and made a *Catholick* of. *Sarah* wrote a few Lines to me about it, and said, *She did think the* English *Friars were the chief Actors of it.* We had a private Way to send to each other. I wrote to her again, and after my Salutation, I said, *Whereas she said,* the Friars were the chief Actors, *she might be sure of that, for they did hasten to fill up their Measures; but I did believe the Lord would preserve the poor Man for his Love,* and that *I was made willing to seek the Lord for him with Tears:* And I desired she would *send him something once or twice a Day, if the Keeper would carry it.* And I told her of the *glorious Manifestations of God to my Soul,* for her Comfort. I told her, *It was much they did not tempt us with* Money.* I bade her *take Heed, the Light would discover it, and many more Things.*

This Letter came to the Friar's Hands, he translated it into *Italian,* and laid it before the Lord Inquisitor, and got the Inquisitor's Lieutenant, and came to me with both the Papers in his Hand, and asked me, *If I could read it?* I told him, *Yea, I writ it. O did you indeed,* says he, *and what is it you say of me here? That which is Truth,* saith I. Then he said, *Where is the Paper* Sarah *sent, bring it, or else I will search the Trunk, and every where else.* I bade him, *Search where he would.* He said, *I must tell what Man it was that brought me the Ink, or else I should be tied with Chains presently.* I told him, *I had done nothing but what was just and right in the Sight of God, and what I did suffer would be for the Truth's Sake, and I did not care:* I would not meddle nor make with the poor Workmen. He said, *For God's Sake tell me what* Sarah *did write.* I told him a few words, and he said, *It was Truth.* Said he, *You say, it is much we do not tempt you with Money.* And in a few Hours they came and tempted us with Money often. So the Lieutenant took my Ink, and threw it away; and they were smitten, as if they would have fallen to the Ground, and went their Way. I saw them no more in three Weeks; but the poor Man was set free the next Morning.

MARGARET SANGER (1879–1966)

Margaret (Higgins) Sanger was born in Corning, New York, to parents who created a home that fostered her ambition and independent thought. One of eleven children, young Higgins considered small families desirable. She became interested in medicine while caring for her sick mother, who died of tuberculosis at the age of forty-eight. While studying nursing in the White Plains Hospital in New York, Margaret Higgins met and

---

*Their own Money, which had now served them about a Year and seven Weeks, was almost exhausted.

married architect William Sanger, and within six months she was pregnant with their first child. The early years of their marriage were complicated by her struggle with incipient tuberculosis. With the improvement of her health came a more settled suburban family life and the birth of two more children. However, both Sangers felt the need for a more involved, active life, so they moved to New York City, where they met other liberals and where Margaret Sanger began contributing articles on sexuality to the socialist paper the New York *Call*. In her nursing work in the city, she saw firsthand the suffering of poor mothers, and decided then to commit herself totally to the birth-control cause.

In 1913 Sanger traveled to Europe to obtain birth-control information denied her in the United States. After returning home, she began in March 1914 to publish a new journal, *Woman Rebel*, which was rejected as "unmailable" by the New York Post Office. Sanger was indicted for violating federal laws and was forced to go into exile in England, where she was influenced in her work by Havelock Ellis. Her return to New York in October 1915 brought a lifelong sorrow, as her small daughter died of pneumonia the following month. When the government decided to drop its charges against Sanger in February 1916, she was able to embark on a lecture tour and to plan her first birth-control clinics.

The following selection describes her imprisonment and legal battle over the first birth-control clinic, located in the Brownsville section of Brooklyn. Following her imprisonment, the movement gathered national force, and in 1921 she formed the American Birth Control League. When physicians began to support her cause, Sanger opened a New York clinic called the Birth Control Clinical Research Bureau, the first of a nationwide series of clinics that were in place by 1938. She continued to raise funds to support the clinics with the help of her second husband, J. Noah Slee, whom she had married after her 1920 divorce from Sanger. Margaret Sanger was still an influential force after World War II, and in 1952 she helped to found the International Planned Parenthood Federation. Sanger died in 1966 in Tucson of congestive heart failure.

Note: Biographical information is from Margaret Sanger, *An Autobiography* (New York: Norton, 1938); Sanger, *My Fight for Birth Control* (New York: Farrar & Rinehart, 1931); James Reed, "Margaret Sanger," in *Notable American Women*, vol. 4, ed. Barbara Sicherman and Carol Hurd Green (Cambridge, Mass.: Belknap Press, 1980).

Margaret Sanger

WORKS BY MARGARET SANGER

Papers: 1890–1966. The Sophia Smith Collection, Smith College, Northampton, Mass.; 1900–1966, Manuscripts Division, Library of Congress.

Birth Control Review. Edited by Margaret Sanger. New York: American Birth Control League; Birth Control Federation of America, 1917–1940.

The Case for Birth Control. New York: Modern Art Printing, 1917.

Family Limitation. New York: [n.p.] 1914. Pamphlet.

Happiness in Marriage. New York: Brentano's, 1926.

Human Fertility. Edited by Margaret Sanger. New York and Baltimore: Planned Parenthood Federation of America, 1940–1948.

Margaret Sanger; An Autobiography. New York: Norton, 1938; Dover, 1971.

Motherhood in Bondage. New York: Brentano's, 1928. Letters to Sanger.

My Fight for Birth Control. New York: Farrar & Rinehart, 1931; Maxwell, 1969.

The New Motherhood. London: J. Cape, 1922.

The Pivot of Civilization. New York: Brentano's, 1922.

What Every Girl Should Know. Reading, Pa.: Sentinel, 1914.

"Why I Went to Jail." In *Together*, February 1960, pp. 20–22.

Woman and the New Race. New York: Brentano's, 1920.

Woman Rebel. Edited by Margaret Sanger, 1914 (self-published).

Why I Went to Jail

Reprinted from *Together*, February 1960. Copyright 1960 by Lovick Pierce (the United Methodist Publishing House).

It was a crisp, bright morning on October 16, 1916, in Brooklyn, N.Y., that I opened the doors of the first birth-control clinic in the United States. I believed then, and do today, that this was an event of social significance in the lives of American womanhood.

Three years before, as a professional nurse, I had gone with a doctor on a call in New York's lower East Side. I had watched a frail mother die from a self-induced abortion. The doctor previously had refused to give her contraceptive information. The mother was one of a thousand such cases; in New York alone there were over 100,000 abortions a year.

That night I knew I could not go on merely nursing, allowing others to suffer and die. No matter what it might cost, I was resolved to do something to change the destiny of mothers whose miseries were vast as the sky. It was the beginning of my birth-control crusade.

[91]

Although the practical idea of giving contraceptive information in clinics set up for that purpose in Holland had met with governmental approval, the New York State Penal Code declared that only a physician could give birth-control information to anyone—and only then to prevent or cure disease. Always this had been held to mean venereal disease. I wanted the interpretation to be broadened to protect women from ill health as the result of excessive childbearing and to have the right to control their own destinies.

As I was not a physician, I would have no legal protection whatsoever if I gave birth-control information to anyone. But I believed that if a woman must break the law to establish a right to voluntary motherhood, then the law must be broken.

I had been a nurse and my birth-control studies in Holland, where clinics had been operated for 38 years, had qualified me to give contraceptive instruction. My sister, who was also a nurse, could assist me.

Dare I risk it?

I did.

Then, as long as I had to violate the law anyhow, I concluded I might as well violate it on a grand scale by including poverty as a reason for giving contraceptive information. The selection of a suitable locality was of the greatest importance.

The Brownsville section of Brooklyn in 1916 was a hive of activity. Although dingy and squalid, it was crowded with hard-working men and women. An enthusiastic young worker in the cause came from Chicago to help me. Together we tramped the streets one dreary day in early fall, through a driving rainstorm, to find the best location at the cheapest terms. I stopped to inquire from an official of a free-milk station about vacant stores.

"Don't come over here." "We don't want trouble." "Keep out." These and other pleasantries were hurled at me as I darted in and out of rooming houses, asking advice, hoping for welcome.

Finally, at 46 Amboy Street, I found a friendly landlord, a Mr. Rabinowitz, who had two first-floor rooms vacant at $50 a month. This was all the money we had (sent from a friend in California) to finance the clinic.

We bought the necessary furniture as cheaply as we could. And Mr. Rabinowitz himself spent hours painting until the rooms were spotless and snow-white. "More hospital looking," he said.

We had printed about 5,000 handbills in English, Italian, and Yiddish.

They read: "Mothers! Can you afford to have a large family? Do you want any more children? If not, why do you have them?

"Do not kill, do not take life, but prevent.

"Safe, harmless information can be obtained of trained nurses at 46 Amboy Street, near Pitkin Avenue, Brooklyn.

"Tell your friends and neighbors. All mothers welcome."

With a small bundle of these notices, we fared forth each morning in a house-to-house canvass.

Would the people come? Nothing could have stopped them!

My colleague, looking out the window, called, "Do come outside and look." Halfway to the corner they stood in line, shawled, hatless, their red hands clasping the chapped smaller ones of their children.

All day long and far into the evening, in ever-increasing numbers they came, over 100 the opening day. Jews and Christians, Protestants and Roman Catholics alike made their confessions to us.

Every day the little waiting room was crowded. The women came in pairs, with friends, married daughters, some with nursing babies clasped in their arms. Women came from the far end of Long Island, the press having spread the word, from Connecticut, Massachusetts, Pennsylvania, New Jersey. They came to learn the "secret" which was possessed by the rich and denied the poor.

My sister and I lectured to eight women at a time on the basic techniques of contraception, referring them to a druggist to purchase the necessary equipment. Records were meticulously kept. It was vital to have complete case histories if our work was to have scientific value. We also gave many of the women copies of *What Every Girl Should Know*, a brief booklet I had written earlier.

Tragic were the stories of the women. One woman told of her 15 children. Six were living. "I'm 37 years old. Look at me! I might be 50!" Then there was a reluctantly pregnant Jewish woman who, after bringing eight children to birth, had had two abortions and heaven knows how many miscarriages. Worn out, not only from housework but from making hats in a sweatshop, nervous beyond words, she cried morbidly, "If you don't help me, I'm going to chop up a glass and swallow it."

I comforted her the best I could, but there was nothing I would do to interrupt her pregnancy. We believed in birth control, not abortion.

But it was not altogether sad; we often were cheered by gayer visitors.

The grocer's wife on the corner dropped in to wish us luck, and the jolly old German baker whose wife gave out handbills to everybody passing the door sent us doughnuts. Then Mrs. Rabinowitz would call to us, "If I bring some hot tea now, will you stop the people coming?" The postman delivering his 50 to 100 letters daily had his little pleasantry, "Farewell, ladies; hope I find you here tomorrow."

On the ninth day, a well-dressed, hard-faced woman pushed her way past the humble applicants, gave her name, flaunted a $2 bill, payment for *What Every Girl Should Know*, and demanded immediate attention. My colleague had a hunch she might be a detective, and pinned the bill on the wall and wrote: "Received from Mrs. —— of the Police Department, as her contribution."

Hourly after that we expected trouble. It came the following afternoon at closing hour. The policewoman again pushed her way through the group of patiently waiting women and, striding into my room, snapped peremptorily, "You, Margaret Sanger, are under arrest."

Three plain-clothes men from the vice squad promptly appeared. They herded our women patients into patrol wagons as though they were the inmates of a brothel. Women began to cry; the infants in their arms began to cry. The clinic soon became a bedlam of screams. The raiders confiscated our 464 case histories, a highly unethical act since the reports were confidential intimacies. They also took our pamphlets.

It was half an hour before I could persuade the men to release the poor mothers, whom I assured the best I could that nothing would happen to them.

Newspapermen and photographers joined the throng. It was a neighborhood where a crowd collected by no more gesture than a tilt of the head skyward. This event brought masses of people into the streets.

I was white-hot with indignation and refused to ride in the Black Maria. I insisted on walking the mile to the Raymond Street jail, marching ahead of the raiders, the crowds following.

I spent the night in jail in so filthy a cell I shall never forget it. The mattresses were spotted and smelly. I lay in my coat, struggling with roaches, crying out as a rat scuttled across the floor.

It was not until afternoon that my bail was arranged. As I emerged from the jail I saw waiting in front the woman who had threatened to swallow the glass; she had been there all the time.

I went back at once to reopen the clinic, but Mr. Rabinowitz came running in to say he was sorry—the police had made him sign ejection papers on the ground that I was "maintaining a public nuisance." In Holland the clinics were called "public benefactions."

Again I was arrested. From the rear of the Black Maria, as we rattled away, I heard a scream. It came from a woman wheeling a baby carriage. She left it on the sidewalk, and rushed through the crowd and cried, "Come back and save me!"

The crusade for birth control was actually under way—with jail terms and hunger strikes, and also with popular demonstrations in our behalf. As I reached the depth of despair and public humiliation, something like a miracle occurred. Help and sympathy sprang up on all sides. Legal aid was proffered. Doctors now rallied to my aid. A group of sympathetic and wealthy women in New York promptly formed a Committee of 100 for our defense. Sympathizers even held a mass meeting in Carnegie Hall.

My trial began in Brooklyn on January 29, 1917. About 50 mothers, some equipped with food and pacifiers and extra diapers for their babies, came to court. Timid and distressed, they smiled and nodded, trying to reassure me. Mingled with them were the smartly dressed members of the Committee of 100.

It surprised me that the prosecution should be carried on so vehemently. To me, there seemed to be no argument at all; the last thing in my mind was to deny that I had given birth-control advice. I had deliberately violated the letter of the law. But my lawyer, Jonah J. Goldstein, was trying to get me off with a suspended sentence.

One by one, the Brownsville mothers took the stand. "Have you ever seen Mrs. Sanger before?" asked the District Attorney.

"Yes. At the cleenic."

"Why did you go there?"

"To have her stop the babies."

"Did you get this information?"

"Yes, dank you, I got it. It wass gut, too."

For days the legal arguments went on. At last, one wintry day, Judge John J. Freschi banged his fist on the desk. "All we are concerned about is the statute," he exclaimed. "As long as it remains the law," he asked my attorney, "will this woman promise unqualifiedly to obey it?"

He turned to me. "What is your answer to this question, Mrs. Sanger? Yes or no?"

The whole courtroom seemed to hold its breath.

I spoke out as emphatically as I could. "I cannot promise to obey a law I do not respect."

The tension broke. Women shouted and clapped. The judge demanded order. When it came, he announced, "The judgment of the court is that you be imprisoned for 30 days."

A single cry came from a woman in the corner. "Shame!" It was followed by a sharp rap of the gavel and silence fell. The trial was over.

The next afternoon I was taken to the Queens County Penitentiary in Long Island City.

I can remember the inmates—pickpockets, prostitutes, thieves— somehow they had heard about me and the birth-control movement. One asked me to explain to them about "sex hygiene." When I asked for permission to do so, the matron said, "Ah, gawn wid ye. They know bad enough already."

But I persisted and got my way. I also taught some of the girls to read and write letters. And I kept up with my own writing, planning ahead the birth-control movement.

The next step? To appeal to the highest court possible.

I was released on March 6. No other experience in my life has been more thrilling than that release. When I stepped through the big steel-barred doorway that gray day, the tingling air of outdoors rushed against my face. In front of me stood my attorney, my friends, and co-workers, their voices lifted in the martial strains of *La Marseillaise*. And behind, from the windows of the penitentiary, were the faces of newly made friends, and they, too, were singing for me.

The case of the Brownsville birth-control clinic began its journey through the courts. It was on January 8, 1918, that the momentous decision came. The New York Court of Appeals sustained my conviction, but Judge Frederick E. Crane's liberal interpretation of the law had the effect of permitting physicians to give contraceptive information to a married person for "health reasons." "Disease" was now to include everything in the broad definition of *Webster's International Dictionary*, not just venereal disease, which had been the original understanding.

This opened the clinics, as well as the doctors' offices, to women for birth-control advice throughout the United States.

BARBARA DEMING (1917–1984)

Barbara Deming began her pacifist political activities following her trip to India in 1959 and her subsequent study of Gandhi's writings. In 1960 she visited post-revolutionary Cuba and discussed pacifism with Fidel Castro. In that same year, at the age of forty-three, Deming became involved with the Committee for Nonviolent Action and began her work with them against racism in the United States and against the Vietnam War. She also worked for civil rights with the Southern Christian Leadership Conference and the Student Nonviolent Coordinating Committee (SNCC).

Deming's experience in the Birmingham, Alabama, jail in May 1963 strengthened her faith in the effectiveness of nonviolent action. There, she tried to communicate with poor white female prisoners who felt threatened by her work with black demonstrators. After her release, she continued the civil rights work for which she had been jailed, and during 1963 and 1964 she joined the Quebec–Washington–Guantanamo Walk for Peace and Freedom. In January 1964, as the walkers passed through Albany, Georgia, distributing their literature, they were arrested and held in the city jail for about a month. *Prison Notes* describes Deming's experience there and the marchers who were jailed with her. The book emphasizes her nonviolent philosophy and its application during this march through the segregated South.

Kate Millett's *Sexual Politics* awakened Deming's active interest in feminism, and until her death from cancer in 1984 she was known and respected for her blend of feminism and pacifism. Late in life she lived openly as a lesbian. Deming stated that she came to see her struggle against patriarchy as analogous to other struggles for freedom. She made her home in the Florida Keys with artist/poet Jane Gapen and wrote a variety of works on her philosophy of pacifism.

Note: Biographical information is from Barbara Deming, *Revolution and Equilibrium* (New York: Grossman, 1971); Leah Fritz, "Barbara Deming: the Rage of a Pacifist," *MS.* 7 (November 1978): 97–101; Leah Fritz, " 'We Are All Part of One Another'— A Tribute to Barbara Deming," *MS.* 13 (December 1984): 41–42; Mab Segrist, "Feminism and Disobedience: Conversations with Barbara Deming," in *Reweaving the Web of Life: Feminism and Nonviolence*, ed. Pam McAllister (Philadelphia: New Society, 1982), pp. 45–62.

WORKS BY BARBARA DEMING

A Humming Under My Feet: A Book of Travail. London: Women's Press, 1985. A novel.

"In the Birmingham Jail." *Nation*, 25 May 1963, pp. 436–437.

Poem and Interview. In *Reweaving the Web of Life: Feminism and Nonviolence*, ed. Pam McAllister. Philadelphia: New Society, 1982.

Prison Notes. New York: Grossman, 1966.

Remembering Who We Are: Barbara Deming in Dialogue with Gwenda Blair. Palo Alto, Calif. Frog in the Well, 1980; reprint, Tallahassee, Fla: Pagoda, 1981.

Revolution & Equilibrium. New York: Grossman, 1971. Essays.

Revolution, Violent and Nonviolent: Two Documents/Barbara Deming, Régis Debray. n.p., n.d. (1968?). "Reprinted from Feb. 1968 *Liberation*."

Running Away from Myself: A Dream Portrait of America Drawn from the Films of the Forties. New York: Grossman, 1969.

To Fear Jane Alpert Is to Fear Ourselves, and Other Letters. New York: War Resisters League, 1977.

Two Essays. On Anger & New Men, New Women. Philadelphia: New Society, 1982.

Wash Us and Comb Us: Stories. New York: Grossman, 1972.

We Are All Part of One Another: A Barbara Deming Reader. Edited by Jane Meyerding, with a Foreword by Barbara Smith. Philadelphia: New Society, 1984.

We Cannot Live without Our Lives. New York: Grossman, 1974.

Prison Notes

From *Prison Notes*. Used by permission of Spinsters Ink.

A letter has come just today from one of my friends, begging us to give up the battle. This second series of arrests has distressed her: "I think you are being wasteful of time, energy, health . . . You are exceeding your mark . . . You have exhausted your *persuasions* (Pritchett* has listened to you, and answered no), and you are now *forcing* them to

---

*Police Chief Laurie Pritchett, Albany, Georgia.—*Ed.*

arrest you, since their minds remain unchanged. . . . The position they have taken all their lives toward what you represent must either be cracked by total conversion (which is more and more out of the question) or—and this I think you ignore like ostriches—find itself *reinforced*. . . . I would have preferred that you move around the obstacle, go your way, walk your walk, deliver your messages. 'To yield,' says Lao-tse, 'is to be preserved whole.' "

I begin to compose a letter to her in my head. We do not hope for anybody's "total conversion." But I shall try to say to her what we do hope.

Dear ——,

I'm sorry that you are distressed by our actions. I'll try to explain what it is that we think we are doing. It is early morning and the yelling back and forth between cells has stopped for a time; all is very quiet. If it will only stay quiet for a little while . . .

You'll excuse my writing on toilet paper. At least it unwinds nicely, like a scroll.

But now I have sat here for I'm not sure how long, not writing at all, just enjoying the luxury of this silence. It is so rare in here that, when it occurs, it's an almost intoxicating pleasure.

This, of course, brings me back to your question: What are we doing here? Why don't we pay our fines and get out? You feel that we have exhausted persuasion—which is the means proper to nonviolent struggle—and by insisting still on trying to have our way, we begin to do a kind of violence both to ourselves and to our antagonists: We are *bound* to be hurt now, and they are *bound* to have to hurt us; we force them to.

But we have not begun to exhaust persuasion. I'm not sure that we are going to win. But it is not blind of us to hope still; it would be blind to give up hope so soon.

We place our hopes in a very particular kind of persuasion, and I don't think you have ever really understood the nature of it. I have never made it clear. And so you ascribe to us the most naïve of hopes. In your letter you try to make me see that we cannot really expect to accomplish a total conversion of our opponents; they are not going to "sit down and reflect mildly on the doctrines of love which have been poured in their ears by twenty-six young strangers." You picture us to yourself as hoping to touch the hearts of our opponents in a very simple and melodramatic way. Isn't this your vision of a nonviolent siege? You see us standing before Chief Pritchett and declaring to him that we think he is being unjust; we are careful not to raise our voices or to clench our fists; we stand there showing ourselves to be the most endearing people, full of love and goodwill. And—hopefully—suddenly—his heart cracks. A small voice inside him cries, "Brothers! I used to be like you when I was a little boy! Teach me to be that way again!"

No wonder nonviolence seems to you no answer to the world's great and complicated problems. I have heard you argue that few people would be able to practice it, and few would be likely to respond. No wonder that you think so.

Every now and then something has happened on this Walk that has borne a remote resemblance to the caricature you hold in your mind. Confronted by people who were treating us as though we were not human, one of us has managed, by a look or a word or a gesture, to assert: I *am* human; treat me as though I were—and has succeeded in making the other do just that.

One day back in October, for example, we were walking single-file through Klan country near Athens, Georgia, and as Yvonne Klein crossed the yard of a small country store, the proprietor came out, screaming threats, his face convulsed. I was walking a little way behind her, and I saw him grab her by the neck. She managed to remain very calm. I saw her turn, slow-motion, and look him quietly in the face; and he dropped his hands. When I caught up with her a little later, she told me that he had had a knife pressed to her shoulder. . . .

You probably read the report in *Liberation* of what happened to the walkers in Griffin, Georgia, the day they refused to cooperate with what they felt to be an unjust arrest and the cops tried to make them walk —first into the nearby jail, then upstairs to their cells—by torturing them with an electric cattle prod. I wasn't there, as you know; I had gone north for a few days. When my friends just took the torture and continued to refuse to walk, all but one of the cops began to feel ashamed, and finally only one man was using the prodder; but he used it savagely and obscenely. Do you remember that two cops, though they did nothing to stop him, began to cry, in spite of themselves? But one moment was described to me that is the particular reason for my recalling the day to you. Once they had been booked, a few of my friends did walk upstairs, but most refused and were carried or dragged very roughly. Eric Robinson was the last to be booked. He was asked by the cops, "Are you going to walk?" He answered that he wouldn't. Eric is about Tom's size and, like Tom, has an almost child's-storybook look about him. He said very quietly, and as though he could believe that they would do what he asked, "Please be careful with me." And to everybody's astonishment, he was carried upstairs very carefully.

Moments like this are the magic moments in a project like ours. And the magic is not a matter of illusion. The extent to which one can affect how others will behave simply by looking for one kind of behavior rather than another—well, who knows the extent? It deserves endless study. I know that I have sometimes felt the power of it to an almost intoxicating degree. I have felt it when we walked up to groups of young toughs along the road—youths who have driven past in their cars and parked to wait for us, clearly hungering for violence; and simply by walking up to them in a friendly way, as though we feared nothing from them, we have been able—well, to bewilder them out of attacking. The Quakers would call it "speaking to that of God in another man." It is not a matter of naïveté, as you seem to suspect. The discipline required is analogous to an actor's discipline. Just as an actor can train himself to believe in the events of a play, and through his act of belief he makes the play real to an audience (and sometimes also to other less experienced actors), so we try to control our fear and to believe in the possibility that our antagonist will behave as though he recognized a human bond between us; and that belief—when we can find it—has an hypnotic quality.

But I had better say rapidly, before you begin to misunderstand me again, that yes, one can expect much too much of such "magic." One can expect too much of oneself, and forget how suddenly belief can fail one. Or one can expect *always* to be able to inhibit violent action in others if one is in control of oneself; and this would be absurd. As you know, we *have* been attacked. Above all, in a situation like our present one, if we hoped to bring about a change in an entire city's policy simply through holding the thought that the change could come—well, we would be lunatics.

There is a very beautiful passage in Proverbs: "As in water face answereth to face, so the heart of man to man." It often does, especially when people act on the assumption that it can; but if it always did, we would have the Kingdom of God on earth. I feel that I have to assure you that we don't believe the Kingdom has come. We do know that men are quite able to look straight at other men and deny to themselves that they are human. To bring others to acknowledge our humanity and treat us accordingly—with justice—we have usually to resort to more than friendliness. We have to rely on *a kind of force*—which I'll try to define and to distinguish from violence.

You chide in your letter that we are now "entering on active behavior" and it looks violent to you; "it cannot any longer be called passive resistance." I'm glad you introduced that term so that I can say I wish it had never been used to describe this kind of struggle. It describes in a literal way, of course, certain tactics, such as "going limp." But it has always been misunderstood to mean that our basic attitude is passive. The word coupled with "passive" is forgotten—"resistance." It is also too bad that "nonviolent action" describes merely what our actions are *not*; and in this term the word "action" is forgotten. We have not suddenly "entered on active behavior"; we have put our faith in it from the beginning. We believe in the power of nonviolent acts to speak louder than words. . . .

Here we are, claiming a basic right, both constitutional and, simply, human: the right to communicate freely with others. And our message seems to us urgent—a message about dangers and about hopes that involve all mankind. (As I tried to plead in the Albany court, it really no longer makes sense for men to use the word "outsiders" about one another: the nuclear age has made us neighbors in a new sense, and we *have* to be able to talk with one another.) But the people of Albany don't want people speaking freely, for a simple reason: they don't want Negroes to be able to speak out. So when we insist, they call us disturbers of their peace. When we disregard the ordinance they have drawn up specially to abridge free speech, they accuse us of defying law and order. Their peace *should* be disturbed; it is a false peace. And the order of which they speak is no true order; there are too many people for whose legitimate desires it allows no room.

Going to jail here has cost us a great deal, but it has also gained us the opportunity to say just this to them more forcibly than we otherwise could have. They would certainly not listen to us if we tried to say it to them in mere words. Nonviolent action is a dramatic technique. Do you remember where in *Hamlet* the prince cries, "The play's the thing"? Hoping to "catch the conscience of the king," he has a drama staged for the king to watch. We go further and try to involve our antagonists as actors in the play, to make it that much more real to them, and hoping to catch if not their consciences—sometimes very elusive—at least that sense in them of what will help or hurt their "image," a practical matter. Or we might possibly catch the consciences of others in the community, without whose acquiescence they cannot behave as they do.

Our hope is to make it hard for them to look away from certain facts. (Gandhi called nonviolence "clinging to the truth.") Like so many others who hold power, they are adept at dismissing pleas, even at persuading themselves that no real discontent exists; and adept, too, at disposing of those who persist in crying that it does. The play into which we draw them must make it hard for them to do this, and it must at the same time make it possible for them to imagine a new situation fairer to us all.

So we try to assert by our actions a number of different things simultaneously. In the first place, we assert: You cannot easily be rid of us; here we are and we refuse to disappear. They throw us into jail—with the gesture of throwing us away. We serve our sentences and immediately turn up again, to repeat the act for which they arrested us. Ideally our numbers would double every time they tried by *their* actions to say: You are not there. But we haven't done too badly. Fourteen of us tried to walk on December 23. After their trial, six more people, drawn to Albany from various parts of the country by news of our struggle, turned up at the courthouse and stood out in pouring rain to protest the sentences. They were jailed. Three days later, another supporter was walking up and down out there, with a sign about the fast and the special danger Ray Robinson was in because of his water fast. The city decided to terminate all the sentences on the same day, January 15, even for this demonstrator, just arrested—hoping we would go away now and let them forget us. But on January 27, seventeen of us were there again trying to walk the forbidden route. And four days before that, you'll remember, Yvonne Klein and the S.N.C.C. worker, Phil Davis, had been arrested for picketing a civil-defense exercise. On February 3, nine more of us were standing with our signs out at Turner Air Force Base. Two of these people had come all the way from Canada to join us. We have word that there is at least one other supporter in town who may decide to take some action. Now and then one of the cops asks nervously how many people we plan to bring in. We are not exactly Hydra headed, but our numbers do increase enough to worry them. . . .

And once we are in jail, we say by our fasting: If you want to lead our lives for us, then don't expect us to help. There is a pacifist clergyman, the Reverend Maurice McCrackin, who refuses to pay taxes because they are spent on armaments. When he was arrested back in 1958, he made the government officials carry him. They could not take possession of his conscience, he told them, but "take the body." Another pacifist, Corbett Bishop, arrested for defying the Military Service Act, went so far as to refuse to walk to the bathroom in jail. They finally threw him out of jail as too much of a nuisance. None of us goes as far as Corbett Bishop, but by our fasting we do declare—though this is not all that we declare by it: We refuse to help you take care of us in here.

By our refusal to cooperate, we keep reminding them of our dissent, refusing to allow them the godlike sense that their will alone exists. We make it psychologically more difficult for them to frustrate us. We also make it inconvenient for them, and we make it expensive. It costs the city something to put us up in jail. When we fast, there are also medical expenses. At the end of the first jail-in the Albany *Journal* estimated that we had cost the city five hundred dollars a day. We tax their minds, their muscles, their pocketbooks. . . .

Our action in fasting, here in jail, cannot help but be in part provocative—it is so *very* uncooperative. And it makes it difficult for the authorities to know just how to behave. (This is especially so for the city doctor, and our fasting has certainly brought out the worst in *him*; he is still so confused and angry that he can hardly bring himself to check on how we are.) But we count on the fact that fasting declares finally a great deal more than defiance, and declares it more clearly than any words could. It communicates how serious we are—gives assurance that we are at least convinced in our own minds that our cause is just, or we would hardly subject ourselves to this and persist in it day after day. It communicates too that we want no victory in the usual sense —are not concerned to see how much punishment we can deal out. We are willing to take on ourselves the brunt of suffering. Having declared this, even without words, it is more possible for us to make the further point: we want justice, but if justice means anything, it means that those who have been opposing us will have rights too. It needn't mean defeat in any real sense for anybody. . . .

There are always what might be called negative advantages to be gained by observing the discipline of nonviolence. Refusal to hit back at an opponent or lie to him or trick him can inhibit him in his resort to violence, break the familiar circuit of vengeance and counter-vengeance. Used as a prudent tactic it is effective. But when those adopting this discipline actually feel a human bond—however frail—with those opposing them and feel a responsibility toward them, and this shapes their vision of a resolution to the struggle, they tap a further source of energy and they can exert still greater pressure. The vision they hold can be to some extent hypnotic. (This, by the way, is a reason why going to jail holds a particular meaning for many of us. Here our sense of being related to all men is greatly sharpened, for we cross a distance that once seemed awesome and separated us from all those whom society has cast out.) . . .

One has time in here to dream, and I dream sometimes that this and other new facts about the present age will make it the age in which people finally decide that nonviolent struggle is the only kind of struggle from which they can hope much. It is of course the age in which we are for the first time able to destroy ourselves entirely if we fail to decide this. "We must abolish the weapons of war before they abolish us," Kennedy acknowledged—though he failed to match the words with any very bold action. Auden has written, "We must love one another or die." It is for the first time in history necessary for us to learn to struggle with one another not as enemies but as members of one human family. It is also perhaps for the first time really possible. Modern communications, as well as all the complex ties that have been established by their means, make us now more effectively that one family. In earlier ages people could tyrannize over one another in convenient isolation; world opinion did not exist as an inhibiting force to be invoked. But now what men in other parts of the world think is a matter of practical concern. And in another sense too it is more realistic than in other ages to appeal to men's consciences—or to their wish to appear to behave with conscience: one could say that it is for the first time in history really feasible to establish just societies, in which men act toward other men—everywhere—with that sense of responsibility which members of the same family show. It is the age of abundance, and it can no longer be argued that some people have to be exploited so that others may live decently. If something is necessary, and also feasible, one can dream that it will happen. Necessity is at least sometimes the mother of invention. One verse of the freedom movement's hymn begins, "The truth shall make us free." Who knows whether or not men will recognize the truth in time?

And who knows whether or not we will succeed in communicating the truth we are attempting to act out here in Albany? At least we can still hope to.*

CHILEAN WOMEN POLITICAL PRISONERS OF THE 1970s

In Latin American countries an important function of literature has traditionally been to reflect the social reality of the people—a social reality that often, during periods of political repression, cannot be expressed through established institutions. Literature is regarded as a source of truth opposing official lies, and as such it is often regarded as a threat to totalitarian regimes. Their lives endangered, writers and artists, along with other intellectuals, often find it necessary to continue their work in exile.

Political prisoners, even if they had not been writers by vocation, often write of their experiences to protest their countries' violations of human rights. In Chile, where intellectual freedom has been repressed since the 1973 military coup of President Salvador Allende's government, male and female resistance workers have been imprisoned and sadistically tortured. For women the experience is doubly traumatic: because women in the Chilean culture are socialized to consider feminine purity essential, a female prisoner who has been sexually tortured may feel unmerited guilt over her own victimization.

*Deming's "letter" ends here, without a signature.—Ed.

[106]

The writings of Chilean women political prisoners are generally collective in nature; the individual writer's life or experience is not emphasized, except as an illustration of the experience of her sister prisoners. The testimony is the prevailing genre, with its descriptions of prison conditions and institutionalized brutality. Thus, the excerpts below do not stress the authors' individuality. The poetry selections come from "Sonia," the pseudonym of a prisoner in Santiago Prison and a participant in a Chilean women prisoners' writing collective. The description of Tres Alamos prison camp is the testimony of "Marta Vera," the pseudonym of a prisoner who spent fifteen months there and wrote of her experiences from exile in 1976. The selection by Chilean resistance worker Gladys Diaz was written with the collaboration of other women inmates. Diaz had been arrested, brutally tortured and imprisoned in Villa Grimaldi, and finally released into exile as the result of an international campaign on her behalf.

Note: Information is from Mario Vargas Llosa, "The Writer in Latin America," *Index on Censorship* (June 1978): 34–40; Robert Pring-Mill, "Poems at Curfew," *Index on Censorship* 7, no. 1 (January–February 1978): 43–44; Comite Jane Vanini, *Women in Resistance* (Berkeley, Calif.: Support Committee for Women in the Chilean and Latin American Resistance, n.d.); Ximena Bunster, presentation at the "Women and Human Rights" session, Women's Studies Conference, University of Pennsylvania, Philadelphia, March 1985.

Poems by Sonia

Translated by Aurora Levins Morales. Reprinted by
permission of the writing collective's correspondent. (Though
the collective could not be contacted, the editor hopes that
this anthology somehow comes into their hands.)

To Celia, A Disappeared Comrade*

The roses will bloom once again in Europe
while back there, far away, they have stopped time
decreeing hunger
decreeing fear
decreeing a state of death.
The aromos bloomed
. . . and no one saw them.

*A former prison mate.—*Ed.*

She Disappeared

Brother, sister, you who survived the horror
of the stadium, Tres Alamos* or Ritoque,*
Tejas Verdes* or Chaiguin*
have you seen my daughter, my brother,
my father, my beloved husband,
my daughter, my sweet daughter.

Wasn't your hand chained to hers—
you must have heard her call me in her pain
when the lash fell on her heart
when the executioner stained her innocence.
Don't you remember her?
I will describe her for you:
She was more beautiful than the sun and the stars
and gave out hope with full hands.
Her eyes flashed like sparks when she dreamed of her country
without flags, the happiness of its people
no longer in chains.
She said goodbye one afternoon (what an afternoon it was)
her smile bleeding, and with a sweet kiss
"See you soon, querida madre"†
Since then, pain is my companion.
Cradling my hope I walk the roadside
with this question on my lips and in my conscience
killing me with blows, day after day.

Poem

They take off the bandage
and the light
wounds my eyes.
The world spins dizzily . . .
stops, then a sheltering hand, a voice
whispers a strange name evoking
stories lost in my childhood. A name
with a smell.
The smell of dampness of the south.

*Prisons and concentration camps.—*Trans.*
†Dear mother.—*Trans.*

Chilean Women Political Prisoners

The smell of forests
and fires made with wet wood,
dispersing
the stench of fear.

She was in front of me
sitting at the foot of the cot.
She had long white hands, blonde hair
tied in two braids, and the eyes of a frightened girl:
such a contrast with her words.

Then came days and days of dead
afternoons, of little figures made from mashed bread,
fragments of sad poetry, tangos,
boleros, sorrows and laughter.

Nights of sudden assault.
Terror.
Terror breathing always through the walls,
through the bars, through the door
that opened from the outside.
Voices far away and close by,
always howling
hope.

On a day like any other they took her away.
Hours later it was my turn. For me
freedom. The freedom of exile (and the world
shattered like a pumpkin).

Today (time is counted now in years)
I found her again: the same timid smile,
her hair loose, the hands hidden
in the folds of a skirt
already old . . .
frozen forever in a blurry photograph.

Under it
a name
        Muriel
a last name, two last names
an age
        22 years
Detained in August of 1974
in Santiago de Chile.
DISAPPEARED.

Life inside the Women's Section

From "Life inside the Women's Section," in *Political
Prisoners, Chilean Women No. 2: Political Prisoners
in the Women's Section of "Tres Alamos" Concentration
Camp*, by "Marta Vera" (London: Women's Campaign for
Chile and Chile Committee for Human Rights, 1976).
Reprinted by permission of Women's International
Resource Exchange (WIRE).

Prison life brings together people of different ages in this case from 17 to almost 60 years old. And from different walks of life: workers, students, housewives, professional women—some are mothers and others are not.

In spite of the differences there are many factors that fundamentally unite them. In the first place they have been detained for struggling for a fairer society which would allow for human development and permit the emergence of a better human being, a whole person. In the second place they share the uncertainty in which they find themselves—not knowing what those who arrested them intend to do with them. Thirdly, and by no means least important, they are united in their refusal to acquiesce, determined to uphold till the last the remnants of human dignity that are left to them. In spite of overcrowding, suffering constant humiliation and nervous strain, being dragged to the lowest levels of human degradation, in spite of imprisonment and torture, the moral resistance of the detainees of the political prisoners has not been worn down.

Imprisonment and torture has not been able to break down the resistance of the Chilean prisoners who collectively benefit as much as they can from the 'minimum freedom' that they have in organising their food and leisure. Inside the camp they have managed to solve their material needs by working collectively and through discussion and study have built up morale establishing a fellowship that makes living together a pleasant experience, forming friendships which makes leaving difficult. All this happens under the watchful scrutiny of the gaolers who see everything, but fail to understand that the political prisoners' determination to carry on their struggle and to continue living has been strengthened rather than weakened.

One might ask what relevance this has to the situation of the political prisoners? How does it manifest itself from day to day?

The uncertainty of the rules of the internal regime permit an elementary level of organisation which is expressed in sporadic meetings to discuss domestic problems such as cleaning, for making a decision with which they are sometimes presented by the authorities, and in planning and organising their lives in productive and cultural activity.

The solidarity between political prisoners is of immense importance in the activities described below. Each person takes on the problems of the others as a practical expression of the political prisoners' concept of the needs and the potential of human beings. . . .

The 'Food Kitty'

In November 1974 we had started to discuss the problems of nutrition. It was clear that the food provided by the camp was deficient in every respect and that eating it for a year or more led to a severe deterioration of health, leaving the prisoners wide open to all kinds of sickness. By this time food was allowed to be brought into the camp. Some of the companeras came from the provinces and therefore rarely had visitors. There were others whose families were in such difficult economic straits that they were unable to bring anything. Other companeras had relatives also in detention. All these situations together with the general need for a balanced diet, were decisive factors in the creation of the 'Food Kitty'. Yet it would not have happened without the solidarity of the prisoners and their collective determination not to give in to defeat.

The 'Food Kitty' had the following objectives:

a) to improve the prisoners' diet with fresh fruit, vegetables, eggs etc. that is with basic foods. For this they pool all the food that prisoners receive individually and share it out in equal portions prepared from whatever there is in the 'kitty'. More often than not these were salads.

b) to work as a team, treating it as a way to get to know each other better, and developing collective and community feeling.

The Food Collective was organised and structured in this way: four companeras are democratically elected as food organisers and everyone else is then organised into groups of 8 or 9 called 'kitchen hands'. The food organisers receive the food on the visiting days when food is allowed to be brought in; they store preserve and distribute the food for the rest of the week, and they formulate the meals. The kitchen hands help in the collection, storage and preparation of the food whenever it is their turn (the rota would depend upon the number of kitchen groups). Both groups work together, daily assessing what to be done, and collectively discussing how to improve the group.

The Food Collective began in this way, and after periodic assessment decided in April 1975 that it should give priority to looking after companeras who were sick, pregnant or breast-feeding, and young children. They did this by reserving for them the most nourishing food.

In May 1975 the new team of food organisers initiated a discussion amongst all the kitchen groups about 'tit-bits'. These are the sorts of food that are not essential and therefore were not included in the kitty (chocolates, cakes etc). Political prisoners have families whose incomes vary substantially, so some receive a much greater quantity and quality of food than others. In terms of the basic objectives of the food collective everyone has the same right to enjoy these delicacies, and it was agreed after frank discussion that these should be shared as well. This meant that all food that came into the camp went into the Food Kitty. Also in May the number of food organisers was increased, electing a chief organiser who reports to the Elders' Council* to co-ordinate the work of the food collective with the other activities of the camp.

In June and July there was a discussion about whether the 'tit bits' were really necessary. In the light of the grave economic situation suffered by the people in Chile, and hence of course the prisoners' families, it was agreed to ask our relatives not to incur this sort of expenditure on our behalf.

The food collective still functions, evaluating its work, improving its techniques, revising its objectives and paying constant attention to the working relationships between the companeras, emphasising the solidarity and the collective enterprise.

The Workshops Committee

In January 1975, a regular course in English was being held, organised by one of the companeras and with 9 per cent of the prisoners participating. Earlier in 1974 classes in gymnastics and the plastic arts had been set up but they had been discontinued by the end of the year

*A representative body, elected by the prisoners.—Ed.

because of lack of participation. Only the English course had survived.

At the beginning of 1975 the idea arose in a general meeting of forming an organisation which would take charge of activities that could be organised in the camp. The idea was approved and three companeras volunteered to implement it. Their job was to consider the physical limitations, the human and material conditions and to work out a programme and present it to the other prisoners. After discussion this programme was accepted, and a Workshops Committee was created to harmonise and develop the cultural, artistic and recreational activities and also to encourage general participation in these workshops. There were workshops in: English, German, Gymnastics, Folklore, Theatre, Plastic Arts, Literature and a Discussion group.* Each workshop has the companera who is most accomplished in the activity and therefore in charge of the development of the workshop.

Thus we began to take part in other activities outside the cell besides that of the Food Collective. Time was short and space was minimal for there were at this time 150 with less than a square yard per person in the interior courtyard; and conditions were difficult.

Yet the activity of the workshops grew and in May 1975 a choral group and a production workshop were formed (more will be said about the latter later on). A study was made of the time available and the workshops were divided into recreational activity, cultural activity and the production workshop. After a deep and lengthy discussion it was agreed that the Production Workshop was the most important and so the hours were reduced for the other's [sic] workshops to give more time to the Production Workshop.

When we moved to Pirque, the workshops had to suspend their activities because physical conditions had changed, and there was a delay of two weeks before they recommenced.

The Discussion Group organised a Talk-in on nutrition during a week specifically devoted to the Food Collective. Later the literary group prepared an analysis of the women's magazine Vanidades (similar to Cosmopolitan) and together with the Theatre Workshop presented this analysis in the form of a play. They chose this magazine as being the

*The Discussion Group was the first to hold discussions on general themes such as abortion, christianity and its role in society, women and the significance of International Women's Year, and so on. Such discussions played an important part in general development of our ideas.

most representative of its type. The study sets out to expose the many subtle ways in which women are ideologically controlled, setting up woman as a sexual symbol, as a consumer package or a marketable article, trivialising women with meaningless quizzes, making 'love' a commercial focal point, distorting reality through the news they present in third rate journalism.

A Sports Group was also organised and every fortnight there was a joint group day when each group displayed its work and everyone joined in the games and songs.

In July 1975 the Library Group was started to organise reading, and making books accessible to everybody. Before this some companeras had received books which they and others who shared their cells had read, but others who wanted to read had no access to books. These books we had were pooled and the majority of books received afterwards were given to the library group. This group organised a system of borrowing and storage and started archives of the daily and weekly press (newspapers and magazines).

During September and October the workshop programme began to even itself out; some lapsed while others survived and grew, developing workshops representing the stronger interests of the group in that they had the greatest support on the return to Tres Alamos. The governor of the camp accelerated this process by banning the Discussion and Choral groups because he considered them to be political. Since intellectual activity is essential, given the importance of maintaining a high morale and good mental health, the library group began to give out weekly press summaries of national and international events, thus giving a broad spectrum of the news and also treating one theme in depth each time. These summaries were given to all the companeras, but after issue No. 6 they were banned because they were considered to be political. For the authorities, the simple fact of thinking or reading a paper together, constitutes a political act which must be suppressed.

We carried on until the end of the year, resisting attack from the authorities, when time began to be given to the preparation of presents for relatives who were not in detention, for children and husbands. This began to have an effect on the attendance and activities of the workshop groups.

In January 1976 the general discrepancy in the level of education among the political prisoners necessitated setting up a course of elementary education in Maths, Spanish, Natural Sciences and Social Sciences and some of the former groups such as French, German and the plastic arts disappeared. Thus the workshops still continued to respond to the needs of the group, having highs and lows depending on the level of repression and the mental and psychological state of the companeras. The Workshops Committee continuing the struggle to develop was reinforced by a realisation of its relevance and importance in maintaining cultural and intellectual activity so that women would not leave the prison having also deteriorated in this respect. . . .

The Production Workshop

Discussion began in May 1975 about the situation of relatives and families outside the camp: some did not have many problems, but others had not enough money for even the basic necessities. There were two types of work done in the camp: the one a permanent and daily and absolute necessity, based on the need to provide money for food for children left outside the camp. The other was voluntary and was combined with cultural and recreational activity as a form of therapy or means of distraction. It was decided after some discussion of this situation that everyone would share the responsibility for providing for the children of the imprisoned companeras. In the earlier discussion three fundamental factors were taken into account; first, the economic situation worsening from day to day; secondly the solidarity which should be manifest in the life shared by the prisoners; and finally to attempt to find the positive aspects of being a political prisoner with the given limitations. A form of organisation was sought to best meet the following objectives:

a) to ease the economic burden of the families of detainees;
b) to supply products to those families with the lowest incomes, more or less defining which products could be made;
c) to create a discipline for working with set hours of work, and maintaining standards of quality and efficiency. In other words developing a respect for manual work

After further discussion it was agreed to set up:

a) an Administrative Committee made up of three companeras who, as well as working, also had the responsibility of looking after the finances, sales and work routine. These companeras worked on the committee for three months

b) a large work section to make the products, with three monitors responsible for technical advice and quality control

c) a Workshop Assembly in which all the companeras participated and which was the only group with the power to make decisions about the objectives of the production workshop

It was agreed to work two hours a day from Monday to Friday, making knitted products such as gloves, mittens, scarves, shawls and hats. As far as wages were concerned, it was decided to pay a wage to all the members of the workshop. A minimum wage was calculated to cover the monthly outlay on soap, toothpaste, shampoo, toilet paper and detergents. Special unemployment allowance was allocated to those companeras whose husbands were out of work, and another compensatory allowance allocated for those whose families were in difficult economic straits and not receiving enough to live on. It was further decided to fix a family allowance for the children left outside the prison. This meant that a prisoner without serious economic problems would receive the minimum wage while another prisoner with a husband out of work and eight children would receive a wage of *twenty times as much*, while both women work the same hours, under the same conditions and with the same degree of concentration. That is from each according to her abilities and to each according to her needs. . . .

Conclusion

There is no conclusion while the arrests continue in Chile, along with the disappearances and the deaths. Torture has become institutionalised.

The above account describes the life of Chilean women political prisoners, explaining the development of their internal organisation and some of the factors which influenced this. Its intention is to show how a small community hemmed in by barbed wire and guns, has evolved a way of life where the collective interests are put first and how women who have been imprisoned for their political ideas strive even in prison to live in accordance with what they believe.

Many human beings whose position is particularly difficult are living their lives this way. To know this reality must deeply wound the conscience of humanity. The lack of conclusion is a call to all peoples and organisations who respect humanity and wish to see the complete restoration of human rights in Chile.

Collective Reflections

From "Roles and Contradictions of Chilean Women in the Resistance and in Exile: Collective Reflections of a Group of Militant Prisoners," presented by Gladys Diaz at the Plenary Session of the International Conference on Exile and Solidarity in Latin America during the 1970s (New York: Women's International Resource Exchange Service, 1979). Reprinted by permission of Women's International Resource Exchange (WIRE).

Yes, our compañeras are winning space; but it has not been easy and it is not enough. There is still a very, very long road to be traveled. Now we have women in the front lines of the working class, there are now women among those who tomorrow will be the vanguard and who will lead decisive battles. And this role has been won fundamentally during these six years of struggle against the dictatorship. Thus we are witnessing the enormous revolutionary potential of the 50 percent of us who are women. Nor has it been a linear process. Like the struggle of the masses, it is a process which advances irregularly. In 1975, only 8 percent of the first women prisoners in Tres Alamos had really done sustained mass work as party members, and only 5 percent had been in high or intermediate leadership positions. The majority of the women had only had experience in rank-and-file conspiratorial activities, or in the reproduction of materials and ideas which others had elaborated. We know that today the situation has improved considerably, but we also know that it could be even better.

The party women have now proved themselves in many battles, like their male comrades, they have had their ordeal by fire. This was at the moment of torture. In the case of the women, this was a difficult moment, but also one of a brutal encounter with the role to which the capitalistic system has assigned us, and one of an equally brutal and cruel encounter with all the contradictions yet to be overcome; all of this we women had to carry with us in the interrogation with the enemy.

Like us, the military have a deep class hatred, but they despise doubly those of us who have committed ourselves to the people's cause. They despise us because we are their class enemies; they despise us because we have dared to break out of the roles to which we had been assigned. Because we have dared to think, because we have dared to rebel against the system. And the ferocity of the military is redoubled in angry and attacking response to the women's emancipation from that traditional role.

They would threaten to bring a woman's children and kill them in her presence, if she did not speak. Or they would already have them there and would make them cry in a neighboring room in order to remind the woman of her basic maternal function. They undressed the women, they ran their hands over their bodies, they raped them, they gave them electric shocks on their naked bodies which had been developed in a context of modesty and virginity. They beat women on the face and on the body in order to mutilate them, because within the conception of femininity, society has given great importance to symmetry, to bourgeois models of beauty. Some women were forced to confront their bleeding, dying compañeros; the torturers hoped that this would demoralize the men, that the women would beg their men to confess. Thus they were forced to weigh their love for their compañeros against their love for the people and the cause of freedom.

This is why we women prisoners in Tres Alamos were proud that 95 percent of us had heroically resisted torture. This sense of proletarian pride was not because we thought ourselves braver, stronger, or as strong as our male compañeros. The sense of pride came from having been able to reject our traditional role at a critical moment. Of having been able to see the priorities clearly as committed and fearless fighters, transcending the tears which we all held back in order not to show weakness.

The women prisoners, despite the fact that most had not had leadership positions, despite the fact that most were very young and inexperienced politically, mastered their limitations, their weaknesses, and took a qualitative leap in their emancipation as women as well as in their revolutionary commitment. Once they lived through the first stage on this second battle front which prison represents, the women went on to live another enriching experience, out of solitary confinement and into the prison community.

There, there were no male compañeros, always so good at organizing and at organizing us; in spite of this, the task of organizing was carried out rigorously and carefully. Discipline, a spirit of sacrifice, solidarity, dignity in the face of the enemy, the creation of activities and workshops to fill the lives of the women and avoid stagnation. Each woman had to contribute what she knew, each one had to be generous with her knowledge, with her experience, and with the maturity she had already achieved. If there was anything of importance learned there, it was how to share, to share food, joys, tasks, knowledge, and pain. And there we did exactly what political prisoners all over the world have done; we converted the prison into a school for well-trained cadres, for combatants, for human beings who were free even behind bars to love more than ever, in those conditions, the freedom which had been so cruelly torn from them.

Just like our compañeros, we women prisoners built our freedom every day. In the absence of freedom of the press, we created wall-newspapers which would be put up and taken down, depending on the degree of vigilance. In the absence of freedom of expression, we responded by creating poems, songs, theatrical works, dances which reflected our lives and hopes. We learned that children are not individual property but rather the children of the collectivity. Miguelito was born in the prison and was freed when he was sixteen months old, when he was already dancing to the song about "el negro José"* and would clap his hands to announce the arrival of the daily meals. Miguelito, along with Amanda, Alejandrito, and so many others lived a new conception of the family. They were the children of one mother and of a hundred aunts. Their feeding, education, entertainment, clothing, bathing, etc., were tasks and responsibilities of the collectivity. The mother's responsibilities toward her child were the same as those of each one of us.

The majority of women reached exile with this cumulus of experience. With the mutilation inherent in the loss of loved ones, with the traumas

---

*"El negro José" is a traditional Chilean song which came to be extremely significant, in a symbolic manner, in the prisons, where it would be sung each time a prisoner or a group of prisoners was released.

remaining from the moments of horror lived while in the hands of the brutal enemy; but also with their hearts overflowing with solidarity received and shared. Externally we were older, but inside we felt renewed by having been able to meet our responsibilities. We arrived at an obligatory but temporary exile, another battle front, less comforting, less gratifying, but as useful as the previous front—as useful and as necessary. This is the temporal space in which the rearguard is constructed and developed, a rearguard which nourishes, which denounces, which propagandizes, which accumulates international forces while basing itself on the actions carried out on the front lines of the battle. An exile in which we must also prepare the conditions for returning to Chile, improved, renewed, strengthened, better than before.

But, what we have just defined as our task is being accomplished with difficulty, with advances and retreats. Once again, in exile, party women face the daily contradictions implicit in being a woman, a worker, a mother, a housewife, and a party militant.

In prison, after having thrown off our traditional role in the torture chamber, we reflected at length on our lives, became aware of many things, wrote to our compañeros who were also in prison or on the outside, in order to communicate our thoughts. We questioned the unproletarian relationship which existed between men and women; we wanted to develop an ideological discussion on that theme. And the debate, which often became collective, began. In the light of the growth achieved, the whole concept of the couple was reformulated. In exile, the topic has been brought up more energetically sometimes advancing the discussion, at other times hampering it, and at still others leading to the breakup of the couple. Because women and men emerged from a rich but difficult experience and because both had grown, but not always in parallel ways. Exile has tended to create an inhospitable framework for discussion.

PART 3

"In the deadly monotony of prison I think we all revert back to childhood": Prison Conditions and Deprivations

*

The six selections in this section were written by women imprisoned under a variety of circumstances and in very different surroundings. In the United States, Union physician Dr. Mary E. Walker was held by Confederates in a converted tobacco warehouse called Castle Thunder, Socialist Kate Richards O'Hare spent time after World War I as a federal prisoner in the Missouri State Penitentiary, and Carolyn Baxter was recently imprisoned in the New York City Correctional Facility for Women. Abroad, American journalist Anna Louise Strong was jailed in Moscow during the cold war, novelist Joan Henry passed a year in a London prison in 1950, and South African Joyce Sikakane was interrogated and detained in 1969 under the Terrorism Act. These women's writings are linked by descriptions of prison routines, environments, and deprivations.

Five general areas of deprivation are cited in Gresham Sykes's classic 1958 study of a male maximum-security prison: liberty, goods and services, security, heterosexual relationships, and autonomy.[1] Researchers who have studied American women's prisons note that Sykes's "pains of imprisonment" also hold true for female inmates.[2] Sykes's categories and the findings of current sociological studies may be used, with caution, as a general framework for discussion of major areas of concern in women's writings about prison conditions. Allowing for differences in time, nationality, and social and political climate, these studies offer insight about the topics repeatedly found in descriptions of conditions in a women's prison.

Letters, journalistic accounts, memoirs, poetry, and fiction by women prisoners are full of accounts of the physical surroundings, routines, and atmosphere within the prison walls. The impulse to describe the prison environment is understandable, since the incarcerated writer knows that it is very strange territory to most of her readers. If she is writing about her first prison experience, she often conveys a sense of apprehension and mystery that allows her reader to identify with her and participate in the prison initiation.

The new inmate is introduced to prison conditions during "reception." This admission process holds so much strangeness, fear, and degradation that it is almost universally described in prison memoirs. It epitomizes the woman's complete loss of autonomy and even identity, if the prison has its way. Current practice in America is for the woman to be physically stripped and searched, then stripped of all material belongings and given a number in exchange.[3] The account of Anna Louise Strong's admission to Moscow's infamous Lubyanka Prison in 1949 is especially moving because this sixty-four-year-old communist sympathizer considered herself a friend to both Russia and China. The Russians, who were not so tolerant of her dual friendships, misinterpreted her plans to enter China and arrested her as a spy. The article she wrote shortly after her release bears the freshness of her incredulity. Joyce Sikakane's narrative, on the other hand, lacks this mystified tone, because she knew all too well not to expect courtesy or justice at the hands of the whites who violently tore her from her home and her son the night of her arrest.

Prison food, at best unvaried and bland, is a constant reminder that the inmate has been deprived of goods and services. For many prison writers, nutrition is a critical issue. Dr. Mary E. Walker, for example, knew that the diet in her Confederate prison jeopardized health and life. Walker, who was never one to observe convention or quietly obey authority, secured a better diet for herself and other inmates. Also true to form, she proudly boasted of her success in her "Statement" printed in the *Daily National Republican*.

Some prison writers have protested the intolerable conditions of forced labor in their institutions. According to her own account and that of fellow inmate anarchist Emma Goldman, Kate Richards O'Hare was quite an efficient and productive seamstress in the shop of the penitentiary at Jefferson City, Missouri. However, O'Hare felt the strain of work and saw that other women suffered. She recognized the value of political prisoners in effecting reforms. Her study, *In Prison*, and her letters to her family, published by her husband, expose the lot of exploited female inmate workers who cannot "make the task."

Scandalous health conditions, often another "given" of prison life, led to O'Hare's major protest via letter to her husband. When she was first admitted in 1919, it was prison procedure to mix healthy and syphilitic women. Though her campaign was successful, her letters show that she considered this unhealthful environment a personal injustice. After her release, she expressed both her anger and her compassion in the *Nation*:

> For fourteen long months I studied that stream of wrecked lives that find their way to prison, and they were not pleasant to look upon, nor did they add to my patriotic pride or peace of mind. They were sinister and revolting: I feared them. But averted eyes and natural repugnance could not relieve me of my personal responsibility nor close my mind to the fact that they are flesh of our flesh, soul of our soul, and that cowardice and prison walls cannot break the human tie that binds us to them.[4]

O'Hare's humanity is evident, but, unlike Goldman, she seems to stand outside the prison, regarding her fellow inmate as the "other."[5]

Inadequate health care is a personal security problem that subtly undermines inmate morale and energy; interrogation, on the other hand, is an immediate and inescapable security concern. With a tone of disbelief and a sense of betrayal, Strong writes her account of her interrogation in Moscow. A tough, matter-of-fact tone characterizes Sikakane's quite different, life-threatening interrogation. Her account recalls the often graphic testimonies, usually oral rather than written, of female prisoners' torture and interrogation in Latin America.[6] And New York poet Carolyn Baxter reminds readers that, although lacking in physical torture, the current American courtroom scene generates psychological violence against poor, minority female defendants.

In an investigation of sex differences in prisoners' responses to deprivations, Lee H. Bowker notes that, although male institutions are "physically more depriving," it is inmates' *felt* deprivation that is crucial in determining their response. Women's greater subjective sense of deprivation may result from socially imposed gender differences and separation from their children.[7] Changed relationships with others disturb the female prisoner; in particular, her anxiety over separation from supportive relationships with those on the outside and from family is acute and is for many inmates the most devastating of prison deprivations.[8] The problems of imprisoned mothers in contemporary American prisons have been well-documented by sociologists. Few prisons make provisions for women with children, and counseling to help disrupted families cope with stress is limited.[9] Most children are cared for by the woman's parents or relatives rather than by the father or foster parents.[10]

The remote, often rural, location of women's prisons compounds the problems of separation by making it virtually impossible for children and other family members to visit, especially if the woman is poor and comes from the city. And the atmosphere for visits is far from ideal: the frequency and duration of visits are restricted, and mothers in most state prisons may not hold their children.[11] A few states have apartments available for conjugal and family visits with eligible inmates, but these are by far the exception.[12] The problem continues after the woman's sentence is up as well: upon their release from prison, most women must return to families with whom they have lost contact but whom they need for emotional support to readjust to life on the outside.

Childbirth in prison is at best a problem and at worst a scandal. Since inadequate medical care, particularly gynecological care, is a common complaint among women in jails and prisons, inmates often receive poor treatment during pregnancy and face a lonely, even frightening delivery. Women are taken to special wards of community hospitals to deliver, since prisons do not have adequate facilities. Inmates claim, however, that they are not allowed to breast-feed or even to see their babies, and that they often receive inhumane treatment under the guise of "security measures."[13] Only a few states provide facilities for incarcerated women to keep their infants in the institution.[14]

"It's a dismal fact: One of the greatest trials of the sentence is the sheer hatred of being cooped up with a bunch of women."[15] Many female prison writers through the ages would agree with this statement; they miss heterosexual relationships and perceive life with female inmates as one of the most offensive prison conditions. Black Panther Assata Shakur, imprisoned at the New York City Correctional Institution for Women, claims that, unlike male prisoners who use the term "brother," "Women prisoners rarely refer to each other as sister. Instead, 'bitch' and 'whore' are the common terms of reference."[16] Carolyn Baxter's poems seem to bear this out, but they also display women's genuine concern for each other and a level of kindness toward fellow inmates that, according to Shakur, is greater than that in men's prisons.[17] Rose Giallombardo's research at the Federal Reformatory for Women in Alderson, West Virginia, indicates that women often object to living with other women because they distrust other members of their sex and dislike living with prostitutes, untidy persons, or those from another race or class. Unlike men, who fear for their lives in prison, American women prisoners, according to Giallombardo, fear disfigurement and verbal attacks by other women prisoners.[18] Negative attitudes of some female prisoners toward their fellow inmates raise complex questions concerning class, race, and gender issues. These negative attitudes are balanced, however, by other women prisoners' very positive expressions of solidarity, as seen in the selections in Part 5.

Some prison writers, like O'Hare, are ambivalent in their responses to sister inmates. Unlike Agnes Smedley or Emma Goldman, who were also imprisoned during the flurry of political trials around the time of World War I, O'Hare did not seem to mix easily with other inmates.[19] Recalling their prison days together, Goldman describes O'Hare's "hauteur," but obviously respects her.[20] Though O'Hare seemed distanced from other inmates by her reserved demeanor and propriety, her very presence in prison testified to the sincerity of her socialism. Her letters show how she expressed her care for her fellow inmates in her dauntless advocacy of prison reforms—but in her writing she maintains her more elevated position as prisoner/reformer.

Another prison deprivation is loss of autonomy. In contemporary American prisons this loss is difficult for male as well as female prisoners. However, it takes a unique form in a women's prison, where a woman not only loses decision-making power, but is also often treated like a child, encouraged to be dependent, and called a girl by the prison administration.[21] Baxter's poems tell the frank reality of a woman's loss of autonomy in an institution where racism and sexism are too often the rule. Patricia McConnel, who had spent time in six jails and in the Federal Reformatory for Women in Alderson, West Virginia, writes:

whatever its purported purpose, its [prison's] actual effect is to destroy all those qualities in a person that might enable her to become an effective human being. Initiative and self-assertion are usually severely punished.

The prisoner has no control over any aspect of her existence; she is expected to surrender any will to direct her own life.[22]

The conditions of today's American women's prisons, often set in "campuses" with light security, may not be as overly repressive as in men's institutions, because women are perceived as less dangerous. However, women's prisons usually offer fewer educational and training programs and impose a repressive, stereotyped expectation of feminine behavior on inmates.[23] Rules and routines cover every aspect of life and must be followed strictly to avoid loss of privileges or "gain time" for good behavior.[24] To a new prisoner, an American women's prison may indeed seem like a totally different world. In their study at the California Institution for Women, Ward and Kassebaum noted that women inmates suffer from anomie, arising from their disorientation in a new environment seemingly without norms, where rules of behavior are unfamiliar and methods for adapting successfully are unclear.[25] Contemporary writers echo the alienation expressed in women's prison literature throughout the centuries and in many nations. Joan Henry's autobiographical narrative mixes humor and pain to illustrate the alienation of her first days in prison. Henry came from her civilized London world that respected privacy to the regulated, utterly impersonal world of Holloway Prison. Her account jars the reader with a hint of the culture shock she felt.

But the greatest deprivation is the loss of liberty itself, a loss for which most people would be psychologically unprepared. The stress Mary E. Walker observes in her cell mate has surely been felt, to a degree, by all women prisoners. Perhaps women prison writers find some relief in expression itself, as did Walker in writing her philosophy: "Whoever passes through terrible trials in the vigor of years ought to thank the Hand that suffered the same to be; for every *terrible experience* develops the powers, so that one can calmly say, 'Strike deep, my heart can bear.'"

NOTES

1. Gresham M. Sykes, *The Society of Captives: A Study of a Maximum Security Prison* (Princeton, N.J.: Princeton Univ. Press, 1958; reprint, New York: Atheneum, 1968), pp. 63–83. A 1977 study by Toch listing seven similar "en-

vironmental concerns"—privacy, safety, structure, support, emotional feedback, activity, and freedom—is cited in Nicolette Parisi, "The Prisoner's Pressures and Responses," in *Coping with Imprisonment*, ed. N. Parisi (Beverly Hills, Calif.: Sage, 1982), pp. 10–11.

2. Rose Giallombardo, *Society of Women: A Study of a Women's Prison* (New York: Wiley, 1966), pp. 93–102; David A. Ward and Gene G. Kassebaum, *Women's Prison: Sex and Social Structure* (Chicago: Aldine, 1965), pp. 3–28.

3. Giallombardo, *Society of Women*, pp. 95–97; Ward and Kassebaum, *Women's Prison*, pp. 10–14; Kathryn Watterson Burkhart, *Women in Prison* (Garden City, N.Y.: Doubleday, 1973), pp. 95–115.

4. Kate Richards O'Hare, "Human Ostriches," *Nation* 120, no. 3118 (8 April 1925): 377–378.

5. See Emma Goldman, *Living My Life*, 2 vols. (New York: Knopf, 1931; reprint, Dover, 1970).

6. See Introduction to Part 2 for a discussion of testimonies by Latin American women.

7. Lee H. Bowker, "Gender Differences in Prison Subcultures," in *Women and Crime in America*, ed. Lee H. Bowker (New York: Macmillan, 1981), pp. 411–412.

8. Separation from their children is the most difficult aspect of imprisonment for the 56 percent of American women prisoners who are mothers with dependent children living at home, according to Ruth M. Glick and Virginia V. Neto, *National Study of Women's Correctional Programs* (Washington, D.C.: National Institute of Law Enforcement and Criminal Justice, 1977), p. xviii. They also found that 73 percent of inmates were mothers. Inmate mothers had an average of 2.48 children, compared with the 1973 census average of 2.18 for all families.

Other studies have cited a higher percentage of women prisoners with dependent children at home. See Coramae Richey Mann, *Female Crime and Delinquency* (University, Ala.: Univ. of Alabama Press, 1984), p. 234.

9. Suzanne B. Sobel, "Difficulties Experienced by Women in Prison," *Psychology of Women Quarterly* 7, no. 2 (Winter 1982): 107–118. Sobel cites a model program at Perdy Institute for Women, Washington (state), which places children in a foster home near the prison and allows inmate mothers to visit and participate in child care.

10. Glick and Neto, *National Study of Women's Correctional Programs*, p. xviii.

11. Mann, *Female Crime and Delinquency*, pp. 203–204.

12. Ibid., p. 204. Mann notes that states with conjugal and family facilities include Washington, New York, California, and Mississippi.

13. Juanita Reedy, "Diary of a Prison Birth," *Majority Report* 5, no. 2 (31 May 1975): 1, 3, presents a graphic account of her poor medical treatment during childbirth while she was incarcerated.

14. Mann, *Female Crime and Delinquency*, pp. 230–231. Mann states that California, New York, and Florida provide facilities for women to keep their infants in the institution.

15. Celeste West, "Kept Women," *Synergy* (January–February 1971): 26–30.

16. Assata Shakur (Joanne Chesimard), "Women in Prison: How We Are,"

Black Scholar 12, no. 6 (November–December 1981): 54–55, reprinted from vol. 9, no. 7 (April 1978).

17. Ibid.

18. Giallombardo, *Society of Women*, pp. 93–102.

19. See Philip S. Foner and Sally M. Miller, eds., *Kate Richards O'Hare: Selected Writings and Speeches* (Baton Rouge, La.: Louisiana State Univ. Press, 1982), pp. 26–27, for further discussion of O'Hare's relationship with women inmates.

20. Goldman, *Living My Life*, 2:677.

21. See Shakur, "Women in Prison: How We Are," pp. 52–53; Angela Davis, *An Autobiography* (New York: Random House, 1974).

22. Patricia McConnel, letter to Judith Scheffler, 6 July 1983.

23. Glick and Neto, *National Study of Women's Correctional Programs*, p. 190; James E. Griffith and Amelia Pennington-Averett, "Women Prisoners' Multidimensional Locus of Control," *Criminal Justice and Behavior* 8, no. 3 (September 1981): 386; Nicole H. Rafter, *Partial Justice: Women in State Prisons, 1800–1935* (Boston: Northeastern Univ. Press, 1985), pp. xxv–xxvi, 177–188.

24. Mann, *Female Crime and Delinquency*, p. 209.

25. Ward and Kassebaum, *Women's Prison*, pp. 25–26. Gabrielle Russier's prison letters, *The Affair of Gabrielle Russier*, trans. Ghislaine Boulanger (New York: Knopf, 1971), also display anomie.

MARY EDWARDS WALKER (1832–1919)

Mary Edwards Walker was born on a farm in Oswego Town, New York, and raised in a family that encouraged independent thought. She claimed that her father's interest in medicine and hygiene had inspired her own career as a physician and dress reformer for women. In 1855 she received her medical degree from the Syracuse Medical College and practiced medicine briefly in Columbus, Ohio, and Rome, New York, with her physician husband, Albert Miller. Her marriage soon ended, and she was legally divorced in 1869. As her interest in dress reform developed, she began lecturing, writing articles for the journal *Sibyl*, and wearing the pants that became her lifelong costume and led to her notoriety and persecution by the press and, at times, by the police.

When her offer to serve as a physician in the Union Army during the Civil War was rejected because of her sex, she worked as a volunteer in Washington, D.C., hospitals. In 1863 she traveled to Chattanooga, Tennessee, and replaced a Union assistant surgeon who had died, but a medical staff examining board declared her unqualified. One staff member described her later as a "medical monstrosity."

Serving as a noncommissioned contract surgeon with the 52nd Ohio Regiment, she daringly crossed enemy lines to treat Tennessee civilians and, some speculated, to spy. On one mission, she was taken prisoner on April 10, 1864, and sent by train to Richmond's Castle Thunder, a tobacco warehouse used to house deserters and political prisoners. One of few women imprisoned there, the five-foot-tall, pant-suited doctor caused quite a stir in the Richmond papers. In August 1864 she was exchanged, she proudly claimed, "for a six-foot surgeon from Tennessee." In October 1864 she was named Acting Assistant Surgeon, U.S. Army, and assigned briefly to the Women's Prison Hospital in Louisville, Kentucky. In 1865 she became the first woman to receive the Congressional Medal of Honor; she wore it proudly even after it was rescinded as unwarranted in 1917. It was reinstated in 1977.

After the Civil War, Walker continued her activities, working for the woman's movement and for dress reform, writing treatises on social issues, and lecturing in the United States and England. She lived mostly in Washington, but returned in her last years to Oswego, where she was considered an eccentric.

Note: Biographical information is from Roberts Bartholow (Asst.-Surgeon, U.S.A.), letter to the editor, *New York Medical Journal* 5, no. 2 (May 1867): 167–170; Sandra L. Chaff, "In Recognition of Mary Edwards Walker," *Women & Health* 6, nos. 1/2 (Spring–Summer 1981): 83–90; Lida Poynter, "Dr. Mary Walker, M.D.: Pioneer Woman Physician," *Medical Woman's Journal* 53, 10 (October 1946): 43–51; Charles M. Snyder, *Dr. Mary Walker: The Little Lady in Pants* (New York: Vantage, 1962).

WORKS BY MARY EDWARDS WALKER

Walker Papers: 1863–1895, George Arents Research Library, Syracuse University, Syracuse, N.Y.; Lida Poynter Manuscripts, including correspondence and an unpublished manuscript on Walker's life, Women's Medical College, Philadelphia, Pa.; Walker Papers, Oswego County Historical Society, Oswego, N.Y.

Crowning Constitutional Argument. Oswego, N.Y., 1907. Pamphlet.

Hit. New York: American News, 1871. Essays.

"Hotel de Castle Thunder." *Daily National Republican* (Washington, D.C.), 25 August 1864.

Isonomy. Oswego, N.Y., 1898. Pamphlet.

A Woman's Thought about Love and Marriage, Divorce, etc. New York: James Miller, 1871.

Unmasked, or the Science of Immortality. To Gentlemen. By a Woman Physician and Surgeon. Philadelphia: W. H. Boyd, 1878.

Hotel de Castle Thunder

From the *Daily National Republican* (Washington, D.C.),
25 August 1864.

Whoever a person is—even if it be a mortal enemy—it is not right to publish all his wrongs without giving him credit for what good he has done. And if it is not right in an individual case, it certainly cannot be in a nation, where peace *ought to reign*, and where it is a sin to make matters any worse than they are, by misrepresenting the deeds of those who happen to be enemies.

While a *guest* at the above "Castle," I am confident that the "bill of fare" was as good, as abundant, and as various as could be afforded. It consisted of corn-bread, rice, peas, and bacon. During the first few weeks we had large rations of bread, etc., sufficient for a laboring man; but soon after the commencement of hostilities, in the "on to Richmond," we had smaller rations of bread, and the bacon was of an inferior quality.

After the Petersburg and Weldon railroads were cut, we received *still smaller* rations of bread and meat, and the commissary was forbidden to sell anything, except by a special order. Our rations at this time consisted of the following: for breakfast, a piece of corn bread, three inches square, and a gill of rice, or of peas; for dinner, a piece of bread the same size, and a small piece of bacon. The *bread* was made with water, out of unsifted meal. The *peas* were always wormy. The *rice* was sometimes good, but generally was musty, or contained vermin. Some rations contained a thousand, which were white, about an eighth of an inch in length, and about the size of a cambric needle. Some contained either a different species of vermin or the same further developed, for they nearly filled the kernel and were black. The *bacon*, in several instances, was so rotten that its odor was unendurable to me after it was served, and would but "just hold together." Occasionally one could see large worm orifices through the best of it. But it was never so bad but that I always found some one who would gladly accept my ration.

As much as the rebs have said against "women's rights," they treated the females in some respects as *equals* of the men, i.e., they gave the same rations.

We had a female servant, and my rice was prepared for cooking by myself, as soon as I found its condition, and was cooked separate from the general mess. I was informed by reliable authority, that there were hundreds in the city that would be glad to be as *well* provided for as we were! Many were in a condition *"next door to starvation,"* and however much we may love the DEAR OLD FLAG, we can but admire the spirit of the rebel soldiers, who, when they were fighting under a sweltering sun to destroy it, divided their scanty rations, and sent to the famishing poor! sent them willingly, cheerfully, aye, even *proudly*! What a lesson!! Flour at this time was $600 and $700 per barrel, beef $5 and $6 per pound, pork $8 and $9 per pound, eggs $10 and $12 per dozen, potatoes $32 per bushel; everything else at the above rates.

Gen. Early sent supplies from Pennsylvania and Maryland *Early enough* to prevent starvation, and *particularly* the ETC. Let no one north of Richmond find fault with Gen. Grant in the face of these *facts*.

In many respects the officials were kind to me, and the chief one, Capt. Richardson, treated me with as much consideration as was possible and consistent with his duties as a commandant. I made no complaint about the "bill of fare" for many weeks, and then not as a *complaint*, exactly, but as a *suggestion*. I sent word to the commissary that it did not "seen [sic] possible for me to swallow another mouthful of corn bread, as I was so tired of it." Two days after he commenced giving all the prisoners rations of wheat bread, and continued them for a number of days, until we were glad to have corn bread again. The wheat bread was always a little sour, caused by its standing so long to rise, and always dry because it had rose so much.

I think it was about three weeks before I left that corn bread was again issued. At this time the longing for vegetables became loud enough to be heard, and I made the remark, that if they "could not afford us some, they *ought* to send us all home;" and suggested that if but one variety could be given, cabbage had more iron and would be better than anything else. Since that time, all the prisoners, except some under punishment, have had rations of cabbage three or four times per week. Each head cost $1.50, and the solid portion was not larger than a coffee cup; one-half of the same was a ration. I shall take no credit to myself for this addition to the "bill of fare;" but one thing was exceedingly gratifying—*we got the cabbage*. Twice in the last three weeks we had rations of molasses—one-third of a gill at one time, and a gill at another. It was as thin as though the first had been made out of a teaspoonful of ordinary syrup, and the last of a tablespoonful.

I have been thus particular in making the above statements, and have gone into *little matters*, as I should have had no patience to have done if *justice*—even to an enemy—had not demanded that truth, which is a "credit" to said enemy, should be told as readily as if it were a *discredit*.

We had the same rations, precisely, as their own soldiers and citizen prisoners, who were confined there for disloyalty, or desertion, or impudence to officers, etc.

But I must tell you about the females. When I arrived at Richmond they did not know what to do with me, as I was the only (what they considered) female *prisoner of war* that they had ever had, who was not dressed in men's attire throughout. They could not send me to "Hotel de Libby,"* because there was no private room. The Castle has four,

*Libby Prison in Richmond.—*Ed.*

expressly for females, with a private hall between them and the central hall of the building. Every one had a large window that opened on the street from the second story of a three-story brick building that sometimes held several hundred prisoners, the majority of whom are deserters from the Confederate army.

There was but one in these rooms when I arrived here—a Miss Manus, from Mississippi, who had been confined for many months as a spy. She was released to be sent home about a week before I left. After I had been there about two months, a large stout Irish woman was brought there, stating she was a cook for the officers of Gen. Wessel's brigade, and that her husband was a private in a Massachusetts regiment. She was sent home on the last flag-of-truce boat. About two weeks before I left a woman was brought from near Petersburg, charged with having harbored Confederate deserters. She left after one night's stay. Another, a Mrs. Green and her husband, were brought from the "Neck" on the Potomac, in Virginia, charged with allowing Yankees to land on their farm. Her husband was 51 years old, and dressed in blue. She was 40, and left four children at home alone, the eldest a girl of 16. Her cries and groans were so deep and bitter, that it almost distracted me, being compelled to hear what nothing but *philosophy* could in any degree *palliate*, and what little of the medicine I could spare without death to myself, could not be received by a stomach that was too old to appreciate a new variety of foreign balm.

I can endure the sight and sound of the greatest agony when I can do aught to relieve the same, but to find a case of the above age and habits of thought, and a woman—I confess it makes me weak to think of it. Whoever passes through terrible trials in the vigor of years ought to thank the Hand that suffered the same to be; for every *terrible experience* develops the powers, so that one can calmly say, "Strike deep, my heart can bear;" so that one can manufacture smiles by the bushel when the heart is breaking; so that, whatever of wrongs or injustice may be met, no glance of the eye can betray aught but a cheerful resignation to "whatever is."

I have written you in great haste, and will now close, thanking Jeff. Davis for my entertainment at the Hotel de Castle Thunder.

KATE RICHARDS O'HARE (CUNNINGHAM)
(1876–1948)

Kate Richards was born to a comfortable middle-class Kansas farming couple, but the drought of 1877 ruined the family financially. She was deeply affected by their poverty and her father's subsequent need to work in industry. At the age of seventeen, finding teaching and book-keeping not to her taste, she joined the International Association of Machinists in order to pursue her love of mechanics. Her work in the shops and her religious sensibility awakened her to the suffering of the poor working class. Hearing Mother Jones speak was one factor that inspired her to study socialist theory and to work with the Socialist Party. In 1902 she married fellow socialist Frank P. O'Hare, and together they had four children and shared a marriage centered on their political and social commitment.

In her active work for socialist causes, Kate Richards O'Hare was particularly sensitive to the plight of poor women and child workers. She wrote for the socialist *National Rip-Saw* and *Appeal to Reason*, lectured throughout the United States, ran on the Socialist ticket in national elections, served as the Party's international secretary, and joined with nonsocialists to promote woman suffrage. With the coming of World War I, O'Hare lectured widely against the war, until a speech in Bowman, North Dakota, in 1917 led to her trial under the Espionage Act. After her appeals of her five-year sentence failed, she was imprisoned in the Missouri State Penitentiary at Jefferson City from April 15, 1919, until her sentence was commuted on May 29, 1920, because of her ill health. She later received a full pardon from President Coolidge. She had intended to conduct a study of prison conditions, but was forced to spend most of her time working in the prison sewing shop. Her letters to her family, which were published by Frank O'Hare, show her efforts to improve prison conditions, including food and sanitation. The intellectual companionship of fellow inmate Emma Goldman was a great boon to her. After O'Hare's release, she worked actively for prison reform and wrote a report and later a book about prison conditions.

After O'Hare's divorce in 1928, she married Charles C. Cunningham. Her prison reform work continued in California, where, as assistant director of the Department of Penology, she succeeded in effecting several necessary changes.

Note: Biographical information is from Philip S. Foner and Sally M. Miller, eds., *Kate Richards O'Hare: Selected Writings and Speeches* (Baton Rouge, La.: Louisiana State Univ. Press, 1982); David A. Shannon, "Kate Richards O'Hare Cunningham," in *Notable American Women*, edited by Edward T. James, vol. 1 (Cambridge, Mass.: Belknap Press, 1971).

WORKS BY KATE RICHARDS O'HARE

Mimeographed copies of O'Hare's prison letters to her family are available in several collections, including New York Public Library; Missouri Historical Society, St. Louis; Schlesinger Library, Radcliffe College, Cambridge, Mass.; The Sophia Smith Collection, Smith College, Northampton, Mass.; Swarthmore College Peace Collection, Swarthmore, Pa.; University of Missouri Library, State Historical Society of Missouri, Columbia, Mo.; University of Oregon Library, Special Collections, Eugene, Ore.

Americanism and Bolshevism. St. Louis, Mo.: F. P. O'Hare, 1919. Author's farewell address before her imprisonment.

"Human Ostriches." *Nation* 120, no. 3118 (8 April 1925): 377–378.

In Prison, being a report by Kate Richards O'Hare to the President of the United States as to the conditions under which women federal prisoners are confined in the Missouri state penitentiary, under the authority of the United States Department of justice and the United States superintendent of prisons. Based on the author's experience as a federal prisoner from April 14, 1919, to May 30, 1920. St. Louis, Mo.: F. P. O'Hare [ca. 1920].

In Prison, by Kate Richards O'Hare, sometime federal prisoner number 21669. New York: Knopf, 1923; reprint, Seattle, Wash.: American Library, no. 30, Univ. of Washington Press, 1976.

Kate O'Hare's Prison Letters. Girard, Kan.: Appeal to Reason, 1919.

Selected Writings and Speeches. Edited by Philip S. Foner and Sally M. Miller. Baton Rouge: Louisiana State Univ. Press, 1982.

Socialism and the World War. St. Louis, Mo.: F. P. O'Hare, 1919. Speech for which O'Hare was indicted.

The Sorrows of Cupid. St. Louis, Mo.: National Rip-Saw, 1912.

Letters from Prison

Letters of 26 April 1919 and 3 May 1919 from The
Sophia Smith Collection, Smith College. Reprinted by
permission of Berta Margoulies O'Hare.

Jefferson City, Mo. April 26, 1919

F. P. O'Hare,
1011 Holland Bldg.,
St. Louis, Mo.

My Darling Sweethearts:

This is Saturday evening, and I will write a part of my letter so it will
not take up too much of my time tomorrow.

We do not work Saturday afternoon, and have almost three hours
outdoors, so I am feeling fine. I am still doing nicely, eat and sleep well,
and do not suffer particularly because of the work. Of course, nine hours
per day at a sewing machine is no light task, but I am perfectly well,
and quite efficient, so manage very nicely.

I hope that none of you are worried about me, for I am really having
a most interesting time. In Emma Goldman, and the dear little Italian
girl,* I have intellectual comradeship, and in my little "dope"† some
one to mother; in the management of the institution very interesting
study, and in the inmates a wonderful array of interesting fellow-beings.

If it were not for being deprived of my loved ones, I could fully enjoy
the new and unusual experience. If I could have my typewriter, and
write more often to my darlings, I would be quite content to do my
work here for a time. It seems so needlessly stupid that I should be
deprived of the opportunity to write, when I have paid the last ounce
of flesh demanded by the state at the sewing machine. There is so much
that I want to write while the impressions are vivid, but perhaps I will
write better for being deprived of the opportunity for a time.

I have received papa's nice letters each day, also the sweet little letters
from Victor and Kathleen, but Gene and Dickie's‡ letters have not come

---

*Gabriella Antolina, political prisoner.—*Ed.*
†In the cell next to O'Hare's was a woman suffering from drug addiction.—*Ed.*
‡The O'Hare children.—*Ed.*

yet. Papa writes me that the twins were lovely, and that he enjoyed their Easter vacation, and that Dick is the dearest and sweetest boy imaginable. I know that you will all be nice and sweet and fine, so that no one can say that mamma has failed as a mother.

I have had so many lovely letters and would like to answer them, but of course it is impossible. The caps Mrs. H. sent are lovely—every one admires them. I thank Dr. H. for the candy, and tell Rosa that I have placed the picture on the wall with my own babies. Someone sent me a lovely box of peppermint candy, which I am particularly fond of. The little leather pocket case with my darlings' pictures in it from the G. Sisters is really my best loved present. It just fits in my pocket and I carry it with me all the time. Of course they can't know how much it means to me, but please do all that words can do to express my appreciation.

I hope that you will make it plain to all my friends and comrades that the only way in which I can express my appreciation for their letters and presents is to do it collectively in my weekly letter to you.

Please write Theresa Malkiel* and tell her to finish the scarf I sent and raffle it for the New York Call.† It is all that I could do to express my loyalty to all that the Call stands for. I got the materials during the last hour of my freedom and fifteen minutes after the cell door had clanged behind me I was busy at work on it. I want this to be my message to all the comrades. Don't waste any time in tears or sorrow over me, but go to work. I want the chances sold for 10¢ each, so every comrade can buy one, and I hope the Call will get a dime for every stitch. Children put x's at the end of their letters to indicate kisses. These stitches are my cross marks, and they are words of loyalty to our cause, and faith in ultimate justice, that I cannot speak or write. Ask Theresa to convey my greetings to the comrades who sent me the beautiful letter from the wedding party. Tell Comrade Kate I send my love, and that after almost eighteen years of married life I can testify that it is not so bad, provided!—you start in early to train your husband in the right way. Be firm! be firm! and never let him forget that he is just a mere man! I can't seem to locate the groom in my memory, but send my love and

*Socialist leader.—*Ed.*
†Socialist newspaper.—*Ed.*

congratulations. I am sure he is all right, or he could never have won a girl like Kate!

Send my letters to Zeuch,* and tell him to write to me often. Give Rella my love, and tell her I am glad she is there to help look after my big boys. I hope that you will not be so busy as to neglect the twins. I want them to have their letter every week, and to either come in, or have some one visit them every Sunday. Just ask the YPSELS† to see that they are not allowed to get lonely, or feel neglected. Kathleen will be all right, and Dick is with you, and I want my baby boys to be looked after. Have the children write to Mother regularly, and send her copies of my letters. Do your best to make her understand that I am all right and not suffering, and that I am merely having a very interesting experience. Her letter was very sweet and beautiful, and I am glad to know that she is a good rebel to the very last.

I receive the Mirror, but not St. Louis Labor. Ask Comrade Hoehn to send it to me. Give him and Billy and Mrs. L. and all the comrades my love, and tell them not to worry about me, but just go on with the work. I am having a rest and a change of work, and will be in fine shape for the campaign.

I have had really one hard experience, and it was pretty bad. That was the Bertillon.‡ I am not prudish, and not supersensitive, but it took all my poise and self-control to go through it without breaking. The men who put me through the ordeal were kindness and sympathy and courtesy itself, but they could not rob it of its trying effects. When you come down, visit the Bertillon room, and thank the man in charge for his kindness to me. Tell him that while it was pretty hard I have recovered from the shock. [I] am wondering how Debs§ will stand it. I am afraid it will be pretty hard on him.

Aside from this there is only one feature that is really revolting, and that is the criminally stupid mixing of the clean women with the frightfully syphilitic. Absolutely no effort to separate them is made. There is an Indian woman here from Alaska, a "federal," who is in the very

*William E. Zeuch, socialist professor and economist.—*Ed.*
†Young People's Socialist League.—*Ed.*
‡A system of classifying and identifying inmates by records of body measurements and markings. Named for Alphonse Bertillon, French criminologist.—*Ed.*
§Imprisoned socialist leader Eugene Debs.—*Ed.*

last stages. Her throat is one mass of open sores, and she bathes in the same tub that I do, and the clean, healthy girls are forced to clean the tub after her baths. There is a white girl in almost as bad condition, who eats at the tables with us, and many of the colored girls are diseased. The dishes are not kept separate and no disinfectants are used.

I have made a formal complaint to the warden, Gov. Painter,* in writing, but so far have received no answer. I am writing to Judge Krum today asking him for legal advice as to my actions. I have asked him to take the matter up with Mr. Fosdick who has charge of the campaign against venereal disease, for the "federals." I think Julia Lathrop, chief of the Government Children's Bureau could do much by personally pressing the matter with the Department of Justice. She is in Washington, and will no doubt be glad to act in the matter. It is a particularly frightful state of affairs, because most of the federal prisoners are young women who are in here for short sentences. I doubt if anything can be done for the state prisoners. Missouri is so backward that I have little hope of anything being done to bring its institutions up to anything humane or modern. "Poor old Missouri."

I would not be telling the truth if I denied that this phase of the situation did not affect me. It does. I can never forget the sickening fact that the country which my ancestors helped to found, and which my father gave his life to protect has forced me to live in constant danger of contamination from the most loathsome of all diseases.

Aside from this one thing I am quite content. I am making the sort of study of criminology that never has been made before, and which could only be made in this way. I am learning things that will be of inestimable value to the world of science, and, in the future, when I speak of crime and criminals I will have a solid basis of hard-won facts on which to stand. I have such a wealth of material now that I think we will have to revise the questionnaire. I feel now that we are not ready to begin the survey. When I get out you must get in, and study the men as I study the women. It is a hard way to serve science and humanity, but it is the only way. I am afraid that you can't get sent up for an "intent," as I have been, so you must discover some crime that can be pinned on you that you do not need to commit.

*William R. Painter, prison warden.—*Ed.*

Send me down that book containing Dr. Barnes' lectures on Nervous and Mental diseases, I have a wonderful opportunity for such studies here. A most interesting case of dementia praecox in the second cell from me, and an interesting case of homicidal mania that promises some lively developments. Ask Dr. Barnes if there has been anything worth while written on Prison Neurosis. I am certainly gathering a lot of interesting material in that line. If there is anything, ask him to send it to me. Also see if he has Hart's Psychology of Insanity. If so I would like to have it for a short time.

I am getting some wonderfully interesting stuff on "wish fulfillments," and the peculiar trend that religious emotions take in prison. Here in this grim cell house the battle between the old orthodoxy of the church, and the newer philosophy of Sir Oliver Lodge is being waged, and the new is winning. These poor victims of society feel that God takes no concern for them and they are not strong enough to stand alone, so they find comfort for their sick souls in the belief that their dead comrades in misery come back to care for and protect them. In the weary hours after the lights are out the cell house is peopled by many ghosts, but they are all kindly, comfortable, amiable ghosts, who flit about all night on errands of mercy and love. There is one, more interesting than all the rest, more kindly and humane; some day I will write her story.

All in all, I find this prison life much like the world outside, only things are intensified here. I feel that most of the wrongs committed against these helpless creatures are wrongs and crimes of stupidity and ignorance, and not the crimes of brutality or even callousness. I will write more of this next time, as my paper is almost full.

I have been so well supplied that there is little left to wish for. Some one supplied me with a higher chair, and it has added 100% to my comfort at the sewing machine, and 20% to my efficiency. I am still waiting for the knife and fork with the soft metal blades. They are in the very back part of the small drawer of the chiffonier. Don't forget the white petticoats, and I want that soft summer corset of mine; I can't remember where it is, but Dickie can find it. Have Dickie get two dozen large kid curlers for me—a paper of pins and two or three sets of little beauty pins. I need the small round point scissors, and some orangewood manicure sticks. You can get all of these at the ten-cent store, except the scissors.

The grocery people do splendidly in sending me food. They certainly use intelligence. I am gaining in flesh, and will soon be quite plump. Oh yes—I need some wash cloths also, and some cheap paper napkins. You might send me the spoon also if you locate the silver.

Send me some small gummed labels, to stick things up on the steel walls, and two or three rolls of pretty crepe paper. Let Dickie choose it. When you come down bring me a 75-candle power light bulb. Don't worry about the lace collars. I have some that will do. Be sure to send Emma the pamphlets, and a copy of World Peace.

It is almost time for chapel, and I must close now. Love and kisses to all my darlings. Be brave and sweet and don't worry—I will be all right. Perhaps Dickie will come down soon.

Lovingly,
Mamma

Jefferson City, Mo., May 3, 1919

F. P. O'Hare,
1011 Holland Bldg.,
St. Louis.

Dear Sweethearts—

Once again the time has slowly drifted past and I may write my weekly letter. Strange it seems to have the days pass and be denied the right to send a word of love to my darlings. I wonder why there should be such a conspiracy against love, while hate is fostered so carefully! Surely we are a mad lot. But no matter—the powers that be cannot take our past from us. In every previous separation of our seventeen years of companionship every day brought its letters and we can be thankful for the memories of the past and the hope of the future.

This is Saturday, and we have a half day free from the stress and the grind of the shop. It is a beautiful day, and we had three hours out-of-doors—so I am feeling quite pleasantly tired. We have only a bare little yard, shut in by high walls; the beautiful hills and river are shut out from us, but we can see the sky, and bask in the sunshine, and get a breath of air free from lint and dust.

I received Dickie's letter today, the first word that I have had from home since last Sunday. I don't quite know just why the whole week should have passed without a letter. But I have not worried over the

[141]

matter. I knew that papa must be very, very busy, or that he had written something that did not pass the censor. Don't get too busy to write, and don't write anything that will not pass, for I need my daily letter after the weariness of the day.

I had dozens of beautiful letters from comrades all over the country with May Day greetings. I wish I could answer them all, but it is impossible. So I must send my thanks in this.

It was a strange May Day for me. Emma Goldman was ill, but little Ella, the Italian girl, and myself wore our colors. It was all that we could do. Emma gave us a bit of red ribbon, and we wore it above our hearts while we bent to the task at the roaring machines. It was a strange sight—yet how typical of our capitalist system. The dirty, grimy shop, whose windows are so high that no sunbeams can ever fall upon its inmates—[Here follow lines blotted out by the censor.] the weary-eyed women, in ugly, shapeless convict garb, each bending like a galley slave to the task, dumb, silent and hopeless. Yet in two hearts at least there burned the fires of revolt and over two hearts there glowed the tiny knots of red ribbon, the world-wide insignia of human brotherhood. There is enough of the ribbon for two tiny bows; one I want you to keep for me. Some day I shall stand with the comrades of all nations in the New International, and I shall want to wear it in memory of this May Day. The other I want you to send to dear old Gene and tell him to keep it until he steps forth a free man, with it upon the heart that has always been loyal to all that it symbolizes.

I received my box of pickles and jam that came from Mrs. K. and everything was very good. When the aroma from my pickled onions was wafted through the cell house, I was a much worried person. Tell Anna W. that I got the Matzos and the cake and enjoyed both. The cake was delicious. Some other comrades sent Matzos, and Emma Goldman thinks it a great joke that the Irish woman should get Matzos, while she, the Jewess, received deviled ham. Mary sent me a lovely dinner from the hotel next day and I enjoyed it fully. I have plenty to eat, but I get so hungry for something hot. My civilized stomach protests at cold food. That is another of the hardships we endure that is merely the result of carelessness and stupidity. There is much of the food served that would be really good if we could get it hot. But the food is sent over from the kitchen at least an hour and a half before meal time, and sits in the shop until it is absolutely cold. Imagine trying to eat beef stew and liver and onions that have stood in the dust and the lint of the shop for hours. It would take no more time or energy to bring the food at meal time, and serve it hot, and it would mean so much to the women in strength and energy and life. If only the women were better nourished the effects of the driven labor would not be so tragic, and if only intelligence were used in the selection and serving of the food they could be nourished and satisfied, as there is enough spent on the food to feed us all well.

I want all the comrades to know that I appreciate and enjoy the things they send. In the deadly monotony of prison I think we all revert back to childhood, the result I suppose of the complete crushing of individual initiative. Meal time and box time are the bright spots in our day. I got the things that Dick sent, and as usual he chose very well. If I can only get my soft bladed knife I will be quite content for the present.

I think it will be useless for you to send me any scientific or technical books for a time at least. I find that the roar of the machinery dulls my brain, and the constant eyestrain of following the endless miles of flying seams makes study difficult, if not impossible. I understand quite fully now why the workers for the most part have scrambled brains. I think it quite possible that if I were compelled to work in an overall factory for a year I might fall so low in intelligence as to vote the Democratic ticket. The pastime that eases the nerve strain most quickly, and causes the time we are locked in our cells to pass most comfortably, is knitting. So I have reverted back to the habits of my pioneer ancestresses, and find comfort and soothing calm in the soft touch of the yarn, and weave my dreams with the flying needles. I have a beautiful sweater for Kathleen almost finished. I need one skein of yarn like the enclosed label, a rich, pretty crimson in color, to finish it. Let Dick send it to me in the next box.

I got a dandy letter from Victor, but have not heard from Gene or Kathleen this week. Try to make them realize that they must write at least once each week.

I got the pamphlets you sent and gave them to Emma. Tell Zeuch I enjoy his letters and found good use for the magazines. Yes, I can have pictures in my cell, but the walls are so dirty that somehow I can't put really beautiful pictures on them. Frank, when you come down, please bring me a half gallon of very light yellow or cream colored paint, and a brush. You know I am quite an expert painter, and I feel sure that Gov. P. will allow me to paint the walls of my cell. The fly specks of many years provide a striking decorative effect, but somewhat out of harmony with my taste.

Prof. Zeuch asks what he can send me. Tell him that a man so painfully learned in the lore of feminine psychology should be able to choose quite scientifically, and I am going to see how much a man can really learn about women from books.

Prof. Zeuch is curious about my little Italian girl, but I understand fully that his interest is entirely scientific. So many have asked about her that I will tell you what I can. We call her Ella Antolin. In type she is like the little girl who played the Tyrolese in our little play, small, dainty, sweet, and naturally clean and refined. She has had little opportunity for education, but is wonderfully bright and absorbs education like a sponge while the vicious, vulgar things with which she is forced into contact do not seem to touch her at all. She was a member of a radical group of young Italians in an Eastern city, and evidently quite active in its work, which seems to have been largely artistic and educational, but of a radical character. The group fell under the suspicion of the D. J.* Ella started to Chicago to find a better job, and on the way the brave, vigilant sleuths discovered some dynamite in her grip in the usual manner in which sleuths find bombs. She was taken to Chicago, and there for many weeks she stood firm through all the brutalities that could be forced upon her. It chills me with horror to hear her tell in her simple girlish way of these hellish weeks she lived there alone and suppported [sic] only by her sublime courage. But she was game to the last and never betrayed even the names of her comrades. She stood her trial, took her sentence, and is serving her time. Her loyalty, courage, poise and sweet cheerfulness makes me ashamed. If I deserve any credit, she deserves a hundred times more. Some day I can write the story of little Ella, and it will be one that will thrill the girlhood of the coming ages. I wish the Ypsels would adopt her and see that she gets her letters and boxes now and then.

Tell Zeuch that Emma laughed when she read his letter and said that a philosophical anarchist is one who is too cowardly to admit his belief,

*Department of Justice.—*Ed.*

and that she is no coward. I can't enlighten him much, for down here in the dregs of life the only philosophy that endures is the philosophy of human brotherhood. I suppose that Emma Goldman and I are far apart in our creeds, but we do not discuss creeds here. They seem so far outside our world. The Emma Goldman that I know is not the Propagandist. It is Emma Goldman, the tender, cosmic mother, the wise, understanding woman, the faithful sister, the loyal comrade. My memories of Emma Goldman will not be of the fiery agitator, but of Emma the healer of sick souls, the valiant supporter of wavering spirits, and the comforter of broken hearts. Emma don't [sic] believe in Jesus, yet she is one who makes it possible for me to grasp the spirit of Jesus, whether it was ever embodied in human form or not.

I must hurry now and finish, for it is almost time for chapel. I loathe it, but must endure it in order to have the outdoor recreation. It is not that I object to the orthodoxy of the services, but I rebel at the ignorance of the man who is supposed to be the spiritual guide for these poor women. He is so dense and stupid and illiterate. I love and revere the human brotherly message of Jesus, and I revolt when a common, coarse poser makes a Billy Sunday of Jesus, and coarsens and brutalizes his message, and does it in English that sets one's teeth on edge. The girls sing very well and that is some consolation.

The plumbers are at work here now, and the worst feature of which I complained last week is being cared for.

This reminds me of such a good joke on Gov. Painter. We worked together on the Senate Committee investigating the minimum wage question some years ago. He always insisted that if only women would be housemaids in other people's kitchens, the social problem would be solved for working women. I made a list of inmates this morning, and found that two-thirds of his guests were house maids. Several girls are here for killing their babies, every one of whom was a house maid, and in most cases they claim that the employer was the father of the baby.

This is my third Sunday away from my beloved ones, and I am wondering how you are spending the day. Dick and Papa will be at the May Day celebration at the Coliseum, and I will be with you in spirit. I hope the twins will be in from school also, for I know that they will enjoy the thrilling activity. I can imagine Victor being chief cook and bottle washer where the eats are dispensed; Gene who is not fond of hard work, but very fond of the ladies, making himself generally agreeable, and Dick, who must have a streak of the banker in him, looking after the money. Papa will be as busy as a cranberry merchant looking after details and the comfort of the ladies. He is particularly strong on ladies. Tell Rella to please keep him in order for me.

There will be many big meetings all over the country this afternoon, and while I am shut away from my comrades I feel serene and happy knowing that never have the divine fires burned so brightly, and that I am serving, even though my place of service is a prison cell. I know that my loved ones will be cared for, that my comrades will be brave and loyal and true to our cause, that the working class will sweep on to victory. I can content myself to step aside for the time to rest from the turmoil and serve the lowliest, most hopeless and most cursed of the human race. And oh! there is so much to do here, so many sick souls and broken hearts, so many bruised spirits and broken lives, and I can, and do, help. The management here is so afraid that Emma and I will teach our isms. We do not need to do that. We only need to serve these poor souls.

And the time will not be wasted for me. I am learning so much. I know now the difference between Hillel and Jesus, Gorky and Wells, Jack London and Galsworthy. Jesus, Gorky and London lived. The others only read of life. I shall have lived also, lived down in the very dregs of life, and when I come back I will reach men and women because of it.

I must close now. Send a message of cheer to the comrades. Remember me to all our friends. I want my children to be very sweet and thoughtful and loving to papa, so he will not be too lonely for me, and papa must be father and mother both to my darlings until I come back. Love and kisses to all my darlings, and be brave and cheerful.

Lovingly,

Kate

(Note—I have taken up the matter of the hygienic conditions, cold food, painting of the cells and other disagreeable matters affecting the eighty women inmates, and changes are, so I understand, now being made. Separate baths are being put in, arrangements are being made to serve food hot—and I feel sure that the warden and management will correct every unnecessary hardship that the women suffer under, largely though [*sic*] mere inadvertence. So do not refer to these matters in case you write to Comrade Kate. Just write her gossipy, cheerful letters.

—F. P. O'Hare)

ANNA LOUISE STRONG (1885–1970)

Born in Friend, Nebraska, and raised in Ohio, Strong was influenced by the progressive thought of her college-educated mother and her father, a clergyman. She was educated at Oberlin and Bryn Mawr, and at the age of twenty-three earned her doctorate in philosophy at the University of Chicago. After working in several positions in the growing field of child welfare, Strong began her career in journalism by covering Seattle's general strike and writing against American involvement in World War I. Excited by news of the Russian Revolution, she went to Moscow in 1921 and traveled throughout Russia to see firsthand the country's development and struggles. From these experiences came her commitment to interpret Soviet issues to the rest of the world.

In 1925 Strong made her first visit to China, a country that she soon came to love. She continued to write on Soviet subjects, while she began to report on the Chinese Revolution to Western readers. Perhaps her most famous work was her 1946 interview with Mao Tse-tung, who explained his "paper tiger" theory of reactionaries (*Amerasia*, April 1947).

Strong was unaware that her positive coverage of Chinese Communist activities made the Soviets uncomfortable. In February 1949, while in Moscow arranging to travel to China, she was suddenly arrested and taken to the Lubyanka Prison. There the sixty-four-year-old prisoner was held for five days of questioning and then deported to Poland as a spy.

On February 24, 1949, Strong returned to New York and was called to testify before a grand jury about her experiences. In March she accepted $5,000 from the *New York Herald Tribune* to write a series of six articles describing her imprisonment. Two of these articles follow. Although she did not blame Russia for the incident and never intended the articles as an indictment of the Soviet Union, the *Herald Tribune* used the articles for their own purposes and editorialized that Strong's work was "one of the most vivid, the most convincing and the most damning documentations of the processes of the Soviet police state."

The articles led her leftist friends, including Agnes Smedley, to reject her. The entire Moscow incident had devastating effects on Strong's work, which was refused publication in Communist countries. She was finally cleared of charges by a statement from Moscow in 1955.

In 1958 she took up residence in Peking and continued to write until her death in 1970. She was buried in Peking and greatly honored as a friend of the Chinese people.

Note: Biographical information is from Anna Louise Strong, *I Change Worlds* (New York: Garden City Pub., 1937); Tracy B. Strong and Helene Keyssar, *Right in Her Soul: The Life of Anna Louise Strong* (New York: Random House, 1983); David C. Duke, "Spy Scares, Scapegoats, and the Cold War," *South Atlantic Quarterly* 79, no. 3 (Summer 1980): 245–256.

WORKS BY ANNA LOUISE STRONG

Papers, 1885–1970, University of Washington Libraries, Archives and Manuscripts Division, Seattle, Wash.

Cash and Violence in Laos and Viet Nam. New York: Mainstream, 1962.

Children of Revolution; Story of the John Reed Children's Colony on the Volga. Seattle: Pigott, 1925.

China's Millions. New York: Coward-McCann, 1928.

The Chinese Conquer China. Garden City, N.Y.: Doubleday, 1949.

The First Time in History; Two Years of Russia's New Life. Preface by L. Trotsky. New York: Boni & Liveright, 1924.

I Change Worlds; the Remaking of an American. New York: Holt, 1935. Autobiography.

I Saw the New Poland. Boston: Little, Brown, 1946.

"Jailed in Moscow," *New York Herald Tribune,* 27 March–1 April 1949. Series of six articles.

My Native Land. New York: Viking, 1940.

Notes on Mao Tse-tung's Talk with the American Correspondent Anna Louise Strong. Peking: Foreign Languages Press, 1968.

One Fifth of Mankind. New York: Modern Age, 1938.

Peoples of the USSR. New York: Macmillan, 1944.

Red Star in Samarkand. New York: Coward-McCann, 1929.

The Rise of the Chinese People's Communes. Peking: New World Press, 1959.

The Road to the Grey Pamir. Boston: Little, Brown, 1931.

This Soviet World. New York: Holt, 1936.

The Stalin Era. New York: Mainstream, 1956.

Tibetan Interviews. Peking: New World Press, 1959.

When Serfs Stood Up in Tibet; Report. Peking: New World Press, 1960; 2d rev. ed., San Francisco: Red Sun, 1976.

Anna Louise Strong

Jailed in Moscow

From "Jailed in Moscow," 28 and 29 March 1949. Reprinted
by permission of Tracy B. Strong.

First Night in Jail

The jail routine of Lubianka closed around me.

I was put first in a tiny cell with only a table and chair and strip of carpet. Leaning my head against the wall, I tried to doze. It seemed hours. Two women entered, a wardress and a doctor.

"Strip," they said.

The doctor listened to my heart and lungs and I wondered, in panic, if she was deciding how much I could stand. They examined my body very thoroughly all over, asking me to bend and stretch and expose various parts, but they did not touch me themselves except as they fluffed my hair back to see what might be hidden at the roots. Seeing that I was shivering, the doctor gave me some clean prison clothing to wear while they examined mine.

First the shoes, with insoles ripped out and laces removed; then the stockings, every seam of which was felt. These were returned quickly. "To keep your legs warm and off the floor," said the doctor, and my tension relaxed. They're not going to be brutes, not yet anyway, I thought.

Nerves Shoot Up and Down

They went over every seam, every button, but tore nothing but the lining of my thick fur cap. My jerky nerves shot up again. In all the next five days my spirits were shooting up and then way down.

I was dressed again in my own now-investigated clothing, all but my shoelaces, watch and brooch. The doctor looked at me, decided that I wouldn't strangle myself with the laces, and returned them.

"You'll feel more decent with them laced," she said. I laced them, and I did.

They put me in another tiny cell that had a narrow bench in it. Again interminable ages passed.

I asked every one, the doctor, the wardress, every person who stuck his nose inside for a moment, what I was there for. They didn't answer. It wasn't their job to know.

[149]

No Prisoner Sees Another

I had just decided that I could sleep on that narrow bench and had lain down when they came and took me to another room. I noticed another bit of technique. No prisoner must be allowed to see another. They looked around each corner, and if any one was there I had to step back till the corridor was clear. In the elevators I had to step to the rear, and they closed iron shutters between me and the operator, so that nobody might see me by chance as we passed various floors.

I didn't care. I didn't want to see anybody except the person who would tell me why I was there and let me out.

Scared and Dazed

From the first arrest to the end nobody laid hands on me. They pointed and I went. I began to think I must be a docile prisoner. Nobody ever called me docile before. I was scared stiff and dazed.

We went to a small, bleak office where a portly man in uniform sat behind a desk. He had two rows of battle ribbons on his chest. He motioned me to a chair with a smile on his face like the keeper of a hotel.

"I am the administrator," he said. I burst out asking what I was there for, but he said that wasn't his job. So I knew he was a kind of warden.

How Is Your Health?

His next words knocked me silly. "How is your health?" he asked. My health? For hard labor in the woods or for what? I replied as accurately as I could. "I'm sixty-three and not as good as once. I've had a bit of rheumatism, my nerves cut up and my legs are bad on long walks. But I get around the world pretty well."

"What do you eat? Have you any special diet?"

"But I won't be here to eat," I cried. "They'll be letting me go!" Smilingly, persistently he learned that I needed a milk and vegetable diet with very little meat.

"Are there any medicines that you have to take?"

"Only vitamins. I had a good kind in my little bag but they took it."

"What kind of vitamins?" he asked.

"Mixed ones," I replied, "but most B-1. I get awfully nervous without it and I know I'm going to get awfully nervous here."

Got Vitamin C

"And Vitamin C?" he inquired. I said that was all right, too. Vitamin C is "the vitamin" for these north-bound Russians and they gave it to me every day, but the B-1 never came. They said they had ordered it and maybe they had. My own expensive mixed vitamins—nearly $40 worth for an expected two years in China—were never given to me. I suppose folks keep poison in little capsules. But did they think I was going to poison myself? Not me. I was going to live!

As I passed through the halls to my cell I saw a clock showing three in the morning. My own watch was not returned till I got to Poland, so from now on there was only empty time.

Cell

My cell was a long narrow room cut in what must once have been a hotel or office building. An ancient hardwood floor, high walls painted green below and white above, a table, chair, strip of carpet, jug of water and thank heaven, a bed! Not a very good one, but I've slept on worse. Flexible iron bands covered with two thin mattresses, a bit bent and bumpy. Clean sheets and an ancient but warm blanket. Two plump pillows.

All that distinguished the cell from a third-class provincial hotel room in Russia was that the big window facing a narrow court had bars outside, and the heavy door had no inside knob but was locked from outside with a peephole in it, so they could look when they liked. I didn't care who looked. I wasn't going to commit suicide or any other little misdemeanors. I was going to sleep.

They told me to tap lightly under the peephole if I had any needs in the night. I tapped often, for the nervous strain put my insides out of order.

Found Washroom Clean

Usually they replied quickly; a man who opened my door and a woman who opened the door to the washroom. Quite decent. Once I had to wait ten minutes; I found they had been cleaning the washroom. That place was really clean, much cleaner than in any Russian provincial hotel.

The bright light in the ceiling bothered me, glaring down in my face. Of course, I thought, they have to be able to see me, and if I can't control the switch I'd rather have it light than always dark. I drew a handkerchief over my face and slept fitfully. Despite my exhaustion the question "Why?" kept racing through my brain. I thought back over my life, years and years, all possible mistakes and errors.

Was it the time I said: "Let the first atom bomb fall on that Press Department. I won't mind then if the second hit me." But every one knew I had a temper. They wouldn't take that seriously. But what if they had?

Sins

All night between snatches of sleep I faced my sins. They all seemed petty, not up to Lubianka standard. "It's crazy," I decided. "They'll find it out in the morning. Maybe in time for me to see that Chinese delegate and get to Manchuria yet." My spirit rose high, jesting: "I bet they just want me to write up their model jail. I'll give it a recommendation. Politest jailers I ever had."

But underneath was the sickening knowledge that you couldn't land in Lubianka without some serious charge. I did not know that already the cables carried the news to the world that I was a "spy."

The Commissar

The gray light came and I knew it was morning. The first, second or third morning? No, I had not yet eaten: it must be the first. It seemed another epoch.

That polite doctor came and asked how I had slept. "Not well," I replied. "The light bothered me."

[152]

"You can have it turned off in the daytime when it is light enough for us to see without it," she offered. So I had it off most of the daytimes, which in this inside room were a dull twilight, suitable for sleeping. So day became my night and night my day.

Breakfast

A woman brought my breakfast, a terrific amount of rice-milk soup, sour milk, half a loaf of bread and a glass of the coffee I had asked for. Weak, of course, nothing to keep you up; the Russians make it with only a teaspoon a cup. I asked for a second glass and got it. I ate part of the rice and milk, but left everything else. The returning waitress seemed pained that I ate so little. "Don't you feel well?" she asked.

"How could I?" I was irritated by these futile attentions. I wanted to come to grips with the man who would tell me why.

Morning passed and lunch. . . . By this time the other correspondents must know the American Embassy must be getting ready to protest. I didn't think it would get them much. Maybe my letter to Molotov would have more luck. I had written him—was it just yesterday afternoon or a century ago?—telling my troubles with that press department and the reasons why I had to go to China. Surely Molotov would know that it was silly to jail me. Maybe? Maybe not?

Jailer Comes at Last

Late in the day a brisk jailer came and said: "The commissar wants you." At last!

We went through a maze of passages, up one elevator, down another, up a third, to what seemed another building. It was the wing where the investigators worked. We went through a string of three offices, with uniformed underlings in each. The last office was bigger, with a large desk, a divan and a long table covered with green felt. I was directed to a seat at one end of the table. At the far end sat the man they called the commissar. At the side of the table between us was a man who seemed a secretary, taking down what occurred.

"What am I supposed to have done?" I demanded. The commissar quelled me with a glance. "I'm asking the questions," he said.

He began with "a bit of protocol," he called it. My name, birthplace, when I first came to the U.S.S.R. It was clear he had never heard of me, except as some one arrested. I had thought I was fairly well known in the U.S.S.R.: My last book on China had sold 300,000 copies. But this man stumbled over my name.

He was a man specialized to the job of getting rid of criminals. I was to him just one more.

How many times in the U.S.S.R.? Over what frontiers? As the bare facts went down—first time 1921, then very often, in all parts of the country, less often since 1937 because more often in China, last arrived October, 1948, with side trip to Budapest in December to a women's congress—I saw them through the eyes of a professional criminal catcher. Why should any American go back and forth to the U.S.S.R. except for subversive reasons? He had no concept of the life of a journalist.

Her Words Froze

I wanted to cry: "But I loved your country! I wanted to write, to explain it to the world!" The words froze. He wouldn't permit them, nor would he understand them. He looked at me, having just learned how to spell my name, as something to be blotted out.

After the "protocol" he rose sternly and pronounced judgment. Some eight thundering words of which I got only the last. "For spying activities."

He was miffed because I was inquiring instead of crushed. "Didn't you understand?"

"I understood that you said I was spying but I wasn't. I didn't understand the rest."

Chucked Out

He repeated the thunder, but I only got one word more: "frontier." He was using some words of law or of denunciation outside ordinary talk. Finally I gathered that I must leave the country, but not in ordinary style. I must be "chucked out" in some disgraceful terrible way. I was not quite sure how.

"We will allow you within reason to choose what country you will be put into . . . You know geography. Choose!"

"I suppose I couldn't choose Manchuria," I faltered.

"That is excluded," he said.

"Then put me on a boat for London."

"A boat? A boat is not a frontier. We cannot put you in the water; we must put you on dry land." This puzzled me till I understood that my passage of the frontier must be secret; there are people on boats.

"It doesn't matter," I said. "Poland or Czechoslovakia."

New Spy Route

It puzzled and annoyed him. It was out of pattern. Probably he was checking the route by which spies travel. Doubtless it is Finland, a country rather anti-Soviet. My choice set him wondering whether in those tried and true pro-Soviet countries, there was a new spy route!

But I was still thinking in the past, that I had friends in those countries. I even knew their presidents. I had book contracts there and local money to help on my passage home. I could not yet grasp that I would contaminate all friends and that contracts would explode in air.

I tried once more to protest that I wasn't a spy and to ask just what was my spying. He said: "Dismissed" very curtly and I went. About midnight he sent for me again.

He had lists of the things to my room. "State at once what clothes you wish to take, and to whom you give the rest. Dispose of your furniture and Soviet money, too. Your American dollars, $613, will be returned to you at the frontier."

Asked for Typewriter

"But you haven't yet explained my crime or heard any defense," I cried. He stopped me. I began to make his list. We bogged down because I couldn't understand the list those men had made of my clothes. "Bring my little typewriter and I'll list what I need and leave the rest," I said. The secretary supported me with, "It will be quicker so."

He dismissed me. I collapsed on my bed, as if torn asunder. Here was a country that for thirty years I had interpreted in a friendly way. Yet an official representing this country, probably patriotic and thinking he was doing his duty, had been looking at me as if he wanted to wipe me from the face of the earth. I was evil to him, to be destroyed.

The Worst

My spirits bumped downhill to the very bottom. Recalling his look, those half-understood words about "chucking me" over the frontier, a horrible picture came. They would take me in a prison car, so that nobody should see me, and dump me not at a station but at the real frontier between two sentries and I had not even a Polish visa. I recalled all those refugees who got stuck between two boundaries and died of starvation. "You know geography," the words seemed sinister. No wonder he was surprised when I chose, in February, the snowy Polish plain!

That night, as in a nightmare, I prayed that I might freeze comfortably to death in snow or die of exhaustion, running, before wolves attacked me. This was of course only fantasy but it came from the real hate and wish-to-destroy that I saw in that man's face. And all the time I knew that he was a patriot stamping out the "enemy." The effect on me of that night has not yet passed.

JOAN HENRY (1914–)

Joan Henry was born in London of a "rather illustrious," though not wealthy family. She writes that she had the "usual over protected childhood and adolescence of that period," but was "shattered" by her twin sister's death at the age of twenty-one.

In 1938 she married an army officer and they had one daughter. That marriage ended during the war and she remarried in 1957.

Her first book, *Women in Prison*, was based on her own prison experiences. The title of its first, British edition was *Who Lie in Gaol*, from a line in Oscar Wilde's "Ballad of Reading Gaol." It was widely publicized and, according to Henry, it helped to effect gradual changes in women's prisons in England. The book was the basis of a 1954 film, "The Weak and the Wicked," starring Glynis Johns. Henry's second prison book, *Yield to the Night*, is a novel about a woman condemned

to death. She worked on the screenplay for the 1957 film that starred
Diana Dors and was released in Britain as *Yield to the Night* and in the
United States as *Blonde Sinner*. Henry also wrote plays for television
and theater.

The selection from *Women in Prison* recalls a year's imprisonment
in England's Holloway and Askham Grange prisons, portraying a naive
inmate adjusting to the jargon, inhabitants, and inflexible routine of a
different world.

Note: Biographical information is from Henry's letter to Judith Scheffler, 21 October
1982.

WORKS BY JOAN HENRY

Commit to Memory. A Novel. London: Cassell, 1948.
Crimson Lake. London: Cassell, 1950.
This Many Summers. London: Cassell, 1947. A novel.
Women in Prison. New York: Doubleday, 1952.
Yield to the Night. London: Gollancz, 1954. A novel.

At Holloway Prison

From *Women in Prison*. Reprinted by permission
of Joan Henry.

In a few minutes I was back in the cell.* I found a single sheet of lined
paper with "H. M. Prison" on the top and a few words telling the
recipient to quote my name and number when replying. I wondered
how I obtained a pen and ink. In a little while the cell door was unlocked
and I was given to understand that it was lunch time; it involved a
similar procedure as at breakfast. This time it was stew in a tin bowl;
mostly soup with a few pieces of meat and a lot of potato, more bread,
and a slab of pudding. I supposed that in a few days I would be hungry,
but at the moment I could only swallow a few mouthfuls. I washed up
the plates and lay down on the bed and tried to think what I would say
in my letter when I eventually got a pen, and to calculate how long it
would be before I received an answer.

*This excerpt begins on the second day of her imprisonment in Holloway Prison.
—Ed.

Time passed by. The cell doors were unlocked, and the pail emptying took place again. Then I was told to pack up my things, which did not take long, as I was moving.

I followed an officer along the passages and through a door. Everything looked just the same, only slightly smaller. I was taken upstairs to the first floor, to the far end. The cell was a bit smaller than my previous one, and the bed was even lower on the ground. The cell was warmer, though, as hot pipes ran through the back of it. I had been given a pen and ink, and when the door was locked once more I sat down to write my letter. There was so much I wanted to say, but so little space on which to say it. I discovered afterward that the fortnightly letter permitted by the regulations consisted of a double sheet, but any special letters—for which you had to book for the governor and which were granted only in cases of necessity—consisted, like the reception letter, of just one sheet. All correspondence was subject to the strictest censorship, and you never received a letter in its envelope.

In the next-door cell a woman began to scream.

"I shall soon get used to it," I wrote. "Naturally everything is very strange at first . . ."

The screams continued, and I heard the next-door cell being unlocked. After a while there was silence.

". . . very strange indeed. You will be able to come and see me in a month from now. . . ."

I made up my bed. The mattress seemed worse than the other one. I heard the other women being let out to go to work. I wished I could go too. Anything would be better than just sitting here.

The hours passed by, and then I heard,

"Exercise! EXERCISE!" The door opened, and I was told to go downstairs. I gave the officer my letter.

The women were lining up in twos on the ground floor. I imagined they were mostly "new girls," like myself. All had red ties. I noticed the girl with the swept-up coiffure, and two very old ladies with white hair, who were standing talking together. I learned later that both were abortionists. They had cells next door to one another and seldom spoke to any of the other prisoners. They were known as "Arsenic" and "Old Lace." Arsenic had a very long, thin nose with a permanent drop on the end of it, and Old Lace had a large, coarse face strangely out of proportion to her narrow, stooping body. She always wore her gray cardigan thrown carelessly over her shoulders in the manner of one accustomed to a sable stole. She was constantly being reprimanded for this. Both of them appeared to have an endless supply of small, gilt safety pins with which they pinned their ties. These were articles much sought after by the other women and sometimes bequeathed to the specially favored by outgoing prisoners. You were not allowed to have such things sent in, and it remained a mystery to me how Arsenic and Old Lace came by their store.

I walked round with a young Indian girl. She was a friendly, naughty little thing with beautiful white teeth in her thin brown face and the large, dark, mournful eyes of her race. Her name was Marie. She had been sentenced to eighteen months.

As we walked round the exercise ground in the cold wind she told me that she was the mother of a baby of six months.

Three officers stood at different points around us.

"Those are the workrooms," said Marie, pointing to a large building ahead of us where a lot of other women were emerging to join us. "I'm going to be a cleaner."

"Will you like that?"

She shrugged her lean shoulders. "Not bad . . . and sometimes you can pick up things . . . I've got a friend in the hospital, she's got T.B. . . . lucky dog . . . Maybe I'll think of some way of going sick myself." Her black eyes twinkled. "It depends which doctor you see . . . One of them is a bit soft."

A woman behind us moved up to say something to Marie.

"In TWOS . . ." yelled one of the officers.

"F . . . . . g mare," said the woman in a loud voice. "Wots it to 'er if we go on all fours like the animals we are now . . . Who she think she is . . . Queen Mary?"

I giggled for the first time since my entry into prison. Arsenic and Old Lace sailed by us, smiling ingratiatingly at the wardress nearest to us.

"Smarmy bitches," growled our friend behind. "Sucking up to them screws . . . Abortion ain't no better than murder in my opinion . . . Respectable women didn't ought to speak to them. . . . I don't know wot my ole man would say at the kind of people I 'ave to mix with here . . .

I didn't ought to be among 'em in the first place . . . just for receiving a couple of blankets.''

Marie began to walk very fast, and I had almost to run to catch up with her.

"The girl with her killed her baby," she said. "But I don't suppose the old witch knows it . . . It doesn't do to talk about people's crimes here . . . Half the time you don't know what they're in for.''

"I suppose not." I felt rather sick.

"What time do we get shut up for the night?" I asked Marie.

"Four o'clock, when we have tea. Fill your pail when you get back to the cell. There's only one hot tap for the whole of this wing. It's hardly worth queuing for that, and you haven't any fags or sweets to bribe someone to get it for you, have you? Ask Miss Mack—she's quite decent—if you can have a couple of books from the library. You *may* get them, though they aren't due till next week. If not, I'll lend you one tomorrow, but don't lose it . . . You can lose remission for that. . . .''

"Thank you very much." It seemed hardly worth the responsibility.

There seemed no opportunity to ask for library books, and I did not know which officer was Miss Mack. I filled my pail as advised and stood in the doorway of my cell waiting for tea. Presently the familiar procession appeared. Warm hay-water, and bread and margarine.

As the cell door closed behind me, I remembered that it was only 4.00 in the afternoon. My door would not be reopened, except for me to be handed a mug of cocoa, until 6.45 the following morning.

Tomorrow would be Sunday. At home I would lie in bed late reading the morning papers. I would see . . . No, NO, had I not resolved to think of nothing that would remind me of the life I had lost? This was to be my existence for eight months . . . until October ninth . . . It had already been worked out on my card, and all I could do was put up with it.

"Thank you." I took the mug of tea and the great slices of bread. I had discovered a bucket on the landing where you could throw unused food.

I drank a little of the tea and ate half a slice of bread and margarine. I rinsed the mug and put the things tidily together. I washed my handkerchief and hung it over the hot pipe to dry. I wondered if I would be given anything to keep my cell clean with. I must ask about it tomorrow.

Tomorrow seemed about a month away. I lay down on the bed. I might just as well undress and get under the bedclothes. There was nothing to stay up for.

I remembered that the previous evening, very shortly after they had been round with cocoa, I heard a voice shouting what I took to be "Teas . . . Teas . . ." It had seemed odd, so soon after cocoa, but I decided that tonight I would refuse the cocoa and have another cup of warm hay-water—anything was preferable to that bitter-tasting stuff.

I lay on my back staring at the ceiling. I thought, This is no dream, this is happening. Even if you sleep, you will wake up and find yourself enclosed in these four walls, and there is nothing in the world you can do about it . . . So what? Nothing is here for tears; self-pity is the least comforting of emotions; it can only lead you back by a road littered with bogus philosophies under a pall of sentimentality to yourself. Maybe there are the lucky ones who can pray . . . yet God has always seemed nearer to me in happiness and sunshine than He has in despair. . . . I closed my eyes. . . . "Our Father which art in heaven, Hallowed be thy name. Thy kingdom come. Thy will be done in earth, as it is in heaven. Give us this day our daily bread. And forgive us our trespasses, as we forgive them that trespass against us . . . but deliver us from evil . . . Amen." . . .

In years to come I knew I would be able to look back and my own tragedy would seem a little comic. I must look so funny in my enormous white nightgown, with my hair tied back with a bit of string, and all of us in blue cotton dresses and ties, like overgrown Girl Guides or Damon Runyon's broken-down Dolls. . . .

At that moment, to my surprise, I heard the sounds of a piano, very badly played, coming from downstairs and raucous voices singing, "Is it true what they say about Dixie?" I learned later that these came from the "Brownies," or young prisoners under twenty-one, and so-called because they wore brown dresses in contrast to our blue ones. They gave more trouble—most of them were ex-Borstal girls—than all the rest of the prison put together, but they were allowed out a bit later than the rest of the women. Strumming on an ancient piano was their favorite form of recreation and a constant source of irritation to the older prisoners.

However, I was amazed at hearing a piano at the moment.

" 'There's just one place for me, near Y-E-U. It's like heaven to be, near Y-E-U . . .' " screamed the girls.

" 'Times when we're apart, I just can't face my heart . . . never stray more than just teu lips away. . . .' "

I shall never hear this tune without thinking of Holloway, for "Near You" haunted my prison days: it seemed to be on everybody's lips, though I had never heard it outside.

After some time the noise—I can hardly call it anything else—ceased and I heard the jangle of keys. I imagined the songsters were being locked up for the night.

Soon came the cry of "Cocoa." I refused it when it came to my cell. I was reserving my strength for a cup of tea.

"Teas . . . Teas . . ." Ah. I rose and went to my cell door. I had not long to wait. I held out my mug with an expectant air . . . A sanitary towel was pushed at me through the door, and I was once more alone. . . .

Light dawned slowly and painfully. "S.T.s" was the cry.

No tea, no cocoa for 6425: she sat down on the bed, a forlorn figure. I could not swear to it, but I think two large tears gathered and fell on the white pad in her hand.

This is a story still enjoyed by the inmates of Holloway, but to me it was one of the most frustrating moments of all time. So in all circumstances is tragedy intermingled with comedy.

JOYCE SIKAKANE (1943–)

Raised in the Orlando district of Soweto, South Africa, Joyce Nomafa Sikakane traces her family's involvement with the African National Congress to her grandfather's activist work as a Lutheran minister. Sikakane was in primary school when the apartheid regime instituted separate Bantu education. She was later sent to a boarding school, where she joined the African Student Association. At the age of sixteen, she was fingerprinted, photographed, and issued a passbook as part of the apartheid system of controlling Africans.

After completing high school, Sikakane worked for two and a half years as a journalist for the Johannesburg *World*, which did not allow her to write stories critical of the government's practices. Her passbook listed her position as file clerk rather than reporter because skilled positions were closed to Africans. In 1966 she became pregnant, but, discouraged from marrying because of the difficulties in finding housing under apartheid, she raised her son alone and lived with her mother.

Sikakane became the first black woman employed by the *Rand Daily Mail*, a liberal newspaper with many African readers, after she quit her job with the *World* because she objected to reporting sensational crime stories. Her new position allowed her to report stories about the effects of apartheid oppression. Though she was employed initially as a free-lance reporter, her work was so well received that the *Mail* offered her permanent status.

In the selection below, from *A Window on Soweto*, Sikakane describes her 1969 arrest and detention under the Terrorism Act for alleged activities with the banned African National Congress. Acquitted at her first trial, she was immediately rearrested, re-tried in June 1970, and finally released in September 1970, after seventeen months in detention. She was unable to find stable employment because banning orders prevented her return to journalism.

Threatened with further government repression, Sikakane escaped from South Africa in 1973. She was reunited with Kenneth Rankin, a Scottish physician she had been engaged to marry in South Africa. They married and moved to Britain, with hopes of someday returning to Africa.

Note: Biographical information is from *South Africa: Trial by Torture—The Case of the 22* (London: International Defence and Aid Fund, 1970); Joyce Sikakane, *A Window on Soweto* (London: International Defence and Aid Fund, 1977).

WORK BY JOYCE SIKAKANE

A Window on Soweto. London: International Defence and Aid Fund, 1977.

Detention

From *A Window on Soweto*. Reprinted by permission of the
International Defence and Aid Fund for Southern Africa.

I was detained on May 12, 1969 at about 2 a.m. We heard knocking and woke to the flashing of torches outside and shouts of "Police! Police! Open the door!" We all got up—my mother, myself and my two brothers —and the police came in. There were three white policemen, one white policewoman and an African policeman, all in plain clothes.

They demanded Joyce Sikakane and I said it was myself and they produced a warrant of arrest under Section 6 of the Terrorism Act. They said they wanted to search the house. They were all brandishing their guns about and so they searched the house and took away whatever documents and personal papers—all my letters for example—they wished. The policewoman was guarding me the whole time.

After about two hours they told me to get dressed, as I was still in my nightie; I did so and was escorted to the car. I was afraid to wake Nkosinathi who was still sleeping, so I left him without saying goodbye.

On the way out of Soweto the car dropped off the African policeman in Meadowlands. I remember him saying "Thank you my baas, you caught the terrorist. I hope you get the information you want out of her."

We drove off to John Vorster Square (Security Police HQ) where another policeman got out, and then on again. When I asked where we were going, the only reply was that I was being detained under the Terrorism Act. I was terrified: I didn't see myself as a terrorist and didn't know why I should be detained under the Terrorism Act.

I was taken to Pretoria Central Prison. They knocked on the big door, the guard looked out and then opened the gate and I was led in. First we went to the office; they spoke to the matron and papers were signed. My engagement ring was taken from me—I was upset about that. Then we crossed the prison yard to another part of the prison. In the yard were about a hundred African women, some with babies on their backs, some sitting on the ground, some with vegetable baskets full of onions, pumpkins and so on, whom I could see were vendors who had been arrested for illegally selling vegetables in the street. As I came into the yard, the policeman shouted to the women to shut their eyes. This was because I was a Terrorism Act detainee, to be held incommunicado, which meant no-one should know who or where I was. I was taken past and up some stairs, where the two policemen escorting me greeted another man as Colonel Aucamp.

He told the matron to take me to a cell. And I heard her ask, "Is she a condemned woman?" as I was shown into a cell with a bright blinding light that made me see sparks.

Aucamp immediately said "No, no, not that one, I made a mistake." So I was taken out and led along to the common shower room, where there were lots of women prisoners, some naked under the showers, some undressing, some waiting their turn. The matron told me to undress, which I did, and got under the cold shower. I could tell the other women knew there was something special about me, being under escort and alone and jumping the queue like that.

After the cold shower I picked up my paper bag of clothes—the matron told me not to dress—and I was led to a cell. It was narrow and high, situated in what I later discovered was the isolation wing. The outer steel door was opened and then the inner barred door; I went in and the matron locked first one and then the other.

So there I was, in this tall narrow empty cell, gazing around. There was a small high hole covered with mesh, for ventilation. And it was very cold: May is the beginning of winter in South Africa and we had already had some frost. Suddenly I heard women's voices coming from outside in the yard, talking. I was horrified to hear them talking about their love affairs inside the prison—the experienced women telling the freshers what to expect, how some were chosen as husbands and some as wives, and generally describing the whole scene to them. It gave me a real fright, standing there naked. I at once got my paper bag and put my panties on!

When I looked around at the contents of the cell all I saw was a damp sisal mat, rolled up, and three grey blankets, also damp and smelling of urine. That was all. I just sat down on the mat and waited.

It wasn't until 7 o'clock that evening that the cell door opened. There was a white wardress and an African woman prisoner in prison uniform, who shoved a plate of food through the door, along the floor, together with a galvanised bucket. All the time the wardress stood between me and the prisoner, so I should not be seen. Then they left, locking the doors behind them. But I heard them open the next cell and then I knew I wasn't alone: if the next cell was occupied I wasn't the only woman detainee.

From then on the pattern of prison life was always the same. In the morning at about 7 a.m. the cell door was opened, the shit bucket and empty plate taken out and a plate of porridge and cup of coffee put in. There was a bucket of sometimes warm water too, to wash oneself and one's underclothes. Lunch was usually about noon, though it could be earlier—on Sundays it was about 10.30—and consisted of izinkobe or dry mealies—corn kernels—which had been boiled but were still dry and hard. There was a beverage too, some sort of drink, which the prisoners used to call puza'mandla—drink power! Then at about 2 p.m. came supper, which was soft maize porridge with one or two pieces of meat, possibly pork, in it. That was all until the next day.

For the first few days I didn't eat anything. I was frightened, angry, depressed, wondering why I had been detained, scared of what might happen, and crying most of the time. By the third day, I had cried all my tears out. At least, I think it was the third day. Two huge policemen, with layers and layers of chin, came for me. I asked where they were taking me and they said, to give an account of your sins.

I was driven in a big Cadillac, with a policeman on either side of me and two more in front. We went to the Compol building (police HQ) in Pretoria. Knock, knock again, the police escort identify themselves and we drive in.

Down some corridors to an office. It looks like any other office except it has these wooden partitions. Right facing me is a stone sink and then there's a desk and a few chairs. I can see it's a work room. All along the walls is this wooden partitioning, covering the windows but capable of being drawn back. It kind of encloses the room, insulates it from outside. And just off this room is a sort of gym closet with punch bags —and a huge African policeman with fierce red eyes standing there. While I was being interrogated policemen kept trooping in to practice boxing on the punch bags.

Joyce Sikakane

Interrogation

There was a constant stream of policemen, about fifteen or twenty, coming into the room, as if they were going on stage. They were brandishing guns, holding documents, smoking cigarettes, greeting me, some scowling at me. They all looked different, some like bulldogs, some like Alsatians, some like timid cats. Some of them behaved with great politeness, like perfect gentlemen. I think this performance was just put on to confuse me, for the next thing was Major Swanepoel coming in. He is the most sadistic and most feared of all the police interrogators; several people have died as a result of his "questioning."

"Have you heard of Major Swanepoel?" he said. "I am Major Swanepoel." All the other policemen gave way to him, treating him very deferentially. Then interrogation began.

They fired questions and statements at me; all of a sudden they were all talking about me and my personal life—all my experiences, which they seem to know better than I did! As they did so they incidentally revealed the extent of their informer network: I found they knew about all sorts of incidents in my career—the story about the Malawian air hostesses being allowed to stay in an all-white hotel, for instance, that I had been working on when I was detained. I also discovered, from things they said, who else had been questioned: Winnie Mandela, wife of ANC leader Nelson Mandela, and Rita Ndzanga, for instance. They had interrogated many other people I knew, and from what they knew I could see they had been tortured to extract the information.

From me they wanted confirmation: that certain things had been done, that I had knowingly participated, and whatever else I could add. From what they know one has to judge what to admit and what to hide and what one might not manage to hide—because it flashes into your mind what risk to others is involved, and also the possibility of being tortured yourself and whether the type of information you have is worth dying for. I knew that in our case what we had been doing was something that would not, in any other country, be considered "terroristic": we were involved with the welfare of political prisoners, helping to make arrangements for families of prisoners to visit their husbands or parents. And so why not admit it? Yes, I did that—so what? We hadn't been involved in anything connected with violence or arms—that would have called for other methods of interrogation. As far as I was concerned they were more interested in getting information about the underground communication network.

The interrogation lasted right through until the following day. They took turns, and took breaks. I was just standing there. I would be tired, I would squat down, I would jump about a bit. I was shown the bricks —the torture bricks on which the men detainees are made to stand. The questioning went on, without food, without anything, till the following morning. Then I was taken back to my cell.

It was about ten days before I was taken again for interrogation. This time it lasted for three whole days because this time they were concerned with taking a statement. Under the Terrorism Act a detainee may be held until a statement to the satisfaction of the Commissioner of Police has been given, and the purpose of the interrogation is to obtain such a statement which can then be used against you or someone else. They still ask questions: anything you admit goes down on the statement.

This time my interrogation took place on the third floor of Compol building, and the interrogators were Major Botha and Major Coetzee. They were trained and experienced political officers. Oh, they were courteous gentlemen, but I could sense hatred—they hated every bit of me. But they had to get what they wanted from me.

They put the proposal that I should be a state witness, giving evidence for the state against the others. I asked why should I do that? and they said, well, you're young, you're an intelligent girl, you have a fiancé outside the country. If you are afraid to give evidence because of what your organisation will do to you, we can always give you another name and find a job in one of our embassies abroad—say in Malawi or London, where you can join your fiancé!

All the time, because of what they wanted out of me, they were at pains to explain that they were not against Africans or black people in general. They were only against communists. They argued that people like myself, young, intelligent, pretty, etc., were being misled by communists. They, on the other hand, were offering me a chance. I found this insulting. How could they sit there, admit that apartheid was a repressive system, which they did while maintaining that racism occurred all over the world. What hypocrites I said inside me to say communists had misled me into wanting to change the system. I didn't need any communists to tell me apartheid is evil. I know. Nor would I join the enemy camp for the sake of self preservation.

So I told Major Botha and Major Coetzee I was not interested in their offer. They said in that case you are going to be here a long time. Others had given evidence, they said. If you refuse we have lots of other evidence we can use, the others are willing.

In the end they took a statement. Under the law it's supposed to be made of one's own volition—but I wondered how, under the circumstances of indefinite detention under the Terrorism Act, anything can be called of one's own volition. I came to the point when I agreed to some of the things they said—well, if you say that, yes, it's so.

After they had taken the statement Major Coetzee said "Well, Joyce, we think you should think seriously about our offer. We will transfer you to another prison, so you can think over the offer." Then they repeated their offer of a job in London. I didn't bother to reply yes or no, I just kept silent. And I was taken back to my cell.

In Nylstroom Prison

About a week later I was transferred to Nylstroom prison. I didn't know the exact date, not having a watch or calendar. Being taken to Nylstroom had some irony, in that one of my "offences," one of the things I had done which led to my being detained, was that at one time I had been part of a group of women who had been to visit prisoners at Nylstroom. It is a women's prison in the Transvaal, north of Johannesburg, and there were political prisoners there from the Cape, who had not heard from or about their families for years. A letter enquiring about their families had been smuggled out by one woman and when it reached us we decided to go as a group to visit the women in Nylstroom. And now I was going to be an inmate of Nylstroom Prison.

In Nylstroom, although still a detainee, I was given a bed with a mattress. There can be proper facilities if they wish it. The bed was part of the better conditions promised me if I would consider giving evidence, and in fact the sheets were even starched. You can imagine how I felt sleeping in starched sheets! I itched all over. The food was the same, just a few spoonfuls more perhaps. But the cell was bigger than at Pretoria, and a different shape. This one was squarer, wider with a lower ceiling, unlike the high narrow Pretoria one. And there was a window through which I could see out and altogether there wasn't the terrible confined and depressed feeling as in Pretoria. And there was a table and a chair!

The matron used to bring me books to read, all crime stories and thrillers which gave me terrible nightmares. One day I complained that I couldn't read the books, so she brought another collection, amongst which was one by (I think) J. M. Miller, an author who wrote about the Resistance movement against the Nazis in Europe, and this book was about the escape route over the Pyrenees, and how the Resistance functioned. I had my suspicions that the book had been put there to encourage me to try to escape—only to be found hanging from a window, or perhaps shot—but anyway it certainly boosted my spirit of resistance too. I did not intend to risk an escape bid, nor to commit suicide—although there were many times, particularly at night, when I was so lonely and depressed I felt anything would be better than this. I had a game to play at such times, a "blindman" game when I shut my eyes and pretended I was blind—not able to see the walls, the bars and the rest.

At Nylstroom, instead of proper exercise, the matron used to take me to an isolated yard where I could sit or jump around—all alone. I just used to sit there for about 30 minutes. I was so depressed, I didn't feel like jumping around. I felt I had no strength. So I just used to sit or lie on the ground, watching the red ants going in and out of their holes. I watched them carrying their food and corpses of dead insects, and I used to count them. It was a beautiful game, counting ants. I had been too long in solitary confinement.

Every so often, the Special Branch officers used to come and ask "Have you thought it over? Will you agree?" and I used to answer "When are you releasing me? When are you charging me? I want to go back home." About every ten to fourteen days they came and said the same thing. I replied as I did before. It was after a long, long time when on the last of these calls, they came and said "Well, we have come to take you."

I said, "Where are you taking me?" "We are taking you home."

Of course I was taken back to Pretoria Central, to the same cell I had occupied before. But there was one remarkable change: on the wall was now written the name Shanthie Naidoo. Shanthie was my friend and now I knew she had been detained too.

That same afternoon the cells were opened, first mine, and then four others, and we were taken out. I'll never forget the feelings of that moment, a kind of muted consternation, when we five women all saw each other. There was Winnie Mandela, Rita Ndzanga, Martha Dhlamini, Thokozile Mngoma—and of course we each half expected, as our interrogators had said, that the others had agreed to give evidence. But they hadn't. I remember we hugged each other hard: it was too good to be true. We felt this was a moment of victory and we were together. Shanthie was not there: they were playing the same game with her as they had with me, trying to make her agree to give evidence against us.

We were then led to the office where security police were waiting, and there was no doubt about their hostility. We were, they said, to appear in court tomorrow, and we would be charged (though we were not told what the charges were). Then we were taken back to the cells. We asked to be allowed to stay together but this was refused, and we did not see each other again until we were taken to court. But that night we were singing freedom songs—singing our lungs out, each in our separate cell.

The next day we were taken to court, where we met the men who were being charged with us. Again there was this muted feeling of consternation: what the police had said and what we now realised was true. Now it was a question of seeing how everyone was, who had sold out and who was still battling. There were some of the people who weren't there; we guessed from this that they had agreed to give evidence, but because of what we had been through we didn't feel like saying anything against them. It was just too bad—bad luck.

In court there was real jubilation—hugs and kisses and clenched fists. Our relatives were also there in the public gallery when we came into court, and we learned that they had instructed a lawyer to defend us. We were charged under the Suppression of Communism Act. It was 1 December—seven months since I had been arrested. There were 22 of us altogether, five women and 17 men. Among them Lawrence and Rita Ndzanga, both trade unionists. During the 1960's Lawrence was national secretary of the Railway and Harbour Workers Union, and until its banning an executive member of the South African Congress of Trade

Unions (SACTU). Rita was secretary of the Toy Workers Union. The apartheid regime embarked on the full-scale repression of the progressive labour movement and in 1963 both Lawrence and Rita were banned, which means being subject to restriction orders, not allowed to continue working or travel outside one's home district. Both had been detained at the same time as myself, and brutally assaulted by the security police. Another of the accused was Peter Magubane, my news photographer colleague with the *Rand Daily Mail.* ...

On Trial

As it turned out, the trial rebounded on the government, because instead of the evidence being to the liking of the state, it exposed the state's methods of getting evidence and demonstrated the bravery and resistance of the men and women on trial. There was good coverage in the white press and also internationally, and there was an observer from the International Commission of Jurists. The quality of the evidence made fools of the Special Branch and their accusations, it made fools of the whole Terrorism Act and all the conspiracy laws of South Africa because, as our lawyer pointed out, some of the acts alleged had taken place when one of the accused was still a toddler, so how could he be held responsible by association?

And because the evidence was so ridiculous and the publicity so bad, the state decided to abandon the case, to withdraw the charges. This was 16 February 1970. We could not believe it when we heard the judge say "You are acquitted!" We began to leave the court in single file, between two rows of police, to go and meet our relatives, who were already singing and celebrating. The police refused to let us out and instead took us to a room, where Captain Dekker announced that he was detaining us again. There was a great protest: I remember shouting and I threw a fist at him, but I'm not sure if it landed. The police confiscated everything we had, including all our legal documents, and we were whisked off under guard, back to Pretoria Central.

It all happened so quickly that we hadn't had time to get used to the idea of being free. Nor had we really believed in the acquittal—it just couldn't be true. In any case we had been told so many times during interrogation that we were going to spend 15 years in jail if we were lucky, more if we were not, and we had come to accept imprisonment. So we weren't surprised to be taken back to detention.

But it was just as bad. I went back to the same cell, and there I stayed for the next four months.

This time there was no exercise, or only very occasionally. There were constant battles between us and the matron and the other officers because we kept demanding to be released, as the court had released us. A magistrate came fortnightly to hear our complaints, as a matter of routine, and we demanded to know why were were detained since we had already been tried and acquitted. We complained about conditions in the cells and demanded to be allowed various things. It all fell on deaf ears; the magistrate thought it was all our fault: "Why did you bring yourself here?" he would ask.

Nothing was improved: they didn't clean our cells, or give us cloths and polish so we could clean them ourselves. The food was just the same, and we could spend a week inside without any exercise, just the door opening three times a day to bring in the food and take out the shit bucket. We used to call these buckets SB's—the same name as we gave the Special Branch.

All the loneliness, emptiness and isolation came back, and so did the need to play games. But this time there were no ants to count.

Sometimes at night we would hear screams and the clatter of SB's on the concrete floors—the noise of prisoners fighting in their cells. Then there would be silence, following by dogs barking, then men's voices and running footsteps towards where the screams had come from. And the next thing we would hear was the sound of real screams, screams of terror, screams of women being sjambokked. Then the screams would die out and we would hear the dogs being taken back and the men's voices, before everything died down to silence again.

Because we had no contact with the other prisoners we never got to know what the fights were about. But more painful than the screams was listening to the cries of the babies, all day and all night. Many women committed to Pretoria Central had small babies, or were pregnant, so throughout the jail there was this terrible forlorn crying, babies crying for their mothers or because they were hungry. It appeared that the women were taken off to work and the babies were just left in the cells, but we couldn't enquire about anything, so we didn't know why things were happening.

Except when condemned prisoners were going to be hanged, then we could hear singing coming from the men's section in the early hours of the morning, long, never-ending hymns. This meant the men knew a hanging was about to take place.

CAROLYN BAXTER (1953–)

Harlem-born Carolyn Baxter has been active as an artist in several media. She is a published poet whose works draw upon her experiences as a black woman and as an inmate in various prisons, including the New York City Correctional Institution for Women, where she participated in the Free Space Writing Project.

Baxter is also active in theater work, as an actress, director, and playwright. As a professional musician, she plays drums, conga, and bass. She has studied at New York City Community College and at Bard College. Her concern for the difficulties faced by ex-inmates in the community led her to work as a counselor for the NAACP's Project Rebound.

Note: Biographical information is from Judith Scheffler's interview with Carolyn Baxter, March 1985; *The Light from Another Country: Poetry from American Prisons*, ed. Joseph Bruchac (Greenfield Center, N.Y.: Greenfield Review Press, 1984).

WORKS BY CAROLYN BAXTER

The Light from Another Country: Poetry from American Prisons. Edited by Joseph Bruchac. Greenfield Center, N.Y.: Greenfield Review Press, 1984. Poems by Baxter are included.

Prison Solitary and Other Free Government Services: Poems by Carolyn Baxter. Greenfield Review Chapbook no. 41. Greenfield Center, N.Y.: Greenfield Review Press, 1979.

Songs from a Free Space: Writings by Women in Prison. Edited by Carol Muske and Gail Rosenblum. New York: Free Space Writing Project of the N.Y.C. Correctional Institution for Women, n.d. [197?].

Street Celebrity. Work-in-progress. Collection of poems.

Carolyn Baxter

Five Poems

From *Prison Solitary and Other Free Government Services*.
Reprinted by permission of Carolyn Baxter.

Lower Court

She opens her mouth, a switchblade falls out, along
with a .22 automatic, a few shells, crumpled one
dollar bills, some change in attitude (she's uncomfortable)
now.
Her pimp steps in,   slaps her,   see jugular
vein separate from neck muscle.

She opens her mouth wider, crumpled one dollar bills
fall out, along with prophylactics, 10¢ perfume, lipstick,
a newspaper clipping for a pair of $30 boots, a whip,
an explanation for the forged driver's license/a
picture of her favorite group, "The Shantells."

She closes her mouth,   The lights dim
in the courtroom.   As her pimp turns her left ear
with his fist, activating last night's streetreel of how
hot it was on the hoe stroll, projected out her eyeballs,
/smell of tricks.

             Legal Aid Lawyer says: Cop Out!
                    She does.

Another nite.
Trapped between gavel/wood.   Making it possible for
her to hit the streets.
Sound of her heels cut grey morning air,
/recite her life back, (in the) same order.

Toilet Bowl Congregation

(Holding cell in Criminal Courthouse, 100 Centre St.)

I

The toilet bowl congregation, preaches sounds of a
cheap hotel, pacing, bitching, broken neon hopes,
pictured in steelbars/cracked wht. paint,
contrasting 2 transients in red/blk. micro miniskirts,

racing words from each other's mouth, on who's pimp
will show/up with bail money first.

"Fas'll be here first!"
"Uhhahh! Smokey will."
"Bitch, you tryin to say my niggah ain't good as yours?"
An ain't on his J.O.B.!"
"Huh! Thas rite Hoe."

As they convince cheap perfumed falseness off each other
with their hands. First the platinum, then red/blonde
streaked wig flies off, while adhesive eyelashes fall like
lead rose petals, a blouse cut off rolling on the
floor, a dress slashed quickly, as officers enter backward, slow motion,
stopping the fight.

On the floor, blk, bloody, bald, a 90 lb knock-kneed
deception of a cheap prostitute

II

Congregations expression; unchanged still as innocent
bystander,
the stud broad, flinched a shoulder, holding her
zipper—juvenile still sleeping,
the nut, never stopped pacing,
murderer, extremely bored.

I tossed a wad of toilet paper by her hand,
waited a min, extended a hand (to help her up.)
got cussed out, sat back down on the bench,
thought—Dizzy Bitch!

(walking out)
handcuffed/belly chained, on our way to Riker's Island.
Another slave's
blood christened cement . . . Again!

35 Years a Correctional Officer

Ms. Goodall does not drink, swear, or masturbate.
"It's against God's will," she says.

Ms. Goodall does not gamble, gets paid to be slick
an' creep around after 1:00 AM to listen for
creaking beds, so she can give out incident reports

to anyone she catches by the creaks
of their bed "Masturbating!"
"It's against God's will," she says.

So I lay naked on floor, along with cold
tile, I feel like a private under the bunk,
hiding from the enemy.

/as her Sears/Roebuck crepe soles creep by the door—
I wanted to ask, what's the difference between a
creaking bed/a manic breathing heavy under the door.

Cell M 591

Dick Gregory in benefit for Fred Hampton,
Civil rights law suit, and Attica Defense Fund poster.

I've antagonized it, with four different kinds of tape.
It keeps falling.
        I slap its corners.
            It falls.
                I slap its corners.
             It
               keeps
                   falling.

Like a reality
that's died, demanding rest.
And I won't let it!!

On Being Counted

Standing next to the radiator, watching the room,
Do my tarot cards for the 1000th time.
I hear the radiator whispering, how stupid I was to
trade your warmth for his.
And I brood over you not letting me steal your hands.
To dry up my pains.

I smell lemon powder, thinking of my name.
Trying to remember femininity.
I can't sleep until I pay my personal digits to
Washington.

2

It's lights out,
yawns, coughs, and dreams from different realities.
Pack up the day, and seek refuge in the night.
Traveling down dark invisible roads.
Hoping to tap a stranger on the back.
Only to find it's their old friend.
Freedom.

I lay down, thinking thoughts that
were one time real,
But are now like houses that have been torn down,
and families that have moved away.

3

I smell the questioning flashlights,
walking down the hall, closing the storage doors
on dead lives,

demanding I recite the patented number, stamped on
my ass,
which is presently subletting the space
my soul used to own.
I'm also asked where I got my map of the justice system.
I say the judge traded it for my birth certificate.
The interrogator smiles, saying he'd never trade his,
and that I'm getting prettier with age.
Not mentioning ugly with time.

4

The dark highlights my barren existence,
that's gushed from me so far.
And I wonder, how there's even a corpuscle of patience
left.
The closing door joins the lock in the key
of finality, in three years from today time.

5

Spotlight invades my public privacy.
Like a peeping tom, inspiring me to sleep insomnia.
I turn to the radiator for some warmth, as I mumble

I feel like I gotta vomit.
The cold radiator yells, not on me bitch.
I have to live here too.

Joining the moon singing do you know the way to
San Jose.
In two part cruelty.

Asking do I know the words to nobody knows da
trouble I seen.

6

So I hum, off key thoughts, that were one time,
real.
But are now like houses that have been torn down
and families that have moved away.

P A R T 4

". . . above all, one must live as a full person at all times"*: Psychological Survival through Communication and Relationships

*

Days are spent in pleasant distractions: soap operas, prison love affairs, card playing and game playing. A tiny minority are seriously involved in academic pursuits or the learning of skills. An even smaller minority attempt to study available law books.[1]

Assata Shakur's description of the coping mechanisms she observed at New York's Correctional Institution for Women at Riker's Island emphasizes escapism, but it is not the whole story. In their 1977 national study of women's correctional programs, Glick and Neto discovered that the women they questioned possessed more self-esteem than they expected.[2] As Nancy Stoller Shaw states, "This discrepancy between prisoners' orientations and the realities of prison life produces a permanent struggle for self and social control. It is ironically tragic that prisons aim to crush the very characteristics that women need in the struggle for a dignified existence."[3] Women prison writers have articulated this conflict, which is felt by the majority of incarcerated women, and not only by those who are educated or politically oriented.

Prison literature by women illustrates two major ways female prisoners attempt to cope with imprisonment: relationships and communication by writing and other means, such as wall tapping. These coping strategies are not unique to prisoners, of course, but the acute stress of a prison environment increases the pressure to find a means to cope. Whether a woman is confined alone in a dungeon or with others in a "campus" institution, she shares the need, common to all prisoners, of withstanding the pains of imprisonment. The means by which an in-

*Rosa Luxemburg, letter to Emanuel and Mathilde Wurm, from Wronke fortress, 16 February 1917. The Wurms were friends of Luxemburg's and members of the German Social Democratic Party.—*Ed.*

mate survives psychologically and maintains self-respect and integrity is a prominent topic in women's prison literature.

Whether historical or modern, American or international, women's prison texts reveal the writers' common impulse to adjust to prison through communication and relationships. The texts are strikingly down-to-earth, often differing from the writings of male prisoners, who share women's need to communicate but generally choose a more abstract, theoretical, and philosophical style. Jack Henry Abbott's recent *In the Belly of the Beast*, for example, presents graphic details about prison conditions and practices, but he sets them within the context of a cerebral discussion of politics based upon his prison reading.

Women prisoners, too, can write in a more cerebral mode; certainly German Social Democrat Rosa Luxemburg gained international renown for her theoretical works on politics and economics. When faced with absolute isolation and denied any reading or writing material, male and female prisoners alike demonstrate the human mind's incredible capacity to maintain alertness and power. German-American Erica Wallach, imprisoned in East Berlin, discovered her impressive will and her latent intellectual resources. Her narrative describes her astonishing display of the human ability to create a vastly varied world of the mind when bereft of all human contact. Most women's writings in this section, however, illustrate a more general reliance upon communication and relationships to cope with life in prison.

The research of Cohen and Taylor on methods of psychological survival of long-term inmates in an English maximum-security men's prison sheds light on women's as well as men's methods of coping with imprisonment and their motivation for writing as a means of communication.[4] The researchers found that reading and writing are particularly important to long-term prisoners because such activities provide goals for achievement and an outlet for expressing what is happening to them. "Relatives do not know how it is inside in quite the same way that Serge or Solzhenitsyn know," the inmates told them.[5] This sense of kinship with prison writers from the past can be very significant for female inmates as well. The study found that inmates do not automatically and totally accept society's demeaning labels, nor do they accept the "inmate" as their only role. Instead, they achieve their perspective through considering the prison experience and what it means to them. Cohen and Taylor quote Hilde Bluhm's study of the auto-biographies of concentration camp survivors:

> Those . . . who embarked on a study of the concentration camp proper, turned towards that very reality which had threatened to overpower them: and they rendered that reality into an object of their "creation." This turn from a passive suffering to an active undertaking indicated that the ego was regaining control.
>
> . . . the association between self-observation and self-expression became a most successful means of survival.[6]

This survival mechanism applies to female as well as male prisoners and explains much about their motivation to confront and express the pains of imprisonment and their rejection of the all-encompassing label of prisoner.

Writing opens a substitute universe to the prisoner, as demonstrated so vividly in the selections that follow. If they were lucky, the women were permitted to write in prison, although the amount of writing was sometimes restricted and the content censored. Rosa Luxemburg, for example, was allowed the relative luxury of writing from her isolated cell. In this way she continued an unusually rich life through her lyrical correspondence with her lover, Hans Diefenbach, and her dear friend Sonja Liebknecht. Even in translation, Luxemburg's letters are a marvelous expression of humanism and culture from the pen of an isolated woman who revels in her ability to find beauty in memories of travel, in books, and in observation of the most sparse plant and animal life around the prison.

Other women, such as Erica Wallach and Eugenia Ginzburg, were not so fortunate, yet even without the means to write they discovered their strength by mentally composing poetry. Women's prison memoirs tell us that wall tapping, that ancient medium of prison communication, sustained several prisoners in isolation by enabling them to expand their sense of self. Indeed, wall-tapping episodes are among the most vivid and riveting of all prison literature, and those narrated by Ginzburg, Wallach, and Russian revolutionary Vera Figner rank among the best. Wall tapping allowed them to establish contact with fellow sufferers and thus escape through imagination during long periods of solitude. Through their tapping, these women gained victory over their captors. Figner explains that her very sanity was saved when she dared to defy the ban on tapping and later overheard comments of awed respect from her comrades.

Human relationships provide perhaps the most important means of coping with prison's deprivations. This method of survival is accessible to a broader range of female inmates, as it includes those without the education or background of the women prisoners who express themselves through writing. Recent research in American prisons recognizes the importance of relationships for inmates and explores the forms those relationships take. Sociologists who have studied the nature of male and female prison subcultures cite the significance of "imported norms, values, and beliefs," especially for women prisoners, who bring female sex-role conventions with them to prison.[7] Giallombardo explains that male prisoners establish a rigid "inmate code" of behavior and a defined system of social roles.

> In contrast to the male prison, however, the evolution of an informal social structure in the female prison to withstand the deleterious effects of physical and social isolation is in many respects an attempt to resist the destructive effects of imprisonment by creating a substitute universe —a world in which the inmates may preserve an identity which is relevant to life outside the prison.[8]

This social structure may take the form of various support systems consistent with relationships the women knew on the outside. Friendships between women are one form, as are lesbian alliances. In general, homosexual contact in male institutions tends to be coercive and power-oriented, whereas women usually form alliances based on the need for affection and support.[9] Researchers identify the characteristic system of interpersonal relationships among American female prisoners as the "kinship group," with inmates assuming pseudofamily roles of both sexes, including parents, children, grandparents, aunts, and cousins.[10]

Writing by women prisoners clearly exhibits the concern for personal relationships demonstrated by the general female prison population. Women prisoners' lack of, need for, and joy in human companionship are major themes in their literature. Their works show the many paths taken to fulfill this need.

The diary of Confederate blockade-runner Catherine Virginia Baxley tells the poignant story of one woman's battle against formidable stress when she faces the permanent loss of the major relationship in her life outside prison. Her story underscores the essential role of relationships in the woman prisoner's life and the pain a prisoner experiences when she finds no prison associations to mitigate her loss. Baxley was a flamboyant prisoner by all accounts. Her brash manner embarrassed her fellow Confederate spy and inmate in the Old Capitol Prison, Rose Greenhow, who referred disparagingly to "the woman Baxley."[11] William E. Doster, provost marshal of Washington, called Baxley "the most defiant and outrageous of all the female prisoners."[12] However, Confederate prisoner Virginia Lomax frankly admired Baxley's boldness: "Nothing seemed to damp her spirits, and to fear she was a stranger."[13]

Baxley's diary reveals her own perception of the inner turmoil that often found release in harassing her jailers. Unlike Greenhow's memoirs, Baxley's unpunctuated and almost indecipherable diary entries, kept in an interleaved copy of Tennyson, were not meant for publication.[14] The voice lacks pretense. Amid echoes of the Complaining Screamer and the Daring Rebel, readers hear mostly the undisguised voice of a woman coping with an imprisonment made almost unbearable by the death of her only son.

In a gruesome coincidence of fates, Baxley watched as her son, a wounded seventeen-year-old Confederate soldier, was carried into the prison where she was passing the sweltering Washington spring days. Baxley swore that the young man, who had contracted typhoid, was being fed improperly, and she was so vociferous in her complaints that officials finally denied her access to the prison hospital. She saw her son only just before he died in the arms of Mrs. Surratt (later hanged for conspiracy to assassinate Lincoln). Virginia Lomax marvels at Baxley's ability to regain her spirits, "but every night, before retiring, she would fold the torn and faded 'jacket of gray' worn by the youthful soldier and place it tenderly beneath her head."[15] Readers of Baxley's diary learn that, whatever outward cheer she possessed, stress and grief had disturbed her emotional equilibrium, so that diary entries show a growing sense of despair and abandonment. We witness the process of grief, heightened by this mother's confinement and the relentless heat.

The search for human companionship takes several forms in the following selections. Anick, the autobiographical heroine of French prison novelist Albertine Sarrazin's *The Runaway*, may scorn relationships with her fellow inmates, but she asserts her female sexuality and longing for her lover Zizi, incarcerated in a men's prison. Their love affair gives her a sense of completeness and traditional femininity that reinforces her sense of self.[16] In the poetry of Puerto Rican Nationalist Lolita Lebrón, imprisoned for twenty-five years in the Federal Reformatory for Women in Alderson, West Virginia, a deep loneliness for her homeland and her people is mitigated by love for her sister inmates and joy in retaining the freshness of life's passion, even in prison. Norma Stafford, a working-class woman and a lesbian, writes poetry that resonates with an honest yearning for emotional and physical contact to combat prison's sensory deprivation. Celebrating the magical healing power of love's many levels, Stafford's poems are at once both intimate messages to beloved individuals and glorifications of female spiritual and physical energy. During her twenty years of isolation Vera Figner found solace in her intense friendship with another imprisoned woman revolutionary. Her loving description of their close bond leaves no doubt that this cherished friend transformed prison life for her.

Through communication and interpersonal relationships, women prison writers cope with the pains of imprisonment and gather strength to proclaim their personal identity and integrity. Giving birth to self and freedom is Norma Stafford's image of the woman prisoner's power to survive. It is a birthing process that only a female prisoner could envision:

> blessed relief   the emergence of me
> when i finally walk out those gates.

NOTES

1. Assata Shakur (Joanne Chesimard), "Women in Prison: How We Are," *Black Scholar* 12, no. 6 (November–December 1981): 53; reprinted from vol. 9, no. 7 (April 1978).

2. Ruth M. Glick and Virginia V. Neto, *National Study of Women's Correctional Programs* (Washington, D.C.: National Institute of Law Enforcement and Criminal Justice, 1977), pp. 163–172.

3. Nancy Stoller Shaw, "Female Patients and the Medical Profession in Jails and Prisons," in *Judge, Lawyer, Victim, Thief: Women, Gender Roles, and Criminal Justice*, ed. Nicole Hahn Rafter and Elizabeth A. Stanko (Boston: Northeastern Univ. Press, 1982), p. 266.

4. Stanley Cohen and Laurie Taylor, *Psychological Survival: The Experience of Long-Term Imprisonment* (New York: Pantheon, 1972), pp. 73–74, 134–146.

5. Ibid., pp. 73–74.

6. Hilde O. Bluhm, "How Did They Survive?: Mechanisms of Defense in Nazi Concentration Camps," *American Journal of Psychology* 2 (1948): 3–32, quoted in Cohen and Taylor, *Psychological Survival*, pp. 137–138.

7. Lee H. Bowker, "Gender Differences in Prisoner Subcultures," in *Women and Crime in America*, ed. Lee H. Bowker (New York: Macmillan, 1981), pp. 411–412. For a discussion of women's responses to imprisonment, see also James E. Griffith and Amelia Pennington-Averett, "Women Prisoners' Multidimensional Locus of Control," *Criminal Justice and Behavior* 8, no. 3 (September 1981): 375–389; Timothy F. Hartnagel and Mary Ellen Gillan, "Female Prisoners and the Inmate Code," *Pacific Sociological Review* 23, no. 1 (January 1980): 85–104; David A. Ward and Gene G. Kassebaum, *Women's Prison: Sex and Social Structure* (Chicago: Aldine, 1965), pp. 70–74.

8. Rose Giallombardo, *Society of Women: A Study of a Women's Prison* (New York: Wiley, 1966), p. 103.

9. Bowker, "Gender Differences in Prisoner Subcultures," p. 414. See also Giallombardo, *Society of Women*, p. 141.

10. See Gary F. Jensen, "The Incarceration of Women: A Search for Answers," in *Women and the Law: A Social and Historical Perspective*, ed. D. Kelly Weisberg (Cambridge, Mass.: Schenkman, 1982), 1:248–249; Coramae Richey Mann, *Female Crime and Delinquency* (University, Ala.: Univ. of Alabama Press, 1984), pp. 220–221; Giallombardo, *Society of Women*, pp. 158–189; Bowker, "Gender Differences in Prison Subcultures," p. 415. Bowker writes that kinship groups were observed as early as the late 1920s and that they are found throughout the United States and abroad. Esther Heffernan, *Making It in Prison: The Square, the Cool, and the Life* (New York: Wiley-Interscience, 1972) is an extended discussion of social systems in women's prisons.

11. Rose Greenhow, *My Imprisonment and the First Year of Abolition Rule at Washington* (London: Richard Bentley, 1863).

12. William E. Doster, *Lincoln and Episodes of the Civil War* (New York: Putnam's, 1915), p. 84.

13. Anon. [Virginia Lomax], *The Old Capitol Prison and Its Inmates. By a Lady, Who Enjoyed the Hospitalities of the Government for a "Season"* (New York: Hale, 1867), p. 142. Lomax notes that she has changed the names of inmates. Her reference to "Mrs. Johnson" may be taken to mean Baxley because Lomax and Baxley were imprisoned in the Old Capitol at the same time and their accounts often coincide, particularly in Lomax's description of the death of "Johnson's" son in the same prison.

14. See Robert A. Fothergill, *Private Chronicles: A Study of English Diaries* (London: Oxford Univ. Press, 1974), pp. 128–153, for a discussion of distinctions between diary and autobiography in their relation to time. Fothergill explains that a diary presents life as a process with the self moving through time, while an autobiography regards life retrospectively from a given point in time and presents the past according to the writer's own design. Perhaps this distinction in form may help to explain the differences in Baxley's and Greenhow's works.

15. [Lomax], *The Old Capitol Prison and Its Inmates*, pp. 148–149.

16. For a further discussion of Sarrazin's work see Elissa D. Gelfand, *Imagination in Confinement: Women's Writings from French Prisons* (Ithaca, N.Y.: Cornell Univ. Press, 1983), pp. 214–238; Gelfand, "Albertine Sarrazin: The Confined Imagination," *L'Esprit Createur* 19, no. 2 (Summer 1979): 47–57; Gelfand, "Albertine Sarrazin: A Control Case for Femininity in Form," *French Review* 51, no. 2 (December 1977): 245–251.

CATHERINE VIRGINIA BAXLEY (1810?–?)

Biographical information about Confederate blockade-runner Catherine Virginia Baxley is scant, but she was said to be about fifty years old during her first imprisonment in the Old Capitol Prison, Washington, D.C., from December 30, 1861, to June 2, 1862. Arrested in Baltimore on charges of "carrying information to Richmond," she was held first in the "Greenhow Prison" (Rose Greenhow's home at Sixteenth Street in Washington, used as a women's political prison), and then moved to the Old Capitol Prison. There she, Greenhow, and a third Confederate spy, Augusta Morris (Mason), were at first allowed to mingle but afterward separated. All three were released and sent to Richmond on June 2, 1862, when they signed a pledge not to return north of the Potomac River during the war. In August, Jefferson Davis ordered payment of $500 to Baxley for services to the Confederacy.

Baxley did not keep her pledge long and was again imprisoned in the Old Capitol in 1865. The following selections are from her manuscript diary and notebook (February 14, 1865 to July 2, 1865), written in an interleaved copy of Tennyson's *Enoch Arden*—a gift from Post Commandant Colonel Colby. They describe her painful meeting with her son, a wounded soldier in the Old Capitol, and her struggle with intense feelings of abandonment following his death.

Note: Biographical information is from William E. Doster, *Lincoln and Episodes of the Civil War* (New York: Putnam's, 1915); Ishbel Ross, *Rebel Rose: Life of Rose O'Neal Greenhow, Confederate Spy* (New York: Harper & Bros., 1954); *The War of the Rebellion: A Compilation of the Official Records of the Union and Confederate Armies*, 2d ser., vol. 2 (Washington, D.C.: Government Printing Office, 1897), pp. 237, 271, 1315, 1321.

WORKS BY CATHERINE V. BAXLEY

Diary and Notebook, 14 February–2 July 1865.

Letters to William H. Seward, Secretary of State, and Edwin M. Stanton, Secretary of War, and others, January–April 1862, written from the Old Capitol Prison concerning her imprisonment. In *The War of the Rebellion: A Compilation of the Official Records of the Union and Confederate Armies*, Washington, D.C.: Government Printing Office, 1897, 2d ser., vol. 2, pp. 1316–1321.

Catherine Virginia Baxley

At the Old Capitol Prison

From Baxley's diary and notebook, 14 February 1865–2 July
1865. Reprinted by permission of the Rare Books and
Manuscripts Division, New York Public Library, Astor,
Lenox, and Tilden Foundations.

About 5 or half past five O'clock April 5—cannot sleep* get up and
sit with my face pressed against my bars—in a little while perceive an
ambulance train winding round the South East corner of the Capitol
passes in front of my windows   I perceive the Gray Uniform so dear to
my heart   poor wounded Rebels & Prisoners   God pity you   I kiss my
hand   one, two, the third ambulance is approaching   two bodies on
Stretchers   I see a pair of clasped hands raised toward me   a voice calls
"Alls lost   Our Cause is hopeless and I am badly wounded"   I am too
near-sighted to recognize the features, and turn from the window half
broken hearted little dreaming it is my own and only child. In a couple
of hours the *Asst. Supt* who is a *brute* in half human form comes in to
my room and in the most brutal & unceremonious manner informs me
my son is wounded and a prisoner at the Lower-or Old Capitol Prison.
God help me now   my only child   I beg   I plead implore to be taken
to him. I have [not] seen my child for two years   he is but a child
[indecipherable]. . . .

This confinement is very tedious very *very* irksome—I have exhausted every thing which could afford a few moments relief to the
mind   counted over and over again the small diamond shape lozenges
in the India carpet the pains [*sic*] of glass in the window—one of the
panes has been struck by a stone and rays strike out from the Centre
like a halo   I have counted the bars in the window blinds, two up and
down down and up again   There is an intolerable smell of whiskey in
this room which annoys me exceedingly and at last I have discovered
the cause   my lamp. Some new fangled Yankee oil I suppose. The guards
watch my every movement but are polite and even kind—for an hour
I have been watching the movements of two spiders   a large and small
one   they have finished weaving their web or *Snare* and are trying to
trap or coax the unwary flies to enter   three or four have been caught

*Baxley uses very little punctuation in her diary.—*Ed.*

but some are wiser more politic not to be trapped I moralized as I watched and will profit in the future. . . .

for 18 mos. incarcerated in Fort Delaware   Exchanged only in Sept. 64—this creature Wilson is a husband and a father   tis he will not take me to my wounded child. I ask permission to write   it is granted but the letter *is not sent*—what Monstrous Cruelty—Col. Wm P. Wood the Supt. proper at length arrives   comes immediately to my room   for two days I have been waiting for you   take me to my son is again the burthen of my cry and he is human—I shall never forget him   I meet my son—Mr. Wood has him brought up to Carroll Prison that I may nurse him—but has to leave immediately, when Brute Wilson's tyranny again commences   I am not allowed to go to my child   a door only at the foot of the Stairs separates us   I beg to be allowed to call through the door and ask him how he is   dont grieve Ma   I am better   The excitement attendant upon Mr. Lincoln's death affects him seriously— they repeat carelessly in his presence the threats of the mob to tear the prison down and murder the prisoners   on saturday he has a hemorrhage on the day of the procession he has a congestive chill   daily he grows worse   I— . . .

For behold thou hast loved   know my childs days nay—his very hours are numbered—Friday night April 22 my darling my beautiful boy leaves me *all alone*   a few minutes before his death he asked me "Ma" is this my birth day—again "kiss me Ma like you used to when I was a little fellow and hold my hand Ma while I sleep—a sleep from which only the trump of the arch Angel will awake him. . . .

6 O'clock June 15th   I have been feverish and excited all day—feel really quite unwell   if I only had something to read—They have changed my room to day from No. 25–to 23—something of an improvement— but oh how dull   monotonous   my brain seems on fire   my very ears tingle—and to make matters worse my glasses have fallen from the window-sill to the balcony and are broken and I cannot see across the street without them. Misfortunes come in flocks   A [indecipherable] Car has toppled over just in front of the window. came men   carrying the engine and tender [indecipherable]   one of the employers saved himself by jumping   there is quite a crowd collected trying to explore this capsized Car—such a trifling thing would have quickened my pulse

sometime since   now I am not at all excited   I am becoming apathetic indifferent to everything—I watch the arrival of the trains hoping to see some familiar face   I scan eagerly every passerby   not one look of recognition   am I quite forgotten? . . .

> The world too Soon exhaleth the dewy freshness
> of the hearts loving flowers—
> We water them with tears, but naught availeth,
> They wither on through all lifes later hours.

> Liberty. In dungeons brightest thou art
> Madame Roland . . .

12 O'clock at night   later perhaps for the chickens are crowing. Sultry snoring outside my door but I cannot sleep   Oh! God how utterly desolate and lonely I feel   have been reading my darling boys diary. Oh! how much I have lost   my child my child   I saw you murdered deliberately murdered before my eyes by cruel unrelenting and base men and your wretched mother powerless and impotent to aid you. . . .

June 17th. Still a prisoner   I watched the day dawning from the window of my pent-up room   tis dull and gloomy—Oh! I begin to feel as if bereft of all hope   a few poor homeless Gray jackets are washing themselves at the pump beneath my window and wiping upon the remnants of what were once pocket handkerchiefs   poor fellows   *perhaps* some wife or Mother is watching hoping praying for their return   I am *all alone*   no one to watch for   None to watch wait and hope for me —tis sad   tis bitter bitter bitter—Oh! that God would give us hearts of flesh   bowels of Compassion—

VERA FIGNER (1852–1942)

Vera Nikolajevna Figner spent an isolated childhood, first in the home of her wealthy, strict father in Kazan, Russia, and later in a restrictive girls' boarding school. During her youth she developed a very close bond with her mother. However, it was her Uncle Kuprijanov who first inspired her desire to help the uneducated masses. After marrying Alexei Filipov, a young magistrate who encouraged her interest in medicine, she began work in 1870 at the University of Zurich. There, she and her sister Lydia actively studied socialism with a group of women students, the *Fritschi*, who, as revolutionaries, eventually all sacrificed their freedom and—many—their lives. As Figner's involvement in the revolutionary cause increased, she and her more conservative husband realized their differences and were later divorced.

In 1876 Figner returned to Russia to put her revolutionary theories into practice. After disillusioning attempts to educate the peasants as a peaceful preparation for reform, in 1879 she helped to found the People's Will, a revolutionary group that used terrorist methods. In 1883 she was arrested for her part in the assassination of Tsar Alexander II and was imprisoned in St. Petersburg's Peter and Paul Prison for twenty months before her trial. Because the execution of women was frowned upon, Figner was sentenced to life imprisonment and taken to the infamous Schlüsselburg Fortress prison in 1884. There she passed twenty years of solitary confinement, of which the first five were without even paper or pen. She and the only other woman prisoner, Ludmilla Wolkenstein, were kept isolated and saw each other only during their half-hour walk every other day. Her fellow revolutionaries all died or went insane under the terrible prison conditions. Figner's own most bitter grief was her separation from her mother.

In 1904 Figner was given amnesty and exiled to Archangel in Siberia. After she was allowed to leave Russia in 1906, she lived for eight years in Paris and Switzerland, where she worked for Russian prison reform and wrote her memoirs. She returned to Russia in 1914 and two years later began working in St. Petersburg with an Amnesty Committee for Tsarist political prisoners. She spent her final years in Moscow, where she was greatly respected by the Russian people and by international political activists, including Emma Goldman.

Note: Biographical information is from Margaret Goldsmith, *Seven Women Against the World* (London: Methuen, 1935), pp. 119–151; Ethel Mannin, *Women and the Revolution* (New York: Dutton, 1939), pp. 116–121; Amy Knight, "The Fritschi: A Study of Female Radicals in the Russian Populist Movement," *Canadian-American Slavic Studies* 9, no. 1 (Spring 1975): 1–17; Barbara Alpern Engel and Clifford N. Rosenthal, eds., *Five Sisters: Women Against the Tsar* (New York: Knopf, 1975); *Encyclopaedia Britanica*, vol. 9 (1972), s.v. "Figner, Vera Nikolaevna."

WORKS BY VERA FIGNER

Autobiographical writings, compiled and translated from the Russian by Barbara
 Alpern Engel and Clifford N. Rosenthal, eds. In *Five Sisters: Women Against
 the Tsar.* New York: Knopf, 1975.
Memoirs of a Revolutionist. Translated by Camilla Chapin Daniels et al. New
 York: International, 1927; reprint, Westport, Conn.: Greenwood Press, 1968.

The First Years

From "When the Clock of Life Stopped," in *Memoirs
of a Revolutionist.* Reprinted by permission of
International Publishers, New York.

My own spirit was stifled and crushed during these years. And whom
would Schlüsselburg not stifle and crush? What comforting thought had
we, members of The Will of the People, brought with us to Schlüsselburg? The revolutionary movement had been defeated, its organisation
destroyed, and the Executive Committee had perished to the very last
member. The people and society had not supported us. We were alone.
The noose of autocracy had been drawn more tightly, and we, passing
out of the life of the world, had left no heirs to carry on the struggle
which we had begun.

Schlüsselburg gave me something, however, which I had not foreseen,
for which I had not prepared myself. The very last joy in my life had
been my mother, and they took her away from me—the only person in
the world who made life real and worth living, the only one to whom
I, fallen into the depths of the abyss, could cling. Joy died within me,
but, dying, left behind it a keen and bitter grief. While I was free, I had
not lived with my mother, and had thought of her only occasionally.
But then I had had my country to think of; my revolutionary activities
occupied my mind; there were strong attachments and friendships; there
were my comrades. And now there was no one, nothing. And my mother,
that final loss, the loss of the very last thing dear to me, became, as it
were, the symbol of all my losses, large and small; of all my deprivations,
both great and petty.

Never did I regret that I had chosen the path that had led me to this
place. It was *my will* that had chosen that path—there could be no

[193]

regret. Never once did I regret the fact that I was deprived of delicate underclothing and fine garments, wearing instead a coarse rag and a convict's gown with a brand on the back. I did not regret but I suffered. Only the thought of my mother filled my mind—her image and no other, and my overwhelming grief at being separated from her. But that grief absorbed and included all of my sufferings, all of my griefs; the grief of my crushed and wounded spirit, and the grief of my oppressed and humiliated body. And thus, symbolised in the loss of my mother, it assumed the caustic bitterness of all my losses, all my deprivations, and became vast and uncontrollable, as do all feelings which are never freely expressed but lie hidden in the dark depths of the subconscious. Destruction threatened my darkened mind.

But when one step more would have carried me to a point beyond all chance of recovery, an inner voice said, "Stop!" It was not my fear of death that spoke. Death was quite desirable; it was linked with the idea of martyrdom, which in my childhood Christian traditions had taught me to regard as sacred; while later the history of the struggle for the rights of the oppressed had strengthened this idea in me. It was the fear of insanity, that degradation of the individual, the degeneracy of his spirit and flesh, that halted me. But to stop at this point meant an effort to regain a normal outlook on life, to become again spiritually whole. My friends helped me to do this.

A dim light began to dawn in me, like the little flames of the wax candles on Palm Sunday. The dumb walls of Schlüsselburg began to speak; I was able to communicate with my friends.* They spoke tenderly, sent me loving messages, and Schlüsselburg's icy crust melted in the warmth of their affection. Other influences were brought to bear, stern words, lessons. Once my neighbour, a man whom I had not known before, asked me what I was doing.

"I am thinking of my mother and weeping," I replied.

My neighbour rebuked me in strong terms. He asked me if I had ever read the *Memoirs of Simon Meyer*, the Communard, and I remembered the scene on board ship, when the ship was rolling badly, and they began

_____
*A reference to the system of communicating messages by tapping on the walls.—*Translator.*

to shave the heads of the Communards. He put before me as an example this Simon Meyer, one of many thousands of Communards. He read me a lecture. I was startled and hurt and angry. I had read the *Memoirs of Simon Meyer*, and I remembered the scene on board ship, and many others. "Why this sermon?" thought I. "I don't need his sermons!"

But that was precisely what I did need. If my neighbour had sympathised with me, had begun to console me tenderly, his words would have been of no avail; they would have coincided with my mood. But he censured me in no uncertain terms; he showed me plainly what my duty was, and he vexed me. And this vexation was salutary; it was in contrast with my customary frame of mind, shattered it, made it incongruous. In solitude a trifle sometimes grows to unwonted dimensions; it sticks in your consciousness, and will not be dislodged. So it was in this case. I could not get my neighbour's words out of my mind. The wall between us every day reminded me of our conversation; and each time I recalled it with an unpleasant feeling of irritation and annoyance. In this way my grief and longing were interrupted, and the annoyance served a useful purpose.

But there was something else, infinitely greater, which raised me out of my depths.

The trial had been the last, conclusive act of the revolutionary drama in which I had taken part. My social activity had ended there. After receiving my sentence, I had felt myself no longer a public character but only a human being. The strain under which I had lived during the years of freedom, and while awaiting the trial, which had heretofore been subdued and repressed, now collapsed; there was no task for my will, and the human being awoke within me. This human being might now suffer without check or self-control, and thus yield to the onslaughts of sickness and death. I forgot that once having undertaken a public career I could not again be just a human being; that I was both more and less than a human being, and that the public task I had chosen was not yet solved. The fact that we as a revolutionary body had inscribed the name of The Will of the People on the history of our time, and that Schlüsselburg, the Russian Bastile, would play its part in the minds of our contemporaries, and cover us with its glory, never occurred to me, or to my friends. We were too humble to imagine it. But in the fifth year of my imprisonment, after a hunger strike which had ended unsuccessfully and before the set time, when I came nearer death than ever before in my life, and longed to die, but was forced to live in spite of myself; when my spirit was full of despair and disappointment, and my nerves utterly shattered, I heard these words, spoken by one of our comrades there, a man more gifted than any of us. He was speaking not to me, but about me, and I chanced to overhear him. He said, "Vera does not belong to her friends alone, she belongs to Russia."

These words raised me to a height that one cannot contemplate, a terrifying height; a height that is oppressive, and imposes obligations above one's strength. But these words, spoken and overheard, placed an ideal before me, an unattainable ideal, but for all that, one to which I was bound to aspire. They gave my will a task: to strive to be worthy, to work on myself, to struggle, and to overcome myself. To strive, to overcome, to conquer myself! To conquer sickness, and madness and death!

But how was I to struggle, how prevail? To prevail meant to disperse the darkness hanging over my spirit, to drive away everything that kept the light from my eyes. That meant to forget. I tried to forget. I drove away recollections; I buried them all in a grave. For ten years I buried them, for ten years I tried to forget. For ten years in my consciousness my mother was dying; and my longing for my native land, for activity and freedom, was dying. Grief was dying, and love too. The snow fell, and covered the past with its white mantle. And I? I was alive. I was well. . . .

I Acquire a Friend

Early in January, 1886, knowing that Ludmila Alexandrovna Volkenstein, one of my co-defendants in the Trial of 14, was also in the Fortress, I asked the inspector why they did not permit me to take my walks in company with one of the other prisoners. The inspector was silent for a moment, and then said, "We can grant you this privilege, only you mustn't . . ." He bent his forefinger and tapped on the door jamb, imitating our fashion of carrying on conversations by tapping on the wall. I replied that I did very little tapping.

The interview went no further, and I was left in solitude as before. But on January 14, when they took me out for my walk, and the door into the little enclosure which we called "the first cage," opened, I beheld an unexpected figure in a short cloth coat, with a linen handkerchief on her head, who swiftly embraced me, and I recognised with difficulty my comrade Volkenstein. Probably she also was as shocked by the change in my appearance, due to my convict garb. And so we stood, embracing one another, and not knowing whether to rejoice or to weep.

Up to this time I had seen Volkenstein only during the trial. We had not met previously, and had known each other only by hearsay. Ludmila Alexandrovna's sincerity, her simplicity and warm-heartedness at once enchanted me. It did not require much time for us to form such a friendship as was possible only under the conditions under which we were living. We were like people shipwrecked on an uninhabited island. We had nothing and no one in all the world save each other. Not only people, but nature, colors, sounds, were gone, all of them. And instead there was left a gloomy vault with a row of mysterious, walled-in cells, in which invisible captives were pining; an ominous silence, and the atmosphere of violence, madness and death. One can see plainly that in such surroundings two friendly spirits must needs find joy in each other's company, and ever afterwards treasure a most touching remembrance of the association.

Any one who has been in prison knows the influence that the sympathetic tenderness of a comrade has on one's life while in confinement. In Polivanov's memoirs of his imprisonment in the Alexey Ravelin, there is a touching picture of Kolodkevich, hobbling up to the wall on crutches to console him with a few tender words. A brief conversation through the soulless stone that separated the two captives, who were dying from scurvy and loneliness, was their only joy and support. The author of the memoirs confessed that more than once Kolodkevich's kind words saved him from acute attacks of melancholy, which were tempting him to commit suicide. And indeed, loving sympathy works veritable wonders in prison; and were it not for those light tappings on the wall, which destroy the stone barrier separating man from man, the prisoner could not preserve his life or his soul. Good reason was there for the struggle to maintain the system of tappings, the very first struggle that a captive wages with the prison officials; it is an out-and-out struggle for existence, and every one who is walled up in a cell clutches at this device as at a straw. But when those sentenced to solitary confinement are permitted to meet their co-prisoners face to face, and to replace the symbolic tapping with living speech, then the warm-heartedness and kindness expressed in the tones of the voice, in an affectionate glance, and a friendly handshake, bring joy unknown to one who has never lost his freedom.

I do not know what I gave to Ludmila Alexandrovna, but she was my comfort, my joy and happiness. My nerves and general constitution had been completely unstrung. I was physically weak, and spiritually exhausted. My general state of mind was entirely abnormal; and lo! I found a friend whom prison conditions had not affected so profoundly and painfully as they had me; and this friend was the personification of tenderness, kindness, and humaneness. All the treasures of her loving spirit she gave to me with a generous hand. No matter how gloomy my mood when we met, she always knew how to dispel it in one way or another, and how to console me. Her smile alone, and the sight of her dear face dispelled my grief, and gladdened my heart. After a walk with her I would come away reassured and transformed; my cell did not seem so gloomy to me, nor life so hard to bear. Straightway I would begin to dream of our next meeting. We saw each other every other day; prison discipline evidently found it necessary to dilute the joy of our meetings by making us pass a day in complete solitude. But perhaps this fact only made our longing to see each other more keen, and accentuated our "holiday mood," which was so pleasant to recall afterwards. . . .

The Punitive Cell

Like most of those who are newly-imprisoned, and find themselves in unfamiliar and malevolent surroundings, during the first years I was crushed and seemed to find my only refuge in silence, resigning myself to the lot of one who has been tied hand and foot. But this attitude of mine was not due merely to a realisation of the impossibility and fruitlessness of any resistance or struggle; another element mingled with it.

Whoever, like myself, has at some time been influenced by the spirit of Christ, who, in the name of His idea has endured abuse, suffering, and death; whoever during his childhood and youth has made of Him an ideal, and regarded His life as an example of self-sacrificing love, will understand the mood of the newly-condemned revolutionist who has been flung into a living grave for the cause of liberty. After his trial, the sentenced prisoner experiences a peculiar emotion. Calm and radiant, he does not clutch convulsively at that from which he is departing, but looks firmly ahead, fully conscious of the fact that what is coming cannot be escaped or averted.

The ideas of Christianity, which are implanted in all of us, consciously or unconsciously, from our very cradles, and also the lives of all martyrs for ideas, create in such a prisoner the consoling consciousness that the moment of his test has come. A trial is given to the strength of his love and the hardiness of his spirit, as a fighter for that good which he has longed to attain, not for his own transitory self, but for the people, for society, for future generations. One can understand that in such a mood we can have no thought of engaging in a war of words or of action with a band of jailers and executioners. Did Jesus resist when they abused and struck Him? Any thought of such an action seemed a profanation of His pure spirit and gentle dignity.

And yet, notwithstanding this mood of non-resistance, after six months of separation from my friend Ludmila I came into conflict with the prison régime, which might have had tragic results.

A few days before Whitsunday, at nine o'clock in the evening, when the inspector was making his customary survey of the prison, looking through the peep-hole in every door, Popov called to me with a loud tap from his cell, which was below mine and several doors removed. I was tired. The day had been long and wearisome and empty. I wanted to lie down on my cot and go to sleep, but I did not have the heart to refuse, and I answered. But when Popov began to tap, his sentence broke off in the middle of a word. I heard a door slam, steps rang out in the direction of the exit, and everything was silent again. I understood. The inspector had taken Popov to the punitive cell.

The punitive cell was the place to which the inspector threateningly referred when he said: "I'll take you off to a place where not a living soul will hear you." Not a living soul—that was terrible to think of.

Here we prisoners were all together under the Fortress roof; all around were friends, each in his stone cell, and that was protection and defence. If you should cry out, your cry would be heard. If you should groan, they would hear it. But "off there?" There "not one living soul will hear you."

I knew that not so very long ago, Popov had been taken "off there," and that they had beaten him cruelly. The thought that he would again be put in that terrible place, that he would be alone, and that a whole pack of gendarmes would again fall upon him, an unarmed man, this thought flashed through my mind and seemed so horrible that I made my decision: I would contrive to be put there too; he should know that he was not alone, and that—if they were going to torture him, he had a witness.

I knocked on the door, and asked them to call the inspector. "What do you want?" said he, angrily, opening the little window in the door.

"It is unjust to punish one, when two were talking," said I. "Take me to the punitive cell also."

"Very well," said the inspector promptly, and unlocked the door.

Then it was that I first saw the interior of our prison as it looked lighted up at night: the little lamps along the walls of our tomb; the forty heavy, black doors standing there like coffins set on end, and behind every door, a comrade, a captive, suffering alone; dying, sick, or waiting his turn to die. Hardly had I passed along my "Bridge of Sighs," and approached the stairway, when my neighbour called out: "They're taking Vera to the punitive cell!" and scores of hands began to beat madly on the doors, and voices shouted, "Take us too!"

In the midst of the gloomy surroundings that stirred me so deeply, the sound of the familiar and unfamiliar voices of invisible people, the voices of comrades, which I had not heard for many, many years, awoke in me a certain morbid, flaming joy: we were separated and yet united; our spirits were one.

But the inspector flew into a fury. When we came out into the court-yard accompanied by three or four gendarmes, he raised his fist, which clutched convulsively the bunch of prison keys. With his face distorted from rage, and his beard quivering, he hissed at me: "Over there, just make a sound, and I'll show you!"

I was afraid of this man. I had heard of the cruel corporal punishments that the gendarmes had inflicted at his command, and the thought came to me: "If they beat me, I shall die." But I replied in a voice that sounded so calm that it seemed to belong to somebody else: "I am not going there to tap messages."

The broad wooden gate of the citadel yawned open before me, and my fear was replaced by ecstasy. For five years I had not seen the night sky and the stars. Now this sky was above me, and its stars shone down on me. The high walls of the old citadel gleamed white and the silvery radiance of the May night poured into the deep, square, well-like space enclosed by them. The whole plaza was overgrown with grass. It lay thick and fresh and cool, lightly brushing one's feet, and it had the allurement of the dewy expanse of a *free* field. From wall to wall stretched a low, white building, while in the corner a single tree loomed dark and tall. For a hundred years this splendid creature had grown there alone, without comrades, and thus solitary had spread about it, unhindered, its luxuriant crown. Keys grated, and with difficulty, as though the lock had grown rusty, they opened the outside door of the prison, which led into a dark, tiny antechamber. I smelled the musty odour of a cold, damp, uninhabited building. Before us stretched the naked stones of the broad corridor, at the far end of which glimmered a little night lamp. In the cold twilight the dim figures of the gendarmes, the indistinct outlines of the doors, the dark corners—everything looked so ominous that the thought suddenly flashed into my mind that this was a real torture dungeon, and that the inspector had spoken truly when he said that he had a place where no living soul could hear one. A moment later they opened a door on the left, and thrust in a small lighted lamp; the door slammed, and I was alone.

I was in a small, unheated cell, which had never been cleaned. The walls were dirty, and here and there crumbling from age. The floor was of asphalt; there was a small stationary wooden table with a seat, and an iron bench on which there was no mattress, nor any kind of bedding.

Silence.

In vain I waited for the gendarmes to come back and bring a mattress, and something to put over me; I had on a thin, cotton chemise, a skirt of the same material, and a prison gown, and I began to shiver from the cold. How could one sleep on the iron lattice-work of that cot, thought I. But no bedding ever arrived; I had to lie down on this Rakhmetov bed.* However, it was not only impossible to sleep, but even to lie for long on the metal bars of the bench. The cold wafted up from the floor, from the stone walls, and penetrated one's body in contact with the iron bars.

The next day they took even this away. They raised the cot and fastened it with a padlock for the rest of the time. At night one had to lie down on the asphalt floor, in the dust. It was impossible for me to lay my head on the floor, which was very cold, not to mention the filth that covered it. In order to save my head, I had to sacrifice my feet: I took off my rough boots and made a pillow of them. My food was black bread, old and hard. When I broke it, all the little holes within were filled with bluish mold. I could eat only a little bit of the crust. They gave me no salt, to say nothing of towels or soap.

When I went to the punitive cell, I had not planned to speak at all; I had gone there only that it might not be so terrible for Popov to be alone. But Popov had no intention of remaining silent; the very next morning he began to call me, and I was weak enough to answer. But hardly had he begun his tapping again when the gendarmes forestalled him by snatching up staves and beating furiously on our doors. A din beyond all imagination arose. One who has not spent many years in the silence of a prison, whose ear has not grown unaccustomed to sounds, cannot imagine the pain experienced by an ear grown tender through the constant stillness.

Unable to stop their furious beating, I became angry and hysterical, and began myself to beat with my fists on the door behind which the gendarmes were raging. This was beyond one's strength to endure. And yet again and again Popov attempted to send messages, and evoked torturing battles with the gendarmes through the door. At last the patience of the gendarmes was exhausted. All at once the hellish din broke off abruptly. The heavy footsteps of the inspector rang through the corridor, and some mysterious preparations and an ominous, whispered conference broke the eerie stillness.

*Rakhmetov is one of the characters in Chernyshevsky's novel, *What Is To Be Done?*, who advocates and practises an extremely Spartan mode of living.—*Translator.*

"Now they are going to open Popov's door," thought I, "and begin to beat him. Can I possibly be a passive witness to this savage punishment? No, I can't endure it."

I began to call for the inspector.

"You want to beat Popov," said I in a strained, hard voice, as soon as he opened the little window in the cell door. "Don't beat him! You've beaten him once already—they may call even you to account!"

"We didn't beat him at all," said the inspector, quite unexpectedly beginning to justify himself. "We tied him, and he resisted, that's all there was to it."

"No, you beat him!" I retorted vehemently, feeling firm ground beneath my feet. "You beat him. There were witnesses, too. He will not do any more tapping," I continued. "I shall tell him, and he will stop."

"All right!" blurted out the inspector.

I called Popov, and told him that such a struggle was more than I could endure, and begged him to stop tapping. . . . Silence again.

The next day they brought me tea and a bed, but gave none to Popov, and I dashed the tea on the floor at the feet of the inspector, and refused to use the bed. But I broke off a piece of bread, and pointing to the mould, said to him: "You're keeping us on bread and water; just take a look then at the kind of bread you feed us."

The inspector flushed. "Give her some other bread," he ordered the gendarmes, and within five minutes they brought me a piece of fresh, soft bread.

For three more nights I lay on the asphalt in the nasty filth, in the cold, with my prison boots for a pillow. I lay there and thought, and thought. . . . What should I do next? It was evident that in the future there would be frequent occasions for collisions with the authorities. Under what circumstances, then, ought I, under what conditions would it be possible and expedient for me to resist the prison administration? By what methods should I struggle against it, how voice my protest? Must I always defend a comrade? My first impulse said, "always." But was one's comrade always right? I had lived through a test and it had been severe. I surveyed everything that had happened during the past few days; I examined my own conduct and Popov's, and asked myself: Do I wish, and have I the strength, to use Popov's methods in my struggle? He was a man with a constitution of iron, great self-control and an immense capacity for resistance, tempered in the Kara mines and the Alexey Ravelin; a cool, obstinate warrior of steel. When his jailers insulted and abused him, he repaid them in like coin. Rough treatment by the guards, noisy scuffles with the gendarmes, did not bother him at all. They bound him, and beat him; several times they beat him cruelly; and he bore it all, and took no revenge; he could still go on living. But I? I could not have done so. Plainly our ways were bound to diverge. I did not have enough strength, enough nervous energy, for the kind of warfare that he was waging; and from a moral point of view, I did not want to start a protest that I could not consistently carry out. Now was the time for me to map out my future conduct, to choose a firm position, to weigh all the conditions, both within and without, and to decide once and for all how I should act, so that there might be no opportunity for weakness or wavering. Petty daily quarrels, rough skirmishes ending in humiliation, were repellent to me, and I decided to reject such methods of warfare. I had learned the measure of my strength, and knew exactly what I could, and what I wished to do. I decided to endure everything that could be endured; but when some cause should arise worth defending with my life, I would protest in its defence, and protest to the point of death.*

On the fifth day of my imprisonment in the punitive cell the inspector said to me: "Prisoner Number Five has been given a bed, and a few other things."

Exhausted, and weakened as though by a wasting illness I was able at last to lie down on my bed, and it was high time; there was an incessant roaring and ringing in my ears, and I felt dazed and dull, half asleep and half awake. As I lay there in the twilight in a half-lethargic state, I suddenly heard singing. A pleasant, rather light baritone voice of unusual timbre was singing, and its quality reminded me vaguely of some one or something, I did not know which. It was a plain little folk song, and its motif simple and monotonous. Who was singing? Who could be singing in this place? I wondered. Could some workman have been admitted to the building on a repair job? That was impossible. And where did the sound come from? It seemed to come from the outside. Were they repairing the roof of the building?

---

*Fifteen whole years passed before life offered me such cause.

The mystery of this unknown singer confronted me for a long time, even after I had been released from the punitive cell. It was some time after this that I suddenly recalled his name, Grachevsky, after he had passed out of this life by committing suicide. And indeed, I learned afterwards that he was in the old prison at the same time that I was there.

Two more days went by.

"Time for your walk!" said the inspector, opening my door. My term of punishment was over.

"I will not go if you are releasing only me," said I, withdrawing into the corner, and added fearfully: "You surely wouldn't drag me out by force?"

The inspector appraised my frail, bowed figure in the corner from head to foot, shrugged his shoulders, and said with a contemptuous air: "What is there to drag!" And he added: "Number Five has left already."

And so I followed.

When I came back to my old cell after my walk, I moistened the slate board, and looked at myself in its small, mirror-like surface. I saw a face that in seven days had grown ten years older: hundreds of thin little wrinkles furrowed it in all directions. These wrinkles quickly disappeared, but not the impressions of the days which had just come to a close.

ROSA LUXEMBURG (1870?–1919)

Polish-born Rosa Luxemburg was raised in a middle-class, intellectual Jewish family in Warsaw. Her socialist political interests, beginning in high school, led her in 1889 to Zurich, where she studied at the university and completed a doctoral dissertation on Polish industrial development—the first of her many works on political and economic theory. In Zurich she met Leo Jogiches, a fellow socialist who was her lover until 1907. Together they founded the Social Democratic Party of the Kingdom of Poland, which opposed nationalism and advocated internationalism and solidarity with the Russian proletariat.

When Luxemburg moved to Berlin in 1898, she began work with the German Social Democratic Party, in which she became a powerful activist and theorist. Her opposition to World War I led to her imprisonment between February 1915 and November 1918 "for her own protection," with only a brief period of freedom in 1916. She was imprisoned in the Women's Prison in Berlin and the fortresses of Breslau and Wronke. Despite her ill health, she not only wrote letters from prison, but also continued her theoretical works. Although Luxemburg was a leader of the German Spartacus Association, which became the German Communist Party, she was unable to prevent the Berlin uprising of January 1919. The result was political retaliation and the assassination of Luxemburg and her associate Karl Liebknecht on January 15.

The following letters to Luxemburg's young lover Hans Diefenbach and to her close friend Sonja Liebknecht, wife of Karl Liebknecht, show how she attempted to live fully through appreciating literature and the natural world, even within prison.

Note: Biographical information is from Stephen E. Bronner, *The Letters of Rosa Luxemburg* (Boulder, Colo.: Westview Press, 1978); Elzbieta Ettinger, ed., *Comrade and Lover: Rosa Luxemburg's Letters to Leo Jogiches* (Cambridge, Mass.: MIT Press, 1979); Margaret Goldsmith, *Seven Women Against the World* (London: Methuen, 1935).

WORKS BY ROSA LUXEMBURG

The Accumulation of Capital. Translated from the German by Agnes Schwarzschild. New Haven: Yale Univ. Press, 1951.

Comrade and Lover: Rosa Luxemburg's Letters to Leo Jogiches. Edited by Elzbieta Ettinger. Cambridge, Mass.: MIT Press, 1979.

The Crisis in German Social Democracy: The Junius Pamphlet, by Karl Liebknecht, Rosa Luxemburg, and Franz Mehring. Translated from the German. New York: Socialist Publication Society, 1918.

The Industrial Development of Poland. Translated from the German by Tessa DeCarlo, with an Introduction by Lyndon H. LaRouche, Jr. Campaigner Publications, 1977. Originally published as Luxemburg's Ph.D. dissertation, Zurich, 1898.

Letters from Prison. Translated from the German by Eden Paul and Cedar Paul. Berlin: Pub. House of the Young International, 1921.

Letters to Karl and Luise Kautsky from 1896 to 1918. Edited by Luise Kautsky. Translated from the German by Louis P. Lochner. New York: McBride, 1925.

The Letters of Rosa Luxemburg. Edited by Stephen E. Bronner. Boulder, Colo.: Westview Press, 1978.

Reform or Revolution! 1899; reprint, New York: Pathfinder Press, 1970.

Rosa Luxemburg

The Russian Revolution, and Leninism or Marxism? New Introduction by Bertram D. Wolfe. Ann Arbor: Univ. of Michigan Press, 1961.

Letters to Friends

Wronke 1/15/17

[To Sonja Liebknecht]

... Oh, today there was a moment in which I felt bitter. The whistle of the locomotive at 3:19 told me that Mathilde* was departing, and on my usual "promenade" along the wall I paced back and forth like an animal in a cage, and my heart was convulsed with grief that I could not get away from here as well. Oh! Only to get away from here! But it doesn't matter. Immediately thereafter my heart was given a slap and had to heel; it has already learned to obey—like a well-trained dog. Let's not talk of me.

Sonitschka, do you still remember what we planned for after the end of the war? A trip together to the south. And we will do that! I know that you dream of going with me to Italy, that most exalted land. I, on the contrary, am planning to drag you to Corsica; that's even better than Italy. There, one forgets Europe, at least modern Europe.

Think of a broad, heroic landscape with the strong contours of mountains and valleys. On high, nothing except barren rock formations which are a noble grey; below, luxuriant olive trees, cherry trees, and age-old chestnut trees. And above everything, a prehistoric quiet—no human voices, no bird calls, only a stream rippling somewhere between rocks, or the wind on high whispering between the cliffs—still the same wind that swelled Ulysses' sails. And if you do meet people, they will fit exactly into the landscape.

For example, suddenly, from around the bend of a mountain path, a file of people and animals will appear—the Corsicans always travel behind one another in stretched-out single files, not in crowds like our peasants. Usually, a dog runs in front, then slowly along comes a goat

*Mathilde Jacob, Luxemburg's secretary and friend.—*Ed.*

[207]

or a little donkey laden down with sacks of chestnuts. Then, there follows a large mule, on which a woman, with a child in her arms, is riding side-saddle, her legs dangling straight down. She sits erect, immobile, slim like a cypress. Alongside, a bearded man is walking in a quiet firm stride. Both are silent.

You would swear: it's the Holy Family. And you encounter such scenes all the time. I was so moved every time that, instinctively, I wanted to sink to my knees as I always must before perfect beauty. There the Bible and antiquity are still alive. We must go there and do it the way I did it: across the whole island on foot, rest at a different place every night, and start out early each morning to greet the sunrise. Does that tempt you? I would be happy to show you this world.

Read a great deal. You must also progress intellectually, and you can do it—you are still fresh and flexible. And now I must close. Be cheerful and calm on this day.

Your

Rosa

Wronke i. P. 3/30/17

D. H. [To Hans Diefenbach]

With a great effort, I had just regained my composure, when a despair gripped me which was far blacker than the night. And today, once again, it is grey instead of sunny—a cold east wind. . . . I feel like a frozen bumble bee. Did you ever find such a bumble bee in your garden in the first frost of an autumn morning? It lies on its back, quite numb as if it were dead, with its little legs tucked in and its fur covered with hoar frost. Only when the sun warms it through, do the legs slowly begin to stir and stretch. Then the little body rolls over and finally, clumsily, rises into the air with a buzz. I always made it my duty to kneel down by such frozen bumble bees and, with the warm breath from my mouth, bring them back to life. If only the sun would awake me, poor soul that I am, from my cold death! In the meantime, like Luther, I'm fighting the devils inside me—with an inkwell.* That's why, as a sacrifice, you must withstand a barrage of letters. Until you have loaded your large gun, I will so bombard you with my low-caliber one that you will be

---

*Martin Luther is said to have thrown an inkwell at the devil.

in fear and trembling. By the way, if at the front you have been loading
your cannon with the same speed with which you have been writing
your letters, then I'm not at all surprised by our present retreat at the
Somme and Ancre. It will surely be on *your* conscience should we have
to conclude peace without annexing beautiful Flanders.

I thank you very much for Ricarda Huch's little book on Keller. Last
week, when I felt most wretched, I read it with pleasure. Ricarda is
really an extremely bright and intelligent person. Yet, her style, which
is so very etiolated, reserved, and controlled, seems to me somewhat
contrived; her deliberate classicism suggests something pseudoclassical
to me. Someone who is really rich and free in his mind can be natural
at any time and allow himself to be carried away by his passion without
becoming untrue to himself.

I also reread Gottfried Keller; the *Zurich Novellas* and *Martin Sa-
lander*. Please don't go up the wall, but I maintain that Keller cannot
write either novels or novellas. What he always presents are only *stories*
about things and people long since dead and gone. I am never involved
when something happens. I only see the narrator rummaging up beautiful memories in the manner of old people. Only the first part of *Der
grüne Heinrich* really *lives*. Just the same, Keller always does me good
because he's such a wonderful guy and, with a fellow whom one loves,
it's nice to sit and chat about insignificant things and little remembrances.

I have never experienced a spring more consciously or more intensely
than the last one—perhaps because it followed the year in jail, or because
by now I know every shrub and every little blade of grass with an
exactitude which allows me to follow the development of each. Do you
remember how a few years ago, by a blooming yellow bush, we tried to
figure out what it was? You made "the suggestion" that we identify it
as "laburnum." Naturally, it wasn't. How glad I am that three years ago
I suddenly threw myself into botany! And I did it the way I do everything,
with all the fervor I possess, with all of my self. The world, the Party
and work vanished. Night and day, I was filled with this one passion:
roving in spring meadows, collecting armfuls of flowers, then going
home, sorting them, identifying them, and mounting them in books.
How intensely I lived all that spring! As if in a fever! How I suffered
sitting by a new little plant, for a long time not knowing how to cat-

egorize it. Sometimes I would nearly faint in those instances, and Ger-
trud would angrily threaten to "take the plants away." But I now feel
myself at home in the green kingdom. I've conquered it, in storm and
in passion—and what one seizes with so much ardor grows deep roots
within one.

Last spring I still had a partner on those hikes: Karl Liebknecht.
Perhaps you know how he had been living for so many years. Parlia-
mentary sessions, commissions, conferences; hurry-scurry, continually
on the go, from train to tram and from tram to automobile, all his
pockets stuffed with note pads and all his arms full of newly bought
newspapers which he would never have time to read. His body and his
soul were covered with the grime of the street, and yet there was always
that genial young smile on his face. Last spring, I had convinced him
to take a little rest, to remind himself that a world exists outside the
Reichstag and the Landtag. Many were the times that he sauntered
through the fields and botanical gardens with Sonja and me. How he
enjoyed himself—like a child—looking at a birch tree with new catkins!

Once we hiked across the fields to Marienfelde. You know the way
—do you remember? We took the trip in autumn and had to walk over
stubble. But, last April with Karl, it was morning and the fields still
carried the fresh green of the winter crop. A mild wind pursued the grey
clouds to and fro in the sky. And the fields now were beaming in the
bright sunlight, now they were darkening like emeralds in the
shadows—a splendid play, and we silently marched along. Suddenly,
Karl stopped and began making strange leaps into the air, while keeping
a solemn look on his face. I watched him amazed, even a bit frightened,
and asked: "What's wrong with you?" "I'm so blissfully happy," he
answered simply, at which point we naturally broke into fits of laughter.

Affectionately,

R.

You unjustly wanted to have me classified as "the most beautiful and
precious stone" in Hindenburg's* pearl necklace. But, according to the
official statement, I am *not* a prisoner of war. Proof: I must pay the
postage for my letters.

*Paul von Hindenburg (1847–1934): To whom the victory over the Russians was
attributed; later commander-in-chief on the Western front. The symbol of German
nationalism, he became president of the Weimar Republic in 1925 and named Hitler
chancellor in 1933.

Rosa Luxemburg

Hänschen [To Hans Diefenbach],

Hello! I'm back again. Today I feel so lonely that I must refresh myself a bit by chatting with you.—This afternoon on my sofa I was taking the siesta which the doctor prescribed for me. I was reading the newspaper, and at two-thirty I decided to get up but then, immediately, I fell asleep unawares and had a wonderful dream which was very vivid but of indeterminate content. I know only that someone dear to me was there that I touched his lips with my finger and asked: "Whose mouth is this?" He answered: "Mine."—"Oh, no!" I cried laughing. "Why, that mouth belongs to me!" I awoke still laughing over this nonsense and looked at my watch: It was still two-thirty. My long dream had, in fact, only lasted a second. But it left me with the feeling of having had a precious experience, and then, comforted, I went back into the garden.

There, I was to have another beautiful experience: a robin sat down on the wall behind me and sang a little song to me. In general, the birds are now completely involved with family concerns; only now and then can one be heard for a short moment, as with today's robin, which has visited me only a few times early in May. I'm not sure whether you know this little bird and its song. Like so much else, I really got to know it only here, and I love it incomparably more than the renowned nightingale. The ringing recital of the nightingale reminds me too much of a prima donna, of audiences, of noisy triumphs, and of enthusiastic hymns of praise. The robin has a tiny, delicate little voice and it gives forth a singularly intimate melody which sounds like an up-beat or a bit of reveille. In the jail scene from *Fidelio*, do you know the distant trumpet call of deliverance which seems to pierce the darkness of night? The robin's song sounds something like this, only it has a soft, tremulous tone of infinite sweetness, like a misty remembrance lost in a dream.

My heart trembles in delight and pain when I hear this song and at once I see my life and the world in a new light, as if the clouds were to disperse and a new bright sunbeam were to fall on the earth.

Because of this soft little song, today I felt at peace with myself. Immediately I regretted all the wrongs I ever had done anyone and all the harsh thoughts and feelings I ever had. Once again, I resolved to be good, simply good—at any price. It's much better than "being right" and keeping accounts of every little insult. And then I decided to write you, today, right away, even though, since yesterday, a writing pad with seven resolutions has been sitting upon my table. The first reads: "Do not write letters." You see, that's how I keep to my own "ironclad" resolutions! That's how weak I am! If, as you write in your last letter, the stronger sex like women the most when they show their weakness, then you will now be delighted with me: Here I am! Oh, so weak! More so than I could wish.

By the way, there your babe's mouth speaks truer than you could imagine, for I just recently experienced this in the funniest manner. Surely, at the Copenhagen Congress, you saw Camille Huysmans, the tall youth with the dark curly hair and the typical Flemish face? Now, of course, he is the big mover at the Stockholm Conference.* For ten years, the two of us both belonged to the International Bureau and for ten years we hated each other—as far as such a feeling is possible for my "dove's heart" (the term was coined by Heinrich Schulz MdR!!!† . . .). Why? It's difficult to say. I believe that he cannot stand politically active women. For my part, I suppose his impertinent face got on my nerves. Well, it so happened that, during the last session in Brussels, which took place towards the end of July 1914 in the face of the approaching war, we found ourselves together for a few hours. We were at an elegant restaurant and I was sitting by a bunch of gladiolas which were on the table. I lost myself looking at them and did not take part in the political talk. Then the discussion turned to my departure, at which point my helplessness in "mundane things" became an issue. My eternal need for a guardian who would take care of my ticket, stick me on the right train and retrieve my lost handbags—in short, they brought up all those shameful weaknesses which have given you so many happy moments.

Huysmans silently watched me all the while, and within an hour, the ten-year hatred was transformed into a glowing friendship. It was laughable. At last he had seen me in my weakness and he was in his element. Right away he decided to take my fate in hand. Together with Anseele,‡ that delightful little Walloon, he dragged me to his house for supper, brought in a little kitten, and played and sang Mozart and Schu-

*The reference is to the socialist Stockholm Peace Conference.
†MdR is the abbreviation for Member of the Reichstag.
‡Edouard Anseele (1856–1938): One of the founders and leading members of the Belgian Workers' Party and a member of the executive committee of the Second International.

bert for me. He owns a fine piano and possesses a nice tenor. It was a new revelation for him that musical culture should be my life's blood. He played Schubert's *Limits of Mankind** very nicely and he sang the closing verse, "And with us play the clouds and the winds" a few times in his funny Flemish accent—with the deep throaty L, something like "cloouds"—with deep emotion.

Afterwards, naturally, he took me to the train, carrying my suitcase himself. He even sat in the compartment with me and then suddenly decided: "Mais il est impossible de vous laisser voyager seule!"†—as if I really were a baby. I was barely able to talk him out of accompanying me, at least to the German border; he jumped off just as the train was getting under way, still calling "Au revoir à Paris!" For in two weeks we were to hold a congress in Paris. That was on the 31st of July. But, as my train pulled into Berlin, the mobilization was in full progress, and two days later poor Huysmans' beloved Belgium was occupied. I had to repeat to myself: "And with us play the clouds and the winds. . . ."

In two weeks, a full year of my imprisonment will be over, or—if you disregard a short interval—two full years. Oh, how much good an hour of harmless chatter would do me now! During visiting hours, of course, we hastily discuss business matters and, most of the time, I am on tenterhooks. Apart from this, I neither see nor hear a human soul.

Now it's 9 p.m., but naturally it's light as day. It's so quiet all around, only the ticking of the clock, and from the distance, the muffled barking of a dog. Isn't it strange how it reminds you of home when in the country you hear dogs barking at night? Instantly I imagine a comfortable peasant's farm house, a man in shirt sleeves standing on the doorstep chatting with a neighbor's wife, his pipe in his mouth. From inside, the bright voices of children and the clatter of dishes. Outside, there is the smell of ripe wheat and the first diffident croaking of frogs. . . .

Adieu, Hänschen

mid-November, 1917

My dearest Sonitschka [To Sonja Liebknecht],

Soon, I hope to get another chance at sending you this letter, and I seize the pen with longing. How long now have I had to forego the lovely

---

*Based on Goethe's poem.
†"But it would be absolutely impossible to allow you to travel alone."

custom of at least chatting with you on paper! But I couldn't help it; the few letters which I was permitted to write I had to save for Hans D[iefenbach] who, after all, was waiting for them. Now it's all over. My last two letters had been written to a dead man; one has already been returned to me. I still cannot comprehend the fact that he's dead. But, let's rather not talk about it. I prefer to settle such matters with myself alone, and when someone, "sparing my feelings," wants to prepare me for the bad news and "comfort" me through his own lamentation, as N. did, this irritates me unspeakably. That my closest friends still know me so little! That they so underestimate me! That they fail to comprehend: the best and most delicate approach in such circumstances is to tell me quickly the short and simple words "he is dead"—that offends me. But enough of that.

What a pity for the months and years which are passing and in which we could be spending so many beautiful hours together, in spite of all the horror which is taking place in the world. You know, Sonitschka, that the longer it takes, and the more the basenesses and atrocities occurring every day transgress all limits and bounds, the more calm and resolute do I become. Just as I cannot apply moral standards to the elements, to a hurricane, a flood, or a solar eclipse, and instead, consider them only something given, an object of research and knowledge, these are obviously, objectively, the only possible paths of history, and we must follow them without getting diverted from the basic direction. I have a feeling that this whole moral mire through which we are now wading, this huge madhouse in which we are living, can overnight, with the wave of a magic wand, be transformed into its opposite, transformed into something extraordinarily great and heroic and—if the war should last for another few years—it *must* be transformed. . . .

When you get a chance, read *The Gods Are Athirst* by Anatole France. I consider the work to be so great primarily because, with a genius' insight into all of human nature, it says: Just look! The most enormous events and the most monumental gestures are made from these miserable figures and these everyday pettinesses in the decisive moments of history.

We must take everything that happens in society the same way as in private life: calmly, generously and with a mild smile. I firmly believe that, in the end, after the war, or at the close of the war, everything will turn out all right. But apparently we must first wade through a period of the worst human suffering.

Apropos, my last words awake a different idea in me, a fact which I would like to share with you because it seems so poetic and touching. Recently, I read in a scientific work on the flight of birds—which until now has been a fairly puzzling phenomenon—that it was observed how different species which are usually deadly enemies, making war on one another and eating each other, peacefully make the great trip south across the sea, flying next to one another. Gigantic flocks of birds go to Egypt for the winter. They fly high up like clouds and darken the sky. Among these flocks, right between birds of prey—hawks, eagles, falcons, owls—there are thousands of little songbirds like larks, golden-crested wrens, and nightingales, who fly without any fear in the midst of the birds of prey which normally pursue them. On the trip, therefore, a tacit truce of God seems to rule; all strive for the common destination and at the Nile fall down half-dead from exhaustion, there to divide back into species and groups of compatriots. Moreover, it has been observed that on this trip "across the great pond" large birds transport many smaller ones on their backs. Thus, flocks of cranes have been seen passing on whose backs tiny migrating birds were merrily twittering! Isn't that charming?

. . . In an otherwise tasteless and pell-mell collection of poems, I recently discovered one by Hugo von Hofmannsthal.* In general, I don't like him at all; I feel he is affected, overly refined and obscure—I simply don't understand him at all. But, I liked this poem very much, and it made a strong poetic impression upon me. I enclose it for you. Perhaps it will give you pleasure as well.

I am now deeply interested in geology. You probably think of it as a very dry science, but that is a mistake. I read the material with a feverish interest and passionate satisfaction; it broadens one's intellectual standpoint enormously, and it conveys a more unified, all-encompassing conception of nature than any other science.

I would like to tell you a great deal about it, but for that we would

---

*Hugo Von Hofmannsthal (1874–1919): Major modernist writer and poet, Hofmannsthal's best-known work is perhaps his play, *The Tower*. He was also the librettist of Richard Strauss' *Rosenkavalier* and *Salome*.

have to talk, while strolling on the Südende field in the morning, or walking each other home a few times on a quiet, moonlit night.

What are you reading? How is it going with *The Lessing Legend*? I want to know everything! Write—if possible—immediately through the same channels or, at least, through official channels without mentioning this letter. I am also silently counting the weeks until I see you here again. That will be soon after New Year's, won't it?

What has Karl written? When will you see him again? Send him a thousand greetings from me. I embrace you and firmly press your hand, my dear, dear, Sonitschka! Write soon and extensively.

Your Rosa

Breslau, mid-December, 1917

[To Sonja Liebknecht]

. . . It's a year now that Karl's been in Luckau. During the past month, I've thought of this often, and exactly one year ago you were visiting me in Wronke, where you presented me with a beautiful Christmas tree. . . . This year I had ordered one. But they brought me a real shabby one, with branches missing—no comparison with the one of last year. I don't know how I will fasten the eight little candles I bought. This will be my third Christmas in jail. But don't you take it too hard; I am as calm and cheerful as ever.

Well, yesterday I thought: how strange that I continually live in a happy state of intoxication for no particular reason. So, for example, I am lying here on a stone-hard mattress in a dark cell, around me the usual quiet of a cemetery; one imagines oneself in the grave. From the window, the reflection of the lantern—which burns all night in front of the prison—is drawn on the ceiling. From time to time, one hears, quite muffled, the distant rattling of a passing train or, from nearby under the window, a sentinel clearing his throat; he is slowly taking a few steps in his heavy boots in order to move his stiff legs. The sand rustles so hopelessly beneath his steps that the whole desolation and inescapability of existence rises from it into the damp, dark night.

There I lie, quiet, alone, wrapped in those manifold black scarves of darkness, boredom, confinement, and winter—and, at the same time, my heart beats with an incomprehensible, unknown inner happiness, as if I were walking over a blooming field in radiant sunshine. And I smile at life in the darkness as if I were aware of some magical secret which might confute the lies, the baseness and the sadness and transform them into sheer brightness and felicity.

And at the same time, I myself am searching for a reason for this happiness. But I find none, and again I must smile at myself. I believe that this mystery is nothing other than life itself; the deep darkness of night is beautiful and soft as velvet if only one looks at it properly. And in the rustling of the moist sand beneath the slow, heavy tread of a sentry, a beautiful little song of life is also singing—if only one knows how to listen properly. In such moments I think of you, and I would so much like to share this magical key with you so that, always, in every situation, you will be able to perceive the beauty and happiness of life, so that you too will live in a state of ecstasy as if you were crossing a multicolored meadow.

Of course, I wouldn't dream of feeding you on asceticism and imaginary joys. I do not begrudge you any real sensuous happiness. I would only like to add to that my own inexhaustible inner cheerfulness, so that I shouldn't worry about you and so that you walk through life in a mantle studded with stars which will protect you from all that is petty, trivial, and frightening.

You picked a beautiful bunch of black and pink violet berries in Steglitz Park. For the blackberries either elders come to mind—their berries hanging in heavy, thick clusters between large, feathery fronds, surely you know them—or, more likely, privets: thin, dainty, upright panicles of berries with slim, longish, green little leaves. The pinkish-violet berries hidden beneath little leaves could be those of the dwarf medlar; they are really red, but in this late season they are already a bit overripe; they begin to rot, and so they often appear reddish-violet. The leaves resemble those of the myrtle: small, pointed at the ends, dark green, and leathery on top, rough below.

Sonjuscha, do you know Platen's *Lethiferous Fork*?* Could you either send or bring it to me? Karl mentioned once that he had read it at home. The poems by [Stefan] George are beautiful. Now I know where the verse originated which you used to recite during our walks in the fields:

---

*August Graf von Platen-Hallermünde (1796–1835): A poet of the Biedermeier period. Platen's works include *Sonnets from Venice* and *The Romantic Oedipus*.

"And under the rustling of the stalks of grain!" When you get a chance, would you make a copy of [Goethe's] "The New Amadis"? I love that poem so very much—naturally, thanks to Hugo Wolf's *Lied*—but I don't have it here. Have you read further in *The Lessing Legend*? I have again taken up Lange's *History of Materialism** which always excites and refreshes me. I would very much like you to read it.

Ach, Sonitschka! I have experienced an acute pain here. In the yard where I walk, military wagons often arrive, packed full with sacks, or old uniforms and shirts often spotted with blood. . . . They are unloaded here, passed out in the cells, mended, then reloaded, and delivered to the military. The other day, such a wagon came drawn by water buffaloes rather than horses. This was the first time that I saw these animals up close. They are built sturdier and broader than our oxen, with flat heads, their horns bent flat, their skulls rather resembling the skulls of our own sheep; the buffaloes are completely black with large soft eyes. They come from Rumania, they are trophies of war. . . . The soldiers who drive the wagon say that it was a very hard job to catch these wild animals and even more difficult to use them, who were so used to freedom, as beasts of burden. They were beaten frightfully to the point where the words apply to them: "Woe to the defeated." . . . About a hundred of these animals are said to be in Breslau alone. Moreover, used to the luxuriant pastures of Rumania, they receive miserable and scant fodder. They are mercilessly exploited in dragging all kinds of loads, and so they perish rapidly.

Anyway, a few days ago, a wagon loaded with sacks drove into the prison. The cargo was piled up so high that the buffaloes could not make it over the threshold of the gateway. The attending soldier, a brutal character, began to beat away at the animals with the heavy end of his whip so savagely that the overseer indignantly called him to account "Don't you have any pity for the animals?" "No one has any pity for us people either!" he answered with an evil laugh, and fell upon them ever more forcefully. . . . Finally, the animals started up and got over the hump, but one of them was bleeding. . . . Sonitschka, buffalo hide

*Friedrich Albert Lange (1828–1875): A left Kantian; Rosa is referring to his *History of Materialism*, which was published in second edition in 1876 and widely read by socialists.

is proverbial for its thickness and toughness, and it was lacerated. Then, during the unloading, the animals stood completely still, exhausted, and one, the one that was bleeding, all the while looked ahead with an expression on its black face and in its soft black eyes like that of a weeping child. It was exactly the expression of a child who has been severely punished and who does not know why, what for, who does not know how to escape the torment and brutality. . . . I stood facing the animal and it looked at me; tears were running from my eyes—they were *his* tears. One cannot quiver any more painfully over one's dearest brother's sorrow than I quivered in my impotence over this silent anguish.

How far, how irretrievably lost, are the free, succulent, green pastures of Rumania! How different it was with the sun shining, the wind blowing; how different were the beautiful sounds of birds, the melodious calls of shepherds. And here: this strange weird city, the fusty stable, the nauseating mouldy hay mixed with putrid straw, the strange, horrible people—and the blows, the blood running from the fresh wound. . . . Oh! My poor buffalo! My poor beloved brother! We both stand here so powerless and spiritless and are united only in pain, in powerlessness and in longing. . . .

Meanwhile, the prisoners bustled busily about the wagon, unloading the heavy sacks and carrying them into the building. The soldier, however stuck both hands into his pockets, strolled across the yard with great strides, smiled and softly whistled a popular song. And the whole glorious war passed in front of my eyes. . . . Write quickly. I embrace you, Sonitschka.

Your Rosa

Sonitschka, dearest, in spite of it all, be calm and cheerful. That's life, and that's how one must take it: courageously, intrepidly and smilingly—in spite of it all.

EUGENIA SEMYONOVNA GINZBURG (1905?–1977)

Eugenia Ginzburg's first book, *Journey into the Whirlwind*, describes the author's eighteen-year imprisonment in Stalin's prisons and Siberian labor camps. It has been compared with Solzhenitsyn's *Gulag Archipelago*. Ginzburg, who described herself as a naively dedicated and loyal

Communist, was expelled from the Party, arrested in 1937 in Kazan, and charged with belonging to a terrorist organization. The former history professor and writer on the staff of *Red Tartary* was separated from her two sons and her husband, a Communist official who was also arrested and later died during his imprisonment. One son died of starvation; her surviving son joined her in Siberia after eleven years.

In her first prison, in the "cellars at Black Lake" in Kazan, she was interrogated and kept isolated from everyone but her cell mate, Lyama. The selection below describes how Ginzburg began communicating with prisoners outside her cell when she deciphered the ancient code of wall tapping by recalling an explanation in Vera Figner's memoirs. In one of her subsequent prisons, in Yaroslavl, she endured solitary confinement by recalling great Russian poetry and mentally composing her own poems.

In 1939 Ginzburg was transferred from prison to the Siberian hard-labor camps. She discusses her experiences in the gold region of Kolyma in her second book, *Within the Whirlwind*. While working as a nurse there, she met and fell in love with her second husband, Dr. Anton Walter. After her release she spent a period of time in exile in the Soviet Union with her son, dissident novelist Vassily Aksyonov, who learned from her of the great, forbidden Russian writers. She was finally "rehabilitated" in 1955. In 1976 she traveled to Paris, where a PEN Club reception honored her.

Note: Biographical information is from "Love and Death in the Gulag," *New York Times Magazine* (June 7, 1981): 26; Harrison E. Salisbury, review of *Within the Whirlwind*, by Eugenia Ginzburg, *New York Times Book Review* (July 12, 1981): 10, 38.

WORKS BY EUGENIA GINZBURG

Journey into the Whirlwind. Translated by Paul Stevenson and Max Hayward. New York: Harcourt Brace Jovanovich, 1967.
Within the Whirlwind. Translated by Ian Boland, with an Introduction by Heinrich Böll. New York: Harcourt Brace Jovanovich, 1981.

Eugenia Semyonovna Ginzburg

The Walls Come to Life

Suddenly they stopped summoning me for interrogation. The empty
prison days fell into a kind of regular routine, marked by the issue of
hot water in the morning, the fifteen-minute walk in the prison yard
(during which we were followed by guards with rifles and fixed bayo-
nets), the meals, the washroom. The interrogators seemed to have forgotten my existence.

"They do it on purpose," said Lyama.* "It's three weeks since I was
last called. They hope prison life will drive you crazy, so that, in sheer
desperation, you'll sign any old nonsense."

But I was so shaken by my first experience of Black Lake "justice"
that I was glad of the unexpected respite.

"Well, let's make sure we don't go crazy," I said to Lyama. "Let's use
our time to find out all we can about our surroundings. You said yourself
that the great thing was to establish contact—and he's still tapping,
isn't he?"

The prisoner in the cell to our left was still tapping on the wall,
regularly, every day after dinner. But I had been too exhausted by the
interrogations to listen properly to his knocking, and Lyama despaired
of ever getting the hang of the prison alphabet.

One thing, however, we had noticed. On the days when our neighbor
went to the washroom before us—this we could tell by the sound of
the footsteps in the corridor—we always found the shelf sprinkled with
tooth powder and the word "Greetings" traced in it with something
very fine like a pin, and as soon as we got back to our cell, a brief
message was tapped on the wall. After that, he immediately stopped.
These knocks were altogether different from the long sequences our
neighbor tapped after dinner, when he was trying to teach us the alphabet.

After two or three times it suddenly dawned on me:

" 'Greetings'! That's what he's tapping," I told Lyama. "He writes

*Ginzburg's cell mate at "Black Lake," her first prison in Kazan.—*Ed.*

and taps the same word. Now we know how we can work out the signs for the different letters." We counted the knocks.

"That's right!" Lyama whispered excitedly. "The tapping comes in groups with long and short intervals. And he tapped out nine letters in all: g-r-e-e-t-i-n-g-s."

During the long months and years I spent in various prisons, I was able to observe the virtuosity that human memory can develop when it is sharpened by loneliness and complete isolation from outside impressions. One remembers with amazing accuracy everything one has ever read, even quite long ago, and can repeat whole pages of books one had believed long forgotten. There is something almost mysterious about this phenomenon. That day, at any rate, after deciphering the message "Greetings" tapped on the wall, I was astounded to find a page from Vera Figner's memoirs whole and fresh in my mind. It was the page in which she gave the clue to the prison alphabet. Clutching my head, myself astounded by my own words, I recited as if talking in my sleep:

"The alphabet is divided into five rows of five letters each. Each letter is represented by two sets of knocks, one slow, the other quick. The former indicates the row, the latter the position of the letter in it."

Wild with excitement, interrupting each other and for once forgetting the guard in the corridor, we tapped out our first message. It was very short:

"W-h-o-a-r-e-y-o-u?"

Yes, it was right! Through the grim stone wall we could sense the joy of the man on the other side. At last we had understood! His endless patience had been rewarded. "Rat-tat, tat-tat-tat!" He tapped like a cheerful tune. From then on, we used these five knocks to mean "Message understood."

Now he was tapping his reply—no longer for a couple of idiots who had to have the word "greeting" repeated a hundred times, but for intelligent people to whom he could give his name:

"S-a-g-i-d-u-l-l-i-n."

"Sagidullin? Who's that?" The name meant nothing to Lyama, but it did to me. Much more boldly, I tapped:

"Himself?"

Yes, it was he—Garey Sagidullin, whose name for years past had not been mentioned in Kazan without an "ism" tacked on to it: Sagidul-linism.

It was the heading of a propaganda theme. "Sagidullinism," like "Sultan-Galeyevism," stood for the heresy of Tartar "bourgeois nationalism." But he had been arrested in 1933. What on earth was he doing here now?

Through the wall my bewilderment evidently was sensed and understood. The message went on:

"I was and I remain a Leninist. I swear it by my seventh prison"—and startlingly: "Believe me, Genia."

How could he know my name? How could he, through the wall, in spite of all the strictness of our isolation, know who was next door? We looked at one another in alarm. We had no need to speak out loud. The thought was in both our minds. He might be a *provocateur.*

Once again he understood and patiently explained. It appeared that in his cell, too, there was a chink between the window boards, and for a long time he had watched us walking in the yard. Although we had never met, he had once caught a glimpse of me at the Institute of Red Professors in Moscow. He had been brought back to Kazan for re-examination on additional charges. It looked like the death sentence.

From then on, though outwardly nothing had altered, our days were full of interest. All morning I looked forward to the after-dinner hour when the guards were changed and, as they handed over their human cattle, were for a while distracted from peeping through spy holes and listening at doors.

Garey's brief messages opened a new world to me, a world of camps, deportations, prisons, tragic twists of fate—a world in which either the spirit was broken and degraded or true courage was born.

I learned from him that all those who had been arrested in 1933 and '35 had now been sent back for "re-examination." Nothing new whatever had occurred to justify this, but as the interrogators cynically put it, it was a matter of "translating all those files into the language of '37"—that is, replacing three- and five-year sentences by more radical ones.

An even more important objective was to force these "hardened" oppositionists (whose opposition in some cases had consisted in advancing untested scientific ideas, such as Vasily Slepkov's methodological research in the field of natural science) to sign the monstrous lists, concocted by the interrogators, of those whom they had "suborned." The signatures were obtained by threats, bullying, false accusations, and detention in punishment cells (the beatings began only in June or July, after the Tukhachevsky trial*).

Garey hated Stalin with a bitter passion, and when I asked him what he believed to be the cause of the current troubles, he replied tersely:

"Koba." (This was Stalin's Georgian nickname.) "It's his eighteenth Brumaire. Physical extermination of all the best people in the Party, who stand or might stand in the way of his definitely establishing his dictatorship."

For the first time in my life I was faced by the problem of having to think things out for myself—of analyzing circumstances independently and deciding my own line of conduct.

"It's not as if you were in the hands of the Gestapo." Major Yelshin's† words rang in my mind.

How much easier and simpler if I had been! A Communist held by the Gestapo—I would have known exactly how to behave. But here? Here I had first to determine who these people were, who kept me imprisoned. Were they fascists in disguise? Or victims of some supersubtle provocation, some fantastic hoax? And how should a Communist behave "in prison in his own country," as the Major had put it?

All these anguished questions I put to Garey, ten years my senior in age and fifteen as a Party member. But his advice was not such that I could follow it, and it left me still more puzzled. To this day I cannot understand what could have prompted him, and Slepkov and many others who had been arrested in the early thirties, to act as he advised me to do now.

"Tell them straight out, you disagree with Stalin's line, and name as many others who disagree as you can. They can't arrest the whole Party, and by the time they have thousands of such cases on their hands, someone will think of calling an extraordinary Party congress and there

*Mikhail Tukhachevsky, 1893–1937, Soviet military leader who, together with Gamarnik, Yakir, Uborevich, and other members of the Soviet High Command, was executed in 1937.
†Ginzburg's interrogator.—Ed.

will be a chance of overthrowing him. Believe me, he's as much hated in the Central Committee as here in prison. Of course it may mean the end for us, but it's the only way to save the Party."

No, this was something I could not do. Even though I felt obscurely, without having any proof, that Stalin was behind the nightmare events in our Party, I could not say that I disagreed with the Party line. I had honestly and fervently supported the policies of industrializing the country and collectivizing the land, and these were the basic points of the Party line.

Still less could I name others, knowing as I did that the very mention of a Communist within these walls would be enough to ruin him and orphan his children.

No; if the demagogic habits of mind I had been trained in were so deeply rooted in me that I could not now make an independent analysis of the situation in the country and the Party, then I would be guided simply by the voice of my conscience. I would speak only the truth about myself, I would sign no lies against myself or anyone else, and I would give no names. I must not be taken in by Jesuitical arguments which justified lies and fratricide. It was impossible that they could be of service to the Party I had so fervently believed in and to which I had resolved to dedicate my life.

All this—very briefly, of course—I transmitted to Garey. I had mastered the technique of tapping so thoroughly, by the end of a week, that Garey and I could recite whole poems to each other. We no longer needed to spell everything out. We had a special sign to show that we had understood, so we could use abbreviations and save time. A blow of the fist meant that a warder was about. I must confess that he used this signal much more often than I did, and I would surely have been caught if it hadn't been for him. However interesting the conversation, he never ceased to be on the alert.

I was never to set eyes on this man. He was eventually shot. I disagreed with many things he said and I never had a chance to discover exactly what his political views were. But I know one thing for certain: he endured his seventh prison, his isolation, and the prospect of being shot with unbroken courage. He was a strong man, a man in the true sense of the word.

ERICA GLASER WALLACH (1922–   )

German-born Erica Glaser had married American Robert Wallach and was living in the United States when she decided to travel to East Berlin in 1950 to learn what had become of her adoptive parents, Noel and Herta Field. Former League of Nations and State Department official Field, his wife, and his brother had disappeared mysteriously behind the Iron Curtain. In August 1950 Erica Wallach was arrested in East Berlin and taken to the Schumannstrasse Prison, where she was relentlessly interrogated. She spent more than two years in East German prisons until she was tried before a Soviet court-martial in January 1953, found guilty of espionage, and sentenced to death.

Wallach was transferred to Moscow and in July her sentence was reduced to fifteen years' imprisonment in the labor camp at Vorkuta, a coal-mining center where she worked constructing roads and railroads. Her only communication with her husband and relatives was through monthly postcards sent from the camp.

In October 1955 she was released by the Soviets, who stated that the charges against her had been mistaken. She refused the compensation offered for her imprisonment. At the age of thirty-three she was finally reunited with her family, who had been living in Virginia; her children had been only six months and two years old when she was arrested. Doctors were shocked to find that her health, which had been poor at the time of her imprisonment, had actually improved. The following excerpts from her prison memoirs illustrate Wallach's point that humans are remarkably capable of surviving and overcoming adverse conditions. She writes, "there is no doubt in my mind that the five years added something to my life rather than took away from it."

Note: Biographical information is from the *New York Times*, 18, 19, 28 October 1955.

WORK BY ERICA WALLACH

Light at Midnight. Garden City, N.Y.: Doubleday, 1967.

Erica Glaser Wallach

House of Horrors

It was Sunday night, an hour after "bedtime," which meant it was
probably eleven o'clock. I was lying on my cot, without sleeping, determined to ruin my nerves and my health even more than They did.
And I could proudly say that I had succeeded, considering that I had
been in prison only eight days. I was a nervous wreck and a physical
horror—a fact that gave me my only satisfaction. It had been a good
day for my nerves, with no activity, no conversation; there was ample
time for the imagination to work.

All the prisons I came to know were famous for their terrifying silences; but Sundays were even more silent, cruelly silent. A Sunday in
prison is like stale water—dirty, smelly, immobile, and yet deep and
frightening.

Usually nothing happens; no questioning, no opening and closing of
doors. The hours from one meal to another seem endless. Never is the
prisoner more aware of the ticking away of time, of the senselessness
of his existence, of life going on in the outside world, of being buried
alive.

I had spent the day brooding over all the sad things there were to
think about, trying to figure out why I was here, counting on my fingers
how old I would be if I were given the twenty-five-year sentence I had
been promised the day before, wondering what my children would look
like then, and other equally pleasant things. Looking around me, I saw
again my ugly home, a cell dimly lit and furnished in solid gray, with
high ceiling, thick stone walls, cement floor, a small table and stool of
heavy wood fixed to the wall, to prevent one from using them as weapons; an iron bed also fixed, the heavy bucket in the corner. And in the
cell Ratbit, a cross between a rat and a rabbit, as gray and ugly and
cheerless as its home—I, or what was left of me.

In my mind, I was seeing my husband warming the bottle for the
baby, when I heard the key in the door. For years to come this sound
would immediately bring a faster heartbeat, trembling, nausea—symp-
toms generally summarized in the word fear.

What could it be? I was still naïve enough to believe that I would not be questioned on Sunday nights. An eternity passed before the key turned twice, the iron bolt was pushed back, and the heavy door opened noiselessly.

"Please, lady, do you want a bath?" The tall, serious warden from Silesia, from then on called "Bathing Master," was standing in the door; behind him was "Zille," a typical young Berliner, with a twinkle in his eye.

I almost laughed; it sounded so funny in this setting, as though the valet in a hotel were saying, "Madame, your bath is ready." But I caught myself in time. How could I have laughed here, in the "house of horrors," as I had named my present domicile. I was very proud of this clever thought; it was one of my strongest weapons against myself, a continuous source of self-pity and self-destruction. It worked this time, too. What could he mean—a devilish torture of some kind? Tears came to my eyes. "Bathing, now? But it is the middle of the night." My voice was barely audible. "I know it is late," said Bathing Master, "but we couldn't get the water hot before." "So that's what it is, boiling water," I thought, and with the greatest readiness for martyrdom, I put my bare feet on the stone floor, keeping the scratchy, dirty gray blanket wrapped around my body, dressed only in pants and bra. "Knock when you are ready!" Bathing Master and Zille withdrew discreetly.

I put skirt and blouse on hastily with trembling hands, stepped into my sandals, knocked timidly, and followed my two butchers to the slaughterhouse, noting with satisfaction that every bone in my body hurt from the cold, hard cot. Not a sound, except for the heavy steps of the men and the slight squeak of my sandals. How many gray doors did I pass? I tried to count but lost track. We went down steep steps into an enormous cellar, and a vision of the torture scenes in *Darkness at Noon* suddenly came to me. How I wished then that I had not read the book just before my arrest. There is no better weapon against yourself than fear.

"Here, please. You can undress in this room and hang up your clothes, and then come to the shower." Bathing Master started fiddling with the knobs.

A real shower! I was stunned and just stood there watching him from my doorless dressing room.

"I am afraid you will have to undress if you want to take a shower," he said. "You can't very well wash with your clothes on, can you?"

"I was waiting for you to go out," I said, offended.

"We have to stay in here; regulations, you know."

"Oh yes, of course." Nothing could have shocked me by then. I took my four items off and ran for protection under the shower. I felt utterly naked in the air, but the water seemed to cover me.

Bathing Master had turned his back, still adjusting the various handles. Zille filled the doorway, trying hard to look past me and yet see me.

"Is the water right?" Bathing Master asked.

"Yes, thank you, just right."

"Not too hot?"

"No, thank you, just right."

"Do you want some more hot water?"

"No, thank you, it is just right."

Poor Bathing Master, he turned his head half right, half left, but did not dare turn around completely. It was Zille, of course, who found his wits first; he put both hands in his pockets, feet wide apart, head back, and relaxed into a broad smile.

"My, are you ever brown! You look as though you had white pants on."

"I'm just back from the Riviera," I said tearfully.

Bathing Master could not stand it any longer. He turned around, lit a cigarette, and stared openly at me too. "Doesn't the warm water feel good? Just take your time and scrub yourself properly. God knows when you will have an opportunity again."

I obeyed. When the time was up, I dried myself with a rough rag and followed my guardians back to Cell Number Seven.

That was the beginning of my career as a public nude. I was to become so accustomed to it that, looking back on this inoffensive little scene, I would wonder why I had even for a second hesitated to take off my clothes. As a matter of fact, the whole thing meant really nothing compared to matters of far more importance which preoccupied me. I had already lost the feeling of being human, much less a woman. And my jailers obviously were not men. I had forgotten that the world still

existed, that life around me went on, that the fact that I had lost awareness did not mean that others no longer thought. "Caraway," my in-
terrogating officer, was to remind me of that. Soon everything changed,
and what followed provided ample time and opportunity to think back
with nostalgia to this short period of human kindness and comfort.

At that point, I did not yet know that horror, fear, mental torture are
not physical facts but creations of one's own spirit. They were not forced
upon me by outside acts or conditions, but lived within me, born of the
weakness of my own heart. If I was beaten, it hurt. That was a fact—a
physical fact. And there were many other physical facts, other tortures.
But everything else was a matter of my own attitude, my will power,
my fantasy. I alone was responsible for the reaction of my nerves, for
the impressions outside factors made on my mind, for the repercussions
of these impressions on all parts of my being—and on my actions. I did
not need to be shaken up by the unknown; I did not have to see horror
where no physical act of horror was committed; I did not have to break
if I did not want to. I wanted to then because I still believed that it was
harder to be a hero than to be a weakling; because I still believed that
I could save my miserable life by being a coward. . . .

We were quietly sitting on our bunks, and Helga* was telling us the
recipe of her favorite chocolate cake. Breakfast was over, the bucket had
been emptied, the officers had made their rounds, and it was not yet
time for interrogation. The prison was ominously silent.

Suddenly we thought we heard a door being opened far away. At once
we dropped the chocolate cake and listened—the automatic reaction of
every prisoner, who so desperately needs to know what goes on around
him. Yes, there it was again: the door was closed, another one opened.
A strange noise came from very far away.

"Perhaps some people are taken to the doctor?" Frieda asked hopefully. She had demanded to see a doctor ever since she had arrived.

"Doubtful. Perhaps a barber for the men. They have to shave them
sometimes, you know." Helga was the most practical of us.

"Listen, there is another door, and they seem to be coming closer."
I strained my ears.

---

*Helga and Frieda were Wallach's companions in the Russian prison in Karlshorst,
outside Berlin.—*Ed.*

"Yes, they are coming closer. Oh, my God, that sounds like an animal. What *is* that sound?"

"Someone gone crazy, that's what it sounds like."

"Shut up. There, that's the next cell. There it is again. Listen. It's a man screaming. I know it is."

"Don't be silly. Probably some hysterical female. Let's not get excited."

The door was shut again, and again there was deadly silence. Everyone waited in horror. And there it was again: the keys, the next cell opened. Nothing for a minute, and then—there was no question about it—a man screaming, then another, screaming with pain.

Closer and closer it came. Cell after cell was opened on our corridor, and after a minute of silence, wails and screams would pierce the silence. The guards went back and forth on their checking tours, opening the lid every few seconds. We stood in utter terror; no one spoke a word. What was there to say?

Now they were just a few cells away from us, and we could hear voices, women's voices: "No, no, I didn't, please, oh please . . ." And then the horrible screams. So women got it too. There was no escape for us.

"Oh, Lord," Frieda whispered. "I can't stand physical pain. Let me out, let me out of this hell!" She was beginning to get hysterical.

"Shut up," Helga said. "Let's find out what this is all about. They are two cells away from us now. Listen!"

Heavy boots went to the door, many of them. The key was turned in the lock. "No," a man yelled, "I did not knock!" "I didn't knock either," came another voice. And then a heavy thumping, over and over again, and the most ghastly roars of pain: "Stop it, ooohh, stop!"

So that was it: Knocking. Knocking on the wall with the alphabet system—the only communication a prisoner had with his neighbors. We knew it was what our jailers feared the most and punished mercilessly. Now that we knew, it was almost an anticlimax. But we had to consult quickly, make a plan of action.

The punishment commando was next door to us. We could not hear a word, but the screams of the two men spoke a clear enough language. And now the boots were in front of our cell, the key turned in the lock, and in walked Natchalnik and five or six other people. I couldn't have been more surprised. However, he did not give me time to meditate. Without a sign of recognition or emotion of any kind, he stormed halfway into the cell, looked the three of us straight in the eye, one after the other.

"Who knocked?"

"I knocked." I stood in the middle between Helga and Frieda, directly facing him.

There was a slight movement of surprise among the others crowded in the cell, but no sign of anything appeared on Natchalnik's face.

"With whom?"

"Both sides."

"How often?"

"Twice."

"With what purpose?"

"To obtain information."

"Did you?"

"No."

"Why not?"

"They did not know how to knock."

"You do know?"

"Yes."

"Who taught you?"

"Long experience."

"How long?"

"Eight months."

"*Tak*. Did the other two knock?"

"No."

"Lie down. On stomach."

I did. The other two girls were told to make room, and Natchalnik got into position. It took only a second. I heard the hard-rubber club swish through the air and immediately felt the burning pain on my derrière. Three times he hit, and, although I made the greatest effort to relax, knowing that the pain would be more bearable if I did, I thought my whole backside was on fire. I had promised myself not to scream. It seemed terribly important at the time, and I managed. Not a sound came from my lips, and I was very proud of my achievement.

How is it possible that a human being can be so conditioned that his greatest pride is in being a perfect victim? Not once did it enter my mind that it would be a more natural reflex to defend myself, to fight my attacker. I could not have won, of course. But I did not even have the desire.

"Get up."

I stood facing him, no hatred in my soul, no emotion other than the thought: "I did it; I got through it without screaming."

"Erica. You are still here. How are you?"

"Fine, thank you."

"This was a lesson, Erica. Only a sample of what might happen if you ever thought of knocking again. I was particularly lenient with you because you told the truth. I respect that. Therefore, I did not hit you hard. I do respect you rather much, Erica. Cigarette?" Natchalnik offered us each a cigarette and was gone.

A very quick investigation of my hindquarters proved that he had drawn blood. The marks of the club were enormous, and we wondered what it might be like if he were not lenient. For a few days, it was painful for me to sit, and I slept on my stomach. But the scars healed beautifully, and the whole frightening incident became one more thing of the past. . . .

My joy was indescribable when I was shown into Cell Number 61. I knew at once that it was bad enough to be my permanent home. My worry that I would be sent to Russia vanished. I was in a German prison, * buried deep in a cellar; I felt secure.

Number 61 was a square hole, five feet by five feet—I could tell because it was not quite long enough for me to stretch out completely. The ceiling was so low I could touch it with my fingers, and each side of the cell was filled with a wooden box to be used as a bed, so that the actual space to walk in was a little quadrangle in the middle, which measured exactly one step across and two steps from the back of the wall to the door. I soon discovered that I could make it in three little steps by walking it diagonally back and forth, changing corners and sides so as not to get lopsided. In the middle of the cell, back against the wall, stood the inevitable bucket. There was no corner in which to hide it or me on it. However, whenever I needed it, I pulled it all the

* Hohenschoenhausen Prison.—*Ed.*

way to the door which prevented the guards from seeing anything except my face right opposite theirs, and, by the time they finished screaming at me, I was finished too.

Number 61 was to be my home for over a year. I sweated in it in the summer and froze in the winter. Since it was tiny and had practically no air, it became so stifling during the summer that even when I sat perfectly still the sweat would run down my body. Sometimes I thought I could not breathe in it another minute. When it got colder and colder—there was no heating except in the halls—I could not get warm even with the most violent exercise, which was, of course, forbidden. But I loved my home and when, for unknown reasons, I was moved out for a few days and put into a large, light cell with a window full of blue sky, I went into a decline, could not face the blue sky and the air of freedom, developed a horrible lumbago, and revived only when I was put back into my beloved little haven, Cell Number 61.

I lived a full, almost complete life during this eternal year. Acquaintances were timidly struck up, friendships developed, even love affairs ensued—all through the thick prison walls. To keep my balance, I followed a rigorous schedule for the entire day. I had learned to judge the time almost perfectly, and I kept strictly to my hours, from the ten-minute exercises in the early morning to writing poetry and books in my head in the evening. I made myself review all the knowledge I had ever acquired and went back to school, having regular half-hour lessons each of French, English, Latin, history, geography, literature, algebra, history of art, and music. I was able to piece together the eight verses of Goethe's *Erlkoenig*, which I had often heard but never memorized. It took me one entire year, and almost as long to recollect the states of the United States. It was hard work because my brain was out of training, and I had no way of checking anything or storing away my painfully acquired information except in the deep-buried regions of my mind. I had always been convinced I had an extremely poor memory. I found it could be trained better than a puppy; it became remarkable. I composed thirty-six poems in prison which, years later, I was able to write down without hesitation. And when the student of medicine next to my cell knocked on the wall a four-verse poem dedicated to me, I could repeat it to him word for word the next day. I never once lost track of the date or the day of the week.

For relaxation, I made menus for a week of freedom—but only shortly before prison mealtime—and I designed dresses. I have always hated to cook and have never in my life made a dress or planned a menu for more than one meal at a time. I composed songs for my children, and I played chess.

The only possession I was ever allowed to have in the cell was my very small and by now paper-thin handkerchief. It served as washcloth, bandage, and toothbrush as well as handkerchief—and chessboard. I pulled threads crosswise to make barely visible squares on it. With the white threads I made the white chess figures and with gray threads from my skirt, the black figures: tiny dots for the pawns, big dot for the queen, very big dot for the king, flat big dots for the rooks, straight thread for the bishops, loops for the knights. The whole thing was so small that I could easily hide it with my knee from the spying guard; the figures stuck to the chessboard, and when the door suddenly opened, I could quickly crumple the whole game in my hand with the figures inside, and any inspection revealed only a harmless handkerchief. I played against myself for hours and hours, one game often lasting for days, sitting on my cot, facing the door, one knee pulled up, moving the figures with my right hand or scratching my knee with it if the spy hole showed the slightest danger. It was never once discovered.

For every half hour of sitting, I walked for half an hour—three steps across, three steps back, fast, very fast.

"Where are you going?" Farm Horse asked. Only officers were allowed to speak to the prisoners.

"Home," I replied without stopping my walk.

Whatever reality could not supply I filled in with memories. I relived my whole life, every detail of it, in those years behind bars, and I got a great deal of pleasure out of it. How lucky I was to have had such a happy childhood, such a wealth of interesting experiences, such an abundance of all the beauty life can provide.

The lack of beauty in prison—music, a good smell, something pretty to look at—was sometimes harder to bear than loneliness and loss of love and freedom. Number 61 was particularly bad in this respect. It had no spots or unevenness on the walls that might have provided me with a painting like the one I had in Schumannstrasse's Number 7—a beautiful replica of the angel in the foreground of Leonardo's *Madonna in the Grotto,* a combination of spots and roughness. It had nearly killed me to leave it. Karlshorst, too, had an abundance of portraits, landscapes and, with the help of the brown wood, oil paintings. Number 61 had nothing. Only if I half closed my eyes could I make some abstract designs out of the black and gray of the bucket. Otherwise everything, including the guards who handed me my food or took me to interrogation, was gray, musty, and ugly. I therefore wrote music of my own and put words to it; I painted pictures in brilliant colors—in my mind. I was equally untalented in all three arts, but had I been given a piano, pencil and paper, brush and paints, I knew I could have produced masterpieces. I even developed a voice. For some odd reason, perhaps due to a strange cough deep down in my chest which started in Number 61 and stayed with me ever after, my voice had become very deep, a man's baritone, and when I sang Negro spirituals with all my might until I was forcefully stopped, I could hear in myself Paul Robeson as he stood downstairs in the hall of our hospital in Spain, big and beautiful, singing up to us, the wounded and me, in his tremendous, moving voice.

The re-creation of music I knew was one of the hardest but most satisfactory of my occupations, although I never did get all the pieces of the various symphonies, concertos, and suites together. Sometimes I worked systematically on symphony after symphony of Beethoven's; on Bach's six suites for cello; on everything I had ever heard and loved. It often took me months to find the beginning bars of each work; some I never found. Sometimes a piece of music would sing in my ears, and I had to classify it, hold on to it, until I found where it belonged. When a whole passage of *Eine Kleine Nachtmusik* suddenly sang in my ears, I was overjoyed.

ALBERTINE SARRAZIN (1937–1967)

Abandoned at birth and given the name Albertine Damien by the Bureau of Public Assistance in Algiers, Sarrazin lived her brief life under several names. In 1939 she was adopted by an aged couple who named her Anne-Marie R. She was a talented and precocious but rebellious child, and her adoptive parents sent her to a reformatory for girls, where she acquired the nickname "Anick." Her parents revoked the adoption when she continued to have trouble with the law. At the time of her death, following an operation in 1967, she had been a prisoner for almost one-third of her life.

During her imprisonment in France for prostitution and theft, she became known to the French public as an author. The autobiographical novels *The Runaway* and *Astragal* have been translated into English. Sarrazin's other writings in French include poetry, *Journal de Prison 1959* (1972), and *Lettres à Julien 1958–60* (1971).

Sarrazin's writings drew extensively upon her prison experience. She married Julien Sarrazin, a prisoner who had helped her escape from Amiens prison in 1957; their story provided the material for *Astragal*. Her 1961–1962 imprisonment in Amiens, Soissons, and Compiègne prisons underlies *The Runaway*, which gives considerable insight into women's prison conditions. The following excerpt from that novel shows how the heroine, Anick, adapts to prison life by focusing on her personal symbols of love, freedom, and resistance. Her obsession with plans to escape with her lover Zizi are symbolized by the recurring image of the runaway mare, *la cavale*.

Note: Biographical information is from Elissa D. Gelfand, *Imagination in Confinement: Women's Writing from French Prisons* (Ithaca, N.Y.: Cornell Univ. Press, 1983); Josane Duranteau, Introduction to *Lettres à Julien*, by Albertine Sarrazin (Paris: J.-J. Pauvert, 1971); Karel Weiss, ed., *The Prison Experience: An Anthology* (New York: Delacorte, 1976), p. 82; Hervé Bazin, Preface to *Romans, Lettres et Poèmes*, by Albertine Sarrazin (Paris: J.-J. Pauvert, 1967).

WORKS BY ALBERTINE SARRAZIN

Astragal. Translated by Patsy Southgate. New York: Grove Press, 1967. Originally published as *l'Astragale*. (Paris: J.-J. Pauvert, 1965). A novel.

The Runaway. Translated by Charles Lam Markmann. New York: Grove Press, 1967. Originally published as *La Cavale* (Paris: Société Nouvelle des Éditions Pauvert, 1965). A novel.

(Sarrazin's other works have not been translated into English.)

These Penitential Precincts

Like a fat shrew fixed in her habits, the prison yawns, howls, eats, and sacks out every day at the same hours.

Except that sometimes it suffers an attack of stomach pains, and then its internal organism is beset by disruptions as unforeseeable as they are disastrous. A girl makes a break, during her transfer to another prison or while she's in detention, or even after being sentenced, but in any event some of the shit always sticks to her shoes. Others, shadows, take her place; it doesn't really make a great deal of difference to us. No one comes here to make friends, but rather to do her time. That, in fact, is why the idea of a prescribed penalty has always seemed illogical to me: that rather archaic sliding scale of the courts, combined with the arbitrary freedom of juries to render verdicts, doesn't please me.

Any more than solid citizens are pleased by the surprises they have when they awaken after one of our visits. The scales are in balance.

I am neither logical nor balanced, nor am I the sociable type, and I have no hope of becoming so; I feel quite uncomfortable among my little sisters in stir, who have their own way of reshaping society.

Like every other inmate with any self-respect, I should make it a practice to read aloud every letter from a friend, carry my beloved's photograph in my bra, show it at the slightest pretext, while my eyes grow nostalgic and damp; or, when things become clannish, show my letters, with a slight pout, to whoever is my best friend at the moment. But I prefer to have some respect for my mail.

This savage part of me is compensated for by my nice qualities, artistic talent, good spelling, a fortune in postage stamps. Oh, I could do very nicely without drawing tulips on their letters, writing letters for them, and then stamping them. It's only that, since I can't do without smoking and drinking Nes, I have to pay my way. So I curse my perpetually being broke and the paths that have led me to it.

I am at the end of my rope, what could possibly make things worse? There are little irritations where my vanity is concerned, more clearly defined anguishes of heart and body, but my private little star shines on without pain. And, in the end, laughs can always triumph over everything.

And how is it possible not to laugh? There are times when you're compelled to wear the clown's suit yourself and be the funny clown, the sad clown.

After the dishes are washed, I go to empty the dirty water: holding the huge, greasy, overflowing basin in both hands, I have to stick my toe in the john door, open it the rest of the way with one shoulder, and then, with vast relief, dump the lot. Generally I get my feet soaked. I have an engraved wedding ring of platinum and a few stones, rather worn but I love it very much because I have never seen another like it except on my man's finger and because it came from a very old jeweler's shop somewhere in France. Not having been made to my measure, this ring is a bit large, and I didn't want to pay much more than it had cost me to have it made smaller.

Consequently, whenever I wash the dishes or myself, I put it on a different finger; but on the middle finger this wedding ring loses all the charm of a slightly over-sized piece of platinum sliding up and down and round the symbolic finger, and I always put it back on the symbolic one as soon as I'm dry. One morning I must have plugged myself into the wrong circuit, my automatic switch failed to function: the clink of the wedding ring on the seat of the john, repeated as the ring tumbled down through the plumbing, was a terrible shock. In a flash I was back at the door of the workroom, banging away with the broom handle, banging and hammering hard enough to break the locks.

The girls, thinking it was an outbreak of some shameful and insane malady that I had kept secret from them, refused to turn a head or lift a hand: in cases like that it is dangerous to irritate the lunatic; after the crisis a good slug in the kisser will take care of everything.

The matron came running almost immediately, which proved that the silence that ordinarily followed our drumming on doors or floors was absolutely deliberate on her part: the matrons don't answer because they're too lazy to climb the stairs, but, if one throws a scare into them by pounding just a little harder than usual, then they'll come.

I explained what had happened. The matron threw up her hands in irritation and helplessness: but good God, I wasn't pointing a gun at her. I didn't even ask her to go head first into the shit-pipes, as normally I would have wanted to do. No, I simply asked her for my ring, and that was all. Suddenly that hunk of metal had acquired infinite size and importance: it was a barrel of jewelry, a universe of jewelry in which I had lived until that morning, stuffed with love and dishwater, and from which I had suddenly been thrown out; I, who never open my mouth to a matron unless I absolutely have to, would have kissed this one's feet if it would have persuaded her to allow me to go shovel through all the shit in the cesspool.

I didn't have to go so far as that: she was really touched, and she led me right downstairs, opened the courtyard door and let me out on my own.

I located the cesspool that was fed by the workroom johns; desperation made me so strong that I yanked off the stone cover as if it had been a feather, and, kneeling on the very edge of the pit, my torso dangerously bent over the edge, I looked. Obviously, it wasn't going to do me a bit of good to look . . .

Then the tears splashed out, irresistibly, and a river of them rolling down my cheeks and plunging down below mingled with the shit in a miserable blend, while the matron kept tugging at my denim sleeve and ordering me to scram out of there. I went back to the workroom with my running eyes and my naked fingers and went right to work on a feverish letter to the Superintendent, asking him to send an emergency alert to the cleaning force and recover at all costs the precious object that I had so tragically lost. All this "because of the monetary as well as the sentimental value" that it had for me, and so on. Somewhat calmer now, I reread the letter, taking particular pleasure in the part that contained the reference to the monetary value: that should really scare the shit out of him, the way the shit is always scared out of all of them by any accusations of error in accounting, requests for transfers of money, any letter mailed with more than one stamp and accompanied by a return receipt—in short, by anything that raises the question of the prison's financial responsibility. But on the other hand I knew something about the speed of the complaint procedure—and at lunch, at eleven o'clock, I had seen my letter lying on the ground-floor table with others of lesser urgency—and so I decided to take direct action: during our afternoon exercise I got some of the girls to help me move the stone (in my panic in the morning I had pinched my hand and now I could not move a finger), and every one shoved her face in the hole, in relays, each one yelling whenever she saw anything shiny. It is unbelievable what one can see in a cesspool, especially when there are fifteen dames above it! Tons of food, first of all, both food that had been prepared and food never eaten: bread, peelings, yogurt jars, jam jars, all kinds of containers; rags, dishcloths, napkins, dish towels, and so on . . .

It was little Mauricette who spotted it.

Yes, there is a good God: there it was, on the surface between a yogurt jar and a banana peel, miraculously saved from the greasy water that we had poured down by the bucket all morning in the hope of flushing it out: my wedding ring, spared and radiant.

I leaped for the broom, tore a yard of wire off the clothesline, fastened it to the broom handle, and made a hook at the other end; then, kneeling as comfortably as I could and aiming with as much precision as possible, in order not to knock the ring into the muck, I managed to fish it out in triumph while the whole courtyard and garden rang with cheers.

The only false note came from the matron: feeling cheated out of her part in the salvage operation, she threatened to deliver my letter to the administration anyway. As calmly as I could, I pointed out to her that, in order to be logical, she should at the same time deliver a second letter canceling the first: "If you will take me back up to the workroom, I'll write it right away."

She shrugged and went away, after having reminded us to put everything back as it had been. I put back the stone and the wire, but I kept the ring. . . .

In the old days, I screamed, I broke things; I broke everything except the prison that watched me passively and confidently. Now I don't scream any more: it is I who watch the prison, I study the old contraption; I'm learning to detach the shouting part of myself, to peel it away without breaking the skin. And, when I have my belly full of thinking about the joint, I simply put a heavy foot down on the analysis in progress, get up, and go to the window to watch the sparrows in the courtyard.

I dream, and my flights into fantasy became more frequent; I'm coming to enjoy them, and I almost don't mind being where I am . . . I set up ingenious detours, strict barriers for the times I'm sick at heart.

Even more than the utter lack of any interest in my daily life, constant association with no one but the matron contributes to my taste for imaginary escapes. I'm not undertaking anything, I'm not getting hold of anything: I want only to remain entirely within myself and to keep this Me far away from here, somewhere where nothing and no one can make it other than what I want it to be.

In a walled, barred cell, where the grub would be shoved in to me through a slanting hole—and not an anti-germ partition like the one in the office here—in a cell where I would not have to yak or fake, it seems to me I would be able to tell exactly where I am more quickly; but here there's always that matron. . . .

A fixed date for discharge is an obsession; but a split is not. A split is for tonight, or another night, or next month, or next year; it takes root, even if not in detail, as a background figure that leaves the rest of the mind detached and alert; it is discreet, like a friend who sits with you without talking; you continue whatever you're doing without bothering about her, yet you remember all the same to give her a smile now and then.

I wonder what my friend the runaway mare will be able to tell me when I make up my mind to ask questions. In every friendship, especially at the outset, there is a secret anxiety, a fear of being betrayed or disappointed by the friend, a fear of your own potential to betray or disappoint. So I keep myself as busy and aloof as I can, lest my friend the runaway should suddenly decide to talk.

This triangle household of the runaway and ourselves makes itself quite at home on my bed, the runaway caressing my mind and Zizi* caressing my heart. We wait attentively, long after darkness has fallen. . . .

But Zi writes: "Darling, the summer is slipping away rapidly . . . When I think of the possibility of letting you down, because I may not be able to find a way out, it drives me up the wall and I want to sit and howl like a baby . . . Try to understand, baby, that all I have at the moment is my teeth, and I can't gnaw my way through walls."

When I read that, I too feel as if I'm about to bawl.

Treacherously the thought of giving in returns, hovering above my resolution . . . It would keep Zizi from being upset, it would mean that for him and for us there would be just the time to be served, these years

*The lover of narrator, Anick; the character represents Julien Sarrazin.—Ed.

[242]

whose every season is winter and that compel us to re-invent sunshine by dreaming of it . . . Oh, no, I can never keep hope alive that long!

I'll be released first, that is almost certain; but I know too well that I'll come back here every day to share . . . What idiocy, to share! It is always impossible to share in the sense of making burdens lighter: a rap cannot be borne as a cart is pulled: if two of us are serving time, the time is doubled. And all the rap we've already served, and that's a long time, can't compensate for anything, can't help in any way, as long as it continues, for us or for others, as long as it has not been eliminated. If we succeed in escaping from it, other guys and other girls will still be caught in it at the same instant; our rap rolls us and erodes us in an endless tide, and those years—like a thick substance that has to be gulped down—will turn into a liquid and evaporate little by little: even memory will have no trace of them.

We always forget stir very soon—why?

Because—at least as far as I'm concerned—I never "realized" my prisons; I never saw them as anything but intervals, as pretexts for doing things that had no relation to them and to the purpose that had been assigned them; in these penitential precincts I've made jokes, if I have suffered it has never been in my conscience, I've observed what was around me, I've also learned to love better . . . Nor have I ever thought that all these days were bringing me closer to freedom: I have always left jail with the feeling of unfinished business; perhaps because release has already put me on the road toward re-imprisonment; but above all because, since for me the concept of expiation has no validity, it seems to me that I must go on paying until I have accepted it . . . in other words, for a very long time to come.

I confected too much adventure out of my prisons: I could not believe that for the others, the men in the Palace of Justice and the Bureau of Prisons, there is nothing of adventure, there is only a chronology and red tape; and that all this red tape will shape the conclusion of the adventure, regardless of what I may have in mind at the moment.

This is why I always concentrate on making a break.

If I gave in, I would give in too much, and I would need a kick in the ass on the final day; already I feel almost frustrated at the thought of throwing away this jumble of fabricated prothèses with which I make myself prop up the absurd and plunge further into it . . .

I toss on my mattress in the dark: "Zizi, you absolutely have to find the tools, prison is beginning to get me down, you have to move fast . . ."

Because in no time we'll be separated . . . And it does no good for Zizi to write: "I'll come and get you no matter where I am," I say to myself that it is precisely here that action must be taken, that there is no other reason for our transfer.

Let the force of things not be greater than our own strength! Let the summer last a little longer! If I accept autumn, then what reason will I have to refuse winter? Warming my feet on the radiators in December, I will be collecting material so as to be patient in spring, and so on . . . But I know that I'm just spinning daydreams in a vacuum: at the thought of staying here, a pang of eternity twists my guts, exactly like when I was a child contemplating the eternity of the catechism, the horrible eternity of the Good Lord.

LOLITA LEBRÓN (1919–)

Puerto Rican Nationalist Lolita Lebrón, known in Puerto Rico as *una Hembra*, a complete woman, was sentenced to fifty years for her part in an armed demonstration in the U.S. House of Representatives on March 1, 1954. Born in the western town of Lares, Puerto Rico, she had lived in the United States for six years and was employed in a sewing machine factory in New York at the time of the demonstration. She led three male Nationalists who, waving a Puerto Rican flag from the visitors' gallery and crying "Viva Puerto Rico," opened fire at random onto the floor and wounded five congressmen. Lebrón, the first to fire, stated in a letter found after the incident that the violent demonstration was in support of independence for her people. She was willing to die for her country in carrying out this mission.

Lebrón was imprisoned for twenty-five years at the Federal Reformatory for Women at Alderson, West Virginia, where she actively worked to secure the rights of women inmates. Pardoned under the Carter administration, she was released in September 1979 and returned to Puerto Rico.

Note: Biographical information is from Gloria F. Waldman, "Affirmation and Resistance: Women Poets from the Caribbean," in *Contemporary Women Authors of Latin America*, ed. Doris Meyer and Margarite Fernandez Olmos (Brooklyn, N.Y.: Brooklyn College Humanities Press, 1983), pp. 33–57; *Women Behind Bars* (Washington, D.C.: Resources for Community Change, 1975), p. 21; Edward F. Ryan, *Washington Post*, 2 March 1954, quoted in Kal Wagenheim, *The Puerto Ricans: A Documentary History* (New York: Praeger, 1973), pp. 204–207.

WORKS BY LOLITA LEBRÓN

Poems. Translated by Gloria F. Waldman. In *Contemporary Women Authors of Latin America*. New Translations, edited by Doris Meyer and Margarite Fernandes Olmos. Brooklyn College Humanities Series. Brooklyn, N.Y.: Brooklyn College Humanities Press, 1983. Also reprinted in *Voices of Women: Poetry by and about Third World Women*. New York: Women's International Resource Exchange, 1982. Originally published as *Sándalo en la celda* (Sandalwood in the cell) (Cataño, Puerto Rico: Editorial Betances, 1974).

Four Poems

"To the Prisoners Playing" and "I Have All the Passion of
Life" are from *Voices of Women*; reprinted by permission of
Gloria F. Waldman. "Alone" and "I Have Seen You" are from
Contemporary Women Authors of Latin America; reprinted
by permission of Gloria F. Waldman.

To the Prisoners Playing

Those beloved voices I hear
are my own sounds,
the smoke
that in a burning echo
murmurs to the land . . .
I sing of the pain
and of the joy
of this world.

Those beloved voices! My sisters!
Confused in melodies of
upheaval, tears, and sobs,
passion and troubles,
and a spring
of complaints and misfortune.

How many times, at their simple echoes,
has my breast opened up
to pure light and reflection

through which I see their faces
like bunches of exquisite and ripe fruit.

In my heart I see all the sun
from their sad, not quite lit eyes,
sheltered within the boundaries
of the earth.

Because I know that in seeing it,
in its mistiness,
it holds all the fire
of the auguries of the splendor
of God,
in his depth and profundity.

I love them with the beating
of my black and blond plumage,
for they are my rainbow,
the treasures yielded by
the shadows and beams of light
on these walls.

They are my wounded and bound birds,
with hollow flesh, stone-like calluses
between their terrible fists
and painted mouths gagged
in deafening confinement.

I love them with the beating
of my black and blond plumage,
for they are my rainbow,
the treasure yielded by
the shadows and beams of light
on these walls.

They are my wounded and bound birds,
with hollow flesh,
stone-like calluses between their terrible fists
and painted mouths gagged
in deafening confinement.

I hear them in the field on Labor Day.
What a tumult!
The tired sun reaches its zenith
as the cloud clears and the worn-out dream
erupts in the back and forth of their laughter . . .

Lolita Lebrón

They drag themselves through
the furrowed dust of talk
and hooch.
They are the very blood and veins
that run through the river of the world.

They are the wound
that the powerful of the earth inflict.
Yet we never see the decayed reflection
of their guns on these walls.

They are the victims of drugs
who have made millionaires of the "pure ones,"
haunting skeletons of doom
that shine like the gold and copper
stolen from us by the Yanqui colonizers.

I Have All the Passion of Life

I have all the passion of life.
I love the sun and the stars
and the seeds.
Everything fascinates me:
water, brooks, groves,
dew and cascades.

I adore looking at the
flowing streams: this clear
proof of beauty;
this joy in my marrow,
in my sight,
this knowing about what's hidden,
and this sensation of seeing
what is clear.

Whoever denies life its joy,
the wealth of its complexity,
its rainbow-like countenance,
its downpour and its universe
of beauty, its generous giving,
the caress, the grain
with fruit and delicacies,
the bud, the flower, pain and laughter;
those who deny life its measure

of joy
are the unseeing ones.
Nor have they drunk from
life's overflowing cup of passion.

I have all the rapture,
the savoring.
That's why they stare and ask:
"Lolita, what do you see of
any beauty?
What do you like? The sky?
These sterile and arid mountains,
these hours so full of ugliness
and injustice,
with endless sighs
and the pushing and the shoving?"

"Why do you sing and laugh, Lolita?
Is your face really lit up
with the joy of life?
Are you mad, Lolita?"

Alone

I'm quiet, like the still water
in the solitude of my cell.
I move serenely towards the sea
with my stillness and my leaping . . .
Alone. Only the voice of the rain
can console my suffering.
"The rain is Your voice." I feel
all your kisses and embraces.
But in the prison now,
a push and a shove is more fitting.
I am a wanderer
in long ago deserts.
Only human, my wounds
ache within my heart,
For I have loved all deeply
and they have no compassion.
Alone, yes, let me be alone . . .
It's not the first time that it is so.
I have been the wanderer
forever without a home . . .

Lolita Lebrón

I Have Seen You

I have seen you as I searched
in the shade
of this terrifying and cold silence.
Some furniture falls to pieces . . .
and I'm left with the cell,
bereft of warmth and humor.
Everything is so alone. So disquieting.
Love has gone so far away from my eyes . . .
And there is no chirping from the birds
to make me smile away my sorrow . . .
"I am trembling, compañero,
with painful and exhausting uneasiness!"
My shoulders hurt . . . as if sinking under
the weight of tortured rock.
The hour is dark.
The day silent with a moan
hidden in its great burden.
Even prayer is wounding: in the depths of my entrails
pain tearlessly weeps.
I like forests and gardens.
The waterfalls with their tiny crabs,
their rocks,
their murmurs and bubbles,
their radiant streams,
the thought of their mysteries,
with flowers and plants surrounding them.
Their aromas.
And how I loved the washerwomen,
scrubbing upon the rocks
with a box of bluing at their side.
How they remind me of mama!
Here, jail is like a tempest,
heavy and hard-hearted . . .
A ruin that reeks of death
and unspeakable pain.
It is the white bear's domain.
Keys and blows, headcounts,
injustices and schemes.
Undisclosed tortures
from an unwritable book.
The real story of death,
unwritten, without pages.

NORMA STAFFORD (1932?–   )

Norma Stafford was the youngest of ten children in a poor farming family of the Tennessee hill country. As a young woman she experienced hardships as a result of classism and sexism. Although she was able to begin nursing school in Alabama, she was aware of her socioeconomic differences with the staff. Her training ended when the school learned of her lesbianism and forced her resignation. After a brief marriage failed, Stafford began a ten-year relationship with a woman. During this time Stafford began writing bad checks and running from the law. She describes her amusement that police consistently ignored her homosexual relationship and insisted that she reveal the identity of the man for whom she broke the law. Once, during a relentless interrogation, she was forced to fabricate a story about a lover and his car in order to get some sleep.

Stafford was imprisoned in several county jails and in Alabama and California state prisons for five and a half years. In 1972, during her imprisonment at the California Institution for Women, she participated in the beginning of the Santa Cruz Women's Prison Project. Through the project, a large volunteer staff brought college-level classes to the women, who received credit from the University of California at Santa Cruz. In this supportive setting, Stafford began for the first time to write prose and poetry and to recognize her gift as a writer.

After her parole in 1973, Stafford became active in giving public readings of her poetry and in working to support the Santa Cruz Women's Prison Project.

Note: Biographical information is from Karlene Faith and Jeanne Gallick, Introduction to *Dear Somebody: The Prison Poetry of Norma Stafford*, by Norma Stafford (Seaside, Calif.: Academy of Arts and Humanities, 1975); "Writings of Norma Stafford," *Crime and Social Justice*, no. 2 (Fall–Winter 1974): 54–56.

WORKS BY NORMA STAFFORD

Dear Somebody: The Prison Poetry of Norma Stafford. Seaside, Calif.: Academy of Arts and Humanities, 1975.

"Writings of Norma Stafford." *Crime and Social Justice*, no. 2 (Fall–Winter 1974): 54–56.

Norma Stafford

Seven Poems

From *Dear Somebody: The Prison Poetry of Norma Stafford.*
Reprinted by permission of Norma Stafford.

[untitled]

may i touch you?
that is what i have missed
more than anything else
a warm human touch.

i will not touch you hard.

[untitled]

i am smiling
for no particular reason
i do this at times
like now when i am alone
silence all around me
where many people
have suddenly shut their mouths
in sleep behind locked doors.

In Santa Cruz

Sitting warming her back in the spring sun
that dared to force its way through the cafe blinds
an ivory-handled walking cane leaned against her thigh.
The beauty of all her ages was upon her.
Seven face lines bore a hard east to west direction,
made a sharp right turn at her ear
then disappeared into the north.

Nibbling toast past her old woman's black whiskers,
hands lined like two roadmaps
gave a delicate tremble, then
lifted her cup of Sanka
and sent it chasing after the toast.

I said to her, "My sister, the growth rings of a tree
know many secrets of this life,
but the tree does not speak.
These lines that you wear
are your growth rings, hiding the
knowledge you have gained while
traveling this life for almost a century.
Tell me what you know."

She carefully wiped her almost invisible lips,
took her cane and walked away from me
leaving on her empty seat
bits of bark and one oak leaf.

for barbara whitaker

in private shadows of slumber
animated by mysteries of moonlight
arose a woman
the photographer's dream
would cause agonized envy
in the master of canvas
renowned wielder of
the magic brush

edges of fantasy
stroking reality
       you
turning in slow-motioned
movements of my mind
revealing all beauty
and true essence of woman
witnessed alone
by this sleeper's eyes.
in the private shadows of slumber.

sensuous lady soft sweet sister
sharing a moment
in the millenniums of time
curled together
in mysteries of moonlight
   warming my life   healing my mind
      private
          in the shadows of slumber.

Norma Stafford

Woman Soldier

Sweet sweet woman soldier
swift sure female warrior
gentle hands warm eyes tending your child
determined hands deadly eyes aiming your weapon
soft lips smooth skin beauty
long lashes veiling the knowledge pride
and self-worth blazing in your eyes of all colors
laughter at party time dancing with your lover
death at battle time for your unbelieving enemy

Entering into battle heavy with child
expensive coiffure wearing levis Arpege
laces boots sneakers barefoot with uncombed hair
giving off the healthy body odor
of determined female sweat.

Comrade in arms my sister
battling daily we were like two bees
stinging the Power in many places
dodging his armies we were alert and cunning

he was confused swatting wildly
slapping places he could not see
looking everywhere trying to pin down
to eliminate the source of his discomfort
a false god perched on his tower
we made him turn move run
screaming curses at his soldiers
ordering them to "seek out and destroy."

You and I my comrade beloved friend soldier woman
survived many years in this battle
before our instinct tuned to his danger
became clouded with fatigue and slept
letting us wake up here
among the other prisoners of war.
I see you smile in here
when that same confused angry power
curses and swears at our resistance
we still cause him pain
never allowing his overstuffed body
to know the luxury of total relaxation.

Lying in your captive labor bed
womb straining sweat pouring
you deliver your child
within these concrete walls and steel bars
because your infant is born of you/in here
she is labeled numbered and her mug-shot is taken
before she has breathed before the cord is cut
she has a number and she is called criminal
but you and I know you have delivered to us
another awesome female warrior.

I hear your deep woman's laughter
ring out through every cell block
and my heart is strengthened
my courage renewed because you are here
just as you are everywhere noble warrior
goddess of Death to the Power
giver of life sweet sweet woman soldier.

This Is Not The End

notes of the score

you say that i am fixed in my black and white state
watch the smoothness of my runs
see my blackness blur
in the taut acrobatics of the violin strings
never am i fixed
neither in black, white, or gold or brown
hear me sing in the heat of the sun
whose rays change me to the golden hue
            that is light
to reach the darkest depths of your life
like ginger i penetrate the air.

the black bars that try to encase me
are only my soft resting place
smell the sweet air of freedom that i bring
weep as i touch the red blood of your heart
laugh as i rub the softness of your feet
never again say that i am fixed.

Norma Stafford

[untitled]

the contractions are coming harder now
all my efforts are more concentrated
i feel the wall thinning
more endeavor goes into my efforts
the pushing the straining the pain
bearing down from everywhere
will end
blessed relief   the emergence of me
when i finally walk out those gates.

PART 5

*"I sense the great weight of the society/
pressing down on the little box of room I lie in/
alone/forgotten/like my sisters in prison":
Solidarity with Other Women*

*

Solidarity, as seen in women's prison literature, is not restricted to "revolutionary rhetoric," but probes more deeply the issues of women's friendships and support systems. Although some writers, such as Albertine Sarrazin, Gabrielle Russier, and Rose Greenhow, disdain fellow female prisoners and desire to set themselves apart from the general prison population, a large body of prison literature by women clearly announces its support for the female society of a women's prison. The backgrounds and circumstances of these writers differ, but the women unite in their advocacy of women's causes and their proud statements of camaraderie. The writers included in the following selections begin by acknowledging the same need for communication and relationships expressed in the writings in Part 4, but they carry that concern one step further. Starting at the personal level of recognized individual need and vulnerability, they move to statements of collective strength. These selections declare pride in unity and especially in female solidarity.

The issue of women prisoners' solidarity is not clear-cut. For instance, both sociologists and inmates have noted that women in American prisons today differ from incarcerated men in their responses to poor prison conditions, with women showing less militancy and confrontation with authority.[1] Black Panther Assata Shakur complained in 1978 that "a striking difference between women and men prisoners at Riker's Island is the absence of revolutionary rhetoric among the women. . . . The women at Riker's seem vaguely aware of what a revolution is but generally regard it as an impossible dream. Not at all practical."[2] On the other hand, Coramae Richey Mann cites several incidences since

1971 of riots and demonstrations in which women have demanded their rights and have protested prison conditions.[3] Some researchers find a rise of politicization among women prisoners, and predict that unrest in women's prisons may increase in the future.[4] Women prison writers had been expressing their feelings of sisterhood and anger at abuses of human rights long before the recent era of prison riots and militancy, but the theme of female solidarity is more prominent in current prison literature than in older writings.

British suffragette Lady Constance Lytton's prison memoirs present an especially fascinating early narrative of this spirit of sisterhood. In her late thirties, this upper-class, unmarried, and childless woman developed a profound interest in prison reform, which she explained as an emotional substitute for "what maternity there lurks in me."[5] Enraged that she had been given preferential treatment when imprisoned with other suffragettes, she posed as a working-class suffragette during her next imprisonment in 1910, and, at great expense to her health, exposed the class injustices of British prisons. Her love for the women inmates she met is evident in the "Dedication to Prisoners" in her memoirs:

> Lay hold of your inward self and keep tight hold. Reverence yourself. Be just, kind and forgiving to yourself.
>
> In my ignorance and impudence I went into prison hoping to help prisoners. So far as I know, I was unable to do anything for them. But the prisoners helped me. They seemed at times the direct channels between me and God Himself, imbued with the most friendly and powerful goodness that I have ever met.[6]

Lytton did, indeed, help her fellow prisoners, contrary to her modest self-assessment. After Lytton's death, Mrs. Coombe Tennant, one of the first women appointed to the position of visiting justice in the prisons, stated that Lytton "was denied an active life in the tussle of things," but "her thoughts lived, and were worked out by others. . . . [S]he had a share in altering the world and shaping thought among women."[7]

The writings of female political prisoners have long served as the voice of their sisters, who are silenced by repression, lack of education, or institution-bred apathy and despair. The testimony literature of Latin America dramatically serves this function today. Socialist Kate Richards

O'Hare, imprisoned in the Missouri State Penitentiary in 1919, explained that political prisoners serve their silenced cell mates by looking beyond personal deprivations to condemn widespread abuses affecting the general prison population:

> Behind prison walls I had experiences that come to but few persons who have the ability to evaluate their educational worth. With the clang of the prison gates behind me I was thrown back two thousand years to the position of a female hostage of the Imperial Roman Empire, sold into slavery because she had dared to challenge the power of Rome. Day by day, week by week, month by month I re-lived all that long and bitter way that women have trod since the day when Jesus said, "Let him who is without sin . . . cast the first stone." In the months I spent in prison were compressed all that womanhood has endured from the slave marts of Rome to the deadly grind of the ultra-modern sweat-shop.[8]

Similarly, American journalist Agnes Smedley, imprisoned in the New York Tombs during World War I, voiced the plight of the women she met there. Her prison sketches, "Cell Mates," depict the courage of her fellow political prisoners, birth-control activist Kitty Marion and Russian revolutionary Mollie Steimer; equally memorable are her sketches of the prostitute and the forger who could not write but boasted colorful personalities and stories of their own. Through writing, Smedley gave individuality to nameless petty criminals behind the Tombs' walls.

Social protest in the American labor and civil rights movements has led to the imprisonment of women from varied racial and ethnic backgrounds. Several have written of their experiences in works that promote the cause of women's solidarity. Ericka Huggins, Angela Davis, and Emma Goldman, for example, strikingly illustrate the power of women's prison literature to articulate the continuity of the personal and the political. Elissa D. Gelfand has written that French women prisoners are twice criminal, because their crimes violate the law as well as social codes of acceptable behavior for women.[9] Taking her point one step further, one can state that many imprisoned American women are thrice criminal, since from birth they have borne the burden of classism and racism as well as sexism.

In contemporary American prisons, the supportive atmosphere of writing workshops, organized by outside universities and prison associations or by the inmates themselves, encourages male and female inmates to write poetry and fiction. The creative work of these groups displays the collective aesthetic that H. Bruce Franklin views as part of the heritage of black American literature.[10] Published in workshop anthologies or prison newsletters, these works not only bear the names of individual authors, but also carry the force of voices united in protest.

Both men's and women's institutions conduct writing workshops, but the collections published by women's groups show the perspective of women writers toward their lives on the outside and their imprisonment. An example is *Songs from a Free Space: Writings by Women in Prison.*[11] The voices of eleven women writers blend to describe the lifestyles that brought them to prison ("Hard rain washes my tears / As I walk in the night / Two years doing my sidewalk act" ['Lady,' by Fannie James Rogers]), and the lives they lead in prison ("Ten Ways of Looking at Prison Lunch [with apologies to Wallace Stevens]," by Gloria Jensen). The preface of the volume boldly announces the collective purpose:

> this anthology is a crime. A crime of conspiracy, an informed, fully-consenting adult decision to commit poetry, an invention of the imagination that will never tear down the bars or break the system's back, but has ripped off some room for people to "breathe together" (another definition of "conspiracy") and pulled off a heist of institutional supermind, liberated the space as a continuum. This anthology is about possibilities. It is nothing flashy—not an act of realpolitik—just a homey little crime among friends.

This declaration of women prisoners' intention to reclaim self-respect and undermine the system's power, even in a "friendly" way, is a recent development that negates the traditional "fallen woman" stereotype. The poems are unmistakably women's, yet the concept of collective publication has nothing exclusively to do with their being female; it has intriguing parallels with the tradition of black American protest as well as the celebrated rebelliousness of male prison literature that seeks to change society.[12]

A new dimension in women's prison literature is the definition of the word "prisoner," as illustrated in Ericka Huggins's poetry. Although some women prison writers of the past have defended themselves by proclaiming their *differences* from other women inmates, Huggins destroys barriers and proclaims a camaraderie in her opposition to sexism, racism, and classism. Her poetry possesses a breadth of vision that regards the woman's prison experience as a paradigm of the woman's position in society. While imprisoned in Connecticut in 1970–1971 during her trial as a Black Panther, Huggins used her poems as a medium to make a revolutionary statement: women inside and outside bars face the same oppression and must not be divided by an adversarial relationship imposed by society. Her poems share the assertive energy of black women poets like Nikki Giovanni and Sonia Sanchez. In Huggins's call to solidarity for all women, imprisonment is metaphorically associated not with romantic transcendence but with the poverty and degradation produced by any social system in which one group controls another. Her poems' concerns are completely opposite the self-justification of Madame Roland's memoirs: rather than defending herself by insisting that she differs from her fellow inmates, Huggins proclaims that *all* women are prisoners.

Writer and editor Patricia McConnel's short piece of fiction about her experiences in American prisons of the 1950s is her protest against inhumane policies and acts of institutionalized brutality that abuse lawful power. She affirms each woman's right to be treated with dignity, whatever her crime. Her stories are about women's survival. They originated in her personal struggle and her observations of others, and they deal in a very real way with her own pain and outrage. Almost thirty years after her imprisonment, McConnel has achieved a distance and perspective that she feels is best conveyed through fiction. Even when they are in pain, her imprisoned characters sing—for singing, throughout her stories, symbolizes "the indestructibility of the spirit." She writes:

> An extremely important element in my motivation to write these stories is to give the reader some sense of the reality of this form of societal madness—that these are real human beings being destroyed by a machine designed and run by madmen, for the most part. In spite of this dark theme, most of the stories are life-affirming in some way. I am impressed, all these years afterwards, at the resiliency of the spirits of the women I knew.
>
> My stories are about women struggling to preserve their wills, their self-respect, in a system intent on destroying them.[13]

McConnel tells the reader that if women inmates are united, even if only in spirit, they can mitigate the cruelties of the system and find a measure of freedom. Her description of her fiction provides an interesting counterpoint to Lytton's earlier "Dedication" to the prisoners she loved. Both works are more than their authors' personal accounts of the pains of imprisonment, written for an intimate family audience or the public; they are messages of love, encouragement, and hope for the women they knew and respected in prison.

NOTES

1. See Coramae Richey Mann, *Female Crime and Delinquency* (University, Ala.: Univ. of Alabama Press, 1984), p. 210; Ruth M. Glick and Virginia V. Neto, *National Study of Women's Correctional Programs* (Washington, D.C.: National Institute of Law Enforcement and Criminal Justice, 1977), p. 172.

2. Assata Shakur (Joanne Chesimard), "Women in Prison: How We Are," *Black Scholar* 12, no. 6 (November–December 1981): 54; reprinted from vol. 9, no. 7 (April 1978).

3. Mann, *Female Crime and Delinquency*, pp. 210–211.

4. Gary F. Jensen, "The Incarceration of Women: A Search for Answers," in *Women and the Law: A Social Historical Perspective*, ed. D. Kelly Weisberg (Cambridge, Mass.: Schenkman, 1982), 1:250. The need for further research on the extent of politicization in women's prisons is noted in Freda Adler and Rita James Simon, eds., *The Criminology of Deviant Women* (Boston: Houghton Mifflin, 1979), pp. 310–311.

5. Lady Constance Lytton, letter to her mother, 24 February 1909, in *Prisons and Prisoners* (London: Heinemann, and East Ardsley, Yorkshire: EP Publishing, 1914), p. 33.

6. Lytton, *Prisons and Prisoners*, p. x.

7. Mrs. Coombe Tennant, J.P., letter to Lytton family, quoted in Betty Balfour ed., *Letters of Constance Lytton* (London: Heinemann, 1925), pp. 265–266.

8. Kate Richards O'Hare, "Foreword," *In Prison* (New York: Knopf, 1923), p. 19.

9. Elissa D. Gelfand, "Women Prison Authors in France: Twice Criminal," *Modern Language Studies* 11, no. 1 (Winter 1980–1981): 57–63.

10. H. Bruce Franklin, *The Victim as Criminal and Artist: Literature from the American Prison* (New York: Oxford Univ. Press, 1978), pp. 250–251.

11. Carol Muske and Gail Rosenblum, eds., *Songs from a Free Space: Writings by Women in Prison* (New York City Correctional Institution for Women: Free Space Writing Program, n.d.).

See the Annotated Bibliography of writings by women prisoners in this book for entries on contemporary anthologies and newsletters from women's prisons.

For further information on prison publications, see Russell N. Baird, *The Penal Press* (Evanston, Ill.: Northwestern Univ. Press, 1967).

12. For a discussion of these traditions, see H. Bruce Franklin, *The Victim as Criminal and Artist*.

13. Patricia McConnel, letters to Judith Scheffler, 1 April 1983; 6 July 1983; 2 March 1985.

LADY CONSTANCE LYTTON (1869–1923)

Constance Georgina Lytton, daughter of British diplomat Robert, first earl of Lytton, was born in Vienna and spent much of her childhood abroad with her family. Educated at home, where she was not encouraged to pursue a career in her interests of music and journalism, Lytton led an uneventful life of service to her family. After her father's death she remained unmarried and devoted herself to her mother, her friends, and domestic interests, especially flower arranging.

The turning point of Lytton's life came in 1906 when she inherited £1,000 from Lady Bloomfield, her godmother and great-aunt. Seeking a public cause to support, she became interested in the British folk-dancing and -singing revival, and through it coincidentally met British suffragettes in 1908. Her interest in prisons drew her to their work, since many of them were being imprisoned. Gradually she came to accept the suffragettes' militant tactics. She served as a movement lecturer and agitator for four years, despite her delicate health and her distaste for public life. She was imprisoned a total of four times: twice in Holloway Prison outside London, in Newcastle, and in Walton Jail, Liverpool. As Lady Constance, she received preferential treatment and was not forcibly fed when a test of her heart revealed its weakness. Outraged at this injustice, Lytton disguised herself as working-class suffragette Jane Warton, was arrested during a demonstration in Liverpool in 1910, and was imprisoned in Walton Jail, where she was forcibly fed without examination. Though she successfully exposed the class injustices of prison treatment, she suffered impaired health for the rest of her life. After a stroke of paralysis in 1912, Lytton spent her last eleven years as an invalid, cared for by her mother and admired by fellow suffragettes. During the first two years of that period she wrote *Prisons and Prisoners* with her left hand.

Dr. Mary Gordon, a psychologist and the first woman prison inspector, described Lytton and the suffragette movement: "Such spiritual upheavals are always irrational, and irrational human types are swept into them as high priests. Con was seized and used. She was both flame and burnt offering."

Note: Biographical information is from Betty Balfour, ed. *Letters of Constance Lytton* (London: Heinemann, 1925); E. Sylvia Pankhurst, *The Suffragette Movement: An*

Intimate Account of Persons and Ideals (London: Longmans, Green, 1931); Emmeline Pethick-Lawrence, *My Part in a Changing World* (London: Gollancz, 1938); *The Europa Biographical Dictionary of British Women*, ed. Anne Crawford et al. (Detroit: Gale, 1983).

WORKS BY LADY CONSTANCE LYTTON

Papers. Suffragette Fellowship Collection, Museum of London (50.82/119). For details, see the Annotated Bibliography in this anthology.
"Japanese Art of Arranging Cut Flowers." In Maria T. Earle, *Pot-pourri from a Surrey Garden*. London: Smith & Elder, 1897.
Letters of Constance Lytton. Selected and arranged by Betty Balfour. London: Heinemann, 1925.
Prisons and Prisoners: Some Personal Experiences. London: Heinemann, and East Ardsley, Yorkshire: EP Publishing, 1914; reprint, Boston: Charles River Books, 1977.

Disguised as Jane Warton

From *Prisons and Prisoners*. Reprinted by permission of
Adam and Charles Black, Publishers.

"Under a Government which imprisons any unjustly, the true place for a just man (or woman) is also a prison."

I was sent to Liverpool and Manchester to join in working an Anti-Government campaign during a General Election in January, 1910. Just before I went, there came the news of the barbarous ill-treatment of Miss Selina Martin and Miss Leslie Hall, while on remand in Walton Gaol. They had been refused bail, and, while awaiting their trial, their friends were not allowed to communicate with them. This is contrary to law and precedent for prisoners on remand. As a protest they had started a hunger-strike. They were fed by force, in answer to which they broke the windows of their cells. They were put in irons for days and nights together, and one of them was frog-marched in the most brutal fashion to and from the room where the forcible feeding was performed. These facts they made known to their friends at the police court on the day of their trial.

I heard, too, of another prisoner in Liverpool, Miss Bertha Brewster, who had been re-arrested after her release from prison, and charged with breaking the windows of her prison cell, which she had done as a protest against being fed by force. She had been punished for this offence while in prison. She did not respond to the summons, and when arrested on a warrant, three and a half months later, she was sentenced to six weeks' hard labour for this offence.

I felt a great wish to be in Liverpool, if possible, to get public opinion in that town to protest against such treatment of women political prisoners. If I failed in this, I determined myself to share the fate of these women.

When I was in Manchester, Mary Gawthorpe was ill with the internal complaint which has since obliged her to give up work. She saw me in her room one day. We had been distressed beyond words to hear of the sufferings of Selina Martin and Leslie Hall. Mary Gawthorpe said, with tears in her eyes, as she threw her arms round me: "Oh, and these are women quite unknown—nobody knows or cares about them except their own friends. They go to prison again and again to be treated like this, until it kills them!" That was enough. My mind was made up. The altogether shameless way I had been preferred against the others at Newcastle, except Mrs. Brailsford who shared with me the special treatment, made me determine to try whether they would recognise my need for exceptional favours without my name. . . .

I joined the W.S.P.U.* again, filling up the membership card as Miss Jane Warton. The choice of a name had been easy. When I came out of Holloway Prison, a distant relative, by name Mr. F. Warburton, wrote me an appreciative letter, thanking me for having been a prisoner in this cause. I determined that if it were necessary to go to prison under another name, I should take the name of Warburton. When I went to Newcastle, my family raised no objection. Now nobody was to know of my disguise, but Warburton was too distinguished a name; that would at once attract attention. I must leave out the "bur" and make it "Warton." "Jane" was the name of Joan of Arc (for Jeanne is more often translated into "Jane" than "Joan") and would bring me comfort in distress. A family sympathetic to our cause, who lived in the suburb near Walton Gaol, were informed that a keen member, Miss Warton, would call at their house in the afternoon before the protest meeting, to investigate the outside of the gaol and the Governor's house by day-

*Women's Social and Political Union.—*Ed.*

light, and that she was ready to be arrested if she could not obtain the release of the prisoners. . . .

I accomplished my disguise in Manchester, going to a different shop for every part of it, for safety's sake. I had noticed several times while I was in prison that prisoners of unprepossessing appearance obtained least favour, so I was determined to put ugliness to the test. I had my hair cut short and parted, in early Victorian fashion, in smooth bands down the side of my face. This, combined with the resentful bristles of my newly-cut back hair, produced a curious effect. I wished to bleach my hair as well, but the hairdresser refused point-blank to do this, and the stuff that I bought for the purpose at a chemist's proved quite in-effective. A tweed hat, a long green cloth coat, which I purchased for 8s. 6d., a woollen scarf and woollen gloves, a white silk neck-kerchief, a pair of pince-nez spectacles, a purse, a net-bag to contain some of my papers, and my costume was complete. I had removed my own initials from my underclothing, and bought the ready-made initials "J. W." to sew on in their stead, but to my regret I had not time to achieve this finishing touch.

All this sounds simple enough, but I suppose it was due to my preoc-cupation of mind that I have never known a day's shopping fraught with such complications and difficulties. At the frowzy little hairdresser's shop, the only one that seemed to me inconspicuous enough for so important a part of my disguise, the attendant was busy, and I had to return in an hour's time. I told him that I was going [on] a journey and wanted the hair short, since that would be less trouble. He cut it off. Then I wanted what remained to be worn in a parting, with the hair falling straight on either side. This part of the process was most absurd, for that way of wearing my hair was obviously disfiguring to me. "Ah! now that looks very becoming," said the hairdresser, and with that I left the shop in haste.

The eye-glasses I had first bought made me feel giddy from the quality of the lens. I had to take them back and have the glasses changed to the weakest possible. At the first place, in spite of all my protests, the shopman insisted on elaborately testing my sight, afterwards requiring me to wait for half an hour or so while he fitted up the glasses. So I went to another shop, and in self-defence invented the story that the glasses were for stage purposes, for a friend of mine who had very good sight, and that if she was not to trip up in her part the glasses must be as nearly plain as possible. This time I was more successful with the lens, but the grip of the folders was still galling to the very large bridge of my nose.

When I had finished this errand I was startled to see walking along the street one of my kind hostesses, whom I had parted from early that morning, professedly to return to Liverpool without delay. I took refuge down a side-street until she had passed by. Then I had strayed into the more opulent quarters of Manchester, in my search for another spectacle shop. All the shops were of a high-class order, and Jane Warton could find nothing to her requirements. On inquiry for a "cheap" draper, three different people recommended me to a certain shop named "Lewis." A sale was on there and Jane found that it was the very place for her. So many Miss Wartons were of the same mind that the street was blocked with customers for some distance down; but I was obliged to wait, for no other shop was of the same description. The hat was a special difficulty; every article of millinery was of the fashionable order, warranted to cover half the body as well as the head. This did not suit Jane. Finally she succeeded in getting the right one of stitched cloth, with a plait of cloth round the crown. Before leaving Manchester I realised that my ugly disguise was a success. I was an object of the greatest derision to street-boys, and shop-girls could hardly keep their countenances while serving me. . . .

[Lytton, masquerading as Jane Warton, was arrested during a demonstration in Liverpool and imprisoned in Walton Jail.—Ed.]

At last the longed-for moment had arrived, and I was taken off to my cell. To my joy there was a window which opened a little bit; at night it was lit by a gas jet that was set in the depth of the wall behind the door, the passage side, and covered in by a thick glass. I was ever so tired—I laid down and slept.

The next day was Sunday (January 16), but they did not ask us to go to chapel. For several days I did not wear my cap and apron in my cell, but did not in other ways continue my protest against the clothes. The cold seemed to me intense, and I wore the skirt of my dress fastened round my neck for warmth. The Governor, accompanied by the Matron, came to see me, but he was in a temper about our having broken his windows, so I said nothing. He was in a fury at the way I had fastened my skirt. I answered that it was for warmth and that I would gladly put on more clothes and warmer ones if he gave them to me. Later on the Senior Medical Officer came in. He was a short, fat, little man, with a long waxed moustache. I should have said he disliked being unkind; he liked to chaff over things; but as I looked at him I thought I would rather be forcibly fed by anyone in the world than by him, the coarse doctors at Newcastle and the cross little doctor I had seen the night before. I said I had not asked to see him, but he made no examination and asked no questions.

I lay in my bed most of the day, for they did not disturb me, and I tried to keep warm, as I felt the cold fearfully. They brought me all my meals the same as usual, porridge in the morning at 7, meat and potatoes mid-day at 12, porridge at 4.30. When they were hot I fed on the smell of them, which seemed quite delicious; I said "I don't want any, thank you," to each meal, as they brought it in. I had made up my mind that this time I would not drink any water, and would only rinse out my mouth morning and evening without swallowing any. I wrote on the walls of my cell with my slate pencil and soap mixed with the dirt of the floor for ink, "Votes for Women," and the saying from Thoreau's *Duty of Civil Disobedience*—"Under a Government which imprisons any unjustly, the true place for a just man (or woman) is also a prison"; on the wall opposite my bed I wrote the text from Joshua, "Only be thou strong and very courageous." That night I dreamt of fruits, melons, peaches and nectarines, and of a moonlit balcony that was hung with sweetest smelling flowers, honeysuckle and jessamine, apple-blossom and sweet scented verbena; there was only the sound of night birds throbbing over the hills that ranged themselves below the balcony. On it there slept my sister-in-law, and on the balustrade, but making no noise, was a figure awake and alert, which was my brother. My dream was of a land which was seen by my father in his poem of "King Poppy," where the princess and the shepherd boy are the types etherealised. I woke suddenly. I could sleep a little in detached moments, but this dream had made the prison cell beautiful to me; it had a way out.

The strain was great of having to put on my shoes, which were too small, every time I was taken out of my cell to empty slops or to see the Governor. The Matron was shocked that I did not put the right heel in at all and every day I was given another pair, but they were all alike in being too small for my right foot.

The next day, Monday (January 17), the wardress took my bed and bedding away because I would not make it up, but lay on it in the day-time. I told her if she wished she must roll me off, but that I did not intend voluntarily to give it up. She was quite amiable, but rolled me towards the wall and took the bed and bedding from underneath me. There was a little table in my cell which was not fastened to the wall. I turned it upside down and was able to sit in it with my body resting against one of the legs. It was very uncomfortable, but I felt too ill to sit up in the chair, and the concrete floor was much too cold without the bed. Every now and then I got up and walked backwards and forwards in the cell to get a little warmth into me. The Chaplain came in for a moment. He was a tall, good-looking man, of the burly, healthy sort. It seemed to me, from his talk, that he would be very well suited to be a cricket match or football parson, if there were such a thing, but he was totally unsuited to be the Chaplain of a prison, or anyhow of a woman's prison. He thought it wise to speak to me as a "Suffragette." "Look here, it's no good your thinking that there's anything to be done with the women here—the men sometimes are not such bad fellows, and there are many who write to me after they've left here, but the women, they're all as bad as bad can be, there's absolutely no good in them." I did not answer, but I felt inclined to say "Then good-bye to you, since you say you can do no good with the women here."

Presently an officer came and led me out. The manner of nearly all the officers was severe; one or two were friends but most of them treated me like dirt. I was shown along the gangway of the ward, which seemed to me very large, much larger than the D X at Holloway, and went in various directions like a star. I was shown into the Governor's room, which lay at the end of the gangway. It was warm, there were hot pipes against which I was made to stand with my back to the wall, and for a moment, as I put my feet to rest on the pipes, I could think of nothing else but the delight of their heat. The Governor was very cross. I had decided not to do the needlework which constituted the hard labour, for this he gave me three days on bread and water. He would not let me speak to him at all and I was led out, but, before I had got to my cell, I was called back into his presence. "I hear you are refusing to take your food, so it's three days in a special cell." I was taken out and down a staircase till we reached the ground floor. I think my cell was two stories above, but I am not sure; then down again and into a short passage that looked as if it was underground, with a window at the top seemingly only just level with the ground. The door of a cell was opened, I was put inside and the door locked. It was larger than the cell upstairs, and the jug, basin, etc., were all made of black guttapercha, not of tin, placed on the floor. This would have been bad for the ordinary prisoner, as it was quite impossible to tell whether the eating things were clean or not and, in any case, it smelt fairly strong of guttapercha; but as the rule for me was neither to eat nor drink, I was able to put up with it well. The bed was wider than an ordinary plank bed and nailed to the ground, so that I was able to lie on it without being disturbed. Best of all was the fact that it was nearer to the heating apparatus and so seemed quite warm when I was led in. I did not notice at first that the window did not open, but when I had been there six or seven hours it became wonderfully airless. I only left my cell for minutes at a time, when I was allowed to draw water, and the air of the corridor then seemed fresh as mountain air by comparison. I had an idea that Elsie Howey or some of the others would have been put into a punishment cell too. I called, but in vain, my voice had grown weak and my tongue and throat felt thick as a carpet, probably from not drinking anything. I tried signalling with raps on the wall, "No surrender—no surrender," Mrs. Leigh's favourite motto, but I was never sure of corresponding raps, though sometimes I thought I heard them. I could not sleep for more than about an hour at a time, my legs drew up into a cramped position whenever I went off and the choking thickness in my mouth woke me.

Tuesday, January 18, I was visited again by the Senior Medical Officer, who asked me how long I had been without food. I said I had eaten a buttered scone and a banana sent in by friends to the police station on Friday at about midnight. He said, "Oh, then, this is the fourth day; that is too long, I shall have to feed you, I must feed you at once," but he went out and nothing happened till about 6 o'clock in the evening, when he returned with, I think, five wardresses and the feeding apparatus. He urged me to take food voluntarily. I told him that was absolutely out of the question, that when our legislators ceased to resist enfranchising women then I should cease to resist taking food in prison. He did not examine my heart nor feel my pulse; he did not ask to do so, nor did I say anything which could possibly induce him to think I would refuse to be examined. I offered no resistance to being placed in position, but lay down voluntarily on the plank bed. Two of the wardresses took hold of my arms, one held my head and one my feet. One wardress helped to pour the food. The doctor leant on my knees as he stooped over my chest to get at my mouth. I shut my mouth and clenched my teeth. I had looked forward to this moment with so much anxiety lest my identity should be discovered beforehand, that I felt positively glad when the time had come. The sense of being overpowered by more force than I could possibly resist was complete, but I resisted nothing except with my mouth. The doctor offered me the choice of a wooden or steel gag; he explained elaborately, as he did on most subsequent occasions, that the steel gag would hurt and the wooden one not, and he urged me not to force him to use the steel gag. But I did not speak nor open my mouth, so that after playing about for a moment or two with the wooden one he finally had recourse to the steel. He seemed annoyed at my resistance and he broke into a temper as he plied my teeth with the steel implement. He found that on either side at the back I had false teeth mounted on a bridge which [he] did not take out. The superintending wardress asked if I had any false teeth, if so, that they must be taken out; I made no answer and the process went on. He dug his instrument down on to the sham tooth, it pressed fearfully on the gum. He said if I resisted so much with my teeth, he would have to feed me through the nose. The pain of it was intense and at last I must have given way for he got the gag between my teeth, when he proceeded to turn it much more than necessary until my jaws were fastened wide apart, far more than they could go naturally. Then he put down my throat a tube which seemed to me much too wide and was something like four feet in length. The irritation of the tube was excessive. I choked the moment it touched my throat until it had got down. Then the food was poured in quickly; it made me sick a few seconds after it was down and the action of the sickness made my body and legs double up, but the wardresses instantly pressed back my head and the doctor leant on my knees. The horror of it was more than I can describe. I was sick over the doctor and wardresses, and it seemed a long time before they took the tube out. As the doctor left he gave me a slap on the cheek, not violently, but, as it were, to express his contemptuous disapproval, and he seemed to take for granted that my distress was assumed. At first it seemed such an utterly contemptible thing to have done that I could only laugh in my mind. Then suddenly I saw Jane Warton lying before me, and it seemed as if I were outside of her. She was the most despised, ignorant and helpless prisoner that I had seen. When she had served her time and was out of the prison, no one would believe anything she said, and the doctor when he had fed her by force and tortured her body, struck her on the cheek to show how he despised her! That was Jane Warton, and I had come to help her.

When the doctor had gone out of the cell, I lay quite helpless. The wardresses were kind and knelt round to comfort me, but there was nothing to be done, I could not move, and remained there in what, under different conditions, would have been an intolerable mess. I had been sick over my hair, which, though short, hung on either side of my face, all over the wall near my bed, and my clothes seemed saturated with it, but the wardresses told me they could not get me a change that night as it was too late, the office was shut. I lay quite motionless, it seemed paradise to be without the suffocating tube, without the liquid food going in and out of my body and without the gag between my teeth. Presently the wardresses all left me, they had orders to go, which were carried out with the usual promptness. Before long I heard the sounds of the forced feeding in the next cell to mine. It was almost more than I could bear, it was Elsie Howey, I was sure. When the ghastly process was over and all quiet, I tapped on the wall and called out at the top of my voice, which wasn't much just then, "No surrender," and there came the answer past any doubt in Elsie's voice, "No surrender." After this I fell back and lay as I fell. It was not very long before the wardress came and announced that I was to go back upstairs as, because of the feeding, my time in the punishment cell was over. I was taken into the same cell which I had before; the long hours till morning were a nightmare of agonised dread for a repetition of the process.

The next day, Wednesday, January 19, they brought me clean clothes. When the wardresses were away at breakfast I determined to break the thick glass of my gas jet to show what I thought of the forcible feeding, it seemed the last time that I should have the strength required. I took one of my shoes, which always lay at my side except when I moved from my cell, let it get a good swing by holding it at the back of my shoulder and then hurled it against the glass with all the strength that I had. The glass broke in pieces with a great smashing sound. The two wardresses, who were in charge of the whole ward while the others were away, came into my cell together; I was already back in my bed. They were young, new to the work, and looked rather frightened. I told them I had done it with a shoe, and why. "But that is enough," I said, "I am not going to do any more now." This reassured them and they both laughed. They took away the shoes as "dangerous," and brought me slippers instead, and, to my intense relief, I never saw them again. As the morning wore on, one after the other of the officials proclaimed that I had done a shameful thing. On being changed to the cell next door, one of the head wardresses—I never made out exactly who she was— was in a great temper. I had told her, as I did every one of the officials, why I had broken my gas jet. "Broken it, yes, I should just think you had, indeed. And all that writing scribbled over your cell; can't keep the place decent." "I'm so sorry," I said; "I assure you there was nothing indecent in what I wrote on the wall." "No, not indecent, but—" she hesitated and, as the words would not come to her assistance, the remark remained unfinished.

I had not been long in the other cell before the doctor and four or five wardresses appeared. He was apparently angry because I had broken the jet glass; he seized one of the tin vessels and began waving it about. "I suppose you want to smash me with one of these?" he exclaimed. I said to him, so that all the wardresses with him could hear, "Unless you consider it part of your duty, would you please not strike me when you have finished your odious job" (or I may have said "slap me," I do not remember). He did not answer, but, after a little pause, he signed to me to lie down on the bed. Again the choice of the wooden or steel imple- ment, again the force, which after a time I could not withstand, in the same place as yesterday where the gum was sore and aching. Then the feeling of the suffocating tube thrust down and the gate of life seemed shut. The tube was pressed down much too far, it seemed to me, causing me at times great pain in my side. The sickness was worse than the time before. As the tube was removed I was unavoidably sick over the doctor. He flew away from me and out of the cell, exclaiming angrily, "If you do that again next time I shall feed you twice." I had removed my serge jacket and taken several precautions for my bed, but I am afraid one or two of the officers and the floor and wall were drenched. I shut my eyes and lay back quite helpless for a while. They presently brought in fresh clothes, and a woman, another prisoner, came and washed the floor. It seemed terrible that another prisoner should do this, it was altogether a revolting business. Two wardresses came and over-looked her work, one of them said, in a voice of displeased authority: "Look at her! Just look at her! The *way* she's doing it!" The woman washed on and took no notice; her face was intensely sad. I roused myself and said, "Well, at any rate, she's doing what I should be doing myself and I am very grateful to her." The wardresses looked surprised at me, but they said nothing.

The Governor came in for a moment to see me. To my surprise his anger had cooled a little. He had before spoken to me in a rage and, if I asked questions which implied a complaint, had told me they were not proper questions for me to ask, or that I must not argue or raise discussions. After failing to get a definite answer as to under whose authority the forcible feeding was done, I said it surely could not be right for him to allow such a thing in the prison over which he had jurisdiction, unless he had seen it and at least fully realised what it entailed. With apparently some reluctance, he admitted that he had witnessed it. I asked, "And after that you sanction and approve of such a thing being done to prisoners who have committed *only nominal crimes with no criminal object and in defence of a claim which they have no recognised constitutional means to enforce?*" The last italicised part of this remark remained unheard, for the Governor interrupted me with "That is not a fitting question for you to ask." Later, I was had up before him in his room and was severely reprimanded for breaking the glass of the gas-box and "inspection" glass, and for defacing the walls of my cell, but I was dismissed with a caution for glass breaking, and my punishment was reserved for the Visiting Magistrates.

When it was evening the light was lit and the doctor and wardresses came again to feed me. I asked if I could not sit up in a chair and the doctor said "Yes." I told him that I was a small eater, that the capacity of my body was very limited and if only he would give less quantities the result might be better. I also begged that he would not press the tube so far down into my body. He treated the request with contempt, saying that anyhow my stomach must be longer than his, since I was taller than he was. This third time, though I was continually sick, the doctor pressed the tube down firmly into my body and continued to pour food in. At last this produced a sort of shivering fit and my teeth chattered when the gag was removed; I suppose that every vestige of colour must have left my face, for the doctor seemed surprised and alarmed. He removed the tube and told the wardresses to lay me on the floor-bed and lower my head. He then came and lay over my chest and seemed very sorry for what he had done. I told him I should not faint, that I was not liable to this or any form of collapse; I did not mention the slight chronic debility of heart from which I suffered. He called in the junior medical officer, who happened to be passing at the time, to test my heart. The junior doctor, who was in a jovial mood, stooped down and listened to my heart through the stethoscope for barely the space of a second—he could not have heard two beats—and exclaimed, "Oh, ripping, splendid heart! You can go on with her"; with that he left the cell. But the senior doctor seemed not to be reassured and he was kind to me for the first time. He tried to feed me with a spoon; but I was still able to clench my teeth and no food got down. He then pleaded with me, saying in a beseeching voice, "I do beg of you—I appeal to you, not as a prison doctor but as a man—to give over. You are a delicate woman, you are not fit for this sort of thing." I answered "Is anybody fit for it? And I beg of you—I appeal to you, not as a prisoner but as a woman—to give over and refuse to continue this inhuman treatment." After I had lain quiet for some time I managed to clean the cell myself. I took out two pails to the sink, but had only strength to carry them a few yards. As I was journeying like this, getting on very slowly, a wardress told me to take only one at a time; her sympathy was moved to this extent, but no further. I took one pail back to my cell, went on with the other, and then came back for the first. When I had finished this business of washing up—which I was glad to do myself, even if it took half the day, that it might not be given to another prisoner, and also for the better cleaning of the hideous mess—I fell on my bed and lay there till evening; they now left me both bed and bedding, which was a tremendous blessing.

I lay facing the window, which was high up, and very little light seemed to come from it. As the sun went down I saw the shadow of the wooden mouldings fall across the glass,—three crosses, and they were the shape of the three familiar crosses at the scene of Calvary, one in the centre and one on either side. It looked different from any of the pictures I had seen. The cross of Christ, the cross of the repentant thief, and the cross of the sinner who had not repented—that cross looked blacker than the others, and behind it was an immense crowd. The light from the other two crosses seemed to shine on this one, and the Christ was crucified that He might undo all the harm that was done. I saw amongst the crowd the poor little doctor and the Governor, and all that helped to torture these women in prison, but they were nothing compared to the men in the Cabinet who wielded their force over them. There were the upholders of vice and the men who support the thousand injustices to women, some knowingly and some unconscious of the harm and cruelty entailed. Then the room grew dark and I fell asleep. When the doctor came again with his apparatus he had bovril and brandy, and the tube was left for only one second in my body. The next morning, Thursday, January 20, I told him that the brandy, which at first had the effect of warming me, left me freezing cold after about two hours, and I thought it was no use. As for the bovril, I had the strongest objection to it of a vegetarian kind, and I begged him not to give it to me again; he said he would not. It was only when I was sick that I knew what were the ingredients put down my body. That morning it was again milk and plasmon that was given me, and I was horribly sick. The doctor said to me, "You are absolutely not fit for this kind of thing. How could your Union send a woman like you to do a thing of this kind? It is like sending a wisp of wind to fight against a——" I did not hear the end of the sentence, but I think he said "a rock." I was not able to answer, but the next time he came I said to him, "Our Union does not send anyone; service of this kind is absolutely voluntary. In my case not one of the leaders even knew of my action. I did it entirely off my own bat and only told the local organisers."

From the third feeding, when the junior doctor had felt my heart on Wednesday evening, the senior doctor had been much kinder to me; in fact I noticed a change in the way I was treated generally, so much so that I concluded my identity had been discovered or was at least suspected. I left off wearing my hair in a parting, as it was almost impossible to keep it away when I was sick. I brushed it back and did it up in a towel every time when I was fed. I left off wearing my glasses, which were too uncomfortable to be tolerated now that the necessity for them had worn off and they were forcibly feeding me quite happily. I then decided to take the utmost advantage of any privilege, in order to bring the officials to act reasonably, to check their recklessness as much as possible, and to bring them to strain the regulations so far as might be—not, as heretofore, in the direction of brutality, but in the direction of hygiene, if not of humanity. I pleaded afresh with the doctor to try the experiment of giving me less quantity of food, of putting less of the tube into the body, of using less glycerine, which greatly irritated my throat the moment the tube touched it, or to use oil instead of glycerine. He listened to what I said, and though except as to the glycerine—he wiped the tube almost free of it, and called my attention to the fact—there was not much difference in what he did, yet his manner of doing it was different.

When I was at the sink on Thursday morning, two or three other prisoners were there, and they hastily whispered to me, "It *is* your friend next to you, No. 21." The kindness which beamed from all their faces did my heart good, but I could never hear or see Elsie Howey next door, and eventually I imagined that they must have mistaken me for her when I threw back my hair after the third feeding.

That day I thought I would clean my window, through which I had seen such a wonderful vision the evening before. Though the day was generally spent in loneliness, I knew that I might be visited at any hour, so I put off till about 3.30, when the ward was generally quiet for a time. All the furniture in the cell was movable, so I placed the table in front of the window and the chair on the top, then I climbed up. Through the small part of the window that opened I looked down, and in a beautiful red glow of the sinking sun I saw a sight that filled my very soul with joy. In the gloaming light—it was an exercise ground that I looked down upon—I saw walking round, all alone, a woman in her prisoner's dress, and in her arms she carried another little prisoner, a baby done up in a blanket. I was too high up to hear her, but I could see distinctly that she cooed and laughed to her little companion, and perhaps she sang to it too. I never saw maternal love more naturally displayed. The words of the Chaplain came back to my mind—"The women, they're all as bad as bad can be, there's absolutely no good in them." No good in them! and yet amongst them there was this little woman who, at least, loved her child and played with it as only a mother-heart can!

I got down and put the table and chair in their place; I felt amazed, having seen a sight as beautiful as the most beautiful picture in the world.

AGNES SMEDLEY (1892–1950)

As a young woman, Agnes Smedley, who was born in northern Missouri and raised in poverty, regarded marriage as economic slavery. She was determined to escape the life of hard work and childbearing that had killed her mother before age forty. Although she had little formal education, Smedley trained as a stenographer through the assistance of an aunt who earned her own living by prostitution. Her quest to advance herself took her to a normal school in Arizona, where she met and married a Swedish-American civil engineer. After a few years their marriage ended in divorce and Smedley moved to New York City, where she studied at New York University, began to work in journalism, and became actively involved in socialist politics and in Margaret Sanger's birth-control work.

In New York during World War I, Smedley studied with Lala Laipat Rai, an exiled Indian professor, and met with young Indian Nationalists who sought independence from Britain. She was arrested in March 1918 and held in the Tombs for six months, principally on the charge that she had violated the Federal Espionage Act by acting unlawfully as an agent for the Indian Nationalist Party; she learned only later that her Indian associates had some German connections that had precipitated her arrest. An additional charge was her violation of an anti-birth-control law, as a few copies of Margaret Sanger's pamphlet *Family Limitation* had been found in her possession. John Haynes Holmes, Unitarian minister and supporter of Sanger's work, raised Smedley's $10,000 bail. She was released from jail after the Armistice but never tried, and the charges against her were dropped in 1923.

The experience of imprisonment, much of it spent in solitary confinement, influenced Smedley's later writing. She could articulate the thoughts and feelings of her silent sister inmates because she shared their background of poverty. In her autobiographical novel, *Daughter of Earth* (1929), she describes her imprisonment through the experiences of the heroine, Marie Rogers. A more direct description is in "Cell

Mates," an intriguing series of character sketches that appeared in 1920 in the Sunday magazine section of the socialist daily, the New York *Call*.

Margaret Sanger held a small reception in her New York apartment for Smedley after her release on bail. After working on the staff of the *Call* and with Sanger's group, Smedley sailed to Germany and began her career as a foreign correspondent. She is most well known for her firsthand reports of the Chinese Revolution. Smedley's close association with the Chinese Communists caused political trouble for her in the United States during the cold war era and is largely responsible for the eclipse of her work until recently. She died in England from complications following an operation, and was buried with honors in Peking.

Note: Biographical information is from Jan MacKinnon and Stephen MacKinnon, "Agnes Smedley: A Working Introduction," *Bulletin of Concerned Asian Scholars*, 7 (January–March 1975): 6–11; MacKinnon and MacKinnon, "Agnes Smedley's 'Cell Mates,'" *Signs 3* (Winter 1977): 531–539; MacKinnon and MacKinnon, Introduction to *Portraits of Chinese Women in Revolution*, by Agnes Smedley (Old Westbury, N.Y.: Feminist Press, 1976); Margaret Sanger, *An Autobiography* (1938; reprint, Elmsford, N.Y.: Maxwell, 1970).

WORKS BY AGNES SMEDLEY

Papers. 1894–1950. Arizona State University Archives, Tempe, Ariz.

Battle Hymn of China. New York: Knopf, 1943; reissued as *China Correspondent*, London: Pandora, 1984.

"Cell Mates." *Call Magazine*, Sunday supplement to the New York *Call*, 15, 22, 29 February; 14 March 1920.

China Fights Back; An American Woman with the Eighth Route Army. London: Gollancz, 1938; reprint, Westport, Conn.: Hyperion Press, 1977.

China's Red Army Marches. New York; Vanguard, 1934.

Chinese Destinies: Sketches of Present-Day China. New York: Vanguard, 1933.

Daughter of Earth. New York: Coward-McCann, 1929; reprint, Old Westbury, N.Y.: Feminist Press, 1973.

The Great Road: The Life and Times of Chu Teh. New York: Monthly Review Press, 1956.

The Labour Monthly. Korea Handbook. Contributions by Agnes Smedley et al. London: Trinity Trust, 1950.

Letter to Margaret Sanger from the Tombs, 1 November 1918. Margaret Sanger Papers, Cont. 12, Reel 10, Library of Congress.

Agnes Smedley

Portraits of Chinese Women in Revolution. Edited with an Introduction by Jan
MacKinnon and Stephen MacKinnon, with a foreword by Florence Howe. First
ed., Old Westbury, N.Y.: Feminist Press, 1976.

Red Flood over China. Moscow: Co-operative Pub. Soc. of Foreign Workers in
the U.S.S.R., 1934.

Short Stories from China. Translated by Cze Ming-Ting, with an Introduction
by Agnes Smedley. New York: International, 1933.

*Stories of the Wounded; An Appeal for Orthopaedic Centres of the Chinese Red
Cross.* Hong Kong: Newspaper Enterprises, 1941.

Cell Mates

From the *Call Magazine*, Sunday supplement to the New
York *Call*, 15, 22, 29 February, 14 March 1920.

Nellie

My first impression of Nellie was gained when I looked up from my
lukewarm breakfast coffee to listen to an avalanche of profanity in an
Irish brogue. Nellie was swearing at the food, and was showering bless-
ings of wrath upon the wardens and matrons of the Tombs prison, who
she swore by all the angels and the Blessed Virgin, had built the jail and
ran it for their own pleasure and profit.

The matron spoke: "Shut your mouth, Nellie, or I'll lock you in your
cell."

Nellie looked up, took up the matron's words, and set them to music.
She sang hilariously and, finishing her coffee, two-stepped down past
the matron and looked her in the eye, still singing. She two-stepped
down the corridor and around behind the iron gate into the "run," in
which old offenders are locked during the day.

Nellie was short, blocky, square in build. Fifty-three summers had
come and gone without leaving their touches in her hair. She had grown
ugly and scarred, knotted, twisted and gnarled like an old oak. But her
vitality had never waned. Her figure had been permitted to develop,
unhampered by corsets—and it had developed, particularly her stomach
and hips. The expression on her square, scarred Irish face was good-
natured and happy-go-lucky, with a touch of sadness which gripped your
heart at times.

From the North of Ireland, Nellie had come to America while still a girl under 20. And, being pretty and very ignorant, with no means of support, she had, in due course of time, become a prostitute. Since that time she had served innumerable short terms in all the jails in Jersey and New York City. Her offenses generally consisted of intoxication, fighting, or "hustling."

In her day, according to her story, she had been much sought after by "gentlemen," and her "clients" included pillars of the law—all the local judges and such. She told me that once she had been brought by a policeman before one of these estimable personages, and after he had rebuked her and sentenced her to pay a nominal fine, she had made some interesting disclosures in the court room and insisted upon his paying the fine for her.

Nellie had never lost her Irish brogue in all these years, and she greeted those whom she liked with "Top o' the mornin' to ye," and those whom she disliked with a "Well, damn ye, ye're able to git up this mornin' and raise hell, ain't ye?"

The girls at the long bare breakfast table had laughed as Nellie gaily responded to the matron's rebuke. From back of the iron gates Nellie's voice came like a fog-horn from a distance. She was feeling fine this morning, and the girls finished breakfast quickly.

"Come on, give us a jig, Nellie," one called.

She pulled her old dirty blue skirt half way to her knees, exposing [illegible] white stockings, and started to jig. It was an Irish jig, and her old run-down shoes made a sound like fire-crackers on the cement floor. She sang as she danced—Irish songs and songs indigenous to the soil of America and to Nellie's peculiar mode of life. Some of them are unprintable. One of them began:

> "Oh-h-h-h!
> Did you ever have a fight
> In the middle of the night
> With the gur-r-rl you love?"

And so throughout the day Nellie kept the girls at attention, vile in talk, always profane, dipping snuff and brow-beating the matrons. When visitors appeared at the gate and gazed back with round eyes at the strange creatures in the cage, Nellie would call "Oh-h-h! Where did you get that hat!" or "Top o' the mornin' to yet [*sic*], lady; are ye plannin' to break in?"

No one could be depressed for long, with Nellie present. One morning I came in from my gray cell into the dull gray corridor. Life seemed quite as dull and gray as my surroundings. Nellie was sitting on a bench near my door, baking her feet against the radiator. She looked up, and her voice scattered the gloom into a thousand fragments:

> "Oh-h-h!
> Good mornin', O Missus O'Grady,
> Why are you so blue today?"

I sat down by her.

"Ye're a nice thing," she said; "and why are ye in this place?"

"I don't think you'd understand if I told you, Nellie," I replied.

Nellie fixed her eyes on space for a few moments. That expression of sadness crept about her mouth.

"I guess ye're right," she said. "I mighta once. I was a purty gir-rl once"—

I felt that I had inadvertently recalled long-dead summers of a tragic life. But before I had time to rebuke myself, she kicked the radiator and brightly asked:

"And how do ye like this hotel?"

I asked why she was there. She reflected for a moment.

"By the holy mother uv Jesus," she started, "I'm as innicent as a baby."

"What is the charge?"

"Hittin' a man on the head with a hammer," she replied.

"I didn't do it," she reiterated, to my back.

"Why didn't you?" I asked.

She chuckled and took some snuff.

"Jest ye wait till I git out."

Then she told me how it happened. It took a long time, and she went into the family history and her personal relations with all the neighbors. She had been out all night, it seems, and in the early morning had gone home. She stopped at a saloon beneath her flat and reinforced herself with liquor before facing her husband, Mike.

Tim, the bartender, had warned her.

"Nellie," he cautioned, "ye'd better not go home now. Ye'll sure git in a tussel with Mike if ye do."

But Nellie, according to her own statement, was "feelin' like a bur-r-d"; so she "ups and flits up the stairs jist as airy as ye please."

Mike was indignant, as husbands sometimes are. He questioned his erring and reinforced wife. The forewarned struggle ensued. The kitchen suffered somewhat, and Mike retreated down the stairs to the first landing. There a friend opened the door, grasped his predicament, and came to his assistance. Somewhat pressed, Nellie picked up a hammer which was lying on a trunk and laid low the intruder.

When Mike's would-be assistant came to consciousness he got a bandage and a policeman, the former for himself and the latter for Nellie.

Nellie concluded her tale. "They arristed me—an', would ye believe me, it wuz Holy Thursday!"

She had been in the Tombs for a number of months. Once Mike came to see her, and she had asked him for a dollar to buy a little extra food. What he replied I don't know, but when she returned to us she sat down in a corner and cried piteously.

The next morning she came in as usual, to see if I wished to get up for breakfast. I asked her to order some extra food from the restaurant.

"And, Nellie," I said, "order yourself a good breakfast."

She grinned and thanked me. And about an hour later her breakfast bill was sent in to me. Nellie had done as I had asked, and had ordered a *good* breakfast! It included, among a dozen other things, four or five pieces of pie. It seems she had stocked up for the winter. And I paid the bill gladly.

When I saw Nellie last she came around to the iron gate to tell us goodby. She had on a clean white waist, and her hair was combed. She was being released, without going to trial.

"What are you going to do now?" I asked.

Her old face assumed that peculiar expression of goodness and sadness—and of helplessness. I knew she didn't know, and that it didn't matter much what she did. She was turned loose on the streets again. No one met her; no one was waiting to welcome her. She turned and left us, a little stooped, and I heard her old shoes click as she went down the cement corridor.

[284]

Agnes Smedley

May

May sat near the barred gate smoking a cigarette and resting her fat hands on her fatter knees. If convicted of forgery this time it meant eight fingerprints—one for each year she had been in the business. She was no amateur; one isn't an amateur at 45, after passing from the factory and the stage into private business.

May's complaint wasn't so much that she had been caught, but that she had been caught on such a trifle. She had sent cigars to a fictitious son in Camp Upton and given a check to the cigar store, receiving only $10 in change.

Her bail was $500, but her man, Vic, was too cowardly to furnish it. It meant trouble for him if he did. He had managed to keep out of the law's grip for eight years, just as she had managed to keep in it; but as years went by the danger seemed to creep closer. Even when May had been arrested this time he had been with her. But she had explained to the detective that he was a strange man who had kindly offered to carry her packages. So he had escaped the law again.

Of course, she realized that Vic couldn't risk arrest; but it seemed unfair at times; she had always shouldered the blame, and always served time, often for him. Even now he wrote letters declaring that had it not been for rheumatism he would have been down to leave money for her personal expenses; but it never occurred to him to send money by mail. Yet again she would forgive him, as women often do. She had his picture in her purse; it was dim and worn from much handling, and she looked at it with mingled anger and compassion. When any one agreed with her that Vic was a worthless scoundrel, she launched into a long defense which would have wrung tears from any jury who didn't happen to know the facts.

"How you worry about a $500 bail!" I exclaimed. "Mine is $10,000."

"Well," May retorted, "*I* didn't try to swing the world by the tail. All I wanted was a little change."

"Tell me," I asked her, "why did you stop working in a factory?"

"Go work in a factory and find out," was her reply.

"Well, why did you leave the stage?"

"Look at me," she challenged sarcastically, "and look at my figger!"

I looked. It *was* rather discouraging; about five feet high and five feet wide, yellow hair and an accordion pleated chin. Eight years ago she had been thirty-seven. One can't be a successful chorus girl at thirty-seven, after your renowed [sic] cuteness becomes buried beneath a bed of fat.

"Couldn't you do something else besides—this?" I inquired, hesitatingly.

"Yes," she grimly retorted, "I could scrub floors or take in washin', or 'hustle,' or do a few little things like that."

May warned me that a "stool pigeon" would undoubtedly be put in to watch me and try to get information from me, that perhaps one was there already; that maybe she, herself, was one. She was scornful of my "greenness."

"Gawd!" she exclaimed once, "I guess if some bull came in here dressed up like a priest, you'd believe him. Now, listen to me, never trust a man dressed like a priest."

May constituted herself my guardian and carefully kept the other girls out of my cell. "Get out, you hussey, you low-down thief," she yelled at them when they wandered into my cell. And if they didn't get out, she would put them out.

"Don't give them any money," she cautioned me time and again. But when she left, she carried some of my money with her. My "greenness" was very profound.

When taken to court, she wore a hat over which flowed a long black veil.

"Some veil," she laughed. "It ought to be a mask!" But even her jokes were told in a tremulous voice, as if she were telling them to keep from thinking of other things.

When the women returned from court, they told me that a very ugly man had appeared against May and that she, when asked if what he said were true, had replied that "any man with a face like that ought to have a check passed on him." She and the other women had been compelled to walk between the long row of masked detectives, veils thrown back; two of the detectives recognized May. She was given the "Indefinite," which means anything from three months to three years in the penitentiary.

Agnes Smedley

Mollie

For circulating leaflets opposing intervention in Russia, Mollie Steimer, with three men comrades, had been sentenced to 15 years in prison, a $500 fine and deportation to Russia. A good start for a little Russian girl less than five feet in height who had not yet reached the age of 21.

Mollie had come from the Ukraine five years before, and since that time had worked in a waist factory for $10 a week. A few months preceding her arrest she had received $15. She was the eldest of five children. A sister, aged 17, and a brother, aged 14, as well as her father, were all factory workers.

Mollie was sitting in her cell writing when I was put into jail. Her greeting was characteristic of her cast of mind.

"I am glad to see you here!" she said. "I wish the prisons to be filled with the workers. They soon will be. Then we will wake up."

Before her, pasted on the wall, were newspaper photographs of Karl Liebknecht, Eugene V. Debs and John Reed, and, printed in red letters high up on the stone wall, were the words, "Long live the Social Revolution!"

Mollie wore a red Russian smock. Her short hair was glossy black and curled up at the ends. Her face belonged to Russia, and the expression of seriousness and silent determination had first been cast in that country many years before. Her carefully chosen words were expressed with a slight foreign accent. Seldom did she speak of anything save Russia, the revolution in Germany and Austria and the future of the workers in America. She was always looking toward that world which she had described on the witness stand to a judge from Alabama:

> "It will be a new social order," she had said, "of which no group of people shall be in the power of any other group. Every person shall have an equal opportunity to develop himself. None shall live by the product of another. Every one shall produce what he can and enjoy what he needs. He shall have time to gain knowledge and culture. At present humanity is divided into groups called nations. We workers of the world will unite in one human brotherhood. To bring about this I have pledged myself to work all my life."

"Is there any such place as you tell about?" the prosecuting attorney had sneered. Mollie replied:

"I believe those who represent Russia have been elected by the workers only. The parasites are not represented in the Bolshevik administration."

The girls in prison loved Mollie. She talked with them at great length, disagreeing with them and frankly criticizing them if she thought best. At night she would talk gently to some girl who was trying to smother her sobs in the rough prison blankets. After the cell doors clanged behind us in the late afternoon, Mollie would stand grasping the steel bars. In simple, slow words she would talk to the girls. She used English which the most humble could understand, and as she spoke the three tiers would become silent and only an occasional question would interrupt her talk.

Mollie's philosophy of life had not been gleaned from books. A child of the soil, the finely-worded sentiments of the *intelligencia* did not impress her as being sincere. The *intelligencia* had deserted the workers of Russia when the great crisis came, when the workers of that country had challenged. "Peace to the huts, war to the palaces, hail to the Third International!"

With her own hands Mollie had labored for many years, had longed for, but never enjoyed, the beautiful things of life, and little, save the most sordid, bare necessities. Even the possibility of school had been closed to her. About her in the factory she had seen thousands like herself, pouring out their lives for crumbs, suffering, and then dying, poor and wretched. The class struggle to her became a grim reality.

Mollie championed the cause of the prisoners—the one with venereal disease, the mother with diseased babies, the prostitute, the feeble-minded, the burglar, the murderer. To her they were but products of a diseased social system. She did not complain that even the most vicious of them were sentenced to no more than five or seven years, while she herself was facing 15 years in prison. She asked that the girl with venereal disease be taken to a hospital; the prison physician accused her of believing in free love and in Bolshevism. She asked that the vermin be cleaned from the cells of one of the girls; the matron ordered her to attend to her own affairs—that it was not *her* cell. To quiet her they would lock her in her cell. "Lock me in," she replied to the matron; "I have nothing to lose but my chains."

Then the news of the German revolution and of the armistice came.

Outside the whistles shrieked and people yelled. In the prison yard outside some of the men prisoners were herded together as a special favor to join in the rejoicing. The keepers moved about among them, waving their arms and telling the men to be glad. The men stood with limp arms and dull faces, looking into the sky and at each other. A few endeavored to show signs of happiness when the warden came their way.

"Peace has come," Mollie said, standing at my side, "but not for us. Our struggle will be all the more bitter now."

The time came when Mollie's old mother, arising from the sick bed, came with a bandaged ear to the prison to tell her of the death of her father and of her 14-year-old brother. Mollie did not cry. She returned to the cell and quietly sat down on the bed beside me. But once I felt the convulsive trembling of her body. Her words came slowly at last:

"You should have seen my father," she said, "so thin, so worked out! Since he was but 10 years old he had worked 14 to 15 hours each day. He was so worked out, so thin! I knew he did not have the strength to live if he ever became ill."

Then, later: "Our dreams," she said; "how fragile! I have dreamed for years—oh, such dreams! Of my brother and sister in school, of studying, of a new order of society. In one minute my dreams are shattered!"

Through the bars of the cell door, through the dirty windows across the corridor could be seen the tops of unbeautiful, dingy buildings. Outside the windows the great stone wall surrounding the prison obstructed all view of the street. The roar of the elevated train, the rattle of drays on cobblestone pavement, and the shouts of men, disturbed but slightly the misery of the jail. From the tiers below came the shouts and the curses of the old offenders.

"Our dreams—how fragile!" mingled with the curses of the women, and before long it seemed that the women, too, were saying, "Our dreams—how fragile; our dreams—how fragile." At times they laughed it, and at times they cursed and sneered as they said it.

Yet the thought: Can that which is so fragile endure so much? And the doors of the past swung back and revealed dreams which have endured for thousands of years, suffering defeat only to rise again; braving prisons, torture, death, and at last wrecking empires.

Mollie was released under $10,000 bail to await her appeal to the

Supreme Court. I watched her pass through the prison yard. A marshal
walked beside her, talking out of the corner of his mouth. He did not
offer to carry her suitcase, heavy with books. His neck bulged with fat,
his chest was high and his shoulders primitive. Mollie did not listen to
him. Her eyes were looking straight ahead into the distance.

Weeks passed, and in the world outside I met Mollie once more. She
was on strike with the 40,000 clothing workers, and was among the
many pickets arrested. A few weeks afterward she came to see me. Her
shoulders had grown sharp and thin and she cynical. She had been
arrested a number of times upon suspicion; secret service men seemed
to follow her and arrest her as a matter of general principle. At last she
was arrested for alleged distribution of radical leaflets and held at Ellis
Island for deportation. There she went on hunger strike to protest seg-
regation from her fellow political prisoners. A friend, holding her thin,
cold hand, asked if she thought it worth while. Mollie replied:

"Every protest against the present system is worth while. Some one
must start."

Mollie did not object to deportation—provided it was done at once,
and to Soviet Russia instead of to the region under Czarist generals. The
city authorities evidently conferred with Federal agents, and decided to
try her in the city courts instead. She was sentenced to serve six months
in Blackwells Island jail, a place notorious for its filth and barbarity.

A short time has now elapsed since the Supreme Court upheld the
decision of the lower court on the first indictment against Mollie. And
she, frail, childlike, with the spirit which made the Russian revolution
possible, will be taken after her jail term is finished to Jefferson City
prison, where she is sentenced to spend 15 years of her life at hard
labor.*

Mollie's reasoning is something like this: Under the Czar we knew
there was no hope; we did not delude ourselves into believing that he
would release those who worked against the system which he represented and upheld. In America we have been carefully taught that we
live in a democracy, and we are still waiting for some one to feed us
democracy. While waiting, we starve to death or are sent to prison,
where we get free food for 15 or 20 years.

---

*Steimer was imprisoned at Jefferson City when Kate Richards O'Hare was there.—
Ed.

Agnes Smedley

Kitty

Kitty Marion* was serving thirty days for giving a pamphlet on birth control to a Mr. Bamberg, who had come to her office and told her with much feeling of his large family, his low salary and the fear of adding more children to his household. Bamberg turned out to be a "stool pigeon" for the notorious Association for the Suppression of Vice. He justified his existence by making people break the law and then having them arrested. Kitty Marion was one of his victims.

Kitty came clattering down the stone corridors every morning with her scrub pail in her hand. "Three cheers for birth control," she greeted the prisoners and matrons. And, "Three cheers for birth control," the prisoners answered back.

Her marked English accent recalled to mind that she had been one of Mrs. Pankhurst's† militants in London, had been imprisoned time without number and had had her throat ruined by forcible feeding. She holds the record; she was forcibly fed 233 times in Halloway prison.‡

"Dirty work," I remarked one morning, as she came in to scrub the Tombs corridors.

"Not half so dirty as cleaning up the man-made laws in this country," she replied. Then we continued our discussion of peace and change.

The prison physician came in to examine two infants.

"Three cheers for birth control," Kitty called to him from her kneeling position. She held her mop rag in mid air. He turned, and she, scrubbing away, remarked:

"Some way or other every time I see a man the more I believe in birth control."

When visitors or keepers came into the prison Kitty was always heard cheering for birth control. When peace was declared she expressed the hope, in a voice that those who run might hear, that now America would apply a little freedom to her own people and grant women the right of personal liberty. So taken up by the injustice of her imprisonment was she that when her room was infested with vermin she remarked that they reminded her of a mass-meeting of Bamber[sic]'s vice society; and

*British singer, actress, and suffragette.—*Ed.*
†Emmeline Pankhurst, leader of British militant suffragettes.—*Ed.*
‡Holloway Prison, London, where Lady Constance Lytton and other suffragettes were held.—*Ed.*

[291]

when she had been forced to put on a striped dress of the convicted women, she looked at it and remarked, "Ah! blue and white stripes! Now, if there were only a few red stripes and some white stars!"

The matrons were glad when her term was finished. When she left she announced that she had come in a spark but was going out a living flame.

ERICKA HUGGINS (1948–   )

Born in Washington, D.C., to a family she describes as "relatively poor," Ericka Huggins studied to become a teacher and in 1968 joined the Black Panther Party in Los Angeles. As an organizer among Panthers there and in Connecticut, she suffered the loss of her husband, John, who was killed by the FBI in 1969. Shortly afterward, Huggins, the mother of an infant daughter, was herself charged with kidnapping and conspiracy to commit murder, in the death of Panther Alex Rackley. She was imprisoned in Niantic State Prison for Women in Connecticut during her controversial New Haven trial that ended in a hung jury. All charges against her and Panther Bobby Seale were dismissed in May 1971 because the enormous amount of publicity had made a fair trial impossible.

In the courtroom during the trial, Huggins wrote poetry that expressed her pain and her faith in humankind, and belied the prosecution's insistence that she was a ruthless murderer. The poems and her diary made prison officials particularly nervous; they objected not only to the political statements, but also to Huggins's frank expressions of tenderness and unity with her fellow prisoners. Matrons feared these were love letters or "kites" addressed to other female inmates. The confiscation of Huggins's writings led her to join Seale in a suit for their rights as prisoners.

After her release, Huggins continued her social activism; in 1972 she was elected to membership in the Berkeley, California, Community Development Council, an antipoverty agency. She served also as director of the Oakland Community School, a progressive model elementary school in East Oakland, California. In her capacity as the first black member of the Alameda County Board of Education, Huggins worked to improve conditions and educational programs in county juvenile institutions. Most recently she has lobbied the California legislature for

Ericka Huggins

National Action Against Rape. She works with Siddha Yoga Dahm of America Foundation (SYDA), a worldwide organization dedicated to teaching meditation in community organizations, prisons, schools, and agencies.

Note: Biographical information is from Ericka Huggins, letter to Judith Scheffler, 18 July 1985; Donald Freed, *Agony in New Haven* (New York: Simon & Schuster, 1973); Angela Davis, *If They Come in the Morning* (New York: Third Press, 1971); *New York Times*, 7 January–31 May 1971, 20 August 1972; *Black Panther* 11 (February 1974); 20 (February 1980); *Life* 7, no. 13 (December 1984): 145.

WORKS BY ERICKA HUGGINS

"And They Kept Them There Hungry." *Coevolution Quarterly* 3 (Fall 1974): 76.

"before a woman becomes grown." *Crime and Social Justice*, no. 1 (Spring–Summer 1974): 50.

"Excerpts from a letter from Ericka." *Black Panther* 6, no. 3 (13 February 1971): 6.

"For Janice's Babe." *Black Panther* 6, no. 20 (12 June 1971): 2. Poem.

Insights & Poems, by Huey Newton and Ericka Huggins. San Francisco: City Lights Books, 1975.

"I Remember Times." *Black Panther* 13, no. 7 (5 April 1975): 21.

"A Letter from Sister Ericka Huggins." *Movement* 5, no. 8 (September 1969): 7.

Poems. In *Off Our Backs: A Women's News Journal* 1, no. 17 (12 February 1971); 2, no. 8 (April 1972).

Poems and a message from Niantic Prison. In *If They Come in the Morning: Voices of Resistance*, edited by Angela Y. Davis. New York: Third Press, 1971.

"Revolution in Our Lifetime," *Black Panther* 5, no. 28 (9 January 1971): 5.

"We Celebrate All the Fallen Heroes." *Coevolution Quarterly* 3 (Fall 1974): 75.

Six Poems

[untitled]

The oldness of new things
    fascinates me;
    like a new feeling about love,
        about people,
        snow,
    highways that sparkle at night; talk,
    laughter . . .
    that old longing for freedom that this
                place renews— —
it all makes me know that humankind
has longed to be free ever forever
since its break from the whole

    maybe the longing for freedom
    will soon make others homesick
      for our natural state
      not dead
      but living;
      not asking for freedom—but free.

[untitled]

I. Morning drifts in
    bringing pots
      teeth
      arms
      soap

Ericka Huggins

feet dragging to the
bathroom. Another prison camp,
damp Sunday morning—"ladies
if you're going to church please
bring your coats down with you.

                            —ladies,
please come . . . 'lord Jesus
be our guest' . . .
                         —ladies, come
with me, your dresses are too short
                           —ladies, girls
children, robots, degenerates—come
with me."
morning drifts in
bringing misery
    loneliness
    depression

II.   Endless music/sound that covers/disguises
    reality. They sit shift groan squirm
    yell scream moan   pretend
                       to be
  happy. They know they are
not. I know they are not.
Within these walls it is
loneliness that keeps us going,
  hoping for freedom—
    any second
      minute
      day
in the corner a woman sits,
huddles. Maybe crying on the inside for her children,
  her life.

A Reflection on Niantic

brown
fall the leaves of
golden yellow on
cold ground
brown the feet
of the dispossessed
   brown around
   the asphalt
that darkens the
road
   there is no end
      no opening
   the winter comes
      brown is covered
      with snow
         and heavy prison coats
my sisters linger in the night air
   hover by the door
      handcuffed or not
the jail holds their bodies—brown;
   holds their minds—blue.

reflections on sunday *

sounds that come from the soul are always the
   same
      free
   open sounds
   giving the kind that reach out
      and touch . . .
   that's what our sisters did/minimum

*On 13 December 1970 Huggins had attended a concert at the prison. The New Haven Women's Liberation Rock Band played to an enthusiastic audience of women inmates.—*Ed.*

touching maximum/sharing oppression
    and the wish for its
     removal . . .
   feeling these sounds
   seeing them felt on others
   watching faces smile
   really smile for the first time in months . . .
getting high—on the natural power of the
people to resist/to smile/to laugh/to sing
    shout/love/give
      even here . . .
wild hair, funky guitar
long, hairfunky voice (someone said bessie smith
   came to mind)
    hair—all lengths, legs, arms, smiles, music—
   SISTERS—and us . . .
raggedy pea coats, cotton dresses, rocking
                       swaying
                       screaming
      enjoying it—
      crying too—even if not too many
      let tears fall free
   . . . us—black/brown/white/poor—SISTERS—
      and it was all a total exchange
        of energy
      communication
      even if we did not share words
      we all knew their soul-songs were
      saying
        we understand
      we know
      we can see what amerika is doing
      to you—Mother/daughter/child/woman
        of oppression
        we can see, they sang—
      and our voices answered their guitars,
      horns — flute — voice — cowbell — tambourine de-

mand for freedom with an unspoken right on
. . . a feeling there that one day—soon—
    all people will be free . . . and
        we left
        stronger
    able to smile
    till we returned to
        rules that degrade
        schedules that destroy sanity
        racism that they cannot see
        sexism that rapes us of our womanhood . . .
and the locks, keys, windows, walls, doors,
        threats
        warnings
        bribes that harden our hearts and
chain our souls . . .
        the time
        must be
        seized
            venceremos!

[untitled]

I wake in middle-of-night terror
next to the warm sleeping body of my lover
yet alone in the conviction that I am in a prison cell
shut away, suddenly, from all that makes my life.
I sense the great weight of the prison
pressing down on the little box of room I lie in
    alone   forgotten.
How often do women awake
in the prison of marriage,
of solitary motherhood
    alone and forgotten
of exhaustion from meaningless work,
of self-despising learned early,
of advancing age

alone and forgotten.
How many women lie awake at this moment
    struggling as I do against despair,
        knowing the morning will crush us once again
    under the futility of our lives.
And how short a step it is
    —for us—to the more obvious imprisonment
    of bars and concrete
    where our sisters lie
    alone   forgotten.
See now, in this middle-of-the-night emptiness
    how little it matters
    whether we wear a convicts ill-made cotton dress
    or a velvet pantsuit—
We are possessions to be bought and sold,
We are children to be curbed and patronized,
We are bodies to be coveted, seized, and rejected
    when our breasts begin to sag,
We are dummies to be laughed at.

    I sense the great weight of the society
    pressing down on the little box of room I lie in
    alone   forgotten
    like my sisters in prison.
If you hear me
    consider
    how the bomb of human dignity
    could be planted outside your cell
    how its explosion could shake
    the foundations of our jail
    and might burst open the door that separates you
    how we might struggle together to be free.

[untitled]

tall
skinny
plain

tall
skinny

plain i am
ericka, 22,
fuzzy hair
droopy eyes
long feet

  i love people
  love nature
  love love
i am a revolutionary
nothing special
  one soul
  one life willing
    to give it
  ready to die . . .

PATRICIA MCCONNEL (1931–   )

When she was in her early twenties, Patricia McConnel spent time in six jails and in the Federal Reformatory for Women at Alderson, West Virginia. It took almost thirty years for her to recover from her prison experiences; she began writing in her mid-thirties in order "to purge the prison horrors." "Sing Soft, Sing Loud" is the title story of her current work, a collection of short fiction about women in jails and prisons. This work has been supported by a grant in literature from the National Endowment for the Arts (1983).

McConnel explains that her stories are "extremely autobiographical," with authentic incidents, and narrators that either are invented or are composites of herself and the women she knew in prison. "Sing Soft, Sing Loud," based upon an actual incident in the San Diego City Jail, is about a woman's refusal to surrender her will and the consequences of her action. In all McConnel's stories, singing symbolizes "the indestructibility of the spirit."

McConnel, now a professional writer and editor, lives in Utah's Canyonlands district and spends her time "writing and wandering in the desert wilderness." A comic novel about the difficulty of defining madness and sanity is one of her current projects. In 1983 and 1985 her stories were selected for the PEN Syndicated Fiction Project, which publishes winning authors' works in major metropolitan newspapers.

Note: Biographical information is from McConnel's letters to Judith Scheffler, 1 April 1983; 6 July 1983; 2 March 1985.

WORKS BY PATRICIA MCCONNEL

"The Aviarian" (PEN Syndicated Fiction Project winner, October 1983). Appeared in the *Arizona Republic*, the *Miami Herald*, *Newsday*, *Rocky Mountain News*, and the *Chicago Tribune*; also in Available Press/PEN Short Story Collection (New York: Ballantine, 1985).

"Bee Bzzzness in the Red Rock Country" (PEN Syndicated Fiction Project winner, 1985). Appeared in the *Arizona Republic*, the *Village Advocate*, *Newsday*, and the *Chicago Tribune*.

"Holy Night, Silent Night" (first prize winner in Feminist Writers Guild Woman of Promise short fiction contest, 1982). Appeared in *13th Moon* (Fall 1983).

"A Life Full of Murders" (PEN Syndicated Fiction Project winner, 1984). Appeared in the *Kansas City Star* and the *Arizona Republic*.

"The Meeting." *Day Tonight, Night Today* (Fall 1982).

"The Prisoners." *Day Tonight, Night Today* (Winter 1983).

"Rites of Passage, Rites of Spring" (PEN Syndicated Fiction Project winner, 1985). Appeared in the *Village Advocate*.

"The Tourist." *Day Tonight, Night Today* (Summer 1983).

"Whomp Man." *Eidos* (Spring 1984).

Working at Home with Computers: New Options for Women. New York: Bantam, forthcoming (November 1986).

Sing Soft, Sing Loud

I know the moment I lay eyes on this kid she is a sick hype. Partly I know because of the way she is walking, like her legs are gonna buckle under her any second, and the screws are holding her up and pushing her along by her arms. And partly I know because she has what I call "jailface." I only see her for a second when they take her past my cell, but that's enough. Once you seen someone with jailface you know it anywhere. It's a look people get only when they been in and out of jails a while, and you never see it nowhere else. Jailface is nothing that just happens. You do it on purpose so you never let on that you're feeling pain or worry or sickness or fear. What you do is you freeze your face so nothing moves—your eyebrows don't wiggle, your mouth don't twitch or smile or frown. Freeze ain't exactly a good word because it makes it sound like the face goes hard, but actually the muscles ain't hard at all, they're limp, and you don't let them tighten up over nothing at all, ever. The worst thing about jailface, though, is the eyes, because they don't look directly at anything and they don't even focus half the time. You can't look into the eyes of someone with jailface because your look ricochets off a glassy surface of eyeball that would bounce bullets.

You do all this on purpose because the moment a screw knows you're scared or weak she has the upper hand, and she'll jump on you with both feet and won't let up until she's had her satisfaction—which in most cases is to see your spirit dead. But if you're walking around with jailface she can't tell if something is still stirring in there or not. Most likely she thinks by your look that you're already dead, so there's not much challenge, no reason for her to jump on you, nothing alive in there to kill, you see. You learn pretty quick that as long as you are wearing that face anything at all can be going on behind it and you'll be safe.

So now I get to why in this case I know the jailface means the chick is a sick hype—it's because she's black. Black chicks don't get jailface as a general rule. I don't know why. I don't mean to say they suffer any less than anyone else, but somehow they take jail with more style and grace. They sing more, joke more, play more. Maybe that's just how a black chick covers up, something she uses instead of jailface. I don't really know—I never been black, and it's the kind of thing I never feel like I can ask about, but the thing I know for sure is that when a black chick has jailface it is something very very bad she is covering up—like kicking a habit.

Maybe that's more than you really want to know about it but see they don't let us have anything to read around the jail but the goddam Bible and so I have lots of time to sit and think about these things and sort of figure out what is going on in this place. I already read the Bible through twice and I ain't even religious.

So anyway they put this chick in the next cell to mine, and as soon as the screws are gone I hear her moan, "Oh my god, I'm sick, I'm sick."

I say to her, "You want a cigarette?"

She says, "Girl, I'm too sick to smoke," and after that she don't make another sound. When they let us out to supper I go over and look in her cell, but she's lying there with her face to the wall and I think maybe she is sleeping so I don't talk to her. After that I get to playing gin rummy downstairs and I forget about her.

It's about twenty minutes after lights-out when she begins to sing. Real soft, real tender her voice is, and I listen a long time. I think she is going to sing herself to sleep, and me with her, and it's nice in that black tomb to hear a sweet voice singing soft like that. In this jail there's no light at all at night, no windows in our tank where the light can leak in from outside like at home. It's like being in a grave. If you lie with your eyes open you get dizzy because there's nothing to focus on, and it gets pretty lonely because it's so black in here you can't believe there's anyone else alive in the place unless you can hear them. So it's good to lie there listening to her singing.

But instead of going to sleep, her songs start getting more upbeat, more swinging, until finally she is singing Aretha Franklin and Tina Turner and Janis Joplin and a lot of other stuff I am really into, and it feels so good I start singing with her. When she hears me chiming in she starts clapping her hands, and so I clap too, and when the pace wears us out we go back to old funkies like *Cocaine Blues* and *Frankie and Johnny* and finally someone else in the tank hollers, "For chrissake, shut up."

We stop singing and I ask her, "How you feel now?"

"I think I better sing some more. It helps to sing."

"Don't they give you nothing to help you through it?"

"Girl, they don't know I'm sick. I got busted for boosting and they never noticed no marks. If I can keep them from finding out I'm sick, maybe I'll get ninety days for the boosting, but I'll have to take the cure if they figure out I'm a user."

"You want me to sing with you? Does it make you feel better?"

"Lord, yes."

I am feeling sentimental so I sing *You Can't Be True, Dear*, and as soon as she picks up the melody I sing harmony and I gotta say it sounds pretty good. Some of the other tenants get a little upset but we don't pay them any mind and they soon let us be, 'cause everyone is used to drunks raving all night anyway. It's only a token protest.

Pretty soon we are into old and way-out things like *Gloomy Sunday* and *C.C. Rider,* all the songs you learn if you spend a lot of time sitting around in jails, and she is pretty impressed that I know all that stuff and we are having a real party considering the circumstances. Then we hear the door to the tank open and the screw's heels clunking on the cement floor. The footsteps stop somewhere below us and this blowtop voice yells, "Cut out the singing up there or I'll throw you in flatbottom." A screw can't stand to think there's ever ten minutes you ain't doing real hard time—if we was crying or moaning with pain she wouldn't have said nothing.

We wait 'til she leaves and we start up again, but softer now. She says to me once, "I need a cigarette now," and I hand her my whole pack because I figure she needs them worse than me. We have to grope in the dark for each other's hands and when her hand touches mine it is ice cold and she is shaking. She keeps singing louder and I tell her, "You better cool it or she'll put you right in flatbottom."

"What's flatbottom?"

"It's not a nice place. Ain't you been in jail before?"

"Not this one."

"It's a cell on the first tier with nothing in it but a cement floor. No toilet, no water, no cot, no nothing. If you have to shit, you shit on the floor, and I mean you sleep with it, kid. The jailhouse rules say they can't leave you in there more than 24 hours but that's just for show. They leave you there as long as they want. It's not supposed to be for punishment but that's what they use it for."

"What is it for, then?"

"For loonies and people who're likely to hurt themselves or someone else. Sort of like a padded cell only there's no padding, and it's supposed to be temporary until they can move you to the hospital or until you calm down. But the screws use it to get you in line and it works real good that way. So pipe down a little."

But my friend says, "Girl, if I don't sing loud, I'll scream. Now I don't mind if I have to go to flatbottom, but I don't want to start screaming because once I start I won't be able to stop." And so she starts off again and to tell the truth I'm a little scared, but I don't want to leave her stranded singing out her cold turkey alone so I sing with her, but softly. And pretty soon the screw comes back and this time the lights all go on and she comes upstairs and marches straight to this chick's cell.

I'm really sweating it out because I don't know if she heard me singing or not, but I turn to look as she takes the kid out and what do you think? This chick is laughing, she's giggling and doing a little dance step as the screw takes her along the ramp toward the stairs. As she passes my cell she looks my way and says, "So long, girl," and this time I notice how skinny she is.

Then she is gone. I hear the door to flatbottom open and shut and I'm waiting for the screw to come back up for me but instead the lights go out and the tank door clangs shut and it's pitch black again. It is quiet for a minute, and I can't stand it because I know this chick is really hurting now. So I start singing some Dinah Washington stuff, and Lady Day, and in about two minutes she chimes in and away we go again. But when we finish a couple of songs she calls up to me, "You better cool it, girl, or you'll be down here with me."

"Hell, I don't care. I been here three months already just waiting for trial in the federal court, and I'm getting pretty bored."

"Well maybe you don't care, but *I* do. Think how it gonna smell in here in the morning with two of us in here."

"You got a point there," I admit, and I don't sing any more. She keeps right on though, and I never knew one person could know so many songs. The screw pokes her head back in once to tell her to shut up, but I mean the kid is already in flatbottom, what more can they do to her? So she don't pay any attention and keeps right on singing.

After a while the tank door opens again but the lights don't go on. The girl keeps on singing like she don't even hear the screw coming, but over the song I can hear the heels clunk-clunking and they don't stop until it sounds like she is all the way in the rear of the tank. I sit up on my bunk and listen close because I can't figure out what she could be doing in the dark. Then the faucet goes on and I can hear water filling up a bucket and I think *Oh shit, she's going to douse her,* and then I think *Christ, she's going to have to sit in water all night and her sick as a dog already.* I am going to call out to tell her to shut up but then I think *What's the use? She's going to get it now anyway*, and right then I hear the splash.

But I'm not ready for what happens next. This kid screams like someone bayoneted, an awful wail that bounces off the walls of that stinking jail like the shriek of a ghost in a tomb. The echoes of the scream seem to be breaking over me from all sides and I think for a moment she has shattered the walls and the jail is going to cave in on us. I am paralyzed and then I realize the echoes are only in my head—the scream has died away and it is quiet except for the whimpers of some of the women, scared out of their gourds. Then I hear the clunk-clunks working their way back to the door and the clang and the click that mean we are locked up tight again.

From flatbottom I can hear moaning, a soft sobbing like a dog that's been run over and is about to die and it tears at me until I can't stand it any longer and I scream *OH JESUS LET ME OUT OF THIS PLACE!* and I cry loud enough for myself to drown out the sobs of the sick hype in flatbottom and pretty soon I am exhausted and escape into sleep.

In the morning she is gone.

I ask Elsie, the trustee that brings the breakfast cart, if she knows what happened to the chick in flatbottom.

"They moved her to the other tank," she says. "Her face and arms are all blistered, like she got burned. I can't figure it out. They never moved anybody at five in the morning like that before. They woke me up, is how I happened to see her."

It don't take much figuring from there to understand why she screamed like she did, except I never knew water from a tap could be hot enough to blister you.

After breakfast comes cleanup and I go to fill the bucket because it is my day to scrub the cement floor. The only thing is I can't find the box of lye we use for scrubbing the cement. Oh Jesus.

I am pretty depressed when the lunch wagon comes, but I pick up some when Elsie passes me a kite. "This must be for you," she says, "the spade chick you were asking about give it to me. She said she don't know your name but she has a friend over here, and I told her I thought I knew who it was 'cause you were asking after her, so she sent it with me."

I stick the kite in my pocket 'til the screw that comes with the food cart is gone and the tank is shut up tight, then I go to my bunk and read it:

Dear Barbara Streisand,
They took me out of flatbottom cause they was afraid I'd catch cold and give their nice hotel a bad name. I got some friends gonna come bring me some loot today and I'll send you the cigarets I owe you. Hang in there, girl. I'll sing loud enough tonight so you can hear me over there.
Very truly yours,
Angora

I don't know the trustee that comes with the dinner cart, and you got to be careful about trustees around here since half the time they get to be trustees because they're the screws' little stoolies, so I wait 'til the next morning to ask Elsie about Angora.

"Christ, it's lousy," she says. "They won't let her go on sick call because of the way it happened, and she's got a fever and stuff running out of her ear."

"Is she singing?"

"Singing? Have you flipped out? What's she got to be singing about? She don't even sit up or eat."

At lunch time Elsie tells me they let Angora loose, just like that. Just turned her loose, no court, no bail, no nothin'.

I don't forget her soon. After I go to the federal joint, sometimes I sit up at the window after lights-out and sometimes someone is singing out a window across the mall in one of the other dormitories and my heart gets a catch in it and I think for a second it's Angora, or sometimes there's not even any singing and she just comes into my mind and I start singing for her again, this time singing as loud as I can, but I never keep it up very long because I know that it don't matter how much I sing, I can never sing loud enough or clear enough to change what happened to her back there. I just wish I had sung louder at the time, that's all, even though it wouldn't have done any good then either.

Or maybe I coulda got all the women in the tank to sing with us. But to get that bunch of losers (me included) to ever be of a mind to do something all together I'd have to figure out how to unmess our minds and I can't think how to do that, so all this speculating I'm doing just goes round and round in circles. But just suppose I coulda got 'em to do it. Sing, I mean. Just suppose. What could the screws do—throw scalding lye on all of us? Feature this—a house full of alkies and junkies and hookers and boosters all raising the jailhouse roof with song, and Angora singing lead—wouldn't that be something? Of course I know that not even all of us singing at the top of our lungs woulda changed a goddam thing either, but it tickles me to think of it anyway. Those screws—it woulda blown their friggin' minds.

An Annotated Bibliography of Writings by Women Prisoners

*

Compiling this bibliography has been a continuing and fascinating part of the research for this book. Although the bibliography is intended to be as comprehensive as possible, there are doubtless many sources remaining to be identified by the serendipitous route that led to so many of the entries in the following pages. In particular, recent prison newsletters, prison writing workshop anthologies, and chapbooks of prison poetry are difficult to locate and may well have been inadvertently omitted. I would certainly welcome word of any additional entries.

The purpose of this bibliography is to guide the reader who would like to find primary material in English or in English translation by women prisoners. No such bibliography now exists. Even the excellent bibliographies of prison writing compiled by H. Bruce Franklin and Daniel Suvak reveal relatively few works by women. Most works by women prisoners are now rare, out of print, in unpublished manuscript form, or in obscure journals. Many sources are elusive because texts are often not readily identified as prison-related through titles or authors' names.

In order to make this bibliography specific and manageable, I have restricted entries to works written during the author's imprisonment or, later, about the experience. All genres have been included. I have endeavored to include all foreign works translated into English. Concentration camp writings, wartime camp internment writings, works written while in hiding, and captivity narratives are excluded because they constitute large bodies of literature in their own right that would broaden the focus of this bibliography and make the research unmanageable. Several autobiographical works have been written by prisoners in collaboration with a professional author. While these collaborative writings reveal many insights about the prison experience, I have included only works that, to my knowledge, were written entirely by the woman prisoner herself or by a group of women prisoners. Finally, I have excluded works written in prison but about other subjects, without reference to the prison experience. Examples of such writing would be political tracts that do not discuss the woman's imprisonment.

The following bibliographies and reference works have been useful in assembling this bibliography. I am particularly indebted to the work of H. Bruce Franklin and Daniel Suvak.

Barrow, Margaret. *Women 1870–1928: A Select Guide to Printed and Archival Sources in the United Kingdom*. London: Mansell, 1981.

Begos, Jane. *An Annotated Bibliography of Published Women's Diaries*. Pound Ridge, N.Y., 1977.

Dutton, Helen. "Prison Writings of Women." In *Women and Law* microfilm series. Section V: Special Films—Rape/Prison/Prostitution. Berkeley, Calif.: Women's History Research Center, 1972.

Engelbarts, Rudolf. *Books in Stir: A Bibliographic Essay about Prison Libraries and about Books Written by Prisoners and Prison Employees*. Metuchen, N.J.: Scarecrow, 1972.

Franklin, H. Bruce. *The Victim as Criminal and Artist: Literature from the American Prison*. New York: Oxford Univ. Press, 1978; 2d ed., 2 vols. Vol. 2, *American Prisoners and Ex-Prisoners: Their Writings: An Annotated Bibliography of Published Works, 1798–1981*. Westport, Conn.: Lawrence Hill, 1982.

Hinding, Andrea. *Women's History Sources: A Guide to Archives and Manuscript Collections in the United States*. 2 vols. New York: Bowker, 1979.

Kuhlman, Augustus F. *Bibliography of Crime and Criminal Justice, 1927–1931*. New York: Wilson, 1934; rev. ed. by Dorothy C. Culver. Montclair, N.J.: Patterson Smith, 1969.

———. *Bibliography of Crime and Criminal Justice, 1932–1937*. New York: Wilson, 1939; rev. ed. by Dorothy C. Culver. Montclair, N.J.: Patterson Smith, 1969.

———. *A Guide to Material on Crime and Criminal Justice*. New York: Wilson, 1929; rev. ed. by Dorothy Campbell Culver. Montclair, N.J.: Patterson Smith, 1969.

McDade, Thomas M. *The Annals of Murder: A Bibliography of Books and Pamphlets on American Murders from Colonial Times to 1900*. Norman, Okla.: Univ. of Oklahoma Press, 1961.

Philip, Cynthia Owen, ed. *Prison Communications: 1776 to Attica*. New York: Harper & Row, 1973.

Rubin, Rhea Joyce. *Barred Visions: A Bibliography of Materials by Prisoners and Ex-offenders*. Chicago: Chicago Public Library, 1974; rev. ed. 1975.

Suvak, Daniel. *Memoirs of American Prisons: An Annotated Bibliography*. Metuchen, N.J.: Scarecrow, 1979.

Women Offenders: A Selected Bibliography. Olympia, Wash.: Institutional Library Services, Washington State Library, 1970. ERIC (Educational Resources Information Center) document.

Each selection in this anthology includes a bibliography of the author's other works, written in or out of prison, about imprisonment or about other subjects.

Alpert, Jane. *Growing Up Underground.* New York: William Morrow, 1981.
Alpert, active in radical antiwar causes, describes her stay in 1969 in the Women's House of Detention, New York City, as she awaited trial on charges of conspiracy to destroy government property. There is a brief discussion of her incarceration in the State Correctional Institute at Muncy, Pennsylvania, 1975–1977.

Alvarez de Toledo y Maura, Isabel, Duchess of Medina Sidonia. "Eight Months in Franco's Jail." *Nation,* 6 April 1970, pp. 396–399.
A brief account of her imprisonment.

——. *My Prison.* Translated by Herma Briffault. New York: Harper & Row, 1972.
The Duchess of Medina Sidonia's account of her imprisonment in 1969 in the women's prison at Alcalá, thirty miles west of Madrid. She was given a one-year sentence by Franco's court for publicly demonstrating in support of Spanish peasants in Palomares. They sought redress for environmental damage done to their village in the crash of an American B-52 bomber there in 1966.

"The American Microcosm." *Greenfield Review* 7, nos. 1/2 (Fall 1978).
This special double issue, edited by Michael Hogan and Joseph Bruchac, includes poems by prison writers and features the 1976 and 1977 PEN winners. A few female poets are represented, but most works are by men.

Angoulême, Marie Thérèse Charlotte, Duchesse d'. "The Narrative of Marie Thérèse de France, Duchesse D'Angoulême." In *The Life and Letters of Madame Élisabeth de France followed by The Journal of the Temple, by Cléry, and The Narrative of Marie Thérèse de France, Duchesse D'Angoulême,* translated by Katharine Prescott Wormeley, pp. 209–292. Boston: Hardy, Pratt, 1902.
Marie Thérèse, Madame Royale de France, describes events during 1789–1795. The only surviving child of Louis XVI and Marie Antoinette, Marie Thérèse began writing her narrative in 1795 while she was imprisoned

in the Tower of the Temple, and completed it in 1799 while exiled in Vienna. During her imprisonment with the royal family, beginning in 1792 when she was thirteen years old, she survived her father, mother, aunt, and brother. She was released in December 1795.

Arrowsmith, Pat. *Jericho*. London: Cresset Press, 1965.

A novel about persons demonstrating nonviolently against nuclear weapons and the personal consequences of their actions. Arrowsmith wrote this book during a six-month term in Holloway Prison. This was one of her six prison terms for work with the British Campaign for Nuclear Disarmament, the Direct Action Committee against Nuclear War, and the Committee of 100. The book describes the problems peace workers face when they encounter violence or when they disagree among themselves.

————, ed. *To Asia in Peace: The Story of a Non-Violent Action Mission to Indochina*. London: Sidgwick & Jackson, 1972.

"The first draft of the book was written by Pat Arrowsmith in 1969 while serving a six-month prison sentence for organising action in this country [England] against the Vietnam war" (from the jacket). She is also coauthor of one selection:

Arrowsmith, Pat, and Rachel Blake. "Thailand," pp. 127–156. This essay describes the 1968 peace mission of twenty-six persons who traveled from London to Indochina to protest the Vietnam War. Among them were Arrowsmith, a thirty-seven-year-old British peace worker from London, and Rachel Blake, a forty-three-year-old British teacher and painter from London. Both women were arrested by the Thai police and imprisoned in the "monkey house" (police station lock-up) at Udon, Thailand, following an attempted nonviolent demonstration at the U.S. base in Udon. They were subsequently transferred to the monkey house prison section at the immigration office in Bangkok, where they were held two weeks.

Baez, Joan. *Daybreak*. New York: Dial Press, 1968.

In these reminiscences and meditations on her life, singer/songwriter Baez recalls her imprisonment for nonviolent resistance to the Vietnam War. She and her mother were held for civil disobedience at California's Oakland induction center and were imprisoned together twice in the Santa Rita Prison, California. The book describes their warm relationships with fellow inmates—drug addicts, prostitutes and pushers—and Baez's resistance to prison authority.

Baluch, Akhtar. "Preface to Akhtar Baluch's Prison Diary." *Race & Class* 18, no. 4 (Spring 1977): 389–395.

Baluch's diary begins on July 25, 1970, when she entered the Central Prison in Hyderabad, Pakistan, and began a hunger strike. An eighteen-year-old Sindhi college student, she was charged with supporting Sindhi nationalist leaders. Her diary includes letters of support from her family. When moved to the Central Jail in Sukkur in August, she expressed solidarity with fellow inmates convicted of murder. She was freed on December 18, 1970.

———. " 'Sister, Are You Still Here?': The Diary of a Sindhi Woman Prisoner." Introduction and Notes by Mary Tyler (q.v.). *Race & Class* 18, no. 3 (Winter 1977): 219–245.

Barrows, Isabel C. "The Massachusetts Reformatory Prison for Women." In *The Reformatory System in The United States*, edited by Samuel J. Barrows, pp. 101–128. Washington, D.C.: Government Printing Office, 1900.
Included in this article are excerpts from anonymous writings by ex-inmates of the Massachusetts Reformatory Prison for Women in Sherborn. Letters declare that the writers are doing well in their lives on the outside and express gratitude to the prison for its educational and vocational programs and constructive moral atmosphere. One educated ex-inmate compares her relatively negative first impressions about the prison environment and her fellow inmates with her later appreciation for the orderly prison management and the humanity of the other imprisoned women.

Battle, Hellen. *Every Wall Shall Fall*. Old Tappan, N.J.: Hewitt House, 1969.
In 1962 Battle, a young American woman, traveled to Germany to work as an English teacher and to study in West Berlin. In 1965 she was arrested in East Berlin for attempting to help an East Berlin soldier escape. She was imprisoned in East Berlin and in Neustrelitz in the north of East Germany. After being sentenced to four years of hard labor, she was transferred to Hohenschoenhausen prison and Bautzen penitentiary. She writes of her fellow inmates and her deepening Christian faith. She was released in 1967, and the soldier she had aided was also released to West Germany.

Baxley, Catherine Virginia. Diary and Notebook, 14 February–2 July 1865. Rare Books and Manuscripts Division, New York Public Library.
Baxley, a Baltimore woman working for the Confederacy, was arrested as a blockade-runner and imprisoned at the Old Capitol Prison, Washington, D.C. There she met her own son, who was dying in the prison.

———. Letters to William H. Seward, Secretary of State, and Edwin M. Stanton, Secretary of War, and others, January–April 1862, written from the Old Capitol Prison concerning her imprisonment. In *The War of the Rebellion: A Compilation of the Official Records of the Union and Con-*

federate Armies, 2d ser., vol. 2, pp. 1316–1321. Washington, D.C.: Government Printing Office, 1897.

Baxter, Carolyn. *Prison Solitary and Other Free Government Services: Poems by Carolyn Baxter*. Greenfield Review Chapbook no. 41. Greenfield Center, N.Y.: Greenfield Review Press, 1979.

Poems of social protest and keen observation of women's pretrial, courtroom, and prison experiences. Baxter's works are also included in *Songs From A Free Space: Writings by Women in Prison*, an anthology compiled by the New York City Correctional Institution for Women (q.v.).

Belfrage, Sally. "Jail." Chapter 9 in *Freedom Summer*. New York: Viking, 1965.

Belfrage, a student volunteer in the 1964 Mississippi Summer Project with the Student Nonviolent Coordinating Committee (SNCC), describes her arrest and imprisonment in Greenwood, Mississippi, for supporting blacks' attempt to register to vote.

Bickston, Diana. *Street Birth . . . or The Little Brown Eyed Girl*. COSMEP Prison Project. Greenfield Center, N.Y.: Greenfield Review Press, 1982.

A collection of poems by Bickston, who began writing in 1979 in a workshop at the Arizona Prison for Women. At the time this book was published, she was incarcerated at the California Institution for Women, Frontera.

Blaugdone, Barbara. *An Account of the Travels, Sufferings & Persecutions of Barbara Blaugdone. Given forth as a Testimony to the Lord's Power, and for the Encouragement of Friends*. Printed, and sold by T.S. at the Crooked-Billet in Holywell-Lane, Shoreditch, 1691.

An early Quaker, Blaugdone was persecuted for her religion throughout her travels. She describes her cruel whipping at Exeter Prison and her attempt to minister to a Catholic inmate while they were imprisoned in Dublin.

Bone, Edith. *Seven Years Solitary*. London: Hamish Hamilton, 1957.

The account of the seven-year, one-month (1949–1956) imprisonment of the author in Communist Hungary, where she was sentenced to prison as an "English spy." Born in Budapest in 1889, Bone was a physician, translator, and former Communist Party member who had resided in England since 1933. She was held in the Conti Street Prison in Budapest until 1954, when she was transferred to a prison in Vác. Her early years in solitary confinement were made easier through her recollection of the examples of prison literature she had read by Silvio Pellico and Vera Figner (q.v.). She describes her delight in teaching herself to read Greek, writing a diary, and studying mathematics; she had won the right to these intellectual pursuits through a "language strike," during which she refused to speak Hungarian to her jailors.

Bonfield, Lynn A. *Jailed for Survival: The Diary of an Anti-Nuclear Activist*. San Francisco: Mother Courage Affinity Group, 1984.

Bonfield describes her imprisonment in the Santa Rita Jail from June 20 to July 4, 1983, for her part in blockading the highway around California's Lawrence Livermore Laboratory for nuclear weapons. Her book describes jail conditions and how the women with her maintained a positive spirit. (Information from Jennifer P. McLean's review in *Women's Diaries: A Quarterly Newsletter* 2, no. 4 [Winter 1984]: 6.)

Boyd, Belle. *Belle Boyd in Camp and Prison*. Edited by Curtis Carroll Davis. New York: Thomas Yoseloff, 1968. Originally published in London by Saunders, Otley, 1865.

Arrested as a Confederate spy, Boyd was imprisoned in Baltimore in 1862, in Washington's Old Capitol Prison in 1862 and 1863, and in Boston in 1864. She became an actress after the war and, in 1886, toured the country to lecture about her war experiences.

Break de Chains of Legalized U.S. Slavery. Durham, N.C.: Triangle Area Lesbian Feminists Prison Book Project, 1976.

A collection of poetry, letters, essays, and artwork by inmates of the North Carolina Correctional Center for Women. Works express solidarity and describe the struggle for justice in prison.

Breshko-Breshkovskaya, Ekaterina Constantinovna (Katerina Breshkov-skaia). *Hidden Springs of the Russian Revolution: Personal Memoirs of Katerina Breshkovskaia*. Edited by Lincoln Hutchinson. Stanford, Calif.: Stanford Univ. Press, 1931.

This volume contains memoirs begun by Breshkovskaia in 1917, when the Russian Revolution made it possible for her to begin to write the experiences that she could not write while in prison. She continued the work during 1921 and 1922 in Prague. The translation was done by several persons over a period of years. Beginning in 1874 Breshkovskaia was held in several prisons, including those in Bratzlav, Kiev, the Sushtchev police station, the House of Preliminary Detention at Petersburg, Litovski Castle, Petrograd, and Irkutsk. She was also exiled to Siberia. She writes fondly of fellow women revolutionaries, including Vera Figner (q.v.).

———. (Catherine Breshkovsky). *The Little Grandmother of the Russian Revolution: Reminiscences and Letters of Catherine Breshkovsky*. Edited by Alice Stone Blackwell. Boston: Little, Brown, 1918.

Breshkovsky, as she wrote her name in America, was a Russian revolutionary. Editor Blackwell notes that this biographical edition combines a translation of a Yiddish account of Breshkovsky's early life with an account of her later life that she dictated through an interpreter to Ernest Poole of the *Outlook*. This volume includes her own writing also, in the form of a translation of her letters to her son from prison in 1909 and to her son and others from Siberia. Emma Goldman recalls having read this book by and about "Babushka" while she was in the Missouri State Penitentiary, 1917–1919 (Goldman, *Living My Life*, 2:661) (q.v.).

Brown, Myra Sadd. Papers. Suffragette Fellowship Collection, Museum of London (50.82/1136).

Autograph letter, to "Sir." Letter to the press, dated 7 May 1912. British suffragette Brown gives an "account of my experience of forcible feeding." Imprisoned in Holloway in 1912, she was forcibly fed despite the fact she had once had a broken nose and had undergone throat and nose surgery.

Autograph letter, to "Sir." Letter to the press, dated 21 May 1912. Brown thanks the press for printing part of her previous letter, but regrets that all was not printed. She gives her motives for her actions leading to her arrest and for her hunger strike.

A declaration regarding forcible feeding, November 1913. Brown gives her reasons for her hunger strike, her previous medical condition, and the effects of her forcible feeding. She made this declaration before a Commissioner for Oaths.

Browne, Martha Griffith. *Autobiography of a Female Slave*. New York: Redfield, 1857; reprint, New York: Negro Universities Press, 1969.

This work includes Browne's account of her imprisonment in Kentucky for attacking the man instructed by her master to whip her. The man had attempted to rape her, and she had attacked him in self-defense.

Bryan, Helen. *Inside*. Boston: Houghton Mifflin, 1953.

Prison memoirs of Bryan, who was sentenced for contempt of Congress and imprisoned in the Federal Reformatory for Women at Alderson, West Virginia, from November 1950 to January 1951. In 1940 she had served as executive secretary of the Joint Anti-Fascist Refugee Committee, an organization that sent aid to Spanish-Republican refugees. She was convicted for her refusal in 1945 to submit her agency's books and lists of contributors and recipients of funds to the House Committee on Un-American Activities. Her account of her imprisonment focuses on the life stories, as she heard them, of socially disadvantaged women serving sentences for federal crimes.

Buber, Margarete (Margarete Buber-Neumann). *Under Two Dictators*. Translated by Edward Fitzgerald from the original 1949 German edition. London: Gollancz, 1949.

Buber and her husband, Heinz Neumann, were German Communists on assignment as translators in Moscow from 1935 until Neumann's arrest by the Soviet Secret Police in 1937 and Buber's arrest in 1938. She was imprisoned in Moscow's Lubyanka and Butyrka prisons and then sent to the Siberian labor camp Karaganda as a "socially dangerous element." In 1940 she was transferred to Ravensbrück, the Nazi concentration camp, where she spent five years. She never saw her husband again.

Buxton, Jane, and Margaret Turner. *Gate Fever*. London: Cresset Press, 1962.

Buxton and Turner were imprisoned in Holloway Prison from April to October 1960 following a civil disobedience demonstration for the Campaign for Nuclear Disarmament. Their book takes the form of letters written from prison to a friend outside, but the authors note that these letters were in fact written after their release, because their frank descriptions of prison conditions would have been censored by prison authorities.

Cassidy, Sheila. *Audacity to Believe*. Cleveland, Ohio: Collins-World, 1977.

Cassidy, a British physician and a Catholic, was thirty-four years old when she traveled to Chile in 1971 to gain further practical experience in surgery. In 1975 she was arrested, tortured, and imprisoned in the Casa Grimaldi, Tres Alamos, and Cuatro Alamos prisons in Santiago for treating a wounded revolutionary. She was expelled from Chile in December 1975 after spending several months in prison.

————. "Tortured in Chile." *Index on Censorship* 5, no. 2 (Summer 1976): 67–73.

The main part of Dr. Cassidy's testimony on January 19, 1976, in Geneva before the United Nations Ad Hoc Working Group of the Commission on Human Rights. She spoke about her arrest, torture, and imprisonment in Chile.

Chevers, Sarah, and Katharine Evans. "Isle of Malta, Anno 1661." Chapter 13 in *A Collection of the Sufferings of the People Called Quakers*, edited by Joseph Besse, vol. 2, pp. 399–420. London: Luke Hinde, 1753.

A narrative written by Evans, and letters from Chevers and Evans to their inquisitors and to their families and other Quakers in England. These two English Quaker women were imprisoned by the Inquisition at Malta while they were on their way to Alexandria in 1661. They were held for three years.

Clitherow, Saint Margaret. "Life of Margaret Clitherow." By her Confessor John Mush. In *The Troubles of Our Catholic Forefathers: Related by Themselves*, edited by John Morris, pp. 333–440. 3d ser. London: Burns & Oates, 1877.

This account of Roman Catholic martyr Margaret Clitherow's life, written by her confessor, "a distinguished secular priest," includes quotations from Clitherow. She was martyred at the age of thirty in 1586 for her adherence to conscience in harboring Catholic priests in her home in York during the Protestant persecution of Roman Catholics in England. A convert from Protestantism, she was imprisoned several times, "sometimes by the space of two years together," during the twelve years that she was a practicing Catholic. She was executed by being pressed to death in the York tollbooth on March 25, 1586. She was beatified in 1920 and canonized in 1970.

Contemporary Prison Writings: 1980. Edited by Jitu Tambuzi and Jeff Elzinga. New Paltz, N.Y.: Tambuzi Publications, n.d. (Not examined. Source: *COSMEP Prison Project Newsletter,* Fall 1980.)

Included in this collection of writing by inmates, community supporters and others involved in the prison system are works by Assata Shakur (q.v.).

Corday, Charlotte. "Letters from Prison." Reprinted in Michel Corday, *Charlotte Corday,* translated by E. F. Buckley, pp. 12, 134–135, 208–214. New York: Dutton, 1931. Also reprinted in Marie Cher, *Charlotte Corday and Certain Men of the Revolutionary Torment,* pp. 83–84, 128–130, 132. New York: D. Appleton, 1929.

Prison letters of the French revolutionary woman who assassinated Marat and was executed by the guillotine in Paris at the Place de la Révolution in 1793. During her brief imprisonment in the prisons of the Abbaye and the Conciergerie, where she occupied a cell previously used by Madame Roland (q.v.), she wrote a letter to her father and a long letter to the Girondist Barbaroux, telling him of her actions and motives.

Crane, Margaret. "Five Vignettes from the Tennessee Prison for Women." *Prison Writing Review* 8, no. 2 (Winter–Spring 1985): 10–22.

Sketches of Crane's prison experiences at the Tennessee Prison for Women, where she was sentenced to one to two years for concealing allegedly stolen goods worth $75. Crane maintained her innocence and held that she was being prosecuted in order to drive her and her mother "out of the county" because of their social activism. Her sketches describe prison conditions and her attempt to provide fellow inmates with legal counseling. She narrates several cases of the women she counseled.

Crisp, Dorothy. *A Light In the Night.* London: Holborn Publishing, 1960.

Prison memoirs by English author and political writer Dorothy Crisp, a regular contributor to the London *Sunday Dispatch* during World War II. In 1958 she was sentenced to Holloway Prison for one year for misdemeanors under the Bankruptcy Act. Her prison memoirs describe conditions in Holloway in order to call attention to the need for prison reform.

D'Arcy, Margaretta. *Tell Them Everything: A Sojourn in the Prison of Her Majesty Queen Elizabeth II at Ard Macha (Armagh)*. London: Pluto Press, 1981.

Irish playwright D'Arcy has been involved in antinuclear and Irish Republican activities, which have influenced the plays she writes with coauthor John Arden. She was imprisoned several times, beginning in 1969. In this book she discusses her stay in Armagh Prison in Northern Ireland. She was imprisoned for refusing to pay a fine for her protest against Armagh prison conditions on International Women's Day in 1979. During her sentence, she joined thirty Republican prisoners for three months in 1980 in their "no-wash protest" in Armagh. She wrote her book at the request of these women to "tell them everything."

Darel, Sylva. *A Sparrow in the Snow*. Translated from the Russian by Barbara Norman. New York: Stein & Day, 1973.

The memoirs of Darel, a Russian Jew, include an account of her arrest at the age of nineteen, and her imprisonment in Leningrad and a series of transit prisons on her journey "home" to Siberia. She had been arrested in 1953 for "escaping" to Leningrad from Siberia, where for over ten years her family had been living in exile as "socially dangerous elements." She wrote this account while in exile in 1953.

Davis, Angela. "Angela Introduces Ericka's New Book." *Black Panther* 8, no. 9 (20 May 1972): 2, 7–8.

Writing from Santa Clara County Jail, California, in December 1971, Davis reviews and praises Ericka Huggins's (q.v.) forthcoming book of poetry, in which Huggins presents the struggle of black women.

———. *If They Come in the Morning: Voices of Resistance*. New York: Third Press, 1971.

In *An Autobiography*, Davis describes the work that she did while in prison on this anthology of writings about the black liberation movement. She contributed several selections, and there are prison interviews with her.

———. "The Soledad Brothers." *Black Scholar* 2 (April–May 1971): 2–7.

From her own prison cell in the Marin County Jail, San Rafael, California, Davis writes a defense of the three Soledad Brothers, including George Jackson. The essay is of interest to those researching Davis's own case, because prosecutors claimed that her uncontrolled love for Jackson motivated her to support a plot by black prisoners to free him.

———. "To Mexican Political Prisoners." *Transcontinental* 6, no. 66 (September 1971): 5.

Davis writes from Marin County Jail, San Rafael, California, on June 14, 1971. Her letter expresses support for Mexicans imprisoned following a demonstration in Mexico City on June 10, 1971.

———. "Walls." In *An Autobiography*. New York: Random House, 1974, pp. 283–346.

A former UCLA professor active in black revolutionary causes, Davis describes her imprisonment in Marin County Jail and Santa Clara Jail, California, in 1970–1971, on charges of murder, kidnapping, and criminal conspiracy. While imprisoned, she fought to take an active part in her own legal defense.

Day, Dorothy. *The Eleventh Virgin*. New York: Albert and Charles Boni, 1924.

Pages 180–218 of Part 2, Chapter 3, of this autobiographical novel describe the prison experience of June Henreddy (Dorothy Day), a young radical journalist who is arrested in Washington, D.C., with a group of suffragists demonstrating for the rights of political prisoners. She spends sixteen days in a workhouse outside Washington, where the suffragists stage a hunger strike.

———. *From Union Square to Rome*. Silver Spring, Md: Preservation of the Faith Press, 1938; reprint, New York: Arno, 1978.

At the age of forty, Day recalls her past life and conversion to Catholicism in this book addressed to her brother. She gives details of her stay in Occoquan Workhouse and the Washington city jail in 1917 for suffrage activity (pp. 81–87). There is also a description of her imprisonment, about 1920, for several days in the West Chicago Avenue Police Station, Chicago. She was mistakenly charged with prostitution, and she writes of the kindness of the prostitutes jailed with her (pp. 98–107).

———. "Jail." In *The Long Loneliness*. New York: Harper & Row, 1952, pp. 72–83.

Day describes her experience in a Washington workhouse and jail after her arrest for picketing in front of the White House in support of suffragists' rights in prison. Sentenced to thirty days' imprisonment, she went on a hunger strike for ten days.

———. "Thoughts After Prison." *Liberation: An Independent Monthly* 2, no. 6 (September 1957): 5–7.

Day writes of family disintegration, materialism, and war from her perspective as an ex-prisoner who is especially sensitive and powerless. She describes the poor with whom she was imprisoned in the 151st Street Police Station in New York City on July 12, 1957. She had been arrested for disobeying the Civil Defense Act, when she picketed instead of taking shelter during an announced air-raid drill in New York City. She and others of the Catholic Workers movement were sentenced to thirty days.

De Beausobre, Iulia. *The Woman Who Could Not Die*. London: Gollancz, 1948.
In February 1932 De Beausobre was arrested by the GPU, the Soviet police, for complicity in the alleged treason of her husband, Nicolay. She was held in the Inner Prison of the GPU and in Boutyrki Prison, and then sentenced to five years' hard labor in the GPU penal camps. Upon her release she learned that Nicolay had been shot. De Beausobre feared living in Russia any longer and was able to immigrate to England because an old friend agreed to sponsor her. Her prison memoirs describe her fellow inmates.

Deming, Barbara. "In the Birmingham Jail." *Nation*, 25 May 1963, pp. 436–437.
Deming describes events leading to her imprisonment in the women's ward of the Birmington City Jail for peacefully demonstrating for racial equality. She relates how the poor white female prisoners initially resented her actions but later came to listen to her beliefs on nonviolence and equality. She also describes the jailing of children who were demonstrating.

———. *Prison Notes*. New York: Grossman, 1966.
A description of her 1964 imprisonment in the city jail of Albany, Georgia, for a civil rights demonstration. There is a discussion of the theory of nonviolent protest, in the form of a letter to a friend who had urged Deming to give up her efforts.

———. *We Are All Part of One Another: A Barbara Deming Reader*. Edited by Jane Meyerding, with a Foreword by Barbara Smith. Philadelphia: New Society, 1984.
This collection includes "In the Birmingham Jail" and selections from *Prison Notes*.

Dergan, Bridget. *The Life And Confession Of Bridget Dergan, Who Murdered Mrs. Ellen Coriell, The Lovely Wife Of Dr. Coriell, of New Market N.J. to which is added Her Full Confession, and an Account of her Execution at New Brunswick*. Philadelphia: Barclay, 1867.
Bridget Dergan (Deignan) immigrated to America from Ireland (about 1864) as a young woman, and was employed by the Coriells as a servant.

This volume contains a letter written to her brother in Ireland from the Middlesex County Jail, New Brunswick, and Dergan's confessions, dictated because she was illiterate. She claims to have murdered Mrs. Coriell so that she "might take her place." The case aroused great public interest, and tickets were issued to five hundred persons to witness her execution in August 1867.

Diaz, Gladys. "Roles and Contradictions of Chilean Women in the Resistance and in Exile: Collective Reflections of a Group of Militant Prisoners." Presented at the Plenary Session of the International Conference on Exile and Solidarity in Latin America During the 1970s. New York: Women's International Resource Exchange (WIRE), 1979.

Chilean resistance worker Diaz presents the collective testimony of her sisters who had been imprisoned and exiled for their work in the Chilean Resistance. Diaz herself had been arrested, tortured, imprisoned in Villa Grimaldi and Tres Alamos, and finally released into exile as the result of an international campaign on her behalf.

Doty, Madeleine Zabriskie. *Society's Misfits*. New York: 1916.

Doty, a young lawyer, voluntarily entered the New York State Prison for Women at Auburn in 1913. Dedicated to prison reform, she posed as "Maggie Martin," a convicted forger, in order to investigate and report on prison conditions for women.

Duras, Duchesse de (Louise H.), née Noailles. "Prison Life During the French Revolution. Written in 1801, the Year IX. of the Republic." In *Prison Journals during the French Revolution*, translated by Mrs. M. Carey, pp. 6–157. New York: Dodd, Mead, 1891.

To fulfill her son's request, the Duchesse de Duras wrote her memoirs upon her release from prison. She was imprisoned in the old convent at Saint-François à Beauvais on October 6, 1793, and transferred to the prison at Chantilly on October 20, 1793. She was again transferred, to the Collège du Plessis at Paris on April 5, 1794, and released on October 19, 1794. The memoirs are dated "Paris, February 11, 1804," and signed "Noailles de Durfort-Duras."

This section of the volume also includes prison writings of her sister-in-law Louise Noailles (q.v.).

Duval, Elsie. Papers. Fawcett Library, City of London Polytechnic, London.

Included are prison diaries from 1911–12 and 1913, and personal correspondence from 1913, 1914, and 1918. Duval, a British suffragette, was forcibly fed in prison. (Not examined; source: Margaret Barrow, *Women 1870–1928: A Select Guide to Printed and Archival Sources in the United Kingdom* [London: Mansell, 1981].)

Dyer, Mary. Letters. In Chapter 5, "New England," in *A Collection of the Sufferings of the People Called Quakers*, edited by Joseph Besse, vol. 2, pp. 196–207. London: Luke Hinde, 1753.

———. Letters. In Appendix 2 of *Mary Dyer of Rhode Island: The Quaker Martyr that Was Hanged on Boston Common June 1, 1660*, by Horatio Rogers, pp. 84–93. Providence, R.I.: Preston & Rounds, 1896.
Dyer's letters to the Massachusetts General Court in 1659, after she had received the death sentence for disobeying an order of banishment from Puritan Massachusetts Bay Colony, and after she was at first reprieved.

Elliott, Grace Dalrymple. *Journal of My Life During the French Revolution.* London: Richard Bentley, 1859.
King George III of England requested Mrs. Elliott, who was known for her beauty and grace in court society, to write this journal. It includes a description of her imprisonment in the prison of St. Pelagie, in the Prison of the Recollets, at Versailles, and in the Carmes prison in Paris. Held under suspicion of espionage against the Republic, she describes her acquaintance with prisoners about to be executed.

Empire! The Creative Writing Journal of New York State Inmates. Edited by Paul Gordon. New York State Dept. of Correctional Services, 1984.
An annual literary arts magazine for inmates of New York State Correctional facilities. The first issue, Fall 1984, contains poems by Althea Sellers and Elly Kessler.

Evans, Katharine. *See* Chevers, Sarah, and Katharine Evans.

Figner, Vera. "When the Clock of Life Stopped." In *Memoirs of a Revolutionist*, translated by Camilla Chapin Daniels et al., Book 2, pp. 179–318. New York: International, 1927; reprint, Westport, Conn.: Greenwood Press, 1968.
A description of Figner's imprisonment in the Schlüsselburg Fortress, from 1884 to 1904, for revolutionary terrorist activity in Russia. She spent much of this period in solitary confinement, communicating through coded wall tappings.

First, Ruth. *117 Days.* New York: Stein & Day, 1965; Penguin, 1982.
South African journalist First was imprisoned without trial under the ninety-day detention law in 1963. She was held in solitary confinement in the women's cells of the Marshall Square Police Station, Johannesburg, and in the Women's Central Prison, Pretoria. Books were not allowed and she was forbidden to write. She was imprisoned longer than any white woman in South Africa before her. Even before her imprisonment she had been served banning orders that forbade her to write and thus ended her

fifteen-year career in journalism. Her activist lawyer husband, Joe Slovo, had previously fled the country, and after her release she joined him in exile in England.

In 1978 she became director of the Centre for African Studies in Maputo, Mozambique. She was killed by a letter bomb in her office in 1982.

Fitzgerald, Tamsin. *Tamsin*. Edited by Richard A. Condon. New York: Dial, 1973.

Editor Richard A. Condon explains that the book is based mostly upon Tamsin's correspondence from prison. A number of brief poems are included. Eighteen-year-old Tamsin was incarcerated from May 1969 to December 1970 at the Federal Reformatory for Women at Alderson, West Virginia. She and her boyfriend, Michael, also imprisoned, were convicted of attempting to hijack an airplane from New York to Havana in order for Michael to avoid the draft.

Flatman, Ada. "Reminiscences of a Suffragette," typescript. Suffragette Fellowship Collection, Museum of London (Group C, vol. 2: 58.87/67).

British suffragette Flatman was imprisoned in Holloway in 1908. She writes fondly of Constance Lytton (q.v.).

Fleming, Amalia. *A Piece of Truth*. London: Jonathan Cape, 1972.

A Greek woman who had been active in the Greek Resistance during World War II, Lady Fleming married an Englishman, Sir Alexander Fleming, in 1953, but returned to Athens in 1962. She was arrested by the military police in 1971 for her opposition to its repression. Her memoirs describe her pretrial experience and her sentence of sixteen months in Korydallos Prison, between Athens and Perama. Her sentence was suspended because she was ill, but upon her return home she was expelled to England.

Flynn, Elizabeth Gurley. *The Alderson Story: My Life as a Political Prisoner*. New York: International, 1963.

Flynn, a labor organizer in the Industrial Workers of the World (IWW), a founder of the ACLU, and later a communist, was arrested in 1951 under the Smith Act and charged with "teaching and advocating the violent overthrow of the government." She spent the years 1955 to 1957 in the Federal Reformatory for Women at Alderson, West Virginia.

Forest, Eva (Genoveva). *From A Spanish Prison*. Translated by Rosemary Sheed. New York: Moon Books/Random House, 1976.

Journal and letters written in 1974 and 1975 from Yeserías Prison, Madrid, where Forest, a psychiatrist by profession and a communist, was imprisoned on charges of terrorist activity against Franco's government. Recipients of letters included her husband, also imprisoned, and their children.

Fortune News. Bimonthly. Edited by David Rothenberg.

A newspaper of the Fortune Society, a nonprofit service and advocacy program for inmates and ex-inmates. Issues include inmates' writings and winning works from the PEN prison writing contest. The April 1979 issue focuses on women.

Fox, Margaret. *The Life of Margaret Fox. Wife of George Fox. Compiled from her own narrative, and other Sources; with a Selection from her Epistles, Etc.* Philadelphia: Association of Friends, "for the Diffusion of Religious and Useful Knowledge," 1859.

A biographical account of the "Mother of Quakerism"—her life, convincement, various imprisonments, and excerpts from letters written during her four-year imprisonment in Lancaster Castle, 1664–1668.

From Women in Prison Here to Women of Vietnam: We Are Sisters. San Francisco: Peoples Press, 1975.

A collection of letters written by women from the California Institution for Women (Frontera) to women political prisoners in South Vietnam. The letters express solidarity and warm wishes in their struggle.

Gannett, Betty. Papers, 1929–1970. Madison, Wis.: State Historical Society of Wisconsin.

Gannett was active in the Communist Party in America from 1923 until her death in 1970. She was a writer, editor, Marxist theoretician, and teacher. Her papers at the State Historical Society of Wisconsin include papers relating to her 1955–1957 imprisonment in the Federal Reformatory for Women in Alderson, West Virginia. She and other party leaders were charged under the Smith Act with conspiracy against the government. (Not examined; source: *The Papers of Betty Gannett: Guide to a Microfilm Edition,* 1976.)

Ginzburg, Eugenia. *Journey into the Whirlwind.* Translated by Paul Stevenson and Max Hayward. New York: Harcourt Brace Jovanovich, 1967.

Ginzburg, a dedicated Communist and a history professor, was arrested in 1937 during Stalin's purges, and imprisoned for eighteen years in Kazan, Moscow, and Yaroslavl prisons, followed by penal camps in Siberia. In this volume, the first of her two books, she describes the prisons and her transfer to the Kolyma camps. Her second book, *Within the Whirlwind,* translated by Ian Boland, with an Introduction by Heinrich Böll (New York: Harcourt Brace Jovanovich, 1981), deals with Siberian camp experiences.

"Girl Delinquent, Age Sixteen: An Undecorated Autobiography." *Harper's* 164 (June 1932): 551–559.

An anonymous autobiographical article by a Chicago teenager, writing from a state penal institution. It deals mostly with the problems faced by the author as a girl growing up on the streets of a slum neighborhood, and how this background led her to prison.

Goldman, Emma. "Letters from Prison." *Little Review* 3, no. 3 (May 1916): 17–18. Reprinted in *The Little Review Anthology*, edited by Margaret Anderson, pp. 62–63. New York: Horizon Press, 1953.

Included are excerpts from letters written by Goldman from Queens County Jail, Long Island City, New York, during her fifteen-day imprisonment in April 1916. She had been arrested in New York in February 1916 for lecturing on birth control. Advocates of birth control enthusiastically supported her in this case, which served the purpose of boosting the birth-control movement.

————. *Living My Life.* 2 vols. New York: Knopf, 1931; reprint, Dover, 1970. Vol. 1: Chapter 12; vol. 2: Chapters 45–49.

A description of her imprisonment in 1893 in Blackwell's Island Penitentiary, New York, for inciting to riot, and from 1917 to 1919 in the Missouri State Penitentiary, for conspiracy against the draft. Includes reference to her friendship with her fellow inmate Kate O'Hare (q.v.).

Gorbanevskaya, Natalya. "Fourteen Poems." *Index on Censorship* 1, no. 1 (Spring 1972): 107–115.

Poems written from 1964 to 1970, excerpted from *Selected Poems by Natalya Gorbanevskaya, with a transcript of her trial and papers relating to her detention in a prison psychiatric hospital*, edited and translated by Daniel Weissbort. Oxford: Carcanet Press, 1972.

————. *Selected Poems by Natalya Gorbanevskaya, with a transcript of her trial and papers relating to her detention in a prison psychiatric hospital*. Edited and translated by Daniel Weissbort. Oxford: Carcanet Press, 1972.

A translator and poet, Gorbanevskaya was confined in mental hospitals because she was a leading dissident intellectual in Moscow. In 1968, during a problem pregnancy, she was transferred, under KGB direction, from her maternity hospital to the Kashchenko mental hospital. She was released, she claimed, because of her pregnancy. She was later diagnosed as schizophrenic and taken to the hospital section of Moscow's Butyrka Prison in 1970 and transferred to a psychiatric hospital in Kazan in 1971. This book includes a poem from Butyrka Prison, letters to her mother and son from Butyrka Prison, and "Free Health Service," a series of notes recording her experience in the maternity hospital and the Kashchenko mental hospital.

Gordon, Helen (Helen Gordon Liddle). *The Prisoner: A Sketch. An Experience of Forcible Feeding by a Suffragette.* Letchworth, Eng.: Garden City Press, 1912.

Gordon writes of her imprisonment for one month (October–November 1907) in Strangeways Prison, Manchester. She was arrested for a suffrage protest in which she broke a post office window. While in prison she was forcibly fed when she demanded to be treated as a political prisoner and protested against prison regulations and food. Her aim in the book is to describe the prison atmosphere and its effect on the prisoner, in order to awaken the public to the situation.

Gratz, Simon. Autograph Collection. "Criminals and their Victims." Case 13, Box 39. Philadelphia: Historical Society of Pennsylvania.

This collection includes writings by two women imprisoned in nineteenth-century America:

Ann Carson, autograph letter, signed, to Hon. Chief Justice Tilghman from prison, 14 February 1822. She writes to request that her bail be lowered. Carson, a Philadelphia belle, was imprisoned several times during her brief life. In 1816 she had been imprisoned in Philadelphia, Harrisburg, and Lancaster prisons pending trial for a series of charges including accessory to the murder of her husband, conspiracy to abduct the governor of Pennsylvania, and bigamy. In 1820 she was convicted and sentenced to two years in the Philadelphia Penitentiary as accessory after a robbery was committed. Released before the expiration of her sentence, she engaged Mrs. M. Clarke to write her "autobiography," so that Carson could earn money for living expenses. She was later imprisoned again in Philadelphia, where she died at the age of thirty-eight, probably from injuries inflicted by other inmates. *The Memoirs of the Celebrated and Beautiful Mrs. Ann Carson* was enlarged and published in its second edition by Mrs. Clarke in 1838.

Mary Mors (Morris), confession, n.d., written in another hand signed by her "mark." She confesses to arson, as "Acsesary and the instrument of the late dredfull fire in Boston."

Greenhow, Rose. *My Imprisonment and the First Year of Abolition Rule at Washington.* London: Richard Bentley, 1863.

Arrested as a Confederate spy, whose home was a center of espionage activity, and whose information had helped the Confederate victory at Bull Run, this popular Washington hostess and her small daughter were imprisoned in the Old Capitol Prison, Washington, D.C., in 1862. She continued her espionage from prison and openly defied Union authorities.

Grey, Lady Jane (Lady Jane Dudley). *Memoirs and Literary Remains.* Edited by Sir Harris Nicolas. London: Henry Colburn, 1832.

Lady Jane Grey (1537–1554) reigned very briefly as Queen of England after the death of King Edward VI, but Queen Mary's claim to the throne was successful and Jane and her husband, Guildford Dudley, were charged with high treason. This collection includes writings of Lady Jane from the Tower of London, where she was imprisoned in July 1553 and executed in February 1554. There are letters to her father and sister Katherine, and a prayer.

Guernsey, Isabel Russell. *Free Trip to Berlin*. Toronto: Macmillan, 1943.

Wartime memoirs of Guernsey, a Canadian civilian who was traveling to South Africa when her ship was captured by the Germans. A prison ship took her and other passengers with British passports to Germany, where she was held in a series of jails during her journey to the Liebenau Women's Internment Camp. After three months there, she was allowed to live in relative freedom in Berlin until, over a year later, she was released to the United States.

Guyon, Jeanne Marie Bouvier. *Autobiography of Madame Guyon. Complete in two parts*. New York: Edward Jones, 1880.

This is the English translation of the French original, dated 1709. Madame Guyon, a French writer on spiritual subjects, was criticized by the Catholic Church for her quietist doctrines and her lifestyle. In 1688 she was arrested and imprisoned in the Convent of the Visitation of St. Mary, near St. Antoine. As the result of a controversy over the quietist doctrines she shared with Abbé Fénelon, she was again imprisoned in 1695 at Vincennes and later in the Bastille, from which she was released in 1703. Her autobiography, she states, was written at the command of her spiritual director.

Harris, Emily. "On the Open Road." *Fortune News*, 23 June 1981, p. 4.

Harris, imprisoned in the California Institution for Women, Frontera, describes what she feels when she jogs around the prison yard and remembers how she and her husband, Bill, were arrested by the FBI while jogging in San Francisco in 1975. Members of the terrorist Symbionese Liberation Army (SLA), they had been hunted by the FBI for one and a half years for their part in the case of Patricia Hearst, a newspaper heiress abducted by the SLA in 1974. They were tried in 1976 for robbery, kidnapping, and assault. This piece received third place for nonfiction in the 1981 PEN prison writing awards.

Henry, Joan. *Women in Prison*. New York: Doubleday, 1952. Published in England under the title *Who Lie in Gaol* (1952).

Henry, a British author, was imprisoned in 1950 for an unnamed offense. She writes of life in two English prisons for women: Holloway and Askham Grange, York.

————. *Yield to the Night*. London: Gollancz, 1954.

A novel written in the first person about a murderess's last days in an English prison.

Hooton, Elizabeth. Letter to Noah Bullock, Derby, England, 1650/51. Swarthmore Manuscripts, Friends House, London; a fair copy made by George Fox is at the Historical Society of Pennsylvania, Philadelphia. Reprinted in Hugh Barbour and Arthur O. Roberts, eds. *Early Quaker Writings, 1650–1700*, pp. 381–383. Grand Rapids, Mich.: Eerdmans, 1973.

Hooton, believed to be the first follower of Quaker leader George Fox, was jailed several times in England and persecuted in Massachusetts for her beliefs. She was imprisoned in Derby jail, England, sometime during Fox's own imprisonment there in 1650–1651. Her offense was reproving a priest. She wrote her letter to Noah Bullock, magistrate or mayor of Derby, admonishing him for jailing her unjustly and warning him to follow God's teachings. This letter and Fox's Derby writings are believed to be the oldest surviving Quaker writings, according to Barbour and Roberts.

Hsieh Pingying. *Girl Rebel: The Autobiography of Hsieh Pingying*. With extracts from her *New War Diaries*. Translated by Adet Lin and Anor Lin. New York: John Day, 1940.

As a twenty-year-old student, Hsieh Pingying left her Chinese village of Hsiehtushan in 1927 to join the Chinese Revolution and to escape her family's plans for her marriage. Her *Autobiography* (1936) tells of her adventures with the army and of the publication in a Chinese newspaper of her letters describing the war. In 1927, when young revolutionaries, particularly bobbed-haired females, were persecuted as Communists, Hsieh Pingying was imprisoned and escaped sentencing only because the judge knew her father. The *New War Diary* (1938) tells of her imprisonment in Japan during the 1930s, but the section about this imprisonment has not yet been translated and is not included in the extracts in *Girl Rebel*.

Huggins, Ericka. "before a woman becomes grown." *Crime and Social Justice*, no. 1 (Spring–Summer 1974): 50.

A poem from Niantic Prison, 1970, about injustices faced by poor black women.

————. "Excerpts from a Letter from Ericka." *Black Panther* 6, no. 3 (13 February 1971): 6.

————. *Insights and Poems*, by Huey Newton and Ericka Huggins. San Francisco: City Lights Books, 1975.

The collection includes poems written in 1970 and 1971, when Huggins, a Black Panther, was imprisoned at Niantic State Farm for Women in Connecticut.

———. "A Letter from Sister Ericka Huggins." *Movement* 5, no. 8 (September 1969): 7.

In her letter dated July 8, 1969, Huggins supports political prisoners in their fight against government repression.

———. Poems. In *Off Our Backs: A Woman's News Journal* 1, no. 17 (12 February 1971); 2, no. 8 (April 1972).

Poems describing Huggins's prison experiences, her identification with women prisoners, and her feminist consciousness.

———. Poems and a message from Niantic Prison. In *If They Come in the Morning: Voices of Resistance*, edited by Angela Davis. New York: Third Press, 1971.

———. "Revolution in Our Lifetime." *Black Panther* 5, no. 28 (9 January 1971): 5.

Hunt, Antonia. *Little Resistance: A Teenage English Girl's Adventures in Occupied France*. London: Leo Cooper, Secker & Warburg, 1982.

Born Antonia Lyon-Smith, the author was an English teenager living in France from 1940 to 1944, during the German occupation. She spent four months in the barracks of a wartime internment camp in Besançon and was later imprisoned by the Gestapo in Gestapo headquarters, Rue des Saussaies, Paris. She was held five months in solitary confinement because the Germans believed she had contacts in the French Resistance. She tells of her illness in prison and the complications she faced when a Gestapo translator saved her life and proposed marriage.

Huré, Anne. *In Prison*. Translated by Emma Craufurd. London: MacDonald, 1965. Originally published in France as *En Prison* (1963).

———. *The Two Nuns*. Translated by Emma Craufurd. London: MacDonald, 1964. Originally published in France as *Les Deux Moniales* (1962).

———. *The Word Made Flesh*. Translated by Emma Craufurd. London: MacDonald, 1967. Originally published in France as *Le Péché Sans Merci* (1964).

Huré, an upper-class French woman, became a Benedictine nun and later left the convent to acquire a doctorate in theology. She was imprisoned numerous times in la Roquette and Haguenau prisons between 1962 and 1971 for robberies, writing bad checks, fraud, and nonpayment of bills. She has written several novels that draw upon her prison experience and use imagery from life in the prison and in the convent. The autobiographical novel *In Prison* is the most directly about prison. *The Two Nuns*, which was very successful in France, is set in a Benedictine abbey for women, and *The Word Made Flesh* is set in a religious school for girls. The novels are abstract and philosophical. (Information from Elissa Gelfand, *Imagination in Confinement: Women's Writings from French Prisons* [Ithaca, N.Y.: Cornell Univ. Press, 1983].)

I Am Waiting to Be Free. Santa Fe, N.M.: Koyemsi Press, 1981.
An anthology of writing from the Women's Penitentiary of New Mexico. It includes poems by Lorri Martinez (q.v.).

Ibarruri, Dolores. *They Shall Not Pass: The Autobiography of La Pasionaria*. Translated from the 1962 Spanish edition. New York: International, 1966.
Ibarruri, a Spanish Communist, explains that this book is not her memoirs, but a "testimony to the traditions of struggle of the Spanish people." In 1931, while working as editor of a Communist newspaper in Madrid, Ibarruri was arrested for helping a fugitive and was held in the Women's Prison of Madrid and Larrínaga Prison in Bilbao until January 1932. She was rearrested shortly afterward in Madrid and released in 1933. She describes her imprisonment with thieves and prostitutes and her attempts to instruct them in Communism. Her difficulty as an imprisoned revolutionary and mother who could not properly care for her children is discussed. She met with Elizabeth Gurley Flynn (q.v.) in Moscow in 1960.

Inside/Out: Poetry and Prose from America's Prisons. Quarterly.
A newsletter. The Summer 1982 issue (vol. 3, no. 1) includes a Special Women's Supplement, with artwork and photographs. Included are poetry, fiction, and drama by Rae S. Stewart, Diane Hamill Metzger (q.v.), La'Shawn Marcella Russell, Diana Bickston (q.v.), and Michele Roberts.

Inside: Prison American Style. Edited by Robert J. Minton, Jr. New York: Random House, 1971.
Most selections in this anthology are written by prisoners themselves, but almost all are by men. It does include two short pieces by Nellie Sloan, who was imprisoned in Corona, a correctional facility for women in southern California. Her husband was a prisoner whose work is also included in the book. Nellie Sloan describes the prison intake process and the prison psychiatric unit.

Invincible Spirit: Art and Poetry of Ukrainian Women Political Prisoners in the U.S.S.R. Translated by Bodhan Yasen. Baltimore: Smoloskyp Publishers, 1977. Text in English and Ukrainian.
This volume contains poetry, letters, and color photographs of symbolic embroidered designs created by Ukrainian women prisoners who have been imprisoned in Soviet labor camps for defending human rights and Ukrainian national rights. The written and embroidered works emphasize

their religious and cultural heritage. The poets are Iryna Senyk, Iryna Stasiv-Kalynets, and Stefaniya Shabatura, and their works were also published in the Ukrainian underground press.

Irving, Addie. Unpublished letters from Sing Sing, 1866. Manuscript Collection, New York Historical Society, New York City. As quoted in Cynthia Owen Philip, *Imprisoned in America: Prison Communications 1776 to Attica*, pp. 79–83. New York: Harper & Row, 1973.

Irving was a thief and a recidivist because it was not easy for women alone, particularly ex-convicts, to earn a living in 1866. While in Sing Sing Prison, she wrote letters to Mrs. E. C. Buchanan, a charitable New York woman who visited and wrote to her. Irving had previously been imprisoned on Blackwell's Island, where, she states, female prisoners were sexually abused and faced temptations that prevented their rehabilitation.

Joffe, Maria. *One Long Night: A Tale of Truth*. Translated by Vera Dixon from the original Russian (1977). Clapham: New Park, 1978.

Born in the United States and raised in Russia, the author married Adolphe Joffe in 1918. Both she and her husband, who was at one time Russian ambassador to Germany, opposed Stalin. Adolphe Joffe committed suicide, but Maria, editor at the U.S.S.R. State Publishing House, continued to protest Stalin's practices. From 1929 to 1957 she endured imprisonment, exile, and incarceration in penal labor camps. Her memoirs, dated Moscow 1958, describe experiences in the camps, in solitary confinement, and in Lefortovo Prison. Only after her rehabilitation in 1957 did she learn of the "liquidation" of her seventeen-year-old son during her imprisonment.

Jones, Mary H. *Autobiography of Mother Jones*. Edited by Mary Field Parton. Chicago: Charles H. Kerr, 1925; reprinted by Chas. H. Kerr, for the Illinois Labor Historical Society, 1972.

Born in Ireland and raised in America, Mother Jones was a major force in the American labor movement from 1880 and was particularly active with striking miners and railroad workers. She describes her several arrests and imprisonments. She was jailed in Parkersburg, West Virginia, in 1902 for speaking in support of the bituminous miners' strike in Clarksburg. In 1913 she was placed under military arrest in Pratt, West Virginia. She was again held under military arrest in 1914 in the Mount San Rafael Hospital, Trinidad, Colorado, and later in Walsenburg Jail, Colorado, for her support of striking miners.

Karsov, Nina, and Szymon Szechter. *In the Name of Tomorrow: Life Underground in Poland*. Translated from the Polish. London: Hodder & Stoughton, 1970; New York: Schocken, 1971.

Karsov, a Polish Jew, was an intellectual arrested by the Communists in Poland in 1966 and sentenced to three years' imprisonment for preparing and distributing dissident literature. Her description of her arrest and imprisonment in Mokotow and in the prison hospital at Grudziadz is interwoven, in dialogue format, with that of Szechter, a Polish Jew and intellectual who married Karsov while she was in prison. She was released in 1968 and their marriage was annulled in London.

Kennedy, Jane. "Detroit Jail Abuse." *Health Rights News* 4, no. 3 (May–June 1971): 10–11.

Kennedy describes conditions in the Detroit House of Correction. As a member of Beaver 55, a radical group opposed to the Vietnam War, she was sentenced to one to four years for a raid and destruction of computer tapes at the Dow Chemical Research Center, Midland, Michigan.

———. "Letter from Prison." *Womankind* 1, no. 1 (May 1971): 16.

Kennedy describes the feeling of powerlessness of women inmates and the effort of women at the Detroit House of Correction to assert their power by changing visiting policies.

———. "Letters from Prison." *Health Rights News* 4, no. 1 (January 1971): 14.

Kennedy describes conditions in the Marion County Jail, Indianapolis, where she spent twenty-four days in July 1970. She was awaiting trial for an alleged raid on an Indianapolis draft board. Her article emphasizes the inadequacy of health care in the jail.

———. "Women in Prison." *Women's Rights Law Reporter* (July–August 1972): 55–57.

Kennedy describes conditions in the Detroit House of Correction. She emphasizes inadequate medical treatment and inhumane punishments.

Kenney, Annie. *Memoires of a Militant*. London: Edward Arnold, 1924.

Kenney, a British suffragette from a working-class background, describes her series of imprisonments, beginning in Strangeways Gaol, Manchester (1905), and Holloway Prison (1906). She was a close associate of Christabel and Emmeline Pankhurst (q.v.).

Kinney, Hannah (Hanson). *A Review of the Principal Events of the Last Ten Years in the Life of Mrs. Hannah Kinney: Together with Some Comments upon the Late Trial. Written by Herself.* Boston: J. N. Bradley, 1841.

Kinney's work includes a brief description of how she spent her imprisonment in Boston Jail for about five months in 1840. Most of the work is devoted to a narrative of the events leading to her imprisonment on the charges of poisoning her third husband, G. T. Kinney. Mrs. Kinney was acquitted of murder charges and went to live with her sister's family.

Kites. Edited by Laverne Hanners. Pine Bluff, Ark.: Women's Unit, Arkansas Dept. of Corrections, 1978.

A collection of poems written by about thirty women in the Poetry/ Creative Writing Workshop conducted by poet Hanners.

Kowalska, Anka. "Poems from an Internment Camp." Translated by Adam Czerniawski. *Index on Censorship* 12, no. 2 (April 1983): 16–18.

Polish poet Kowalska was held in Goldap and Darlowek detention centers from the beginning of martial law in Poland in December 1981 until May 1982. Included here are translations of three poems she wrote in March and April 1982.

Kulkielko, Renya. *Escape from the Pit.* Foreword by Ludwig Lewisohn. New York: Sharon Books, 1947. Originally published in Hebrew.

Memoirs of the war years by a twenty-two-year-old Jewish woman, writing from a kibbutz in Israel in 1946. She gives an account of her courageous attempts to survive in Nazi-occupied Poland until her arrest in 1943, when her forged passport was detected. She was imprisoned in Katowice by the Gestapo and then transferred to a prison in Myslowice. She describes the conditions of her fellow women prisoners. Aided by her sister Sarah, she escaped and in 1944 arrived in Palestine.

Lafarge, Marie Cappelle. *Memoirs of Madame Lafarge; Written by Herself.* Translated from the French. Complete in 1 volume. Philadelphia: Carey & Hart, 1841.

Memoirs of her life, written in 1841, during her incarceration in the Prison of Tulle, for the poisoning of her husband.

Lai Ying. *The Thirty-Sixth Way: A Personal Account of Imprisonment and Escape from Red China.* Translated, adapted, and edited by Edward Behr and Sydney Liu. Garden City, N.Y.: Doubleday, 1969.

This book must be read as Lai Ying's own work with some reservations, because it is unclear to what extent *Newsweek* correspondents Behr and Liu have "adapted and edited" the account that they asked Lai Ying to write. Born into a "bourgeois" family, she was arrested as a Catholic counterrevolutionary in Canton in 1958. She was sentenced to prison for five years and held in Canton's Tsang Pien Jail, Niu Tou K'eng Reform Camp, and New Life United Enterprises, a prison camp where she worked as an artist and member of a theatrical troupe. She was released in 1963 and escaped to Macao in 1966.

Latour, Madame. "Memoir: Containing an Account of the Life in the Prison of the Luxembourg, where she was Imprisoned During the Years 1793 and 1794, in Company with Madame La Maréchale Duchesse de Mouchy." In *Prison Journals during the French Revolution*, translated by Mrs. M. Carey, pp. 159–197. New York: Dodd, Mead, 1891.

Madame Latour wrote her memoirs after her release from prison. She describes her close association in prison with the Duchesse de Mouchy, mother of the Duchesse de Duras (q.v.).

Lebrón, Lolita. Poems. Translated by Gloria Waldman. Reprinted in *Voices of Women: Poetry by and About Third World Women*. New York: Women's International Resource Exchange (WIRE), 1982. Also reprinted in Doris Meyer and Margarite Fernandez Olmos, *Contemporary Women Authors of Latin America, New Translations*. Brooklyn College Humanities Series. Brooklyn, N.Y.: Brooklyn College Press, 1983. Originally published as *Sándalo en la celda* (Sandlewood in the cell) (Cataño, Puerto Rico: Editorial Betances, 1974).

Poems by Puerto Rican Nationalist Lebrón, who was imprisoned for twenty-five years in the Federal Reformatory for Women at Alderson, West Virginia, for her part in a 1954 armed demonstration in the U.S. House of Representatives. Released in 1979, she returned to Puerto Rico.

Lemmé, Janet E. *Conviction*. New York: Norton, 1970.

Lemmé, an American married to an East German immigrant, was arrested with her husband as they attempted to help his sister and brother-in-law escape through Hungary in 1966. They were imprisoned in the Markó Prison in Budapest. Lemmé was sentenced to six months' imprisonment and released in 1967, while her husband was sentenced to eight months. Her account of her experience gives details on prison conditions, her relationship with fellow inmates, and her treatment by Communist officials.

Lermolo, Elizabeth. *Face of a Victim*. Translated from the Russian by I. D. W. Talmadge, with a foreword by Alexandra Tolstoy. New York: Harper & Brothers, 1955.

Lermolo, a Russian woman and wife of an alleged counterrevolutionary, had been living in exile in the town of Pudozh when she was arrested in 1934 for complicity in the assassination of a top Communist official. Stalin himself aided in her cross-examination. She was imprisoned for eight years, at first in the Leningrad jail of the secret police and in the Political Isolator of the secret police in the town of Chelyabinsk.

Letters, dated 1846, from Ohio Penitentiary. In *Memorials of Prison Life*, by James Bradley Finley, pp. 185–186; 188–189. Cincinnati: L. Swormstedt & A. Poe, 1855; reprint, New York: Arno, 1974.

Two anonymous letters, dated 1846, written by female inmates of the Ohio Penitentiary. Addressed to "Beloved Husband" and "Dear Mother," they are heavily moralistic and penitent in tone. Rev. Finley, chaplain of the prison, quotes them in his account of the prison as he knew it.

Lewis, Primila. *Reason Wounded: An Experience of India's Emergency*. New Delhi: Vikas Publishing House, 1978.

Lewis gives an account of her imprisonment in 1975 during the Emergency declared by Mrs. Gandhi's government. Lewis was arrested and held for eighteen months because of her support of a union for poor agricultural workers south of Delhi.

The Light from Another Country: Poetry from American Prisons. Edited by Joseph Bruchac. Greenfield Center, N.Y.: Greenfield Review Press, 1984.

This anthology of recent writing by male and female American prisoners includes poems by Carolyn Baxter (q.v.), Diana Bickston (q.v.), Lorri Martinez (q.v.), Michelle Roberts, Jessica Scarbrough, and Terri Meyette Wilkins.

Lipper, Elinor. *Eleven Years in Soviet Prison Camps*. Translated from the 1950 German original by Richard Winston and Clara Winston. Chicago: Henry Regnery, 1951.

Lipper, a Dutch Socialist working for a Moscow publisher of foreign literature, was imprisoned in 1937 in Moscow's Lubyanka and Butyrka prisons. She spent a total of eleven years (1937–1948) in ten of Stalin's Soviet prisons. She was convicted of counterrevolutionary activity and support of a foreign state against the Soviet Union. As a child she had lived in Holland and Switzerland and she had studied in Germany and Italy. At the time of her incarceration she knew no Russian.

Little, Joanne. Letter. *Off Our Backs: A Women's News Journal* 5, no. 1 (January 1975): 5.

A letter to Madeleine Janover of the *Off Our Backs* staff. Little expresses gratitude for the journal's support and describes her prison routine in solitary confinement, her feelings about her self-defense killing of her jailer, and her growing self-awareness.

———. Poems. *Crime and Social Justice*, no. 3 (Summer 1975): 44.

Two poems written about Little's prison experience.

[Lomax, Virginia]. *The Old Capitol and its Inmates. By a Lady, Who Enjoyed the Hospitalities of the Government for a "Season."* New York: Hale, 1867.

An anonymous description of the 1865 imprisonment in the Carroll and Old Capitol prisons, Washington, D.C., of Baltimore resident Lomax on suspicion of disloyalty to the Union. She describes prison conditions and her fellow inmates, including Mrs. Surratt, who was later hung as a conspirator in Lincoln's assassination. All other names are changed, including her own (she refers to herself as Maria Miller). Lomax states her admiration for the boldness of Catherine Virginia Baxley (q.v.), whom she calls "Mrs. Johnson."

Look for Me in the Whirlwind: The Collective Autobiography of the New York 21. Introduction by Haywood Burns. New York: Random House, 1971.

Defendants in the New York trial of the Black Panther 21 tell their individual life stories, interwoven in this "collective autobiography" written in prison. The Panthers had originally been arrested in April 1969 on a number of charges, but the trial was delayed until September 1970. In May 1971 all were acquitted. Writings by two women, Joan Bird and Afeni Shakur, are included. Bird describes the Women's House of Detention in New York City in 1971.

Luxemburg, Rosa. "Letters from Prison." Translated from the German by Eleanor Clark. *Partisan Review* 5, no. 1 (June 1938): 3–23; "Letters from Prison." Translated from the German by Ralph Mannheim. *Partisan Review* 10, no. 4 (July–August 1943): 362–371.

Letters written by Luxemburg during her imprisonment in Wronke and Breslau prisons, 1917–1918. Recipients were Sonja Liebknecht and Hans Diefenbach.

———. *The Letters of Rosa Luxemburg.* Edited by Stephen E. Bronner. Boulder, Colo.: Westview Press, 1978.

This collection includes letters written between 1916 and 1918, during her imprisonment in Wronke and Breslau. "Red Rosa," a leading intellectual in the German Social Democratic Party, was imprisoned during most of World War I. Recipients of letters include Hans Diefenbach, her last love, and Sonja Liebknecht, her dear friend and the wife of her imprisoned comrade, Karl Liebknecht.

Lytton, Constance. Papers. Suffragette Fellowship Collection, Museum of London (50.82/119).

Correspondence. Typed copy of a letter to her mother, February 24, 1909, written from King's Cross Station, London, to be sent upon her imprisonment in Holloway.

Autographed letter, signed, to her mother, from Lytton's cell in Bowstreet, February 24, 1909.

Autograph letter, signed, to her sister, Lady Betty Balfour, October 11, 1909, from Central Police Court cell, Newcastle.

Autograph letter, signed, to Kitty Marion (q.v.), October 11, 1915 and autograph letter, signed, to Kitty Marion, October 15, 1915. Marion had been seeking the name of an American to write to for assistance and Lytton suggested Madeleine Doty (q.v.). Lytton notes that Mrs. Pethick-Lawrence (q.v.) agreed that Doty was the right person to help Marion.

Notes on her weights while in prison and list of clothes, 1910.

Typed copies of her statements with reference to medical reports, April 1910.

Typed "Detailed Statement of Prison Experiences by Jane Warton (Constance Lytton) Jan. 1910."

Diary of arrest and imprisonment at Walton Jail, 1910.

Statement of Constance Lytton on treatment of Jane Warton.

―――. *Prisons and Prisoners.* London: Heinemann, and East Ardsley, Yorkshire: E. P. Publishing Ltd., 1914; reprint, Boston: Charles River Books, 1977.

Imprisoned for suffrage activity in England, Lytton posed as Jane Warton, a homely working class suffragette, in order to expose the inequality of treatment by class in British prisons. She was incarcerated in Holloway Prison, New Castle Prison, and Walton Jail, Liverpool, where she endured brutal forcible feedings.

Marion, Kitty. Papers. Suffragette Fellowship Collection. Museum of London (50.82/1120.1121).

Autograph letter, signed, to Edith (?), December 10, 1938, from New York City. Marion, a British singer, actress, and suffragette, refers to the enclosed manuscript on her prison experiences, which she wishes to have published in England. She states that she is looking for a ghostwriter.

Typescript autobiography referred to above. It gives an account of her activities with the suffragettes and refers to her series of imprisonments in Holloway Prison in 1909, 1912, and 1914.

Typescript account of Marion's experiences in Newcastle Prison, dated November 14, 1909 (Group C, vol. 3). Marion was imprisoned there with Constance Lytton (q.v.). She writes of forcible feeding.

Markievicz, Countess Constance de. *Prison Letters of Countess Markievicz.* London: Longmans, Green, 1934; reprint, Millwood, N.Y.: Kraus, 1970.

This collection includes letters written between 1916 and 1921, during her imprisonment at Aylesbury, Holloway, Cork, and Mountjoy prisons for Irish revolutionary activity. The recipient of most letters is her sister, poet Eva Gore-Booth.

Martinez, Lorri. *Where Eagles Fall.* Brunswick, Maine: Blackberry, 1982.

A collection of poems by Martinez, a Chicana prisoner at the Women's Penitentiary of New Mexico. She writes of the pain of separation from loved ones.

Mary, Queen of Scots. *Letters of Mary, Queen of Scots, and Documents Connected with her Personal History.* Edited by Agnes Strickland. New York: J. Winchester, 1842.

Letters written by Mary to her supporters and to Queen Elizabeth during her extended imprisonment by Elizabeth in England, beginning in 1568 and ending with her execution in 1587 in Fotheringay Castle where she was last imprisoned.

———. *The Letters and Official Documents of Mary Stuart, Queen of Scotland.* Translated by William Turnbull. Edited by Prince Alexander Labanoff. London: Charles Dolman, 1845.

These letters do not duplicate those in the Strickland collection.

Maybrick, Florence Elizabeth. *Mrs. Maybrick's Own Story: My Fifteen Lost Years.* New York: Funk & Wagnalls, 1905.

Mrs. Maybrick, an American living near Liverpool, England, was convicted in 1889 of murdering her husband by poisoning. She spent fifteen years in Walton Jail, Woking Prison, and Aylesbury Prison, England, during which time she continued to declare her innocence and receive support from American and British political figures. Unlike many nineteenth-century works by convicted murderesses, Maybrick's is an analysis of prison conditions rather than confessions or a moralistic treatise.

McConnel, Patricia. "Holy Night, Silent Night." *13th Moon* (Fall 1983).

A short story drawn from McConnel's prison experience. In her early twenties McConnel spent time in the Federal Reformatory for Women at Alderson, West Virginia, and in six jails.

———. "The Tourist." *Day Tonight, Night Today* (Summer 1983).

A short story drawn from McConnel's prison experience.

McShane, Yolande. *Daughter of Evil.* London: Star/W. H. Allen, 1980.

McShane, a sixty-one-year-old Englishwoman, was imprisoned in Holloway and Styal prisons and Moor Court Open Prison, England, from January 1977 to February 1978. She was charged with aiding a suicide by giving sleeping pills to her ill and aged mother, but in fact her mother never had committed suicide. She writes of prison routine and conditions and of the need for prison reform.

Metzger, Diane Hamill. "Coralline Ornaments." Sedona, Ariz.: Weed Patch Press, 1980. A collection of poems by Metzger, who has been an inmate in Pennsylvania's Prison for Women at Muncy since 1975, and who has also published poems in *Eagles Way, Gravida, Grit,* and *Inside/Out.* Her poetry and fiction have won awards in the Philadelphia Writers' Conference (1969), Writers' Digest Creative Writing Contest (1978), and PEN Writing Awards for Prisoners (1978, 1981, and 1985).

————. "Only Beginning." *Inside/Out* 3, no. 1 (Summer 1982): 2, 7–8. Special women's supplement.

A short story describing the flight and arrest of a woman and her husband, who were accused of killing his ex-wife.

Michel, Louise. *The Red Virgin: Memoirs of Louise Michel.* Edited and translated by Bullitt Lowry and Elizabeth Ellington Gunter. University, Ala.: Univ. of Alabama Press, 1981.

Heroine of the Paris Commune of 1871, Michel published her memoirs in 1886, at the age of fifty-six. They were begun during her third imprisonment, in 1883. She describes her incarceration at the prison of Chantiers and the reformatory at Versailles in 1871, and the Auberive prison in 1872–1873, before she was finally exiled to New Caledonia. She traveled there by prison ship in 1873 and remained in the prison colony for six years, until her pardon in 1880. Again in 1882, she spent two weeks in jail for disturbing the peace. For leading a Paris crowd in an anarchist demonstration in 1883, she was sentenced to six years' solitary confinement. She was sent to the Centrale Prison at Clermont and to Saint-Lazare Prison and pardoned after three years. Writing from prison, she showed particular sensitivity to the plight of poor women prisoners.

Middleton, Jean. Testimony of her imprisonment in Barberton, South Africa in 1968. In *South Africa: The Imprisoned Society*, edited by Allen Cook, pp. 71–72. London: International Defence and Aid Fund, 1974; reprinted from *Anti-Apartheid News*, June 1973.

Middleton, a white political prisoner, describes conditions in the Women's Prison in Barberton, where she was held from 1965 to 1968.

Mikolajska, Halina. Letter from prison. *Index on Censorship* 12, no. 2 (April 1983): 15–16.

A letter from renowned Polish actress Mikolajska, from the Darlowék women's internment center in April 1982. She writes to the director of the Polish Theatre in Warsaw, Kazimierz Dejmek, to thank him for his efforts for her release and to explain her position of conscience that she cannot sign a loyalty oath to satisfy the authorities. She describes the human rights violations experienced by women refusing the oath.

Mitchell, Hanna Maria Webster. *The Hard Way Up: The Autobiography of Hannah Mitchell, Suffragette and Rebel.* Edited by Geoffrey Mitchell, with a Preface by George Ewart Evans. London: Faber & Faber, 1968.

Hannah Mitchell, born in Derbyshire, England, into a poor family, received virtually no formal education. At the age of fourteen she ran away from her family's farm to work in the town's shops. Self-educated, with a lifelong desire to write, she became active in the woman suffrage movement and the Independent Labour Party. She differed from most suffragettes in coming from the working class rather than the middle class. In 1906 Mitchell was arrested with other suffragettes at a Liberal Party rally and charged with obstruction. She was sentenced to three days in Strangeways Prison, Manchester. After one night in prison, she was released when her husband paid her fine. In 1926 she was appointed a magistrate for the city of Manchester, administering the law and trying to correct injustices she had experienced. Her grandson has edited her manuscript, which has not been substantially altered.

———. Typed autobiographical account of Hannah Mitchell (n.d.). Suffragette Fellowship Collection, Museum of London (Group C, vol. 2: 60.15/21).

Nation, Carry. *The Use and Need of the Life of Carry A. Nation. Written by Herself.* Topeka: F. M. Steves & Sons, 1904.

In this autobiography, Carry Nation gives an account of her numerous jailings for destroying taverns in order to protest the sale of alcohol. She was first imprisoned in 1900 in Wichita Jail for "malicious mischief"; she describes in detail the harsh conditions there. She became a public lecturer on temperance, and she helped to pay expenses by selling souvenir hatchets, often from her cell window. Her imprisonments included Wichita (3), Topeka (7), Kansas City (1), Coney Island (1), Los Angeles (1), San Francisco (1), Scranton (2), Bayonne, New Jersey (1), and Pittsburgh (3). Her final imprisonment was in 1904 in Philadelphia, where she opened a saloon door and "a two legged beer keg in the form of a policeman grabbed me."

Nelson, Belle Harris. 1863 Prison Journal. Historical Department, Church of Jesus Christ of Latter-Day Saints, Salt Lake City, Utah.

Belle Harris Nelson, a Mormon, was imprisoned with her infant son in the Salt Lake Penitentiary from May 18, 1883, to August 31, 1883, for contempt of court when she was called before a grand jury and refused to testify against her former husband, Clarence Merrill. She had been a plural wife and had divorced Merrill in 1862 because of his neglect. When Merrill was charged with polygamy in 1883, she refused to give information about their marriage. The journal contains Belle Nelson's letter to the *Deseret News*, 26 June 1883, and describes prison conditions and her visits with Mormon women.

Nevinson, Evelyn Sharp. Papers. Bodleian Library, Oxford University.

The collection includes letters (1892–1955), notebooks and scrapbooks (1907–1927), manuscript drafts, and press-cuttings (1909–1946) of British journalist and suffragette Nevinson, who went on a hunger strike in prison. (Not examined; source: Margaret Barrow, *Women 1870–1928: A Select*

Guide to Printed and Archival Sources in the United Kingdom [London: Mansell, 1981].)

Nguyen, thi Hong [pseud.]. "A Prison Memoir." *Indochina Chronicle*, no. 40 (April 1975): 3–5.

A working-class woman imprisoned in Tan Hiep, South Vietnam, on suspicion of being a Communist, describes the spirited protest of women prisoners who demanded better conditions.

Noailles, Louise. Letters to Monsieur Grelet, her children's tutor; her husband, Louis, Vicomte de Noailles; and Alexis, her eldest son; and extract from her last will and testament. In "Addenda" to the Duchesse de Duras's memoirs (q.v.), in *Prison Journals during the French Revolution*, translated by Mrs. M. Carey, pp. 139–157. New York: Dodd, Mead, 1891.

Louise Noailles writes from the Prison of the Luxembourg, Paris, before her execution on July 22, 1794. She was the sister-in-law of the Duchesse de Duras.

No More Cages: Women's Prison Newsletter. Bimonthly. Women Free Women in Prison Collective, Brooklyn, N.Y.

A newsletter containing letters, poetry, and articles by and about women in American prisons and psychiatric institutions.

No Title at All Is Better than a Title like That! 1, no. 1. Santa Cruz, Calif.: Santa Cruz Women's Prison Project, 1974.

A collection of poems and essays by inmates of the California Institution for Women at Frontera. Writing workshops were conducted by the Santa Cruz Women's Prison Project.

O'Brien, Edna V. *So I Went to Prison.* New York: Frederick A. Stokes, 1938.

In 1933, O'Brien, a New York stockbroker, was arrested and imprisoned in the House of Detention on charges of grand larceny. After her conviction, she was imprisoned in the State Reformatory for Women at Bedford, New York, in 1935, for fifteen months. She was released in 1936.

Off Our Backs: A Women's News Journal 8, no. 2 (February 1978): 9–11.

This issue explores the violation of women inmates' rights at the Bedford Hills Correctional Facility for Women, New York State. Included are articles by inmates Carol Crooks, Laura Carey, Sheila Liles, Alberta James, Lydia Navarette, Delores Smith, and Irma Jean Mitchelle.

O'Hare, Kate Richards (Cunningham). "Human Ostriches." *Nation* 120, no. 3118 (8 April 1925): 377–378.

In this article O'Hare describes deplorable prison conditions and exploitation of prison labor that she observed during her imprisonment at the Missouri State Penitentiary at Jefferson City in 1919.

———. *In Prison.* New York: Knopf, 1923; reprint, American Library, no. 30. Seattle: Univ. of Washington Press, 1976.

Imprisoned in Missouri State Penitentiary from 1919 to 1920 for her protests against American involvement in World War I, Socialist O'Hare planned to do a sociological study of conditions while incarcerated. Her book explains her theories on the role of political prisoners in prison reform, and gives a picture of prison life, based upon her study of fellow inmates.

———. *In Prison, being a report by Kate Richards O'Hare to the President of the United States as to the conditions under which women federal prisoners are confined in the Missouri State Penitentiary, under the authority of the United States Department of Justice and the United States Superintendent of Prisons. Based on the author's experience as a federal prisoner from April 14, 1919, to May 30, 1920.* St. Louis, Mo.: F. P. O'Hare, [ca. 1920].

———. *Kate O'Hare's Prison Letters.* Modern Series no. 1. Girard, Kan.: Appeal to Reason, 1919.

This volume contains sixteen letters from O'Hare to her family. They were written from April 1919 to September 1919, during her imprisonment in the penitentiary in Jefferson City, Missouri. Her letters describe prison conditions, her observations of fellow inmates, and her personal responses to imprisonment.

———. *Selected Writings and Speeches.* Edited by Philip S. Foner and Sally M. Miller. Baton Rouge: Louisiana State Univ. Press, 1982.

This book includes letters written to O'Hare's family and fellow party workers, from the Missouri State Penitentiary (1919–1920). Also included are selections from *In Prison.*

O'Leary, Fran. "Fran O'Leary Reflects on Past Life." *Fortune News* Women in Prison issue (May 1979): 6.

O'Leary, president of the Fortune Society (q.v.), writes about what led her to prison. As a young, jobless woman, she became a prostitute and was imprisoned in New York City's Women's House of Detention, which served as a school of crime. From there she went on to robbery and served time in the Los Angeles County Jail. As a parolee living in New Jersey, she could not find work, but the Fortune Society and her work counseling teenagers helped to keep her from returning to prison.

Pankhurst, Dame Christabel. *Unshackled: The Story of How We Won the Vote.* Edited by Lord Frederick Pethick-Lawrence. London: Hutchinson, 1959.

After Christabel Pankhurst's death in 1958, her executrix found a typescript of these memoirs, which were then edited by Lord Pethick-Lawrence, husband of suffragette Emmeline Pethick-Lawrence (q.v.) and a committed supporter of woman suffrage. Christabel Pankhurst had worked with her mother, Emmeline Pankhurst (q.v.), in the British militant suffrage movement. She writes of her imprisonment in 1905 for protesting at the Liberal Party's rally in the Manchester Free Trade Hall, and in 1907 ior organizing a protest at the House of Commons. In 1908 she was imprisoned in Holloway for inciting the public to riot during a speech at Trafalgar Square.

Pankhurst, Emmeline. *My Own Story.* London: Eveleigh Nash and New York: Hearst's International Library, 1914; reprint, New York: Kraus, 1971.

Emmeline Pankhurst was a major leader of the British militant woman suffrage movement. Her authorship of this autobiography is in question; Martin Pugh, in *Women's Suffrage in Britain 1867–1928* (London: The Historical Assoc., 1980), states that the book was written for her by an American journalist. The Acknowledgements do express Pankhurst's "deep obligation to Rheta Childe Dorr for invaluable editorial services performed in the preparation of this volume, especially the American edition." Pankhurst does not specify the extent of these "services." The book gives general accounts of the numerous imprisonments of suffragettes. There are detailed descriptions of her imprisonment in Holloway (1908) for demonstrating, and of another 1908 imprisonment, when she demanded that suffragettes be treated as political prisoners. In 1913 she was sentenced to Holloway for three years for conspiring to destroy Lloyd George's country house. She went on a thirst and hunger strike and, under the "Cat and Mouse Act," was repeatedly released for ill health and rearrested when she had recovered.

Pankhurst, E. Sylvia. Papers. Suffragette Fellowship Collection, Museum of London.

A report on forcible feeding, April 23, 1912 (Group A: 57.70/12). Pankhurst explains the suffragettes' motives for their hunger strikes (to demand treatment as political prisoners), and describes abuses they suffered in prison. She gives accounts of cases of several individual women, including Constance Lytton (q.v.) and Helen Gordon Liddle (q.v.).

Typed copy of a letter to her mother, Emmeline Pankhurst (q.v.), March 18, 1913 (Group A: 60.15/16). Sylvia Pankhurst was serving two months' hard labor in Holloway and being forcibly fed. She discusses forcible feeding in her letter.

———. *The Suffragette: The History of the Women's Militant Suffrage Movement 1905–1910.* London: Gay & Hancock, 1911; reprint, New York: Source Book Press, 1970.

This history includes Estelle Sylvia Pankhurst's account of her own imprisonment in Holloway (1906) and the conditions she found there. Pankhurst was the daughter of Emmeline Pankhurst (q.v.) and sister of Christabel Pankhurst (q.v.).

——. *The Suffragette Movement: An Intimate Account of Persons and Ideals.* London: Longmans, Green, 1931; reprint, New York: Kraus, 1971.
Pankhurst gives an account of her several imprisonments, among them Holloway (1906), for protesting the imprisonment of suffragettes, and Holloway (1913), where she went on a thirst and hunger strike and was forcibly fed.

Perkins, Josephine Amelia. *The Female Prisoner; A narrative of the life and singular adventures of Josephine Amelia Perkins, a young woman, who . . . for the three years last past . . . has been unhappily addicted to a criminal propensity, more singular and surprising in its nature (for one of her sex,) than can be found on record; in the commission of which she has been four several times detected, twice pardoned on account of her sex, once for reason of supposed insanity, and the fourth and last time, convicted and sentenced to two years' imprisonment in Madison County jail, Kentucky. Annexed is well-written address to parents and children.* New York: C. Harrison, 1839. (Not examined.)

Perpetua. "The Passion of SS. Perpetua and Felicitas." In *Some Authentic Acts of the Early Martyrs,* edited by E. C. E. Owen, pp. 74–92. Oxford: Clarendon Press, 1927.
Perpetua, a twenty-two-year-old Christian martyr and nursing mother who died in the arena of Carthage in 203, tells of her imprisonment and her visions as she awaited execution.

Pethick-Lawrence, Emmeline. *My Part in a Changing World.* London: Gollancz, 1938.
Pethick-Lawrence was raised in a middle class family in Bristol, England. She became a leader in the Women's Social and Political Union (WSPU) in 1906 and was imprisoned six times in Holloway for her suffrage work. Her first imprisonment (1906) followed an attempt to speak in the House of Commons. Another attempt to enter the House of Commons led to her imprisonment for two months in 1909; she gives a tender, admiring account of her association there with Lady Constance Lytton (q.v.). In 1912 she was imprisoned in Holloway and her husband, Frederick, was held in Brixton Gaol for conspiring to commit property damage; while in prison both were forcibly fed.

Phillips, Eugenia Levy. Papers. Southern Historical Collection, The University of North Carolina at Chapel Hill. Chapel Hill, N.C.

In 1861 Eugenia Levy Phillips, wife of Washington lawyer Philip Phillips, was imprisoned in Washington with her sister and daughters for aiding the Confederacy. Her second imprisonment was in 1862 at Ship Island, Louisiana. This collection of Phillips's papers includes her prison journal from Washington, August 23–September 18, 1861; her prison diary from Ship Island, July 4–August 6, 1862; her 1889 account, in manuscript with clippings, of her two imprisonments; and correspondence with her family concerning her Ship Island imprisonment, 1862.

Phillips, Margaret B. "Eleven Days in the Cage." *Focus/Midwest* 10, no. 64 (1974): 24–25.

Phillips was sentenced to seven months' imprisonment for a civil rights demonstration to protest racial discrimination by a St. Louis defense contractor. In May 1974 she spent eleven days in the St. Louis County Jail before her parole. She writes of her feelings about imprisonment and protests the lack of adequate medical care for her fellow inmates.

Pintíg: Poems and Letters from Philippine Prisons. Hong Kong: Resource Centre for Philippine Concerns, 1979.

A collection of poems, letters, political statements, and artwork by female and male political prisoners. Many works are anonymous. Included are "Letter of a Wife to her Husband," "Letter of a Daughter to Father," "Statement on International Women's Day by Female Political Prisoners of Camp Bicutan," and a poem by imprisoned journalist Clarita Roja (Mila Aguilar, pseud.).

Pinzer, Maimie. *The Maimie Papers.* Edited by Ruth Rosen and Sue Davidson. Old Westbury, N.Y.: Feminist Press, 1977.

Ex-prostitute Maimie Pinzer wrote a series of letters from 1910 until 1922 to Fanny Quincy Howe, a respected Bostonian. In her letters, now held at the Schlesinger Library, Radcliffe College, she writes of her family's financial struggles that led to her prostitution. Her account includes a description of her brief imprisonment at the age of thirteen in the Central Police Station in Philadelphia's City Hall and in the Moyamensing Prison. She afterward spent a year in the Magdalen Home. Her offense was incorrigibility.

Poppy. The Women's Unit Newsletter, California Rehabilitation Center at Norco.

Begun in 1980 in the Bright Fires Writing Workshop of California Rehabilitation Center, this newsletter publishes women's poetry, prose, artwork, and interviews with staff. (Source: "Poppy," by Jean L. Samuel, Artist-in-Residence, C.R.C., *Prison Writing Review* 7, no. 2 [Summer 1983]: 19–24.)

Priess, Anita. *Exiled to Siberia*. Steinbach, Manitoba, Canada: Derksen, 1972 (dual language edition: English and German).

Born Anita Enns in 1909 in the Ukraine, Priess was living in Germany at the time of her arrest by Stalin's Russian police in 1946. She was charged with refusing to divorce her German husband and return to Russia. Sentenced to ten years in penal camps, she was first imprisoned in Torgau and then transported to Siberia, where she remained until after the death of Stalin in 1953. The book describes her fellow women prisoners. Priess wrote her memoirs in 1972 in Canada, where she had remarried and found freedom in 1967.

Prison Writing Review. (Incorporating and continuing the *COSMEP Prison Project Newsletter*.)

The COSMEP (Committee of Small Magazine Editors and Publishers) Prison Project, begun in 1974, sends donated literary magazines and small press publications to prison inmates and encourages prison writing through its *Prison Project Newsletter* 1976–1983, now the *Prison Writing Review*, and its Prison Project Chapbook Series of inmates' poetry.

COSMEP Prison Project Newsletter 5, no. 1 (Fall 1980), contains poems by Diana Bickston (q.v.) and poems from the Bright Fires Writing Workshop at the California Rehabilitation Center.

Prison Writing Review 7, no. 2 (Summer 1983), contains a number of poems by women in the Bright Fires Writing Workshop, and by women at the California Institution for Women, Frontera. Recent issues contain poems by men and women from American prisons.

Quarles, Ariel. "Busted." *Moving Out* 7, no. 1 (1972): 68–71.

Quarles describes her three-day stay in a county jail on charges of possession of marijuana. She notes that her purpose in writing is to describe inhumane and sexist practices in the jail system.

Reddy, Snehalata. *A Prison Diary*. Karnataka State, Mysore, India: Human Rights Committee, 1977.

Extracts from the prison diary of Reddy, imprisoned in May 1976 in the Bangalore Central Jail. A leading Indian actress, she was not told specific charges against her, but was held on political suspicion, presumably because of her friendships with socialist leaders. She suffered severe asthma attacks and developed heart problems in prison, and finally received a one-month parole for medical reasons. While on parole she learned of her release, but she died of a heart attack five days later, on January 20, 1977, at the age of forty-four. During her imprisonment and while on parole, she worked to improve the conditions of the poor women she met in prison.

Reedy, Juanita. "Diary of a Prison Birth." *Majority Report* 5, no. 2 (May 31, 1975): 1, 4.

Reedy's diary describes her experiences as a pregnant prisoner who delivered her only child in a hospital under rigidly supervised conditions. On April 30, 1975, she was taken from the Women's House of Detention on Riker's Island in New York to Elmhurst Hospital's "prison suite." She writes that she received poor medical treatment and was kept from seeing her baby and from breast-feeding.

Renay, Liz. *My Face for the World to See.* New York: Lyle Stuart, 1971.

Memoirs of Renay, who was imprisoned for three years in the Federal Correctional Institution at Terminal Island in California. She was sentenced for perjury after refusing to cooperate with government prosecutors in the trial of gangster Mickey Cohen.

Reweaving the Web of Life: Feminism and Nonviolence. Edited by Pam McAllister. Philadelphia: New Society, 1982.

This anthology of works by feminist pacifists includes some works by women who have been imprisoned for civil disobedience against the Vietnam War, racial discrimination, and discrimination against lesbians and gays. These writers include Joan Cavanagh, Jane Meyerding, Barbara Deming (q.v.), Juanita Nelson, Charlotte Marchant, and Joan Baez (q.v.).

Richardson, Mary R. *Laugh a Defiance.* London: Weidenfeld & Nicolson, 1953.

Memoirs of the British woman suffrage movement by a militant suffragette. She was imprisoned in Holloway several times and went on a hunger strike there. She describes in detail her slashing of the Rokeby Venus in the National Gallery to protest the imprisonment of suffragette leader Emmeline Pankhurst (q.v.).

———. "Tortured Women: What Forcible Feeding Means—a Prisoner's Testimony." 8 August 1914. Typed extracts from "The Woman's Dreadnought," edited by Sylvia Pankhurst, 8 August 1914. Suffragette Fellowship Collection, Museum of London. (Group A: 57.116/52).

British suffragette Richardson, famous for having axed the Rokeby Venus in the National Gallery, gives details on several individual cases of forcible feeding and describes a feeding in detail.

Rickett, Allyn, and Adele Rickett. *Prisoners of Liberation: Four Years in a Chinese Communist Prison.* New York: Cameron Associates, 1957; reprint, Garden City, N.Y.: Anchor/Doubleday, 1973.

An account of an American couple's imprisonment in Communist China. "Rick" and "Dell" tell their separate stories in alternating sections of the narrative, assembled in chronological order. They had traveled to Peking in 1948 as graduate students with Fulbright grants. When hostilities broke out between the United States and China during the Korean War, they fell under suspicion. Rick was arrested as a spy and Dell was at first kept under surveillance at home and then imprisoned fourteen months later for assisting her husband in his espionage. They were imprisoned separately in Peking. Dell was held from September 1952 to February 1955 and then deported; Rick followed afterward.

Rigby, Françoise (née Labouverie). *In Defiance.* London: Elek, 1960.

Rigby, a Belgian woman active in the Resistance during World War II, was arrested in German-occupied Brussels in June 1944. Her war memoirs tell of her imprisonment in Saint Giles Prison. She was released in September 1944 when Brussels was liberated. Married and living in England after the war, Rigby founded an agency to aid refugees.

Rock, Shirley. "An Introduction to the Female Offender." *Woman Offender* (March 1978): 9–15.

Rock, an inmate at the Indiana Women's Prison, Indianapolis, discusses issues in female corrections, including theories concerning the rising crime rate among women. She notes that many imprisoned women have been forced to commit crimes because of their poverty, yet few job training opportunities exist for them in prison. She also discusses the need for better health care, education, and programs for imprisoned mothers and their children.

Roland de la Platière, Marie Jeanne Phlipon. *An Appeal to Impartial Posterity: By Madame Roland, Wife of the Minister of the Interior: or, A Collection of Tracts Written by Her During Her Confinement in the Prisons of the Abbey, and St. Pelagie, in Paris.* Translated from the French original. First American edition (corrected). 2 vols. New York: Robert Wilson, 1798; reprint, New York: AMS.

Madame Roland reflects on her childhood, marriage, imprisonment, the Revolution, and the great leaders of the age, as she awaits her execution, which occurred in 1793.

———. *The Private Memoirs of Madame Roland.* Edited by Edward Gilpin Johnson. 2d ed. Chicago: McClurg, 1900; reprint, New York: AMS, 1976.

This volume covers, in a different translation, the same material as Volume 2 of *An Appeal to Impartial Posterity.*

Rosenberg, Ethel. Letters. In *We Are Your Sons: The Legacy of Ethel and Julius Rosenberg,* by Robert Meeropol and Michael Meeropol. Boston: Houghton Mifflin, 1975; reprint, Champaign: Univ. of Illinois Press, 1986.

Letters written between 1950 and 1953, from the Women's House of Detention, New York, and the Death House at Sing Sing, to Rosenberg's imprisoned husband, Julius; their lawyer, Manny Bloch; and their sons, Robert and Michael. The Rosenbergs were executed in 1953 for their alleged conspiracy to give atomic secrets to the Soviets.

——. *The Testament of Ethel and Julius Rosenberg.* 2d ed. New York: Cameron & Kahn, 1954.

The revised and enlarged edition of *The Death House Letters* (New York: Jero, 1953), published during the Rosenbergs' imprisonment to help raise money for their children.

Russell, Martha. Diary. In *The Russells of Birmingham in the French Revolution and in America 1791–1814*, by S. H. Jeyes, pp. 61–103. London: George Allen, 1911.

Extensive excerpts from the diary of Martha Russell, about her captivity aboard a French ship during the French Revolution. With her were her father, William Russell, her sister, and her brother.

Russier, Gabrielle. *The Affair of Gabrielle Russier.* Preface by Raymond Jean, Introduction by Mavis Gallant. Translated by Ghislaine Boulanger. New York: Knopf, 1971. Originally published as *Lettres de Prison* (Paris: Éditions du Seuil, 1970).

This volume includes letters written by Russier to parents and friends from Les Baumettes Prison in Marseilles, where she was imprisoned in 1969. A teacher in a French lycée, Russier was held without trial because of her affair with one of her teenage students; this persecution led to her suicide. Her case drew public attention to the need for reform of the French criminal code, prisoner system, and treatment of women.

Samuelli, Annie. *The Wall Between.* Washington, D.C.: Robert B. Luce, 1967.

Samuelli, a Romanian Jewish woman imprisoned for espionage in Communist Romania from 1949 to 1961, writes of her association with other women prisoners from all social classes. She was held in the Political Women's Penitentiary at Mislea, the transit prison of Jilava, the secret police interrogation prison in Bucharest, and the penitentiary at Miercurea-Ciuc. She explains that her work is not an autobiography or a description of Communist political prisons, but rather a portrayal of how women from varied backgrounds endured imprisonment without admitting defeat. She recounts individual women's stories as she had heard them in the prisons, where reading and writing were forbidden, and where women maintained mental alertness by teaching each other their languages and exchanging life stories. She describes the system of wall tapping by Morse code, used as a medium of communication throughout the prisons.

Sanger, Margaret. Diary entry for 8 February 1917, Margaret Sanger Papers, Cont. 1, Reel 1, Library of Congress.

Sanger, imprisoned for her birth-control activity with the Brownsville Clinic, writes of her incarceration in the Queens County Penitentiary, New York. Although the diary dates only the day of her entrance into prison (8 February 1917), there are entries for three days. She describes prison food and routine, her poor fellow prisoners, and her resistance to fingerprinting by the warden.

――――. *Margaret Sanger; An Autobiography.* New York: Norton, 1938; reprint, Dover, 1971.

Chapters 17–19 describe Sanger's arrest and imprisonment in 1916–1917 in the Queens County Penitentiary, Long Island City, for distributing birth-control information in the Brownsville Clinic in Brooklyn.

――――. *My Fight for Birth Control.* New York: Farrar & Rinehart, 1931; reprint, New York: Maxwell, 1969.

Chapter 14 describes her imprisonment after the Brownsville Clinic raid.

"San Quentin, as a Female Prisoner Knew It." Chapter 5 in *Crime and Criminals*, by the Prison Reform League. Los Angeles: Prison Reform League Publishing Co., 1910.

An anonymous female prisoner, an inmate for several years, gives a detailed description of living and working conditions and race relations in San Quentin. The publication of this account helped lead to some prison reforms.

Sarrazin, Albertine. *Astragal.* Translated by Patsy Southgate. New York: Grove Press, 1967. Originally published as *l'Astragale* (Paris: J.-J. Pauvert, 1965).

A novel written by Sarrazin while she was in prison for burglary, about an escapee who breaks her ankle while fleeing prison, and her love affair on the outside.

――――. *The Runaway.* Translated by Charles Lam Markmann. New York: Grove Press, 1967. Originally published as *La Cavale* (Paris: Société Nouvelle des Éditions Pauvert, 1965).

A novel about an imprisoned woman's impressions of prison life and her preoccupation with plans for escape, symbolized by the recurring image of a runaway mare. Written by Sarrazin during her own imprisonment in France.

Saxe, Susan. "I Argue My Case." *Off Our Backs: A Women's News Journal* 6, no. 10 (January 1977): 4.

Addressed to "Gentlemen of the Jury," this poem protests sexism.

———. "To My Friends." *Off Our Backs: A Women's News Journal* 7, no. 2 (March 1977): 5.

Saxe explains why she decided to plead guilty to charges of armed robbery and destruction of government property when she was captured in 1975 and charged with acts committed in 1970. She states that she is a political prisoner who opposed sexism, racism, and the Vietnam War.

Shakur, Afeni. "Prison Women." *Ann Arbor Argus*, no. 37 (February 1–14, 1971): 8–9.

Black Panther Shakur, charged with conspiracy to bomb a New York department store, describes how the court and prison systems violate the rights of poor women.

———. "The Prisons and Jails Are Filled with Political Prisoners." *Black Panther* 5, no. 2 (July 18, 1970): 11.

Shakur, a member of the Panther New York 21, writes of the inadequate legal counsel given political prisoners. She describes the case of a sister inmate as illustration.

———. "To Our Black Brothers in Prison, Black Panther Party U.S.A." *Black Panther* 5, no. 4 (August 1, 1970): 26.

A poem expressing solidarity with imprisoned black men.

Shakur, Assata [Joanne Chesimard]. "Women in Prison: How We Are." *Black Scholar* 9, no. 7 (April 1978): 8–15, reprinted in 12, no. 6 (November–December 1981): 50–57.

Assata Shakur, a member of the Black Liberation Army, was imprisoned in New York City in May 1973 on a series of charges including bank robbery, attempted murder, kidnapping, and murder. She was acquitted of the first three charges. In this article, she describes her fellow inmates at Riker's Island Correctional Institution for Women and explains how women prisoners' dependency is encouraged.

Sharp, Evelyn. *Unfinished Adventure: Selected Reminiscences from an Englishwoman's Life*. London: John Lane, 1933.

Sharp, a British writer who contributed to the "Yellow Book," includes in her memoirs a chapter on her incarceration in Holloway Prison. Her participation in a militant suffrage demonstration in 1911 led to her sentence of fourteen days. During her second imprisonment of four days in Holloway in 1913, she participated in a hunger strike.

Sharpe, May Churchill ["Chicago May"]. *Chicago May: Her Story*. New York: Macaulay, 1928.

The autobiography of Sharpe, born near Dublin, Ireland, in 1876 and christened Beatrice Desmond. In 1889 she immigrated to America, where she married Albert "Dal" Churchill and began her life in crime with their robberies. Widowed at the age of fifteen, she became active in the underworlds of Chicago, New York, London, and Paris. Her second husband was James Montgomery Sharpe. By 1927 she had been imprisoned a total of fifteen times in the United States, once in France, once in Brazil, and seven times in England, for robbery, prostitution, and blackmail. Two long sentences were served on Blackwell's Island, New York, and in Aylesbury, England, where she knew fellow inmate Countess Markievicz, the Irish revolutionary (q.v.). August Vollmer, Chief of Police in Berkeley, California, suggested she could make an honest living by writing. Following his advice, she dictated her memoirs to the stenographer of her Philadelphia lawyer, Henry John Nelson, in 1928.

Shih Ming. "In a Chinese Prison: A Girl Revolutionist Tells her Experiences as a Captive." *Asia* 37 (Fall 1937): 99–100.
Shih Ming refused an arranged marriage, left her wealthy family and home in Hupeh, and entered the University at Peiping, where she edited two magazines. As a revolutionist and communist leading students in their demand for release of student political prisoners, she was arrested in 1930. This article describes her imprisonment for several months in the women's detention house and in a garrison, where she was tortured. She was released suddenly when a new warlord came to power.

Sikakane, Joyce. *A Window on Soweto*. London: International Defence and Aid Fund, 1977.
Sikakane's work includes a description of her arrest and imprisonment in Pretoria Central Prison and Nylstroom Prison in 1969 under the Terrorism Act in South Africa. Sikakane, a black journalist, was charged with membership in the African National Congress and with various conspiracies. She was finally released but was served with banning orders.

Šiklová, Jiřina. "Save These Books." *Index on Censorship* 12, no. 2 (April 1983): 37–39.
Prague sociologist Šiklová wrote her defense statement from the Prague Ruzyne Prison, where she awaited trial for helping banned Czech writers send their books out of the country. She was arrested in May 1981 and detained until March 1982, pending a trial that was never held. Her statement explains her actions to defend the right of all Czechs to read freely.

Sisters of Inner Connections, eds. *Writing for Rights*. State Correctional Institution at Muncy, Pa., Summer 1981.
The women incarcerated in Muncy Prison have compiled this newsletter, containing poems, essays, news items, letters, and artwork. Most contributors are women at Muncy, but works by inmates from several other

states are included. One of the editors and authors of numerous pieces in the newsletter is Moving Cloud (June Boyd), an inmate at Muncy.

Smedley, Agnes. "Cell Mates." *Call Magazine,* Sunday supplement to the *New York Call,* 15, 22, 29 February and 14 March 1920.

A series of four sketches of the women Smedley met while imprisoned for six months in 1918 in the New York Tombs. She was arrested and charged under the Espionage Act for her involvement with Indian nationalists. Included are portraits of Russian revolutionary Mollie Steimer and British birth-control activist Kitty Marion (q.v.).

————. *Daughter of Earth.* New York: Coward-McCann, 1929; reprint, Old Westbury, N.Y.: Feminist Press, 1973.

Pages 301–334 of Smedley's semi-autobiographical novel describe the arrest and imprisonment of "Marie Rogers" in the Tombs for six months during World War I.

————. Letter to Margaret Sanger, 1 November 1918. Margaret Sanger Papers, Cont. 12, Reel 10, Library of Congress.

Smedley wrote this letter, addressed "Dear friend Margaret Sanger" (q.v.), from the Tombs in New York City, where she was imprisoned during World War I. She describes her hearing, prison conditions, and her meetings in prison with Kitty Marion (q.v.) and Mollie Steimer.

Songs from a Free Space: Writings by Women in Prison. Edited by Carol Muske and Gail Rosenblum. Free Space Writing Project of the N.Y.C. Correctional Institution for Women, n.d. [197?].

This anthology, described as "a crime of conspiracy, an informed, fully-consenting adult decision to commit poetry," contains poems and short essays by eight women: Carolyn Baxter (q.v.), Fannie James Rogers, Gloria Jensen, Juanita Reedy (q.v.), Carole Ramer, Assata Shakur (Joanne Chesimard) (q.v.), Mildred D. Moss, and Deborah Hiller.

Spiridonova, Maria Alexandrovna. Letters. In *Spiridonova: Revolutionary Terrorist,* by I. Steinberg. Translated and edited by Gwenda David and Eric Mosbacher. London: Methuen, 1935.

Russian revolutionary heroine Spiridonova became active in 1906 with her assassination of General Luzhenovsky, who had been devastating peasant villages in the region of Tambov, where she lived. This biography includes her letters from prison in Tambov (1906) and from prisons in the Kremlin and exile in Samarkand, where she was sent for later actions. In *Living My Life,* Emma Goldman (q.v.) describes her awe at meeting Spiridonova in Moscow.

Staal, Madame de (née Delaunay). *Memoirs of Madame de Staal de Launay Written By Herself.* Translated from the 1755 French original by Selina Bathurst. London: Richard Bentley, 1877.

Raised in a convent and well educated, Madame de Staal-Delaunay became lady's maid to the Duchesse du Maine. When her mistress was arrested for conspiracy in 1718, Madame de Staal-Delaunay was taken to the Bastille, where she was held until 1720. She describes the conditions of her prison, her diversions, and her prison love affair.

Stafford, Norma. *Dear Somebody: The Prison Poetry of Norma Stafford.* Seaside, Calif.: Academy of Arts and Humanities, 1975.

Born into a poor Tennessee farming family, Stafford was imprisoned many times in county prisons, and she spent five and a half years in state prisons in California and Alabama for writing bad checks. In 1972 she began to write poetry as part of her work in the Santa Cruz Women's Prison Project at the California Institution for Women.

Stanford, Sally. *The Lady of the House: The Autobiography of Sally Stanford.* New York: Putnam's, 1966.

Raised in poverty on a farm near Baker, Oregon, Stanford was a teenager when first sentenced to two years in the Oregon State Penitentiary in Salem for obtaining goods under false pretenses in 1918. After her parole, she began a bootlegging operation. In 1931 she began her prostitution career in San Francisco and prospered as "madam" of some of the most exclusive brothels in that city. About 1940 she was falsely arrested on charges of involvement in a kidnapping plot, when her brother ran off with an underage girl. She was held in a Livingston jail for sixteen days, until she was released on bail and later cleared of charges.

Steinheil, Marguerite (née Marguerite Japy). *My Memoirs.* French edition, Paris, 1912; English edition, New York: Sturgis & Walton, 1912. No translator named.

Steinheil, a Parisian socialite trapped in an unhappy marriage with Adolphe Steinheil, a painter twenty years her senior, was arrested in 1908 for the strangulation murders of her mother and husband. She was imprisoned in the Saint-Lazare Prison in Paris until her acquittal in 1909. Her case caused a great sensation at the time, and her book criticizes the injustices of the French judicial system.

Stern, Susan. *With the Weathermen: The Personal Journal of a Revolutionary Woman.* Garden City, N.Y.: Doubleday, 1975.

Chapter 16, "Jailtime, December 14, 1970–June 29, 1972," presents Stern's prison experiences. A member of the radical Weathermen group, she was the only woman among the Seattle 7, who were tried for conspiracy in

1970. She was imprisoned in the Seattle City Jail from December 1970 to January 1971; Cook County Jail, Chicago, in March 1971; and Purdy State Institution for Women from April to June 1972. Her book traces her growing involvement in radical politics.

Stevens, Doris. *Jailed for Freedom*. New York: Boni & Liveright, 1920; reprint, Freeport, N.Y.: Books for Libraries Press, 1971.

Dedicated to Alice Paul, this account of the American woman suffrage movement (1913–1919) and the jailing of its participants gives a biographical list of suffrage prisoners. Stevens, a social worker, teacher, and officer of the National Woman's Party, was arrested for picketing on July 14, 1917, in Washington, D.C. Although sentenced to sixty days in the Occoquan Workhouse, she received a presidential pardon after three days. Her account gives details of her imprisonment and prison conditions of the suffragists.

Stirredge, Elizabeth. *Strength in Weakness Manifest: in the Life, Various Trials, and Christian Testimony of that Faithful Servant and Handmaid of the Lord, Elizabeth Stirredge*. Philadelphia: Benjamin and Thomas Kite, 1810.

A description of Stirredge's persecution for her Quaker beliefs. She was persecuted by a clergyman in her parish of Chew Magna, Somerset, England, and imprisoned in Ilchester Gaol in 1683.

Strong, Anna Louise. "Jailed in Moscow." *New York Herald Tribune*, 27 March–1 April 1949.

A series of six articles describing the arrest and imprisonment in 1949 in Moscow's Lubyanka Prison of Strong, an American journalist who sympathized with the Chinese Revolution and Mao Tse-tung. She was charged with spying and held five days for questioning. The *Herald Tribune* printed the series as an exposé of Soviet police state methods.

Suffragette Fellowship Collection, Museum of London.

The Museum of London acquired this collection of papers of militant British suffragettes in 1950. Several of the longer pieces are referenced under the authors' names within this bibliography. In addition, the collection contains many shorter pieces, including brief biographical and autobiographical statements of suffragettes who were imprisoned but who are less well known. Many of these are catalogued in Group C, vols. 2 and 3. The pieces provide details on the suffragettes' experiences in the movement and their imprisonments.

The Suffragist: Official Weekly Organ of the National Woman's Party. July–December 1917.

Issues from this period give extensive coverage of the American suffragists' demonstrations in Washington, D.C., and their subsequent jailing in the District of Columbia Jail and the Occoquan Workhouse in Virginia. The prisoners were released November 27 and 28, when their hunger strike forced the government to commute their sentences. Brief articles by suffrage prisoners include:

Matilda Hall Gardner, "Occoquan," 28 July 1917

Doris Stevens (q.v.), "Justice as Seen at Occoquan," 11 August 1917

Alice Paul, "A Note from Alice Paul," 24 November 1917

Rose Winslow, "The Prison Notes of Rose Winslow, Smuggled to Friends from the District Jail," 24 November 1917.

Talamante, Olga. ". . . from Olga's Prison Letters." *El Gallo* 8, no. 1 (January 1976): 14.

Talamante, a twenty-five-year-old Chicana from California, describes her torture and imprisonment in Azul, Argentina. She had gone to Argentina in 1973 to work with a community center there and was arrested in November 1974 and charged with subversive activities and possession of guns. She was imprisoned for nearly eighteen months, during which time there was an active defense campaign for her in the United States.

Tassin, Ida Mae. *Proud Mary, Poems from a Black Sister in Prison.* Buffalo, N.Y.: Buffalo Women's Prison Project, 1971. (Not examined; cited in Kathryn W. Burkhart, *Women in Prison* [Garden City, N.Y.: Doubleday, 1973].)

Taylor, Mary Ellen. Letters. Fawcett Library, City of London Polytechnic, London.

Correspondence of Mary Ellen Taylor, a British suffragette, with her daughter, Dr. Dorothea Taylor, 1912. In that year Taylor was imprisoned for her suffrage work. (Source: Mary Barrow, *Women 1870–1928: A Select Guide to Printed and Archival Sources in the United Kingdom* [London: Mansell, 1981].)

ten Boom, Corrie. *A Prisoner—and Yet!* Toronto: Evangelical, 1947.

The author writes of her persecution by the Nazis during World War II because her family harbored Jews in their home in Haarlem, Holland. In February 1944 she was imprisoned at Scheveningen with her sister and aged father, who died there. Corrie ten Boom was imprisoned that same year in concentration camps at Vught and Ravensbrück. She was released in December 1944, but her sister died in Ravensbrück.

Tencin, Claudine Alexandrine Guérin de. *Memoirs of the Count of Comminge.* London, 1744. Translation of "Les Mémoires du Comte de Comminge" (1735) in *Oeuvres des Mesdames de Fontaines et de Tencin.* Paris:

Garnier, n.d. (Not examined; source: Elissa D. Gelfand, *Imagination in Confinement* [Ithaca, N.Y.: Cornell Univ. Press, 1983].)

————. *The Siege of Calais by Edward of England. An Historical Novel.* Translated from the French original [1739]. London: Printed for T. Woodward, at the Half-Moon between the Temple-Gates in Fleet Street; and Paul Vaillant, against Southampton Street in the Strand, 1740; reprint, New York: Garland, 1974. Joint author is listed as Pont de Veyle, Antoine de Ferriol, Comte d'.

Claudine de Tencin, a French author, was imprisoned in the Bastille for three months in 1726 for the death of her lover, La Fresnais, who blamed her for his suicide committed in her salon. In this novel she uses her prison experience to depict that of the male protagonist, Monsieur de Chalons, imprisoned by Edward II of England. (Source of biographical data and summary of book: Elissa Gelfand, *Imagination in Confinement* [Ithaca, N.Y.: Cornell Univ. Press, 1983], pp. 34, 111–113, 121.)

Terrero, Jane. Papers. Suffragette Fellowship Collection, Museum of London.

Prison Experiences. Typescript (2 copies) (Group A: 60.15/13 and 50.87/62). British suffragette Terrero gave this paper twice, shortly after coming out of prison.

"The Story of the Two Hunger Strikes" (Group A: 60.15/13). "A ten minute paper given once at Wilburn."

Letter to Mrs. How-Martyn regarding suffragette experiences, 24 January 1928 (Group C, vol. 3: 57.70/11). Terrero gives an account of her arrest and imprisonment in 1912.

Manuscript register relating to prison experience of Janie Terrero (50.82/116). "Containing scraps and extracts from letters to my husband covering the period I was in Holloway for the cause of Women's Suffrage in the year 1912." The letters are copied, in her hand, into a notebook. Also included are notes on her hunger strike and forcible feeding and on prison administration, and letters to her husband and notes written from police court while awaiting trial in 1912. Terrero was arrested March 1, 1912, for breaking windows on Oxford Street, London, and was released June 25, 1912.

Thornton, Alice. "Merely Justice." *Atlantic Monthly* 135, no. 5 (May 1925): 611–623.

This is the second in a series of two papers analyzing Thornton's prison experiences. Here she discusses prison discipline and her work to start a "school" in prison, where she taught female inmates to read and write.

————. "The Pound of Flesh." *Atlantic Monthly* 135, no. 4 (April 1925): 433–446.

Thornton, explaining that she could be classified as an "accidental criminal" whose offense was isolated and "the result of sudden temptation or extreme emotional states," was a university graduate and a skilled worker when imprisoned for several years for her unnamed "one horrible mistake." Her purpose in writing her articulate essay is "to interpret certain aspects of the penal problem." She does this through a description of prison conditions and character sketches of fellow inmates.

Time Is an Eightball: Poems from Juvenile Homes & the Penitentiary of New Mexico. Edited by Bob Henry Baber. Santa Fe, N.M.: Tooth of Time, 1984.
This collection includes poems by girls at the Youth Diagnostic Center and inmates of the Women's Penitentiary of New Mexico. Lorri Martinez (q.v.) is one of the poets represented.

Todd, Judith. *The Right to Say No.* London: Sidgwick & Jackson, 1972.
Todd, a Rhodesian journalist, was imprisoned for five weeks in Marandellas jail in 1972, while her father, the former Rhodesian prime minister, was held in a nearby prison. They were held under the Rhodesian Emergency Powers Regulations of 1970 on suspicion that they were dangerous to the public safety. Todd's book goes into detail about Rhodesian politics and describes her stay in Marandellas and later in Chikurubi Prison Farm, where she went on a hunger strike and was forcibly fed.

Turkow Kaminska, Ruth. *I Don't Want To Be Brave Anymore.* Washington, D.C.: New Republic Books, 1978.
Turkow Kaminska, a noted European singer and actress, and her musician husband, Adi Rosner, were Polish Jews arrested by Stalin's police in 1946. Her memoirs extend from World War II to her return to Poland in 1956. At the age of twenty-six, she was first taken to a Lvov prison in December 1946, where she was held until the spring of 1947 on the charge of attempting to cross the border illegally. In 1947 she was transferred to a prison in Zolotchov, and then to prisons in Kiev and Kharkov. In 1948 she was sentenced to a five-year exile in Kokchetav, one of Stalin's Siberian camps. There, she was reunited with her daughter. They were later transferred to Karaganda, a city where she continued to live in exile until her release in 1952.

Turner, Margaret. *See* Jane Buxton.

Tyler, Mary. *My Years in an Indian Prison.* London: Gollancz, 1977.
Tyler, an Englishwoman living in India, was arrested in 1970 with her Indian husband and imprisoned in Hazaribagh Central Jail in Bihar, and the Jamshedpur jail. They were suspected of engaging in revolutionary activity against the Indian government. She describes in detail her prison

ANNOTATED BIBLIOGRAPHY

conditions and fellow female prisoners. She was released and allowed to return to England in 1975, but her husband remained in prison at the time.

Vasconcellos, Suzanne R. "The Tragedy of the Beast's Offspring." *Crime & Delinquency* 28, no. 4 (October 1982): 518–522.

Vasconcellos's essay is an indictment of the prison system and its treatment of both men and women inmates. She explains little about her own situation, except that she has been sentenced to eleven years' imprisonment for a nonviolent crime.

Vera, Marta [pseud.]. *Political Prisoners, Chilean Women No. 2: Political Prisoners in the Women's Section of "Tres Alamos" Concentration Camp.* London: Women's Campaign for Chile and Chile Committee for Human Rights, 1976.

A pamphlet containing the testimony of a Chilean woman imprisoned for fifteen months in Tres Alamos concentration camp for political prisoners. She wrote from exile in 1976, relating in detail the process of interrogation, the legal situation, and prison conditions. With pride she describes the communal organization of women within Tres Alamos.

Voices from Within: The Poetry of Women in Prison. Edited by Ann McGovern. Weston, Conn.: Magic Circle Press, 1975.

A collection of poems by the Bedford Hills poets: Bernadine Adams, Leonore Coons, Glenda Cooper, Clementine Corona, Susan Hallett, Theresa Simmons, Susan Smith, Constance Walker. They are members of The Long-Termer's Committee at Bedford Hills Correctional Facility, New York. McGovern, who ran a writing workshop with these women, collected and compiled these poems.

von Meck, Galina. *As I Remember Them.* London: Dennis Dobson, 1973.

The autobiography of von Meck, daughter of a pre-Revolutionary Russian landowner and railway president. In 1923, during an attempted escape into Poland, she was arrested and held until 1924 in prisons in Korosten, Zhytomir, and Kiev. She was again imprisoned in 1928 in Lubyanka Prison and Moscow's Butyrka Prison on the charge of espionage for the United States and England. In 1931 she was transferred to Siberian labor camps, where she remained until her release in 1935.

Walker, Dr. Mary Edwards. "Hotel de Castle Thunder." *Daily National Republican* (Washington, D.C.), 25 August 1864.

Dr. Walker, who served as a physician in the Union Army, was imprisoned in 1864 by the Confederates in a Richmond prison known as Castle Thunder. This article describes prison conditions and the treatment of women.

[360]

Wallach, Erica. *Light at Midnight.* Garden City, N.Y.: Doubleday, 1967.

A description of Wallach's five-year imprisonment in East German and Russian prisons, beginning in 1950. A German woman married to an American, she had entered East Berlin to find her foster parents and was arrested by the Communists on charges of spying and held at first in Schumannstrasse Prison.

Walled Garden: Poems from NSW Prisons. Edited by Rosemary Creswell. Sydney, N.S.W., Australia: Ball & Chain Press, N.S.W. Department of Corrective Services, 1978.

This anthology of poems from New South Wales prisons was assembled with the encouragement of the Programmes Division of the N.S.W. Department of Corrective Services. Most poets represented are men, but women poets include Julie Cashman, Patricia Collins, Mary Farrell, and Sandra Willson (q.v.).

Walton, Olive. Diary during imprisonment in Aylesbury Prison, 1912 (typescript). Suffragette Fellowship Collection, Museum of London (Group C, vol. 2: 50.82/1131).

The original diary is in the possession of Walton's adopted daughter. British suffragette Walton was sentenced on March 27, 1912, to four months' imprisonment for breaking windows. Her diary includes a statement given to the WSPU in London, July 1912, on hunger striking and forcible feeding in Aylesbury.

Weisbord, Vera Buch. *A Radical Life.* Bloomington, Ind.: Indiana Univ. Press, 1977.

Vera Buch Weisbord was an American Communist active during the early years of the movement, in the 1920s. She worked for labor causes in New York, New Jersey, and Pennsylvania. In 1929 she was jailed in Gastonia, North Carolina, on charges of murder and conspiracy in connection with a strike. While in prison, she was encouraged by reading the story of Vera Figner's (q.v.) imprisonment.

Wharry, Olive. Prison notebooks. British Museum, London.

Notebooks kept by British suffragette Wharry in Holloway and Winson Green prisons (1911–1914). (Not examined; source: Margaret Barrow, *Women 1870–1928: A Select Guide to Printed and Archival Sources in the United Kingdom* [London: Mansell, 1981].)

Who Took the Weight. Weston, Conn.: Magic Circle Press, 1977.

An anthology of women's prison writing. (Not examined; source: H. Bruce Franklin, *American Prisoners and Ex-Prisoners: Their Writings: An Annotated Bibliography of Published Works, 1798–1981* [Westport, Conn.: Lawrence Hill, 1982], p. 51.)

Williams, Helen Maria. *Letters containing a Sketch of the Politics of France, From the Thirty-first of May 1793, till the twenty-eighth of July 1794, and the Scenes which have Passed in the Prisons of Paris.* Two vols. London: Robinson, 1795; reprinted in *Letters from France*, Facsimile Reproductions, with an Introduction by Janet M. Todd (8 vols. in 2). Delmar, N.Y.: Scholars' Facsimiles & Reprints, 1975.

Williams, a popular English poet living in France during the Revolution, sympathized with the principles of the Revolution and was friendly with leading French intellectuals, including Madame Roland (q.v.). In October 1793, Williams was arrested with her sisters and mother and taken to the Luxembourg prison, according to a decree ordering imprisonment of the English and seizure of their property. They were released in December 1793.

Willson, Sandra A. K. "Prisons, Prisoners and the Community." In *Women and Crime*, edited by Satyanshu K. Mukherjee and Jocelynne A. Scutt, pp. 196–204. Sydney: Australian Institute of Criminology, in association with George Allen & Unwin, 1981.

Willson, released from prison in 1977, now works in the field of women's corrections. In New South Wales she has worked with the Network for Drug and Alcohol Agencies, and in 1979 she founded the first halfway house for female ex-prisoners in that area. The article discusses prison conditions at the Mulawa Training and Detention Centre for Women in New South Wales. Willson criticizes the lack of a classification system, inadequate medical attention and programs for released inmates, and poor inmate–staff relations. She suggests halfway houses as one improvement in the system.

Winsor, Mary. Papers. The Arthur and Elizabeth Schlesinger Library on the History of Women in America, Radcliffe College, Cambridge, Mass.

The Winsor Papers include "My Prisons," a typescript reminiscence of American suffragist Winsor's two prison sentences in 1917 and 1918; newspaper clippings about picketing and prison sentences (1917–1918) and about the prison special train, February 1919. (Not examined; source: letter to Judith Scheffler from Elizabeth Shenton, assistant to the director, Schlesinger Library.)

"Women Incarcerated." Feature issue of *Hunt Walk Talk* (Spring 1985).

This issue of the journal of the men's Hunt Correctional Center in St. Gabriel, Louisiana, focuses on articles and interviews with inmates of North Carolina Correctional Institute for Women and Louisiana Correctional Institute for Women. Included are articles by Jeanette Parker, "The Common Bond" (pp. 95–97, 155), and Deretha Smith, "My Impressions of Prison Life" (pp. 98, 155).

"Women Locked Up." *Women: A Journal of Liberation* 3, no. 3 (1972).

This special issue on confined women includes contributions by women prisoners:

> Teri O'Meara. "View from Within," p. 35. O'Meara writes from a Baltimore, Maryland, prison, where she was sent on prostitution and drug charges. She describes how women prisoners are treated like children and criticizes the lack of work and training programs.

> "South Vietnamese Prisoners Speak" (dated 20 September 1970), pp. 40–43. This document by several unnamed female political prisoners describes their brutal treatment in a South Vietnamese prison, beginning in November 1969. They were held in Con Son Prison and Chi Hoa Prison and severely punished for a hunger strike.

Women's Voices from Soviet Labor Camps. Translated by Lesya Jones. Edited by Bohdan Yasen. Smoloskyp Samvydav Series: Documents of Ukrainian Samvydav. Baltimore: Smoloskyp Publishers, 1975.

Included in this collection are letters to world organizations, the United Nations, and Soviet officials written by Stefania Shabatura, Iryna Senyk, Nina Strokata-Karavanska, Nadia Svitlychna, Iryna Stasiv, and Odarka Husyak. They protest the violation of human rights that occurs in Soviet prison camps, where they were sentenced in 1972–1973 for "anti-Soviet agitation and propaganda."

Wurmbrand, Sabina. *The Pastor's Wife.* Edited by Charles Foley. London: Hodder & Stoughton, 1970.

Wurmbrand and her husband, Romanian Jews who had converted to Christianity, were imprisoned in 1948 by the Russians, who had entered Romania after World War II. Her pastor husband was arrested as a counter-revolutionary and Sabina Wurmbrand was held in secret police headquarters, Bucharest, for questioning about his activities. She was sent to Jilava transit prison and then to forced labor camps near Cernavoda. In the Tirgusor maximum-security prison she worked in the sewing shop. She was released in 1953, but her husband was imprisoned for nine more years.